LICS
IA
SUNGKIANG
HU-NA MENG
INNER MONGOLIA AUTONOMOUS REGION
Tsitsihar
NORTH EAST
Harbin
HSING-AN MENG
KIRIN
Kirin
AREA
HSI-LIN-KUO-LO MENG
CHAO-WU-TA MENG
CHE-LI-MU MENG
LIAONING
Fu-shun
Mukden
Pen-chi
CHA-HA-ERH MENG
JEHOL
Chinchou
An-shan
An-tung
NORTH
Jehol
Kuei-sui
SUIYÜAN
CHINA
PEKING
Tientsin
Dairen
PORT ARTHUR NAVAL BASE AREA
SEA OF JAPAN
KOREA
Paoting
HOPEH
Tai-yüan
AREA
YELLOW SEA
Tsinan
SHANTUNG
SHANSI
EAST
YELLOW
SHENSI
JAPAN
K'ai-feng
KIANGSU
Sian
HONAN
CHINA
ANHWEI
CENTRAL
Ho-fei
Nanking
Shanghai
EAST CHINA SEA
WAN
HUPEH
Hangchow
AND
YANGTZE
AREA
Wu-han
Chungking
CHEKIANG
SOUTH
Nan-ch'ang
Ch'ang-sha
KIANGSI
EICHOW
HUNAN
FUKIEN
Foochow
Kweiyang
CHINA
FORMOSA
AREA
PHILIPPINE SEA
KWANGSI
KWANGTUNG
Canton
Nan-ning
HONG KONG (U.K.)
MACAO (Port)
M
SOUTH CHINA SEA
HAINAN
PHILIPPINES

The
PROSPECTS
for
COMMUNIST
CHINA

TECHNOLOGY PRESS BOOKS
IN THE SOCIAL SCIENCES

THE PROSPECTS FOR COMMUNIST CHINA
By W. W. Rostow and others

LABOR MOBILITY AND ECONOMIC OPPORTUNITY
By Members of the Social Science Research Council

NATIONALISM AND SOCIAL COMMUNICATION
By Karl W. Deutsch

INDUSTRIAL RELATIONS IN SWEDEN
By Charles A. Myers

PRESSURES ON WAGE DECISIONS
By George P. Schultz

THE DOLLAR SHORTAGE
By Charles P. Kindleberger

MID-CENTURY: THE SOCIAL IMPLICATIONS OF SCIENTIFIC PROGRESS
Edited by John E. Burchard

CYBERNETICS: OR CONTROL AND COMMUNICATION IN THE ANIMAL
AND THE MACHINE
By Norbert Wiener

THE MOVEMENT OF FACTORY WORKERS
By Charles A. Myers and W. Rupert Maclaurin

The
P R O S P E C T S
—— for ——
C O M M U N I S T
C H I N A

W. W. ROSTOW

in collaboration with
Richard W. Hatch
Frank A. Kierman, Jr.
Alexander Eckstein

and with the assistance of others at
The Center for International Studies
Massachusetts Institute of Technology

Published jointly by
The Technology Press of
Massachusetts Institute of Technology
and
John Wiley & Sons, Inc., New York

Chapman & Hall, Ltd., London

PREFACE

Like our earlier study, *The Dynamics of Soviet Society*,* this volume tries to serve two purposes. It aims to pull together in the compass of a short volume what we know about Communist China; and it aims to assist in the making of a forward-looking American policy by offering a unified interpretation of Peking's intentions and its ability to achieve them.

Specifically we set out to answer these key questions:

1. What are the operative motivations of the Chinese Communist regime?

2. What are its current intentions with respect to the society of the mainland and to the external world?

3. What problems does it confront in achieving its purposes?

4. What is the likelihood of Chinese Communist success or failure, in terms of the regime's apparent objectives?

5. What are the prospects for change in Chinese Communist society over the foreseeable future?

To answer these questions we have found it necessary to review the modern history of China from the perspective which 1954 affords; to assess the changing human response to Communist rule on the mainland from 1949 to the present; to examine in detail the character of Peking's network of ties to Moscow, and the relationship to the external world implicit in those ties; and to consider the economic foundations for the regime's power aspirations. The interconnection among these elements as they are likely to affect the future course of Chinese Communist society is our ultimate theme in Chapter 16.

The conception underlying the book's structure is the following: Parts 1 and 2 narrate the major facts of modern Chinese history and set out our interpretation of them; Parts 3, 4, and 5 focus intensively on the three great strategic factors likely to determine the future evolution of Chinese Communist society—the interplay between the regime and the people, the Sino-Soviet alliance, and the Chinese economy; Part 6 weaves together our conclusions as a whole. This

* W. W. Rostow and others, W. W. Norton, New York, 1953; Mentor Books, 1954.

method involves a degree of repetition both of fact and argument; but we have felt that an examination of Chinese Communism from different perspectives gave us the best chance of emerging with balanced conclusions.

We have built this synthesis from the full range of materials available to us. We have exploited the considerable possibilities which the Communist press itself offers, the growing monographic materials covering parts of the Chinese Communist performance since 1949, and the rich literature on modern Chinese history, including the pre-1949 history of Chinese Communism. We have not attempted to footnote in detail the sources used, although a bibliography is included in the volume. This is an interpretative essay rather than a scholarly monograph.

It is a general conviction of the Center for International Studies (CENIS) that answers to such basic and difficult questions as those we have posed demand a unified view of a whole society in motion; and that the formulation of such a view must be, in the end, the responsibility of one person. It follows directly that our unified view, however clear it may be, will not be definitive. Any other scholar charged with this task would have emerged with a synthesis somewhat different in emphasis and perhaps even different in substance. And so, although I assume full responsibility for the body of the text and the conclusions, I do so in full awareness that there are alternative ways of looking at the phenomena of Chinese Communist society and that other perspectives may prove more legitimate than mine.

It has been encouraging to us all that on many of the key issues the views of a wide range of experts and observers whom we have consulted have tended to converge. The difference among experts, as is often the case, proved on dispassionate examination to be somewhat less than they sometimes believed. Nevertheless, the selection of materials, their organization, and the character of the conclusions drawn have been inevitably arbitrary.

There has been a wide and comforting consensus among my principal collaborators and myself—so substantial, in fact, that important segments of the text are wholly theirs. Chapter 5 is the work of Mr. Frank A. Kierman, Jr. His historical essay so converged with the main lines of our analysis of current Chinese Communist society that it has been included in Part 3 of this study, in summary form. This is not the simple happy accident it might appear. At every stage in our work we have benefited enormously from Mr. Kierman's rare combination of historical scholarship and contemporary insight, made available to us with endless patience and generosity. He is responsible for a considerable part of whatever virtues this study may have.

This study owes an incalculable debt to Mr. Richard W. Hatch. Working with different materials, we talked out and agreed on the general perspective which suffuses this analysis. The view of the top leadership of Chinese Communism is largely based on his special research. And in his function as editor, besides making the reader's task vastly more easy than it would otherwise have been, Mr. Hatch has extended his contribution far beyond mechanical matters. At many points substantive passages are his. It might be noted that, in editing Part 5, and subjecting himself to the economist's jargon, Mr. Hatch rendered services over and beyond the call of a humanist's duties.

We have profited greatly from the presence in Cambridge of Mr. Alexander Eckstein, now engaged at the Harvard Russian Research Center on a basic study of the Chinese economy. His responsibilities do not extend beyond Part 5, although he has been a most valued critic of the study as a whole. Part 5 has been worked out between Mr. Eckstein and myself. Chapter 12 is our joint work; Chapters 13 and 14 are wholly products of Mr. Eckstein's scholarship. Chapter 15 is solely my work. If Mr. Eckstein were summing up the economic position in relation to the regime's objectives and prospects, his emphasis and interpretation would differ somewhat from mine. His views will be available at book length in the not too distant future.

Part 3 of the study owes much to the painstaking accumulation of evidence on attitudes toward the regime done by Mrs. Elizabeth Whittington, and to her measured evaluation of those difficult materials. In this work Miss Martha Henderson and Miss Ann Murphy have participated in the course of performing their other tasks at CENIS.

Miss Henderson is responsible for developing the detailed bibliography at the end of the volume. The scattered and piecemeal character of research and reporting on Communist China appeared to require and justify this extensive effort.

I have, of course, benefited from the ideas, comments, and criticisms of my CENIS colleagues. Although they have had urgent responsibilities of their own, they have turned aside to educate me and make available their time and working papers. In particular, I wish to acknowledge the assistance of Mr. Benjamin Schwartz, who helped lay out the research plan for this study, and Messrs. K. C. Chao, Ronald Hsia, John Kautsky, Harold Isaacs, Douglas Paauw, and Toshio Tsukahira, and Miss Martha Henderson. Although they bear no responsibility for the final form of this study, their suggestions, often accepted, have contributed to whatever value it may have. Out of their studies of Communism in Asia, Mr. Kautsky and Mr. Tsukahira have made an additional direct contribution to Part 4, there explicitly acknowledged.

In addition we have had the benefit of criticisms from a wide range of academic and other experts. To these readers of an earlier draft, and their wonderful tolerance of this intrusion by an outsider into the field of China studies, we owe a substantial debt: L. F. Chen, S. Y. Chen, Ai-li Sung Chin, Richard Eckaus, John Fairbank, George Kennan, John Pelzel, David Rowe, Raymond Sontag, John Carter Vincent, and Richard Walker. Although they bear no responsibility for the final text their criticisms and suggestions have improved it at many points.

To one of our critics we are particularly grateful. Standing in for the non-expert reader, Miss Harriet Peet examined our initial draft with great care; and her suggestions, both of presentation and substance, have made it a substantially better book than it would otherwise have been.

We have been supported indispensably throughout this venture, accomplished under forced draft, by an admirable secretarial team: Miss Anne Sartorio, its chief of staff; Miss Nancy Lou Grimes, and Mrs. Barbara Mahoney. We have been similarly aided by the untiring and often miraculously swift mobilization of research materials by our library staff: Mrs. Mildred Lamson, its chief; Mrs. Arlene Dagenais, and Mrs. Nan Waldstein.

This book is about Communist China, not about American policy. But we wish to note in this Preface a conviction that is shared by all centrally concerned with this venture.

Militarily and ideologically Communist China, now fully joined to the Soviet Union, presents an enormous challenge to the United States and to the Free World. Peking's pretensions to power in Asia and its claim as a model of theory and practice for Asia are unlimited.

We do not underrate the power and confidence of Peking's top leadership; but we are deeply persuaded that, from the common basis of ultimate humanistic values which, though different in form, ultimately bind the nations of the Free World, there can be fashioned societies whose strength and resilience will ultimately make Communism a tragic aberration of this century. Specifically, it is our conviction that a vigorous Free World policy—political, economic, and military—can contain the military threat of Chinese Communism, defeat its pretensions to political and ideological leadership in Asia, and, in time, diminish or even remove the danger we now confront. But this requires an American policy prepared to join sympathetically in efforts to solve the great revolutionary problems of Asia, and an American people prepared to sustain such a policy: to sustain it not merely with guns and armed men, but also with capital and technique, with energy, and with a sense of human fellowship.

It is our hope that this book may contribute marginally to the development of the understanding and the will which must underlie such an American policy.

W. W. ROSTOW

August 12, 1954

CONTENTS

CHRONOLOGY

THE CHINESE EMPIRE

1848–1865	Great Taiping Peasant Rebellion
1890–1898	Peaceful reform movements
1895	Sun Yat-sen's first revolutionary attempt
1901	Boxer Rebellion
1905	Sun Yat-sen exiled (to Japan)
	Sun Yat-sen's first statement of the *Three Principles of the People* (San Min Chu I) and foundation of the T'ung Meng Hui revolutionary society
1905–1908	Anti-foreign boycotts
1906	Manchu recognition of "constitutional principle"
1911	Collapse of Manchu regime

THE CHINESE REPUBLIC

Kuomintang (KMT)	*Chinese Communist Party* (CCP)
1912 February 12. Chinese Republic proclaimed: Sun Yat-sen proclaimed President, but yields position to Yuan Shih-kai. KMT party succeeds T'ung Meng Hui.	
1916 Sun Yat-sen succeeds to presidency on death of Yuan Shih-kai.	
(A period of ineffectual attempts to unify China, during which Sun Yat-sen unsuccessfully sought substantial assistance from Britain and the United States.)	

1919   Marxist study groups appear, their most prominent leader Ch'en Tu-hsiu, at Peking University.

1920   P'eng Pai emerges as Communist peasant leader. Comintern sends two agents to China to contact Chinese Communists.

1921   Sun Yat-sen is offered the co-operation of the Comintern.

(A period of indecision while Sun Yat-sen considers and negotiates Communist support.)

1921   July. Chinese Communist Party founded at its First Congress in Shanghai, and decides on unofficial cooperation with KMT.

1923   Sun Yat-sen concludes agreement with Soviet Ambassador Joffe for Comintern assistance; and Borodin arrives as adviser to Sun to reorganize KMT.

Sun sends Chiang Kai-shek to Moscow to observe Soviet methods.

1923   CCP officially joins with Kuomintang.

(A period during which the Communists really constitute left wing of the Kuomintang.)

1925   March 12. Sun Yat-sen dies. Chiang Kai-shek becomes nominal Kuomintang leader.

1926   March 20. Chiang Kai-shek consolidates his effectual control of KMT by arresting political workers in army, seizing pro-Communist leaders and Soviet advisers in Canton, thus foreshadowing the end of KMT-CCP cooperation.

1926   The Northern Expedition to the Yangtze begins in July. KMT armies have great success.

December. KMT government moves from Canton to Hankow. A time of peasant movements and strikes.

1926   CCP fails to capture leadership of industrial strikes in Canton, Hong Kong, Shanghai, etc.

1927   March 24. KMT enters Nanking.

March 26. KMT enters Shanghai.

Northern Expedition peters out, with negotiated unification of China under Chiang Kai-shek.

April 12. Chiang Kai-shek crushes the Communist-led unions in Shanghai, decisively terminating any semblance of CCP participation in his regime. "Nationalist Government" set up in Nanking.

July 15. Peasant revolt crushed.
Chiang firmly in power.

	1927	December 11–13. After failure to seize and hold Canton, Communists gather in the south.
	1928	First Chinese Communist army formed under Chu Teh and Mao Tse-tung.

1931   (Japanese invade Manchuria)

(The period of Chiang's war to consolidate the rest of China and defeat the Communists while Japan consolidates occupation of Manchuria.)	1931	November 7. Chinese Soviet Republic proclaimed at Jui-Chin (Kiangsi). It controls 6 districts. It declares war on Japan.
	1932– 1933	Chu-Mao combination achieves leadership of Communist movement.
	1934	November 10. Chinese Soviet Republic dies, its control over the 6 districts broken by Chiang's victories; the Long March begins.
	1935	Long March ends in Shensi; Communists build army and consolidate peasant support.
1936 December. Chiang kidnaped at Sian when his troops demand to fight Japanese instead of Communists.	1936	December. Communists, Chou En-lai as spokesman, and Chiang Kai-shek negotiate United Front against Japanese.

1937   (July. Beginning of war with Japan)

(The period of ostensible collaboration of the CCP and KMT in the United Front against the Japanese)

1938   Nationalist government moves to Chungking in 1938.

1941   January. Communist Fourth Army incident, in effect, terminates United Front.

	1941	Communists begin reconsolidating their hold in North China.

1942 Cheng Feng party reform movement launched by Mao Tse-tung. Initiation of various party reform movements which continued through 1950.

(Period of Communist extension of control over some 300,000 square miles and 95,000,000 people.)

1945 Confirmation of Yalta provisions by Sino-Soviet Treaty.

1946– Marshall Mission: its failure marks official end of KMT-CCP collab-
1947 oration (or truce), and the resumption of civil war.

1949 October 1. Promulgation of the People's Republic (Communist) of China with capitol at Peking.

1949 September 29. Promulgation of the Common Program (the basic policies for Communist China).

December 7. Chiang Kai-shek goes to Formosa.

THE PEOPLE'S REPUBLIC OF CHINA
(Communist)

Internal	*External*
1950 April 30. The Marriage Law. Basic attack on old family system.	1950 February 14. Sino-Soviet Treaty of Alliance.
June 29. Trade Union Law.	
June 30. Agrarian Reform Law. Major instrument for land redistribution which continued until the spring of 1953.	
	November 26. Chinese enter the Korean War.
1951 February 21. Regulations of the People's Republic of China for Punishment of counter-revolutionaries which went on until superseded by "Provisional Methods for Control of	

Counter-Revolutionaries" of June 1952. (These control methods still continue to be publicized and employed.)

March 14. Proclamation concerning the Popularization and Intensification of the *Resist America Aid Korea* Propaganda throughout the country. (Campaign, with many smaller subsidiaries, continued through the spring of 1954.)

May. Production Increase and Economy Drive initiated by Kao Kang in Manchuria, gradually spread from there to South.

October. The 3-Anti, 5-Anti Movements. The 3-Anti part of party reform and reorganization; 5-Anti major urban movement against business class. (Continued to June 1952.)

1952 December. Chou En-lai announces First Five Year Plan for 1953–1957 (extended to 1959). Major move toward industrializing China.

1953 October 1. New "General Line" of Transition to Socialism announced. Major program for 1954: (*a*) November 23. "Order of Government Administrative Council for Enforcement of Planned Purchase and Planned Supply of Grain." (*b*) December 16. Decision on the Development of Agrarian Production Cooperatives.

1951 May. Tibet occupied by Chinese troops.

July 10. Truce negotiations begin at Kaesong, Korea (following Malik speech of June 23 in U.N.).

1952 February. Chou En-lai makes germ warfare charges.

1953 March. Sino-Soviet Trade Agreement.

July 27. Korean War Armistice signed.

December. New Bond Drive.

1954 June. Draft Constitution of the People's Republic of China issued. (Includes abolition of 6 administrative regions.)

1954 April–July. Geneva Conference on Korea and Indo-China. First entry of Communist China into a great power conference.

Therefore, in general, an intelligent prince in his administration relies on force and not on virtue.

Shang Yang, 4th Century B.C., Legalist

When men are subdued by force, they do not submit in their minds, but only because their strength is inadequate.

Mencius, 3rd Century B.C., Confucianist

When the fields are overgrown with weeds and the harvest is bad, the price of corn high and the people short of food and their dead bodies found on the roads, these are what I call human omens. When the official orders are stupid ones, when public undertakings are put in hand at the wrong times and the basic industries are not properly organized, these are what I call 'human omens.' If the (sense of) ritual and righteousness is not cultivated, if the women's and men's apartments are not kept separate and there is sex licence, then father and son are suspicious of each other, rulers and ruled are at cross purposes, tyranny and distress go hand in hand. These I call human omens. They are born of disorder, and when these three kinds come together, peace is dead in that country.

Hsun Ch'ing, 3rd Century B.C., Confucianist

PART

1

PROLOGUE TO COMMUNIST VICTORY

THE STRUGGLE FOR POWER:

1840–1949

THE STRUGGLE FOR POWER: 1840–1949

I. THE BREAK-UP OF MANCHU RULE: 1840–1911

The Chinese domestic revolutionary period begins with the historic Taiping Rebellion, which, mobilizing peasant discontent, began in 1848, reached a military peak which threatened the dynasty late in 1853, and lapsed back to its base around Nanking to disintegrate in 1864. Its history reveals clearly the multiple pressures confronting the Manchu regime in the mid-nineteenth century. It underlines the fact that, in addition to the pressures exerted on China by Britain and the other Western powers, the regime faced important internal prob-· lems.

A long period of peace had united with the introduction of high-yield new crops (kaoliang, corn, sweet potatoes, and peanuts) to produce a sharp rise in population which apparently started toward the end of the seventeenth century. It is estimated that per capita acreage (measured in mou) declined as follows: [1] *

1685	5.43	1766	4.07
1724	4.83	1812	2.85
1753	4.43	1872	2.49

Although there was some expansion of cultivated land over this period, according to these estimates the population rose from about 112 million in 1685 to 300 million in 1872. Since Chinese agricultural society was not based on primogeniture, this increase in population (as, for example, in Ireland over the same period) led to the progressive parceling of land. There is substantial evidence of a fall in the peasant's standard of living and an increase in his consciousness of misery. The progressive pressure of population on the land was one

* Superior numbers refer to the Notes collected at the end of the chapters. See page 44.

of the causes of the Taiping Rebellion. Its actual timing may have been affected by the floods and famines of 1846–1848, which made acute a deteriorating agricultural situation. Unlike Western Europe, which faced a food crisis at precisely this time, China could not turn to the United States as a place of emigration or to the midwestern American wheat fields as a source of food imports.

Since the new Chinese crops which set in motion the changes in land tenure and population came over the Pacific from the western hemisphere, the whole context of the Chinese position in the nineteenth century may be regarded as resulting from contact with the West.

The Taiping Rebellion had even closer western connections. Its remarkable leader, Hung Hsiu-ch'uan, in a curious mystical experience, seized upon aspects of Christianity as drawn from Protestant missionary tracts and united them with older classical and Taoist elements in the Chinese religious tradition. His rebellion was not only a social and economic revolt of the rural poor but also an attempt to seize the dynastic power of China under a quasi-Christian, non-Confucian ideological banner. Some part of the inchoate fervor which marked this rebellion certainly derived from its religious creed.

The social and economic program of the Taiping Rebellion, which linked Chinese rural discontents with a version of Christian ethics, in many ways foreshadowed persistent elements in Chinese revolutionary aspiration. It included, within a primitive version of rural Communism, egalitarian land redistribution. In their social teaching the Taipings advocated equality between the sexes, and, according to Fairbank, "they inveighed against slavery, concubinage, foot-binding, arranged marriage, cruel punishments, and the use of opium." [2]

The Taiping Rebellion reflected western influences in other ways. It arose in the hinterland of Canton, the original locus of intense western contact; and it spread through the lower Yangtze valley, where the British had founded the new commercial base of Shanghai in 1843, and where the weakness of the Manchu dynasty in coping with foreign intrusion was most evident. These were regions where in general the writ of the imperial power was growing weaker. It is almost certainly true that the evidences of dynastic weakness in the face of external pressure helped raise the notion of open revolt as a realistic possibility. The foreign powers also contributed to the persistence of the Taiping Rebellion by harassing the Manchu dynasty. France and Britain were at war with China from 1856 to 1860, investing Peking in the latter year.

In the end, however, the western powers, more frightened of the rebels than of the dynasty, aided the regime in the defeat of the Taipings, which was accomplished in large part by Chinese troops, led first by the Salem adventurer, Ward, and after his death by the British artillery captain, Gordon. In addition, a group of Chinese gentry, mainly from Hunan, contributed significantly to the Taiping defeat. When the full extent of the dynasty's crisis was revealed, these Chinese, called upon for assistance, succeeded in organizing forces capable of dealing with the rebels. Thus the Manchu rulers of China had to accept not only western military assistance but also increased help from the Chinese themselves, whom they had for several centuries largely excluded from military leadership. This episode symbolized the decline of effective Manchu rule over China.

The frustration and defeat of the Taipings resulted not only from the converging efforts of westerners, the dynasty, and certain Chinese gentry, but also from their own lack of effective organization and leadership.

With the failure of the Taiping Rebellion, the leadership of the reform movement in China, such as it was, fell into the hands of the group of Chinese scholar-officials who had figured in the Taiping defeat: notably, Tseng Kuo-fan, Tso Tsung-t'ang, and Li Hung-chang. They and the other Chinese who joined the movement were in general less concerned with agricultural reform than with a direct attack on the other sources of China's national and international weakness—political, economic, and military.

Over the latter decades of the nineteenth century China suffered a series of crushing national humiliations. Japan, Russia, France, and Great Britain all seized portions of the Chinese empire; Germany and the United States shared in the extraterritorial privileges, granted foreigners under duress; and Japan decisively defeated the Chinese in a brief war in 1895, beginning the tragic modern story of Korea. The meaning of Chinese military weakness was underlined when the western powers demanded a massive indemnity for the slaughter of some 242 missionaries and other foreign civilians in North China and Manchuria in the Boxer Rebellion of 1900.

It was significant of the growing depth of the Chinese feeling toward foreigners that the Boxer uprising, unlike the Taiping Rebellion, was directed primarily against foreigners rather than toward domestic reform. This was only in part a result of the tactic of certain Manchu leaders who, following a recurrent pattern in Asia and elsewhere, successfully channeled off widespread domestic discontents into xenophobia. Both the awareness of China's international weakness and a sense of injured national dignity were already spreading downward through the Chinese population.

As a counterpoint to continuing national military and political humiliations, a succession of reformers sought to bring about directly, through the medium of the Manchu regime itself, the changes that promised to transform China into an effective modern state. The most notable expression of such efforts was the hundred days of reform in 1898. The Emperor, acting under the influence of a small group of intellectual leaders, issued a monumental series of reform edicts which touched everything from the techniques of government to the development of science. If implemented, they would have transformed the policy of the Chinese state; and, if persisted in, they would have transformed Chinese society.

The reformers may well have been encouraged in their method of revolution from above by the role of the Emperor in the Japanese Revolution of 1868. To the Chinese intelligentsia and political leaders the Japanese success in creating after 1868 a modern state capable of conducting its affairs with the world on the basis of equality was a primary model; and in Japan the Emperor had proved an effective rallying point for those intent on achieving modernization. China, however, did not have a purposeful and coherent ruling class with independent sources of strength. Moreover, the cyclical concept of Chinese history, with its unstable "Mandate of Heaven," denied to the Manchu dynasty the theological continuity which in Japan took the form of the Emperor's kinship with the sun-god. Above all, the reformers in China failed to carry with them the imperial civil service. There was no Chinese equivalent of the Japanese samurai; and the ties of China's developing commercial middle class were primarily with foreign rather than domestic trade, unlike the situation in Japan in the 1860's. Later, under the KMT,[3] this group was to play an important part in the Chinese revolution; but the reformers of 1898 failed to link it with their movement for national reform. Neither historical tradition nor the geographical, economic, and social structure of China facilitated a clean transfer of total national power to the new aspiring groups at this time.

The Empress Dowager, whose retirement had offered an occasion for the reform effort, returned to smash it. The new edicts were rescinded. Six of the reformers were executed, and the two leading intellectual figures in the movement fled to Japan, and then, via Honolulu, to the United States.

The Reform Movement had not halted revolutionary efforts. Sun Yat-sen, at twenty-eight, had started his revolutionary career in 1894 with his secret Revive China Society—which would amalgamate with others to become the Society of Sworn Brothers in 1905, and finally the National People's Party (Kuomintang) in 1912. Although after the failure of 1898 certain educational and political reforms were fostered by the Manchu dynasty, they failed to satisfy the aspirations of Sun and his followers, who launched ten revolutionary outbreaks before the successful Revolution of October 1911.

The success of the Japanese in their war against Russia in 1905 profoundly affected Chinese political leaders. It dramatized the connection between domestic reform and industrialization; it demonstrated the ability of Asia to cope successfully with western military and political intrusion. Japan exercised, both directly and indirectly, considerable influence over the generation which made the Chinese Revolution of 1911.

The Revolution of October 1911 was detonated and made effective by regional interests opposed to an effort to centralize control over the growing Chinese railway system, and whose easy victory reflected the weakness of the dynastic government. The continuing success of the Revolution thus hinged on an alliance among reform and regional elements to whose cross purposes the tragedy of modern China can largely be attributed.

The reformers sought certain positive substantive changes in Chinese political, economic, and social life, as well as in China's relation to the external world. These had been first summarized by writers like Liang Ch'i-ch'ao and then, in 1905, by Sun Yat-sen's Three People's Principles: Nationalism, Democracy, and the People's Livelihood. Sun Yat-sen's organization, outlawed and hounded by the Manchu dynasty, had attracted the more or less steady loyalty of a substantial group of students, merchants from the coastal cities, overseas Chinese, and a certain number of officers of the Chinese Army. But the dynasty fell only because the reformers' purpose briefly converged with the interests of regional groups who had become powerful through the dilution or destruction of the power of central dynastic rule over their areas. And these regional interests, with their military strength, were important factors in later developments; for, although unified military rule of China briefly emerged from the October Revolution, the armed strength of the country was not controlled by a disciplined political organization loyal to Sun Yat-sen's party or its broad aims.

The meaning of this schism was made evident almost immediately after the Republic of China was formed (January 1, 1912) at Nanking. Sun Yat-sen promptly stepped aside as provisional president in favor of Yuan Shih-k'ai, the general who had founded the first modern military formation in Chinese history, and who controlled much of China's effective military strength. Yuan took firm personal hold of the reins of power, proscribed the Kuomintang as a political party, and began to act in the classic manner of those founding new dynasties. His effort to re-create the monarchy was defeated by widespread resistance in 1915; and he died in failure the following year. There began a painful decade in which *de facto* power remained where it had, in fact, been despite Yuan's brief effort—in the hands of war lords who controlled the particular regions of China with their own military forces.

The meaning of military power in relation to political authority was thus driven home to the Chinese revolutionaries from two directions: first, from abroad, through the inability of China to cope with British, Russian, Japanese, and other western aggression in the decades after 1840; secondly, at home, where the inability of the civil rulers to control the regionally based elements of China's military strength made the revolutionary aspirations of the new republic largely a mockery.

The outcome of the Revolution of 1911–1912 thus posed for the Chinese intelligentsia the following problem: How should central political strength be organized to control the various regions of the country and thus create that unity of Chinese government which was a prerequisite to dignified Chinese foreign relations and effective domestic reform?

II. The Evolution of the Kuomintang: 1911–1945

The weakness of the Chinese national state after Yuan Shih-k'ai's death in 1916 did not bring to an end the Chinese revolutionary movement. As Fairbank points out,[4] the decade after 1911 saw operative in China three forces tending on the whole to accelerate the course of change despite inertia and resistance by regional leaders:

> First, the central power of the dynasty was gone and nothing equally vigorous could be maintained in its place. There was therefore a lessening of efforts at reform or at repression from the top, and widespread opportunity for local change and innovation. Secondly, the foreign powers became absorbed in World War I. Industry in China had a breathing space in which to develop in relative freedom from the pressure of foreign commercial competition. Thirdly, the World War gave Japan an opportunity for political aggression. After ousting the Germans from Shantung in 1914, the Japanese presented to China in 1915 the notorious Twenty-one Demands. This brazen diplomacy backed by the threat of force consolidated the Japanese position in Shantung and Man-

churia but failed to achieve a Japanese protectorate over China. In the process it roused Chinese nationalist sentiment to a new height.

The strength of the underlying aspiration for national dignity and power was reflected in 1915 by the vigorous Chinese response to Japan's efforts to move in on the German positions in China (as incorporated in the Twenty-one Demands) and to make China a Japanese protectorate. Later this emergent nationalism was reflected in the reaction of Chinese students and others in the large cities to the Versailles Treaty arrangements which transferred German holdings in Shantung to Japan. On May 4, 1919, there began widespread demonstrations which gained sufficient momentum to affect briefly the policy of the weak national government in Peking, which conducted Chinese foreign affairs. The May 1919 demonstrations, followed by a partially successful boycott of Japanese imports, revealed to the Chinese themselves and to the world the popular depth of the growing national sentiment. For many Chinese the event has remained a symbolic landmark; and it still figures prominently in Communist versions of modern Chinese history.

In the years after the First World War the reform movement took many directions: political, social, cultural, literary. Chinese intellectuals, stimulated in part by students returned from the West, were eagerly combing the accumulated lore of western ideas and re-examining China's difficult modern experience. A new generation of young men was emerging who took for granted the need for change and even the directions of change, and whose interest was in method and in what should be done first—the problem of priority.

In formal political terms the KMT under Sun Yat-sen remained the principal instrument of revolution; and Sun Yat-sen managed to maintain an unstable intermittent base in Canton. From 1921 he became president of the southern Chinese government, under the unreliable protection of the local war lord. Fundamentally, however, although the revolutionary potential of China was clearly on the rise, the KMT, the principal but not unique instrument for reform, had not solved the problem of effective political and military organization.

In 1923 Sun Yat-sen, influenced by the lessons of Chinese failure and Lenin's success, embarked upon a total reorganization of the Kuomintang, with Soviet agents serving as advisers. Despite its other preoccupations, Moscow had sensed from 1919 that important advantages might accrue to it by association with Chinese revolutionary forces.

It is essential to an understanding of modern China to appreciate the extraordinary impact on virtually all Chinese intellectuals and political leaders of the successful Soviet Revolution. Before the success of the November Revolution, Marxism had made little or no impression on Chinese thought and politics. The Marxist notion that politics, social structure, and culture are reflections of material conditions and economic methods violated much in the Chinese Confucian tradition and experience; and even the Chinese Communists have been and remain rather superficial Marxists, although not the less effective Communists for that. Like Lenin and Stalin they are more nearly political (or power) determinists than economic determinists in their thought and action.[5]

Lenin's practical success, however, coming at the stage of frustration in the Chinese revolution, was a major event with long-lasting consequences. The experience of the first two decades of the twentieth century had impressed on key Chinese revolutionaries the hard necessities of effective political and military organization, and especially the problem of generating effective force to back up political aspiration. Moreover, the possibility of creating immediately in China anything like the procedures of western democracy had receded from the minds of most Chinese reformers, faced by the overriding problem of effective national government, and the massive weight of illiteracy and traditionalism in the predominantly peasant population. They knew that war lords were not going to be overthrown and China unified by parliamentary procedure or by well-meant political aspiration which lacked troops at its command. The need for élitism was recognized both in Confucian tradition and by Sun, after 1905, in his idea of party tutelage. Further, the failure of the western powers to check Japanese imperialism in China as successor to that of Germany had considerably lowered the prestige of the West; while the Soviet Union had made effective propaganda by apparently renouncing Czarist gains in China and along its frontiers. Finally, the example of Japan's revolution had proved impossible on the Chinese scene, owing to profound historic differences in the structure and tradition of the two countries. It was logical, if not inevitable, that Chinese intellectuals should look closely and sympathetically at a method that had succeeded both in seizing the totality of political power for a revolutionary party and in launching a program of what looked like reform in a relatively backward country.

Thus Marxism appealed to Chinese intellectual leaders primarily as providing an appropriate technique for seizing and holding power. Leninism as an intellectual creed had one appeal which Marxism itself could never equal in China. Lenin's theory of imperialism brought to the center of the stage of modern history the problem which most completely obsessed the Chinese intellectuals, as well as other intellectuals in Asia: namely, the problem of the relationship between colonial and other weak Asian states and the western industrial powers. Western political theory had little to say about imperialism; and western practice, with its confusing mixture of aggression, practical self-interest, and authentic missionary humanitarianism, left something to be desired, in Asian eyes. Leninism treated this relationship in terms full of promise for the Asian future, placing the moral blame (ostensibly the scientific cause) for the unhappy facts of the imperialist relationship squarely on the industrial states. It is not remarkable that Asian intellectuals have tended to be influenced by Lenin's version of Marxism. What is remarkable is that so many have not accepted his gross and soothing simplifications.

Against this background Sun Yat-sen entered into an intimate complex relationship with the Comintern and the Soviet Union, formulated in a statement by himself and the Soviet Ambassador, Adolph Joffe, in January 1923. The KMT reorganized itself on a literal model of the Russian Communist Party. The reorganization ranged from the creation of local party units to the reshaping of the top command. It affected groups all the way from the village level (*tang-pu*) to a National Congress and a nominally all-powerful Central Executive Committee. Even more important, perhaps, the KMT began seriously to develop its own military strength, seeking at last a method for subordinating military to civil power. It set up in June 1924 the Whampoa Military Academy at Canton, headed by Chiang Kai-shek, who had been sent to Moscow the previous year to observe Soviet methods.

The fundamental agreement between the Soviet Union and Sun Yat-sen was that the Soviet Union would lend moral support and advice to the KMT, as a unique national party, in its efforts to unify the country under its party banner; and, conversely, that it would not support any effort to seize independent Communist power in China. It was formally agreed in the joint statement that China was at an inappropriate historical stage for Communism. A formula was arrived at which permitted Communist Party members, as individuals, to work within the KMT, which they proceeded to do with great vigor over the following four years. There was no question, however, of the dissolution of the Chinese Communist Party, which, of course, took the ulterior view (as did the Comintern) that it would exploit the possibilities of gaining strength within the KMT, ultimately capture its machinery, and thereby seize total power in China. The period of ostensible KMT-Communist collaboration was marked by interminable if somewhat obscure Communist maneuvers designed to seize and hold strategic posts in the KMT structure and to develop independent popular support.

The KMT, having strengthened and consolidated its base in South China, faced the central task of bringing under control the strong war lord leaders in the northern provinces. Although a Northern Expedition for that purpose had been talked of for some years, it became a realistic possibility only in 1925 after several years of KMT reorganization, in which Soviet guidance played a role. In March 1926 Chiang Kai-shek, then commander of the KMT's principal military formations, emerged as the central figure in the KMT organization at Canton. At this stage, however, KMT political unity was challenged by the clear emergence of Left and Right factions, the Right backing Chiang Kai-shek. This confronted the Soviet government with a hard choice: should it back the Left, with its Communists and Communist-sympathizers, or should it support Chiang Kai-shek, who held out the greater possibility of unifying China soon? Borodin, the Soviet adviser, urged that the Northern Expedition be undertaken under Chiang's leadership with substantial Soviet and Communist support, and that the question of factional power in the KMT be postponed. This priority was accepted in the KMT, despite an abiding mutual distrust between the Left and Right wings.

Aided by the development of its own military arm and given fresh energy for political reform by both Communist and non-Communist intellectuals, effectively organized for the first time, the KMT gained strength. By the spring of 1927, under Chiang Kai-shek's leadership, the Nationalist armies, against little resistance, had gained control over Wuhan (Hankow), Nanking, and Shanghai. Before completing the consolidation of the country, however, the KMT underwent a famous internal crisis. The intellectual reformers, both Communist and non-Communist, had gained increasing political power as the KMT gathered momentum and spread northward. The Left-wing reformers of the KMT itself dominated the headquarters of the government at Wuhan; and the Communists gathered considerable popular support for themselves, within the orbit of the KMT, mainly in the large cities (through the new trade unions) but in certain rural areas as well. In April 1927 Chiang Kai-shek, sensing both the danger of growing Communist political organization and his own military strength, crushed the Communist-led labor movement in Shanghai. In this move he was supported by the Right wing of the KMT, with its foundations in the commerce and banking of the coastal cities. By the end of the year he had eliminated from effective power in the KMT both the Communists and the Left-wing KMT government at Wuhan.

Chiang Kai-shek proceeded to complete the apparent unification of China during 1928. At least formally, the government at Nanking, which he set up to replace that at Wuhan, brought virtually the whole of the country under a single authority. The consolidation was based, however, on quasi-diplomatic arm's-length agreements with the Northern war lords rather than on a solid unification of authority. Chiang's government founded itself ideologically on Sun Yat-sen's Three People's Principles; and it elevated the memory of Sun Yat-sen, who had died in 1925, much as the Communists canonized Lenin in post-1924 Russia. Politically the KMT held that a period of political tutelage was required before effective democratic procedures could be installed in China. The national government operated as the dictatorship of a single party, the KMT, in which Chiang Kai-shek maintained a personal primacy. His effective authority was, however, gravely compromised by considerable regional military autonomy, by a variety of political cliques, and by continued clandestine Communist activities, political and military.

Although Chiang lost Manchuria to Japan in 1931, the KMT made important, and now often forgotten, progress over the decade 1927–1937. The Nationalists gave considerable substance both to the Chinese aspirations for dignified national unity on the world scene and to economic and social progress. Major advances were made in reorganizing relations between China and the foreign powers on the basis of conventional international law. A substantial group of able, often western-trained, administrators brought an unprecedented degree of competence and order to the organization of national affairs. The regime created a unified national currency. Although there were grave weaknesses in Nanking's tax system, the Nationalist government proved capable of financing large civil and military operations. Progress was made in agriculture, industry, transport, and public health. Nationalist-dominated trade unions by no means met western standards of independence and integrity of leadership; but they made distinct progress, notably in skilled trades, where there was no mass of available labor to weaken the workers' bargaining position. And, within the orbit of KMT rule, although often under independent auspices, the underlying social revolution in methods of education, in the position of Chinese women, and in social life and culture generally went forward, especially in the cities.

In evaluating the weaknesses of KMT rule over this period it must be borne in mind that, internally, the Communists were never crushed and difficulties with war lords persisted; and that, externally, Chiang Kai-shek enjoyed peace only for the period 1929–1931. In 1931 the

Japanese moved into Manchuria; in 1932 Shanghai was attacked; and from that time down to 1937, when full-fledged invasion began, North China was progressively infiltrated. During this period Chiang felt that he lacked the military strength to cope alone with the Japanese military threat. The Communists remained a potential threat at his back. In the face of Japanese aggression he was unsupported by the League of Nations and, except for some modest loans, by the western powers generally. Virtually from the beginnings of his consolidated rule he was bedeviled, like his predecessors from 1840 on, with external military pressures, to which was added the heavy burden of dealing with the Communists, who moved increasingly towards military insurrection. Even if his primary interest had been in problems of domestic reform the situation he confronted denied him the freedom to concentrate the resources, energies, and talents of his country wholeheartedly on the substantive problems of Chinese society.

Partially related to these chronic external and internal pressures, the position of Chiang Kai-shek had certain underlying weaknesses the importance of which became clear in the decade after 1937, in which year China came under full-scale Japanese attack:

1. In a military sense the unity of China was more apparent than real. Important areas were still dominated by war lords; and Chiang Kai-shek was too involved in interminable, exhausting, and complex negotiations and military engagements to maintain even the semblance of national unity. This condition proved critical when the central government lost to Japan the coastal area of its basic support and fell back on agrarian inland provinces.

2. The KMT, partly because of the lack of real national unity, was never able to generate in its hands the resources necessary to bring about either an industrial or an agricultural revolution. The loss of sovereignty over Manchuria in 1931 obviously interfered with both these related economic objectives. In addition, the KMT as reorganized after 1927 lacked a political and social conception which would meet deeply felt, if latent, peasant aspirations. It has been conventional to contrast the KMT failure in this regard with the Communist success in the period 1927–1949. This view often fails to take into account the overriding pressures on the KMT to maintain itself against both external and internal enemies. Moreover, it must be pointed out that, while land reform as offered by the Chinese Communists was an effective tactical device for rallying peasant support to their insurrectional cause, it is by no means clear that anything but very large-scale allocations of industrial resources to agriculture could have brought a serious long-run satisfaction of peasant wants. The lack of

a vigorous high-priority agricultural policy on the part of the KMT, within the limit of the straitened national resources it controlled, was probably not the result of purposeful conservative pressures on the national government, although such pressures undoubtedly existed and were felt. Until driven back by the Japanese to Chungking in 1939, the KMT's support was more commercial than agricultural. Although it is true that complex ties existed between commercial and agricultural interests, a simple class-interest analysis does not satisfy all the evidence. Whatever the economic and social interests involved, a group within the KMT was permitted and even encouraged to do what they could about rural reconstruction; and they made important if piecemeal gains. It is probably true that the explosive peasant potential was generally not appreciated by the KMT top leadership, which devoted its limited energies to tasks which were believed to have higher priority than reform. And so, despite some technical and political reforms, the ancient structure of Chinese life at the village level persisted under KMT rule in most parts of China; and this structure, which had been slowly degenerating for a century or more, had within it profound economic and social discontents which ultimately were turned against the KMT by Communist political promises.

3. Chiang Kai-shek never succeeded in eliminating the Chinese Communist movement and its military units, or in denying it some form of minimum base from which it could operate, carry on nation-wide propaganda, and, ultimately, expand the territories it controlled.

4. In the light of post-1945 events it is easy to overestimate the extent to which the politically important Chinese intelligentsia were sympathetic to and cooperated with the Communists. Nevertheless, it is true that Chiang's ideological formulation of Sun Yat-sen's tradition failed to rally support among important groups of the Chinese students and younger intelligentsia. Before 1936 Chiang's failure to resist the Japanese head-on alienated many. More generally, the New Life Movement, begun in 1935, with its ambiguous mixture of Chinese and western values, did not provide a wholly satisfying framework for China's vigorous and well-educated youth. The extreme emphasis on national unity as against immediate reform; the emphasis on discipline as opposed to individual freedom; a persistent strand of mistrust for intellectuals (based in part, of course, on their believed political radicalism); the sporadic but often ruthless use of secret police; the attempt to infuse the Kuomintang with a revised Confucian tradition—these constituted a program which failed to attract the loyalty and respect of many of China's students and intellectuals.

5. Despite his formal acceptance of the Leninist concept of disciplined single-party rule, Chiang Kai-shek was, in spirit and method of operation, in an older tradition of personal paternal autocracy. Chiang's techniques of administration and concentration of authority severely limited his ability to cope with the extremely difficult problems he confronted.

Despite these and other real weaknesses, the decade 1927–1937 saw in China a higher degree of geographic unity, national purpose, and movement toward widely shared national goals than any other time since 1840.

The kidnaping of Chiang Kai-shek in December 1936 by Chang Hsueh-liang, the powerful northern war lord, set off a dramatic series of events which led to a 1937 agreement between the KMT and the Communists to join forces against Japan. The kidnaping both reflected directly and symbolized a widespread feeling (sedulously cultivated by Communist propaganda) that the internal power struggle in China should be subordinated to defense against the Japanese. Up to this point Chiang, acutely aware of Japanese military superiority and of the political insecurity of his domestic base, had avoided a direct military clash with the Japanese, who encroached southward from Manchuria into North China. Perhaps alarmed by the vista of Chinese unity implicit in the KMT-Communist agreement, the Japanese launched full-scale invasion of China in 1937. Chiang's position as unquestioned national leader, created by the 1937 agreement, was confirmed.

Between the invasion of China in 1937 and the Japanese attack on Pearl Harbor in December 1941 Chiang fought a gallant defensive war, attracting worldwide sympathy but little military help except modest assistance from the Soviet Union.

From about 1939, when the Japanese incursions into China were checked and a front was stabilized, a steady process of erosion set in within the Nationalist government. It was in control of a limited agricultural area, but denied the coastal cities whose commerce, industry, and banking had been the primary sources of its funds, its energy, and its most creative administrators. It became increasingly dependent on peasant taxes and peasant recruitment in areas where the traditional gentry and the traditional war lords were strong and conservative. Working increasingly through the gentry, it adopted short-run tax and recruitment policies which exacerbated peasant discontent. This pattern denied it the capability to meet the longer-run aspirations stirred up and given promise of fulfillment by the Communists.

The Nationalist government lacked the military power to remove the Japanese from the communication lines and cities they held. Its leaders were acutely aware that, whereas the setting of the war weakened the KMT position, it was affording opportunities in the North for expansion of Communist strength which would ultimately have to be confronted. Chiang felt impelled to allocate major military formations to containing the Communists within their agreed area. The Communists, in the advantageous position of irresponsible opposition, could promise much for the future. The KMT had to face the responsibilities of a dreary present.

Without centralized sources of food and money and without adequate communication, the power of the central administration weakened. Chiang's control over certain of his regional commanders became increasingly less effective. Lacking the military resources to fight an effective war, lacking the resources to carry out economic development, hamstrung by urgent short-run needs and commitments and thus prevented from considering a serious policy of agricultural reform, the personnel of the administration, with certain notable exceptions, lost zest and morale. Many, discouraged by the insoluble big problem, turned to the easier small one and looked to their personal interests and fortunes. The evidence of chronic financial corruption in the KMT is incontestable. However sanctioned it may have been in the old Chinese tradition, it was a source of weakness and a symbol of decay. The key figures around Chiang were narrowed to those in whom he felt an overriding personal loyalty. Given his awkward circumstances, this criterion of selection is understandable; but it did not place responsibility with the ablest generals and administrators. And those who held power grew older and further away from Chinese popular sentiment. There is no doubt that the government in Chungking became progressively less able to meet its enormous problems and responsibilities.

When the Nationalist government returned to the Chinese cities at the end of World War II in 1945 its representatives were greeted initially with enthusiasm. Chiang was the acknowledged national leader who had kept the faith and triumphed in the company of major power allies who treated China as an equal. It is a major tragedy of modern history that the six years of waiting in the wilderness which had made him an unrivaled national symbol had rendered his administration incapable of building upon this dominant national sentiment, or upon the military strength, international status, and United States economic support he then commanded. In several areas the new government administrators became involved in serious scandals—most disastrously in Formosa. More fundamentally, they failed to act in accord with the high, perhaps impossibly high, expectations of peasant, worker, and intellectual which the war years had stirred in China as throughout the world. The Chinese people are highly sensitive to the presence or absence of vital spirit (the *ch'i*, preservation of which is paramount in Chinese boxing); and it took no time for them to perceive that the Kuomintang was exhausted. In the meantime the Communists had been preserving their *ch'i* by healthful open-air exercise, hard work, simple fare, and a judicious refusal to enter upon extreme military adventures in their highly selective warfare against the Japanese.

It was against this background—almost of an exile government returning awkwardly to a transformed homeland—that the KMT faced the Communist challenge in 1945.

III. The Rise of Chinese Communism: 1918–1945

A. Origin and Early Days: 1918–1923

Almost seventy years elapsed in the West between the publication of the Communist Manifesto and the Russian Revolution. The writings of Marx and various schools of Marxists had been mulled over and debated, and they had become a curious but familiar part of the intellectual furniture of the western world. But at the time of the Russian Revolution few Chinese had read Marx or had followed with any care the elaborate doctrinal and organizational history of the Russian Marxists. The Revolution came as an electrifying event without a history known in China.

By the spring of 1918 a Society for the Study of Marxism had been set up at Peking University; and Communism joined the catalogue of western ideas and institutions over which Chinese intellectuals pored, seeking for the right answer to their nation's awesome problems. During 1919, Marxist study groups spread, including one organized in Changsha by Mao Tse-tung, then a student; and a Marxist weekly began to appear. In 1920 the Comintern, charmed by the apparent momentum of all this intellectual interest, and finding in it confirmation of Lenin's view that Asia had great strategic potential for world Communism, dispatched two agents to China to help create an effective Communist Party there. In the meanwhile Chinese sent to France on war work had formed a Communist unit. In July 1921 the First Congress of the Chinese Communist Party was held at Shanghai, including delegates whose assorted ideologies embraced "biblical social-

ism, social democracy, anarchism, and various shades of Communism." [6] By 1923 Sun Yat-sen was engaged in a total reorganization
of the KMT on the model of the Russian Communist Party, with a
Comintern agent as his principal adviser. Between them the KMT
and the Chinese Communist Party engaged the attention of a high
proportion of the younger Chinese political intellectuals. It is thus
not unfair to say that within five years of the November Revolution
Russian Communist theory and practice had become a dominant influence in the Chinese revolution as far as political organization was
concerned.

In part the attractiveness to the Chinese revolutionaries of the Russian Communist experience can be explained in terms of their recent
defeats and humiliations and their current frustrations. The Revolution of 1911 had failed in its grand purposes; effective power lay
fragmented in the hands of the war lords. The chronic humiliation
of China by the Great Powers continued; and the willingness to recognize an increased degree of Chinese sovereignty only underlined the
extraterritorial violations that remained. Sun Yat-sen's Three People's Principles were a widely acceptable formulation of China's problem and its objectives; but no effective instrument was in sight to
move China toward those objectives. Meanwhile Lenin had apparently translated revolutionary aspiration into the seizure of effective
power; and his example was bound to interest Chinese intellectuals,
ambitious for their country and their program, but little more than
ineffectual commentators on the current scene. Moreover, there were
elements in Lenin's political theory and practice which may have made
his conception of a disciplined one-party state system correctly guiding
the nation on the right historical path easier for Chinese than westerners to accept. The Chinese philosophical tradition contains so
many strands that it is easy to find in it antecedents for almost any
position one chooses.

The following elements in the Chinese tradition made Leninism,
as opposed to the Marxist theory of history, an understandable and
even familiar line of formal approach to the problem of political
power:

1. Political power in China had been for centuries administered by
an intellectual elite; and, as of the early 1920's, the recent efforts of
Chinese reformers to achieve western forms of political democracy had
failed. The notion of a self-appointed elite seizing the state's power
in the name of good purposes was not shocking to Chinese, given their
history and their traditional concepts of politics and state. Sun Yat-
sen's party enunciated this position as early as 1905.

2. The ruling Confucian conceptions had counted on the inculcation of ethical values and a sense of social responsibility in the elite as the primary check on the evil use of political power. The western notion of the dispersion of power and the rule of formal law as the ultimate protection for the individual had never gained formal authority on the Chinese scene.[7] The centralization of authority, a key to Lenin's organizational ideas, was both familiar and sanctioned in traditional Chinese thought. Many Chinese fell in with the notion of a centralized single-party state, without in any way envisioning the full intimate control of village, family, and individual which it came to involve in Communist practice once power was seized.

3. Chinese political thought had for centuries recognized insurrectional revolt as a correct response to bad rule. The revered philosopher Mencius flatly approved it. Chinese history and folklore had long taken the view that bandits in the hills might have a legitimate role in history, overthrowing bad, weak dynasties and founding new dynastic lines. The conception of a secret conspiratorial party of insurrection was not incompatible with procedures familiar in Chinese life. Both the KMT and the Chinese Communist Party had antecedents in the secret societies which, along with family and clan, played so important a part in the organization of Chinese life. Reportedly, Mao Tse-tung regarded *All Men Are Brothers,* the classic Chinese story of an insurrectional band acting in defiance of the ruling dynasty, as his favorite reading when he was plotting for power in the hinterland.

4. Although rigorous economic determinism has largely left Chinese cold, including Chinese Communists, the Hegelian notion (which Marx adapted) of 'correct' historical positions and 'inevitable historical stages' was not alien to Chinese thought.[8] China had a long recorded history, the fluctuations of which were studied as a central part of Chinese education and as a means of prediction. To the stream of history the Chinese applied touchstones of moral judgment. Moreover, the persistent strand of practicality in the Chinese approach to philosophy and political theory made it easy for them to identify (as Communists have come to do) the 'correct' position at any moment of time with what would work in terms of effective power.

5. Finally, Lenin's theory of imperialism not only elevated a problem already high on the Chinese agenda but did so in terms which assuaged hurt feelings and which offered to the backward areas rapid rise in status if they followed the Communist path.

On the whole, it seems that Lenin's concepts of party organization and of imperialism were more acceptable on the Chinese scene than in any western country. By 1923 they had, in somewhat different versions, by and large captured the KMT as well as the Chinese Communist movement. But it should be emphasized that the acceptability of these strands in modern Communism do not imply a general acceptance of Marxism as a philosophy of history or of Communist totalitarian administration as a way of ruling society.

The stylized traditional autocracy of the Chinese Empire, whatever its formal ideology, bore little relation to the administrative practice of Communist regimes after they gained power.[9] The demonstrable attractiveness of Leninism to many Chinese intellectuals should not be translated automatically into the view that Communist practice will necessarily prove acceptable on the Chinese scene, nor into the view that the Chinese Communist rulers are simply another in the long succession of Chinese dynasties.

B. Communist-KMT Collaboration and the Debacle: 1923–1927

By 1923, when Sun Yat-sen negotiated with the Soviet diplomat Joffe the terms of Moscow's assistance in the KMT reorganization, the Chinese Communist Party was already sufficiently formed and effective to extract conditions for its collaboration with the KMT. The essence of the understanding was that, while keeping their organization in being, the Communists would participate in the KMT as individuals; and that they would subordinate Communist objectives to those of the KMT, whose formal ideology at this stage was in any case deeply colored by revolutionary language impossible to distinguish from the emergent Communist jargon. Although Communist propaganda and recruitment objectives accorded high priority to the Chinese armed forces, apparently no move was made at this time to develop distinctively Communist armed units.

Two converging judgments probably determined Comintern and local Chinese Communist acceptance of this subordinate position for the Communists. First, the Communist movement in China was weak, commanding little popular support. Communists judged that collaboration with the KMT, while maintaining the Communist Party's identity, would give it greater opportunities for spreading its doctrine and gathering adherents than going it alone. Second, without question, Moscow's first interest in China was to use it as a counterweight to Japan and the western nations in power politics. A unified China antagonistic to Japan and the western powers but friendly to Russia was (and is) an Asian objective of Soviet policy—although the problem of maintaining a China at once unified and closely tied to Moscow poses its own difficulties for the long pull.

The Chinese Communists were in no position in 1923 to create the kind of China Moscow needed to help it meet its foreign policy requirements in the NEP (New Economic Policy) period. If the Chinese Communists went it alone, they could only further weaken China as a factor on the current world scene, thus strengthening the relative power of Japan and the West in areas Moscow judged to be of strategic importance. The tangled story of Soviet relations with the KMT on the one hand and the Chinese Communists on the other from 1923 to 1927, and the post-1927 course of Soviet policy in China, make sense only in terms of the persistent priority accorded by Moscow to its immediate power interests over its apparent ideological commitments when the two were judged to conflict. This judgment does not imply that Moscow's decisions were coolly made in the light of an agreed strategic doctrine. On the contrary, the evidence of ignorance and confusion about China in Moscow is incontestable, as is the role of Chinese policy as an intraparty political football. Nevertheless, the upshot was a series of Moscow decisions on China which faithfully reflected the priority accorded Russian national interests as then defined.

Moscow's tactic in moving toward this objective was to ride both horses in China as long as possible: to assist the KMT in gaining and consolidating national power, while at the same time preparing the way for the Chinese Communists to seize control of the KMT at the 'correct' stage. In the period down to Chiang's Northern Expedition of 1926 Moscow succeeded in enforcing on the Communists its priority for Chinese unity under the KMT. Communists and their sympathizers did, indeed, make rapid progress within the KMT apparatus and within the leftist Wuhan governmental structure as well as among industrial workers. Moreover, in certain areas Communist leaders had sensed the power of discontent among the poorer peasantry and were developing techniques for harnessing peasant energies within the framework of Communist organization. All this burgeoning Communist activity and infiltration, combined with Chiang's military successes in 1927, appeared to indicate that Moscow might ride the two horses successfully.

It is true that after Sun's death (1925) there were in certain KMT quarters some signs of restiveness with the energetic and quasi-independent role of the Communists. As early as March 1926, in Canton, Chiang Kai-shek had indicated both his willingness and his ability to reduce the number of Communists in points of strategic importance in the KMT and civil structure and to begin to gather control of the KMT into his own hands. Over the following year, however, the

Soviet advisers remained; KMT-Moscow relations remained superficially good; the Chinese Communists, somewhat weakened, nevertheless operated effectively in political support of the Northern Expedition; and Chiang Kai-shek continued to speak in public both the language of an international revolutionary and that of a national leader.

In April 1927, with a good part of the Yangtze conquered, Chiang, reacting to the steady Communist challenge within the KMT, completed the removal of the Communists from the KMT structure, killed many Communist leaders, and did what he could to destroy the Communist organization and the institutions—such as labor unions—it dominated. After a brief attempt to rally around the Left KMT government at Hankow, the Communists found themselves, by default, an outlawed party of insurrection.

The passage in Communist history from 1923 to 1927 was accompanied by a counterpoint of Marxist ideological debate concerning what stage Chinese history was in and, therefore, what the 'correct' line was. And behind this debate lay Stalin's grim struggle, against Trotsky and others, for total Soviet power. The story of these years has been told and argued with passion by Communists and by historians of Communism. There is no need here to rehearse the arguments or to analyze the schismatic politics and maneuvers that produced the Chinese Communist defeat of 1927, which was the outcome of split and confused purposes in Moscow, within the Chinese Communist movement, and within the KMT, resolved temporarily by the man who had effective control over the armed forces on the spot. As late as April 5, 1927—one week before Chiang's decisive *coup* in Shanghai—Stalin made evident the nature of his priorities in China: ". . . at present, we need the Right. It has capable people who still direct the army and lead it against imperialism." Stalin could not envisage, apparently, that these 'capable' men leading the army would crush the Chinese Communist movement. It is clear from subsequent Soviet policy that he never changed his main aim in China: the creation and support of a strong anti-Japanese, anti-western Chinese government oriented to Moscow as far as Soviet diplomacy and bargaining leverage could achieve.

C. The Rise of Mao and the Military Agrarian Base: 1927–1945

The leadership, political and military strategy, and tactics of modern Chinese Communism take much of their shape from the defeat of April 1927—and from the lessons in power it appeared to demonstrate. The rise of Mao and the strategy of military operations from a political base in the countryside emerged from the failure of Communist tactics in the period before and immediately after that defeat.

The first leader of the Chinese Communist Party, when it was formally organized in 1921, was Ch'en Tu-hsiu. It was he who attempted to administer the dual policy of collaboration with the KMT and the building of an independent Communist movement. This policy was opposed by groups both in Moscow and in China who would have preferred seeing the Chinese Communists go it alone, looking as a matter of first priority toward a Chinese Communist revolution. There is no doubt that Ch'en's policy had the overriding support of Stalin. However, in the aftermath of April 1927, amid elaborate dialectical denunciations for his failures of conception and tactics, Ch'en was removed from power and replaced by Ch'ü Ch'iu-pai. The new policy recognized the lack of military strength within the Communist movement and looked to prompt insurrection based on the workers in Chinese cities. Although the new line of the Communist Party was insurrectional, and sanctioned for the first time the building of an independent Communist military force, it still looked to the left-wing political elements in the KMT and to the 'wavering bourgeoisie' for support.

There followed a series of strikes in the cities and insurrectional movements in the countryside. The latter were led by Mao Tse-tung, who by 1927 had come firmly to the conclusion that Communist power should be built on the misery and frustration of the poorer peasants. In the cities the Communists did not do well. They were vulnerable to urban-based KMT police power. They had lost much prestige by their failure and defeat in 1927, which damaged the labor unions they had dominated. Moreover, the KMT developed the so-called yellow unions, which competed with remarkable success against the blandishments of Communist working-class leadership virtually down to 1949.

Neither the efforts at insurrectional revolt in the cities in 1927–1928 nor the related rural uprisings made important headway. Towards the end of 1928 Li Li-san returned from Moscow to succeed Ch'ü Ch'iu-pai. Although Comintern doctrine now sanctioned the build-up of a military agrarian base, Li Li-san's primary interest was in a continued effort to establish a solid Communist base among the urban workers. Li's unsuccessful and costly insurrectional enterprises in the cities, including assaults on Changsha and Hankow, led the Comintern to denounce him late in 1930. He was withdrawn to Moscow and kept in storage until 1945, when he reappeared in Manchuria. He was replaced by Wang Ming (Ch'en Shao-yu), one of the 'returned student clique' brought back from Moscow at Comintern suggestion.

Under Wang's leadership the fortunes of the urban-based Communist movement showed no signs of improvement. Meanwhile Mao Tse-tung, steadily at work along different lines, improved his fortunes in the Communist hierarchy. Although still challenged both in his own rural terrain and in the higher party structure, by 1932 Mao was the leader of the only effective Communist political and military strength in China. Nevertheless, when Wang was withdrawn to Moscow he was succeeded not by Mao but by Po Ku (Ch'in Pang-hsien), who maintained orthodox Comintern conceptions of urban insurrection. Mao did not attain formal leadership of the Party until January 1935.

The rise of Mao stemmed from the fact that he pursued a secondary line of attack on the problem of Chinese Communist power—via rural organization—which over the period after 1927 proved more effective than that carried out under direct Comintern instruction by the succession of Comintern appointees: Ch'ü Ch'iu-pai, Li Li-san, Wang Ming, Po Ku, and Po Ku's successor in 1934, Chang Wen-t'ien. Until events made Mao and his line of approach the only surviving alternative, the Comintern and Moscow clung to the strict Leninist formula that the urban proletariat was the primary if not unique instrument of revolution. From a western point of view Mao's exploitation of peasant discontent appears a wholly consistent adaptation of Lenin's *de facto* opportunism in the pursuit of power. To Communist theorists of the 1920's, imbued with the mystique of the urban proletariat, Mao's tactical flexibility was a painful doctrinal deviation. Its success was hard to swallow.

In his remarkable 1927 assessment of the peasantry as an effective source of revolutionary strength Mao bluntly made his famous calculation as follows: "To give credits where they are due, if we allot ten points to the accomplishments of the democratic revolution, then the achievement of the urban dwellers and the military units rates only three points, while the remaining seven points should go to the peasants in their rural revolution." Mao's insight into what Communist organization might accomplish if it harnessed the discontent of the poorer peasants matured at just the time when Chiang Kai-shek was decimating the central Communist organizational structure, breaking its hold on the KMT, and destroying its independent base in the urban trade unions. Mao proceeded to combine his own political plan for organizing the peasantry under the Communists with the Comintern's 1927 sanction to organize Communist military strength. As early as 1928 Mao had outlined his strategic military-political plan in a statement for the Central Committee of the Communist Party which enumerated the conditions required for the maintenance and development of "separate armed Soviet bases." This formulation, which governed Mao's strategy down to 1949, is summarized as follows by Schwartz:

> The first condition is the existence of a "strong mass base." Although it is not specified, the mass base is, of course, to be a peasant mass base. These peasant masses are to be won by a program of land reform designed to satisfy the basic grievances of the bulk of the peasantry within the areas under Communist control. The second condition is the existence of a strong party, that is, of a party leadership organized along the lines prescribed by Lenin. The third is the existence of a strong Red Army for, in an environment in which military power was decisive, a Soviet base could survive only by possessing its own military force. The fourth condition is the control of a strategically located territorial base, and the fifth condition is that the area in question be self-sufficient enough to maintain its population.[10]

These five conditions reflected lessons which had been learned from the peasant revolts which the Communists organized in the autumn of 1927. Although these had been little more successful than the strikes fomented in the cities, the combination of events had a distinctive result: the Communist rural base of operations was left virtually undamaged at a time when the 'primary' urban proletarian base was seriously weakened.

In May 1928 Mao joined forces with the soldier Chu Teh in Mao's native Hunan. Over the next two years, in the neighboring mountains of Kiangsi, Mao and Chu Teh organized a guerrilla force recruited mainly from discontented peasants. In 1929–1930, aside from two attacks made on the city of Changsha in compliance with Comintern instructions, the new Red Army wandered under difficult conditions through Kiangsi and Hunan mainly demonstrating that it could remain in being.

By the end of 1930 Chiang Kai-shek judged its existence sufficiently dangerous to warrant launching the first of five major campaigns designed to destroy the Communist base. These continued from December 1930 to the important Communist setback in October 1934. Chiang's forces, advised by the German general von Falkenhausen, used scorched-earth tactics to drive the Communists, advised at this stage by a German Communist known as Li Teh, into encirclement, where the advantages of Communist guerrilla tactics could be denied.

The period 1928–1934 is significant in Chinese Communist history for three major reasons. First, Mao and his followers, although militarily defeated in 1934, had worked out the strategy and tactics of armed insurrection based on the support of the poorer peasants. Second, this technique, combined with the almost complete failure of the Chinese Communists in the cities, made Mao's line of approach the ruling strategy of the Chinese Communist movement. Third, the Communists had made their first effort at formally ruling a portion of China when in November 1931 at Juichin, Kiangsi, a Chinese Soviet Republic was proclaimed. In general the laws of this Republic were drawn almost verbatim from the Soviet model. However, the major substantive element in the Communist program within the civil area controlled by the Red Army was land redistribution; and this was carried out by vigorous and often bloody expropriation of land on behalf of the poorer peasantry. In his 1927 appreciation of the revolutionary potential of the peasantry Mao had stressed the violent feelings which could be generated among the poorer peasantry against the rural gentry. At this stage, unlike the later period in Shensi, Communist land reform was ruthlessly executed. Mao gave full play to the emotions that could be released among the poorer peasants by the land-redistribution process.

Mao had begun with about 1,000 men, to whom, in 1928, 2,000 more of Chu Teh's followers had been joined; in the course of 1928, 8,000 other armed peasants had been recruited in southern Hunan. In 1934 the Red Army, going into its fifth major battle, possessed about 180,000 men under arms, of whom about 100,000 broke out of the encirclement of October 1934 to begin the long march to the north.

The extraordinary story of the 6,000-mile march from Kiangsi to the residual Communist base in Shensi has often been told. Fewer than 20,000 soldiers of the 100,000 who had set out a year earlier reached Shensi. Nevertheless, at the end of 1935 a Communist military force continued to exist; and it still held a rural operational base where it could at least symbolically execute its land policy and carry on nation-wide propaganda against the KMT.

In the course of 1936 the political and military situation was transformed when Chiang Kai-shek was forced to agree to the united front against Japan. The reasons for Communist advocacy of this policy represent the convergence of Soviet Russian and Chinese Communist interests:

1. It remained, on strictly Russian grounds, the persistent Russian interest in China that Japanese aggression be opposed.

2. It was the interest of the Chinese Communists that Chiang Kai-shek commit his military resources against the Japanese rather than devote them to destruction of the Communists.

3. It was a Chinese Communist interest to present themselves to the Chinese people, and especially to the intelligentsia, as the most energetic defenders of the Chinese nation against a foreign aggressor.

4. As in the earlier days of Communist-KMT collaboration, an alliance against Japan would offer the Chinese Communists respectable reasons and increased channels for carrying on nationwide propaganda.

5. Operations against Japan would afford the possibilities of extending the area over which the Communist armies, and, therefore, the Communist civil administration, could extend their control.

This whole phase of Chinese Communist policy is characterized by a more temperate political and land-reform policy in the areas it controlled. Both the moderation of Communist relations with the KMT and the modesty of its internal program are to be understood in the context of the worldwide Communist line of 1936–1939. That line sought to mobilize in each country a popular-front domestic program, of a moderate liberal or socialist type, to accompany an external policy of collective security action against Germany, Italy, and Japan. This line fitted peculiarly well the situation of the Chinese Communists, who had been moving toward some such formulation well before 1936, when Chiang was kidnaped.

It was in these years of popular-front policy that western observers first met and reported the performance of the Chinese Communists on an extended scale. Their performance at this phase led to widespread misconceptions concerning their ultimate purposes and the techniques that they would be prepared to apply to attain them.

Over the war years the Chinese Communists conducted guerrilla operations on a substantial scale against the Japanese. In 1937 they held some 30,000 square miles, embracing 2 million people; in 1945 they held about 300,000 square miles, containing 95 million people, or between 20 and 30 per cent of the Chinese population. The Chinese Red Army, decimated in 1934–1935, numbered about 900,000 in 1945. Mao had succeeded in seizing and holding the rural hinterland over a wide area while never permitting his troops to become engaged in a showdown frontal operation with the Japanese where they might have been destroyed.

Meanwhile, Communists made the most intensive efforts to prepare for the postwar struggle for power in China, their preparations including, especially, the following:

1. The publication, as early as 1940, of Mao's *New Democracy*. This book purported to present the theoretical bases of Chinese Communism along lines consistent with Sun's Three People's Principles. It also outlined a popular-front program designed to appeal to the

intelligentsia and even to the commercial and industrial middle class as well as to poor peasants and urban workers. The maintenance of absolute Communist Party control within the New Democracy was concealed, and the role of New Democracy as a transitional stage on the way to 'socialism' and 'communism' was played down.

2. The land program of the Communists was presented as moderate in character, and, while the ultimate goal of collectivization was not wholly concealed, it was played down.

3. Immense effort was made to build up and to indoctrinate a disciplined cadre of party members from the many recruits who joined the Communists in this period. In particular, from the first half of 1942, the Cheng Feng (ideological remolding) Movement was conducted to bring the various new Communist members into line with Mao's version of Lenin's rigid party orthodoxy. Whatever the flexibility of the program the party advertised, there was a hardening, not a relaxation, of dictatorial discipline within the Communist Party itself.

There is no question that the primary objective of the Chinese Communist Party throughout the war years was the pursuit of power in China. Its relations with the KMT, the limited nature of its military operations against Japanese forces, its posture towards the United States and the western allies, its civil policies in the areas it controlled, and its proclaimed program for the future were all geared to this overriding tactical objective. And, by the close of World War II, they had succeeded in laying the foundations for later achievement of this objective.

IV. THE COMMUNIST TAKEOVER: 1945–1949

There are few sequences of modern history about which so much has been written as that part visible to the West of the process by which the Chinese Communists triumphed over the Nationalist government and gained control of the China mainland in 1949. Moreover, there are few international events which have generated in the United States a controversy of equivalent intensity. Despite the extent to which the sequence has been explored and subjected to the heightened examination which comes with public political debate, there remain for the historian a good many unanswered questions. Any attempt at the present time to analyze the process of Communist victory and to weigh the elements which entered into it must be regarded as highly tentative.

Nevertheless, certain main facts are reasonably clear. Objectively examined, the great American debate on postwar China touches less on what happened than on what might have happened if the United States had acted differently at various stages in modern Chinese history. Our purpose here is not to speculate on whether a different American policy in China could have averted the Communist victory, but to summarize the main known facts in this tangled story.

The story of the Communist takeover begins not with 1945 but more nearly with the agreement of 1936–1937 between the Communists and the Nationalist government to end hostilities between themselves and jointly to resist the Japanese invasion. It will be recalled that the Communist strategy of resistance to the Japanese was determined by a convergence of the strategic interests of the Soviet Union and the Chinese Communist belief that an agreement to concentrate on the Japanese in alliance with the KMT would increase the chances for the expansion of Communist power in China. Although Chiang Kai-shek was essentially forced into this agreement, it soon emerged that the situation also offered him unique opportunities to act in the name of the nation as its acknowledged leader in a popular cause. The prestige of Chiang Kai-shek was perhaps at its highest when he led his country in its resistance against Japan in the years immediately following 1937.

The agreement between the Communists and the Nationalist government to concentrate on the common enemy and to accommodate their respective policies to this purpose was incorporated in a series of exchanges and manifestos in 1937, the upshot of which was the following four promises of the Communists:

1. The *San Min Chu-I* [Three People's Principles] enunciated by Dr. Sun Yat-sen is the paramount need of China today. This party is ready to strive for its enforcement.
2. This party abandons its policy of overthrowing the Kuomintang of China by force and the movement of sovietization, and discontinues its policy of forcible confiscation of land from landowners.
3. This party abolishes the present Soviet Government and will enforce democracy based on the people's rights in order to unify the national political machinery.
4. This party abolishes the Red Army, reorganizes it into the National Revolutionary Army, places it under the direct control of the national government, and awaits orders for mobilization to share the responsibility of resisting foreign invasion at the front.[11]

Despite their ambiguities, these promises were judged by Chiang Kai-shek to be at least formally acceptable under the conditions he faced. On September 23, 1937, he issued this statement:

The Manifesto recently issued by the Chinese Communist Party is an outstanding instance of the triumph of national sentiment over every other consideration. The various decisions embodied in the Manifesto, such as the abandonment of a policy of violence, the cessation of Communist propaganda, the abolition of the Chinese Soviet Government, and the disbandment of the Red Army are all essential conditions for mobilizing our national strength in order that we meet the menace from without and guarantee our own national existence.

These decisions agree with the spirit of the Manifesto and resolutions adopted by the Third Plenary Session of the Kuomintang. The Communist Party's Manifesto declares that the Chinese Communists are willing to strive to carry out the Three Principles. This is ample proof that China today has only one objective in its war efforts.[12]

In the course of its first year certain measures were taken on each side which appeared to meet the terms of this agreement; but one decisive element—that relating to the position of the Chinese Red Army—was never put into effect. And, in general, this agreement is to be understood as a tactical truce, agreeable to both sides for different reasons, in the face of the situation posed by Japanese invasion.

From 1937 to the breakdown of negotiations with the KMT at the end of 1946 the Communists were never prepared to place their armed forces under anything like the full control of the Nationalist government. Undoubtedly influenced by the painful lessons they learned in 1927 and 1933–1934 about the meaning of military power, the Communists accorded an overriding priority to maintaining their own military units intact, avoiding encirclement or engagement on fixed fronts.

What emerged, then, from the agreement of 1937 was a kind of diplomatic accord between two powers—one formally sovereign, the other exercising *de facto* sovereignty within flexible boundaries—to abstain from hostilities with each other and to engage a common enemy. Since each of these adversaries looked ultimately to total authority in China, since their boundaries were ill-defined, and since all the movements of their troops carried implications of enlarged or diminished domestic authority, there were bound to be clashes. These began towards the close of 1938, and in January of 1941 chronic mutual suspicion and hostility reached a climax in the New Fourth Army incident, when a headquarters detachment of about 5,000 men of the Communist New Fourth Army was decimated while passing through Nationalist-held territory under circumstances not wholly clear down to the present. It was against this background of conflicting long-run political ambition in China and confirmed mutual hostility amounting at best to an armed truce that the United States confronted the China situation when it became involved in the Far Eastern war. It is doubtful that the American government or the American people had an adequate sense of the historical depth and purposefulness of the antagonism which underlay that situation.

From the end of 1941 to 1947, when the Chinese civil fight to the finish began, American policy with respect to China had two strands: to encourage the unification of China by political means; and to strengthen Chiang Kai-shek's hand in the unification process by American aid and by exhortations to improve the quality and effectiveness of his political, economic, and military administration. During the war years the American motivation was simply that the internecine conflict and the weaknesses in KMT policy and administration grossly lowered the fighting value of China as a military ally in the war against Japan. In the postwar years these same strands of policy had a different foundation. The most responsible United States observers judged that, with such economic and military assistance as the United States was prepared to grant, Chiang Kai-shek could not achieve the prompt and total reconquest of China. It was felt that Chiang, to make good within China his recognized international status as its ruler, would have to enter into political arrangements with the Communists and then, on the basis of an effective economic, political, and social policy, win over to his side the Chinese people.

It should be noted that American policy ruled out at all stages the substantial use of American armed forces on the Chinese mainland in the postwar years, and that no important group of American politicians was prepared to envisage the violation of this limitation.[13] This is, in our judgment, the central fact about American postwar policy in China.

In the immediate postwar period, Soviet, and perhaps even Chinese Communist, estimates of Chiang Kai-shek's strength were such as to make it unlikely in their judgment that a Chinese Communist victory could be promptly achieved in China by military means. The ruling Communists prided themselves on their hardheaded view of power; and when they measured the military strengths of the two sides in China in 1945 the answer was a three-to-one advantage in favor of the KMT. Some such appreciation almost certainly influenced both the Soviet decision to dismantle Manchurian industry as reparations and the brief effort to renew the Moscow-KMT tie, through Chiang's son, Chiang Ching-kuo, early in 1946; it may well have given some substance to the apparent (but, in the end, untested) willingness of the

Communists to form a joint government, short of surrendering full control over their armies, in the early stage of General Marshall's negotiation.

While the United States was assisting Nationalist China, Soviet assistance was given to Communist China in violation of both interallied and Sino-Soviet diplomatic agreements of 1945. In the course of the postwar period the Soviet assistance consisted of three important elements:

1. Delay of Nationalist occupation of Manchuria and assistance to the Chinese Communists in infiltrating the countryside of Manchuria, notably during the Red Army withdrawal in the spring of 1946.

2. Turning over to the Chinese Communists stores of Japanese arms and ammunition.

3. Probably some additional assistance in the form of Soviet-manufactured arms and ammunition and in Soviet military advisers, whose guidance may account for the sharp improvement in Communist staff work noted by observers after 1945.

The degeneration of the uneasy armed truce in 1945 into full-scale civil war and Communist victory took place in a series of stages during which the hopes of each side and their appreciation of their own relative capabilities altered. The decisive factor in that story is military; that is, the *dénouement* came as a result of a civil war in which one side was victorious in the field. For that reason the story is best understood if the military sequence is outlined and if the political and social factors which profoundly relate to it are assessed afterwards. The civil war proceeded in the following three stages:

1. *V-J Day to the cease-fire agreement of January 10, 1946.* In this period the Communists and the Nationalist government sought to move in on Japanese-held areas. Aided by United States transport facilities, which rapidly moved about 500,000 men into key areas, the Nationalist government succeeded in installing itself in the major cities of Central, East, and North China. The Communists made rapid progress in the hinterland of Manchuria and in some parts of North China. Although the Soviet occupation of Manchuria limited to some extent the areas the Communists could take over, they received the surrender of many Japanese units and acquired their arms—in violation of agreement with the Nationalist government. Hostilities began as Nationalist troops sought to clear the lines between the cities they held. The Nationalist government decided, against United States advice based on an estimate of Nationalist capabilities, to occupy Manchuria, as it was legally entitled to do in terms of existing international agreement. Despite this difference in judgment, the United

States backed Chiang's decision early in 1946, both diplomatically and with essential transport facilities. Throughout the latter months of 1945 inconclusive diplomatic negotiations were conducted between the Nationalist government and the Communists against a counterpoint of military operations; and Moscow simultaneously explored the possibilities of special bilateral arrangements with the Nationalist government designed to limit or exclude United States influence in China. It was in this curious, degenerating, military-diplomatic setting that General Marshall arrived in China in December 1945, seeking the unification of the country by political negotiation. On January 10, 1946, he achieved a cease-fire agreement between the Nationalist government and the Communists. In strictly order-of-battle terms, the Nationalist government at this stage had an advantage in troops roughly equivalent to the relative area of China it held, that is, better than three to one.

2. *The failure of mediation: January 1946–January 1947.* In the course of 1946 the Nationalist government persisted in its purpose of consolidating its military hold on all of China, including Manchuria; and at the end of the year substantial progress had apparently been registered. Large numbers of troops had been transferred to Manchuria, and, despite Soviet assistance to the Communists in the period of Red Army withdrawal (spring 1946), the major urban centers were held by the Nationalists. In spite of some relative increase in Communist men under arms, the Nationalist government had 2,600,000 men as opposed to a Communist force of perhaps 1,100,000 at the close of 1946. Similarly, despite the Soviet transfer of Japanese arms to the Communists, the Nationalist advantage in rifles was estimated at better than three to one. The military successes of 1946 did not, however, damage Communist main strength or alter its hold on important rural areas.

This military evolution was accompanied by and intimately bound up with a most complex series of negotiations, sponsored by General Marshall and later aided by Ambassador Stuart until 1947. These were designed to establish terms on which might be created a Chinese national government embracing the KMT, the Communists, and so-called Third Force elements. In the first half of 1946 these negotiations appeared to make some progress in the sense that formulae for political and military unification were discussed in detail, compromises were put forward attempting to meet divergent views, and the procedure in general had the trappings, at least, of serious purpose. The negotiations deteriorated from July 1946; and the Chinese National

Assembly was convened on November 15 without Communist acquiescence or participation.

For no sustained period during the negotiation did military action
cease. The Nationalist troops extended the areas they controlled,
fatally enlarging their commitment to hold fixed points and the lines
of supply between them. The course of negotiation was affected by
the failure to achieve an effective truce, a failure for which there were,
essentially, three deeply rooted reasons:

(*a*) Both the KMT and the Communists were committed ideologically to conceptions of total power in China and looked at all political
formulae in terms of the prospects of their assisting or impeding efforts
to achieve total power. The concept of a continuing political system
of mixed fluctuating power, tolerating several parties, was understood
and acceptable only to a small minority of Chinese politicians (the so-
called Third Force) who took part in the exercise; and their authority,
never backed by the substance of military strength or effective political organization, progressively diminished.

(*b*) In the light of their knowledge of Communist purposes, important and increasingly influential elements in the KMT, including
Chiang Kai-shek, saw no possibility of an acceptable solution without
complete elimination of Communist military strength; and these elements also believed that it lay within Nationalist capabilities to achieve
this end.

(*c*) Given their estimate of relative KMT military strength, the
Communists may have been initially prepared to consider a variety
of formulae which would give them only minority status in a unified
government. They were never prepared, however, to consider a
formula which would effectively deny them control over their own
armed forces. And this ruled out, of course, any meaningful unification of China.

The horizon of short-run ambition of the Chinese Communists and
of Moscow may well have lifted in the course of 1946, not only as
Nationalist military, economic, and political weaknesses were revealed,
but also as American demobilization proceeded and the United States
made clear that it was not prepared to make either Communist domination of Eastern Europe or a Communist victory in China a cause of
war.

The process of disintegration went on until, in December 1946,
General Marshall concluded that no useful purpose could be served
by his remaining on the scene. He left China on January 8, 1947.

3. *Open civil war: 1947–1949.* In the course of 1947 the Communists moved gradually into a general military offensive. Its main pur-

poses were: to isolate the government garrisons in Manchuria by severing rail connections, and to prepare the way for a later repetition of the Manchurian strategy by infiltrating the countryside of Central China. During 1947 the government, despite some surrenders, fully maintained its order of battle advantage.

The Communist strategy consisted in isolating garrisons in cities, maintaining a protracted siege designed to weaken morale and encourage defection, and concentrating superior Communist forces at particular points for the showdown when garrisons were softened up. The Nationalist forces, having gained their forward positions without serious conflict in 1945–1946, were never thrown into major offensive operations; and a lack of unity or of clearly delegated responsibility in command prevented the Nationalist leaders from using the substantial urban garrisons effectively in support of each other when each, successively, was put to the test.

In the course of 1948 the situation moved on to a climax. Wei-hsien and Tsinan in Shantung, Chinchow and Mukden in Manchuria, fell to the Communists with enormous losses in men, equipment, and supplies. By the autumn of 1948 Manchuria and East Central China were lost. In this climactic period (September–November 1948) the balance of force dramatically shifted. By early 1949 government troops numbered 1,500,000; Communist strength, built mainly on KMT surrenders, had risen to over 1,600,000.

The Nationalist forces were seldom effectively reconcentrated thereafter, the bloody and gallant battle of Hsuchow being the major exception. Tientsin and Peiping fell in January 1949. In April a serious plan for defending the Yangtze was rendered ineffective when essential units were suddenly withdrawn to the east before the Communist attack was launched. By July 1, 1949, Mao could proclaim the People's Democratic Dictatorship; and the Organic Law of the Communist regime was put into effect on September 27. The Communists pushed on steadily into Central and South China, past a series of potential and well-advertised defense lines, to complete occupation of the mainland and Hainan (May 1950).

In strictly military terms, then, the Nationalist government suffered its decisive defeat in a campaign for Manchuria, the climax of which was the fall of Mukden on November 1, 1948. In this campaign it was hampered by certain particular logistic weaknesses, notably lack of control over the railway lines running north from Central China and lack of access to Manchuria through the port of Dairen.

It has been argued that at a decisive stage in 1948 the Nationalist forces were short of important types of ammunition owing to the slowness and irregularity of American supply shipments, and that in certain areas small arms ammunition was clearly short.[14] The major weakness of the Nationalist position, however, lay in its commitment to garrison a large number of key urban positions and the lines of supply to them. The Communists, on the other hand, moved freely around the countryside, continuing the military strategy which Mao had developed in the years 1927–1934 in Kiangsi: namely, the concentration at selected points of superior offensive forces based on and provisioned from the countryside and capable of fluid movement. Although the strategic task of the Nationalists was offensive in character—to destroy Communist main strength—its military tactics of garrisoning cities and railway lines were those appropriate only to a limited offensive, like that of the Japanese in China; and they led to a rigid defense of fixed positions, which played into Communist hands. Victory could have come to the Nationalist forces only if they had forced a showdown in the field with the main strengths of the two sides pitted against each other. This had been done with success in Kiangsi in 1934. It was never attempted after 1945. Thus the Nationalists' military tactics dissipated their important initial advantages in numbers of troops and scale and quality of equipment.

These strictly military characteristics of the two armies had a political history and political foundations. The Communist advantages can be summarized as follows:

1. They had developed over many years a political-military method for operating from rural bases; by their temperate land-reform tactics in the Popular Front period and their unceasing propaganda, they had gained limited elements of positive support and widespread passive acquiescence in rural areas; and there had been some increment in support from intellectuals, many of whom had remained in a no-man's land, resisting the courtship of the Communists, harassed or ignored by the KMT, since 1927. This rise in political fortunes was translated in the period 1945–1949 into massive local recruiting which made losses good, and, along with KMT defections, raised the level of the Chinese Communist armed forces from about a million in 1946 to over 1,600,000 in 1949. Communist units were deployed largely in their native regions, avoiding problems of physical adjustment and morale that bedeviled the Nationalists, notably in their Manchurian and North China operations.

2. The policy of the Soviet Union permitted the Communists to acquire from Japanese stockpiles arms necessary for the Manchurian campaign, to infiltrate the Manchurian countryside, and to receive other forms of assistance.

3. Because of their disciplined political structure, and its special history of development from a small unified core, the Communist armed forces were under effective unified command; and beneath that command there was a uniformity in military and political strategy and tactics.

The political and social factors contributing to the weakness of the KMT military position at this time were:

1. Chiang Kai-shek's persistent conviction that serious action on political, social, and economic reform issues must await the prior effective unification of China, if necessary by military means, under the Nationalist government. This conviction led directly to his seeking a military decision in Manchuria at a time when American advisers, at least, strongly counseled that this lay beyond his current effective capabilities. Chiang's tendency to separate military from long-run political and social policy—at the cost of the latter—was perhaps his most fundamental and persistent weakness.

2. The degeneration of standards and morale in the Nationalist administration in the latter days of the Chungking period resulted in carpetbagging urban operations by Nationalist administrators in many areas where they regained control, which progressively diminished the initial postwar prestige of Chiang Kai-shek and his government in China.

3. Chiang Kai-shek's authority—economic, political, and especially military—was dilute in many areas and over various army commands; and within the top leadership of his administration there was no agreement on appropriate military strategy and tactics equivalent to that which informed Communist operations. As the Communists brought their strategy to a climax in attacks on major garrisons, Chiang proved incapable of maneuvering his forces in any effective strategy of mutual support—partly because individual army commanders had a personal vested interest in keeping their units in being as a form of personal bargaining power and as a hedge against Communist victory.

4. In general, the KMT made little effective effort to present to the Chinese people an attractive postwar political, social, and economic program. In particular, the KMT let itself be jockeyed by the Communists into appearing as a war party, unwilling to settle internal differences by negotiation. It failed, therefore, to enlist sympathy and enthusiasm even among those who understood the underlying intransigence and objectives of the Communists. The profound war-weariness of China made this defeat in domestic political warfare serious to the KMT's cause. From the Communist point of view apathy was almost as helpful as positive support for their cause.

5. The Nationalist government was not able to restore production at a sufficient rate and to establish monetary policies which would contain inflation. Although inflation had causes deep in China's war-torn position and KMT administrative weakness, its continued existence was a powerful factor in reinforcing the image of a dynasty which had lost the Mandate of Heaven. It contributed to the wide-spread mood, immensely helpful to the Communists, of belief that the KMT belonged to the past, and, approve of them or not, the Communists were the wave of the future.

Thus, twenty-eight years after its founding, the Communist Party achieved virtually undisputed authority on the China mainland. Exploiting the weaknesses developed in the KMT out of its difficult history, the Communist power tactics, political and military, proved sufficient to gain a clear-cut victory.

At the time of their victory the Communists had already controlled the civil government in various rural Chinese areas for several years; and they had put forward various manifestos outlining a national policy program. Their pre-1949 Popular Front rural practice and their announced program were calculated to gain popular support in a struggle for power; they did not reflect fully either Communist intentions once power had been gained, or the reality of China's inescapable problems. Nevertheless, although the core of their power in the period of takeover was their unified and disciplined armed forces, they had succeeded, as a result of their actions and announced program, in harnessing, to some extent, two major political forces which characterize the Chinese revolutionary movement from its modern beginnings: the old and recurrent aspiration of the Chinese peasantry for land and social reform; and the new, more sophisticated national and international aspirations of the Chinese intelligentsia, stimulated by the challenge and achievements of the western world. These two strands run through the whole modern history of China.

V. SUMMARY

The present position of the Chinese Communist regime, the problems it confronts, and its prospects for continued rule can be understood only in the light of the revolutionary history briefly reviewed above.

The ending of Manchu rule, after almost 300 years of continuous authority, resulted from a process which had many precedents in the dynastic history of China. Internal weaknesses and dissatisfactions combined with increased pressure on China from the outside to destroy the authority of the regime. Such interaction of internal and external pressure has occurred repeatedly in Chinese history; and various theories of dynastic decay have been advanced and debated among scholars of China.[15] The passing of the Manchu dynasty had, however, two central characteristics not shared by its historic predecessors. Externally, the pressures with which China was confronted arose from the whole arena of world power and were of a wholly new kind both in the direction from which they came and in the authority and prestige they carried with them. They resulted in an irreversible drawing of China onto a rapidly changing world scene. Internally, the forces which were set in motion after 1842 tended to transform the agricultural society which had persisted in China over several thousand years of recorded history.

The West confronted China with the challenges of modern military power and with the tasks of large-scale international commerce and industrialization. The western incursion challenged the relevance and viability of Confucian thought and values crystallized and generally operative since the second century B.C.; and it made patently obsolete methods of politics and governmental rule at least as ancient as the Confucian tradition. By weakening the texture of Chinese society and confronting it with other values and systems of organization, the West both stirred latent popular discontent into positive aspiration and made the literate citizens of China examine the realistic alternatives that modern western societies might offer.

In short, we have reviewed not simply a recurrent cyclical pattern around a stable norm but, rather, the first century of a sea change in the structure of a whole society and in its relations to the rest of the world.

Our broad view of this century can be summarized as follows:

1. In the decade before 1911 the political intelligentsia, reacting to the humiliating external defeats and internal failures of the preceding half-century, came to define the Chinese problem as involving three related requirements:

(a) Some kind of democratic reform of the Chinese government—in the pre-1911 period the reformers being split between those who sought to work within the framework of the dynasty and those more radical who looked to its overthrow.

(b) The creation of relations with the external world which would satisfy the deep Chinese aspirations for dignity and status.

(c) The internal reshaping of Chinese society to meet the emerging aspirations of various Chinese groups and classes; a reshaping that touched upon fundamental cultural and ideological conceptions, social structure and mores, and the Chinese economy as well as upon the political machinery itself.

After 1911, and especially after 1915, the first of these problems was transformed into the question of re-creating an effective national state. Thus, the ambiguous but, from the mid-1920's, almost universally accepted Three People's Principles, Nationalism, Democracy, and the People's Livelihood, formulated by Sun Yat-sen as early as 1905, have a special importance. They represented an accepted statement of China's problems and aspirations rather than a clear program for political action. In fact, the political history of China in the past half-century can largely be interpreted in terms of differing views as to how, and in what order, and in what relationship to one another these aspirations should be achieved.

2. From 1898 forward, repeated efforts at the internal reshaping of Chinese society were substantially frustrated by the most profound inertia and resistance to change. A sufficiently strong national government dedicated to these goals did not exist. And China, weak in the face of the external world, was prevented from devoting its full creative energy and resources to substantive domestic problems. China's inability to solve the first and second of its problems, national unity and international independence, thus postponed effective action on the third—domestic reform.

3. In the face of this situation, by about 1923 there emerged in the most responsible segment of Chinese political leadership a consensus that the first priority task of China was to create an effective national government capable of ruling the whole of the country. This required, in particular, that the political leaders learn to unify Chinese military units under effective control. For the next quarter-century the energies of Chinese political leaders were preponderantly devoted to the pursuit of effective domestic power; China's relations with the external world and the promise or substance of internal reform and economic development were almost wholly subordinated to this first-priority goal—or treated as tactical instruments for achieving it.

4. From 1927 two major contenders for national power emerged, the Kuomintang and the Chinese Communist Party: the former, initially the triumphant survivor of an internecine struggle and legitimate successor to Sun Yat-sen's revolutionary party, the latter initially a small insurrectional minority linked to Moscow. Both claimed to seek the goal of national dignity and independence; both were committed to a radical reshaping of China's domestic society; both were committed to the technique of a single disciplined national political party. Although the two parties in fact mainly contended for domestic political

power, beneath the level of the struggle for power the aspirations of various groups for dignity and authority on the international scene and the substance of reform spread and strengthened; and to some extent, by governmental and non-governmental means, some progress towards China's substantive goals was achieved. This progress did not, however, fully satisfy popular aspirations, and the revolutionary momentum of various groups remained the motive force of Chinese politics.

5. The Kuomintang, apparently victorious in 1927, was profoundly weakened in its attempt to consolidate national power and to satisfy the substance of Chinese aspirations by the following key factors:

(a) Chiang Kai-shek proved unable, in the difficult circumstances in which he was forced to operate, to consolidate his military control over China and thereby his effective administrative control. The Communists were never wholly eliminated, and his control over key regions remained uncertain, based on unstable alliances with war lords.

(b) Chiang Kai-shek was confronted in 1931 with Japanese seizure of Manchuria and, then, with its further incursions into Shanghai (1933) and North China. From 1937 to 1945 he faced Japanese invasion. This aggression denied China its principal potential industrial base and forced a diversion of resources and energies to strictly military problems. It drove the KMT out of vast areas of China, forcing the government to operate from a distant rural base in Szechwan from 1939 to 1945. And it imposed all but intolerable strains on the fabric of China's economic and social life.

(c) The domestic sources of Chiang Kai-shek's power and, especially, the character of his own political thought limited the KMT in mobilizing on his side the aspirations of China's peasants for improved economic and social status. Chiang insisted that effective national unity must precede substantial political and economic reform. However correct or incorrect this view may have been as a realistic judgment, it certainly denied him tactically important sources of political strength and support.

These three aspects of the KMT's position produced, during the latter years of the Second World War, a degenerative military and political situation. The consequences of this degeneration of KMT strength and morale were felt strongly from mid-1945, when, in fact, the KMT at last had what might be called objective possibilities for consolidating its rule. The Chinese Communists, aided by the opportunities for expansion during the Japanese War and by the postwar acquisition of Japanese arms and a strategic base in Manchuria (both granted with Soviet connivance), proved able to exploit decisively the relative military and political weakness of the post-1945 Nationalist structure.

6. Thus in 1949 the Chinese Communists were able to create, for the first time since 1911 (or, perhaps, 1916), a national government which soon effectively ruled all of China. Aside from their major asset—which was the weakness of the KMT—the Chinese Communists had two principal strengths denied to Chiang Kai-shek in the period of 1945–1949: first, unified military force; second, a program of political promises designed to harness the support (or passive acceptance) of both a substantial part of the Chinese peasantry and active elements in the Chinese intelligentsia.

The Chinese Communists hold a peculiar place in the sequence of revolution in modern China. We can place Sun Yat-sen as among the first generation of modern Chinese revolutionaries. Born in 1865, he had ties and memories that went back directly to the aftermath of the Taiping Rebellion of 1848–1864. Sun's generation defined China's revolutionary problem, experimented with reform, but never solved the primary problem of establishing a foundation of national authority capable of achieving their purposes. They were concerned with ends more than means.

In these terms, the men who came to power in 1949, like the present top leaders of the KMT, belong to a second generation who have been primarily technicians in the problem of power, concerned with the means for controlling societies rather than with the ends sought by the human beings who compose those societies. Mao Tse-tung is now more than sixty years old. His whole mature life and that of his colleagues has been spent in pursuing domestic power by a mixture of military and political means. Before 1949 the leaders of Chinese Communism had never been previously confronted with responsibility for the full range of China's persistent domestic and foreign problems. Moreover, they are united not only by their own experience of successful insurrection but also by ideological habits which have led them to take the methods and techniques developed by the Soviet Union as a basic if not always overriding model.

Having seized and at least temporarily consolidated national power, they face a future which hinges now on their handling of the postponed questions of substance which for a whole generation of Chinese political history have enjoyed only a derived or secondary priority. They come to this task freighted with commitments to the Soviet Union, to Communist ideology, to methods of political administration, and to agricultural collectivization—all of which affect the manner in which they have proceeded, and, in certain phases of Chinese life, limit their ability to cope with the issues which confront them.

In particular, the following appear to be the key issues on which China's internal evolution will depend in the absence of a major war. Can the Communist regime create relations of dignity with the external world? Can it meet the substantive domestic aspirations—economic, social, and political—which the Communists themselves have mightily stirred up in the Chinese peasantry, the industrial working force, and the intelligentsia? If it cannot meet these aspirations as they existed in 1949, can it either alter them to fit the regime's capabilities or present the facts in such a way that these groups believe that their aspirations are being met? If, as seems likely, it cannot meet them or alter them or persuade the bulk of the Chinese that they are being met, can it maintain effective control by devices of force, threat, propaganda, and incentives which in effect persuade dissatisfied Chinese that no realistic alternative exists to the passive acceptance of continued Communist totalitarian rule?

In substantial part, the following essay is concerned with the manner in which the Chinese Communists have begun to deal with these issues of substance; it is concerned with their successes and their failures, and the forces apparently set in motion by their effort.

Notes for Chapter 1

1. C. C. Chang, *An Estimate of China's Farms and Crops*, 1932, pp. 11–14, quoted in A. K. Chiu, "Agriculture," *China*, Ch. XXXII, H. F. MacNair, ed., Berkeley, University of California Press, 1946, p. 469.

2. John K. Fairbank, *The United States and China*, Cambridge, Mass., Harvard University Press, 1948, pp. 152–153.

3. Used throughout as the accepted abbreviation for Kuomintang, the National People's Party.

4. John K. Fairbank, *The United States and China, op. cit.*, p. 174.

5. For a development of this distinction see W. W. Rostow and others, *Dynamics of Soviet Society*, New York, W. W. Norton, 1953.

6. Quoted from Kisselev, "A History of Communism in China," *The China Illustrated Review*, January 28, 1928, p. 11, in R. C. North, *Kuomintang and Chinese Communist Elites*, Stanford, California, Hoover Institute Studies, Stanford University Press, July 1952, p. 22.

7. The relations developed between the agents of the imperial government at the county (*hsien*) level and the gentry did reflect, in fact (as opposed to theory), a rather subtle distribution of authority; and the impact of autocratic power on the individual was traditionally softened by bribery, family ties, and other instruments for deflecting centralized authority.

8. There are those who have traced a portion of Hegel's inspiration back to the Chinese classics, although not rigorously.

9. For further elaboration of this point see Ch. 5. For a parallel view of Soviet Communism in relation to the Russian autocratic tradition, see W. W. Rostow and others, *op. cit.*, Ch. 7.

10. Benjamin I. Schwartz, *Chinese Communism and the Rise of Mao,* Cambridge, Mass., Harvard University Press, 1951, pp. 189–190.

11. *United States Relations with China, with Special Reference to the Period 1944– 1949* (White Paper on China), Department of State publication 3573, Far Eastern Series 30, August 1949. (Division of Publications Office of Public Affairs, U. S. Government, Washington, D. C.) This official United States translation of the Communist promises differs in important respects from that published by the Central News Agency of Nationalist China, September 22, 1937. The latter makes the Communist commitments much less explicit. Although we are in no position to arbitrate the differences there is no doubt that the Central News Agency translation more faithfully reflects Communist intent, which was, of course, to exploit the agreement so as to enlarge its own relative power position in China, and to avoid the surrender of any important prerogatives in the areas held by Communist forces.

12. *Ibid.*, p. 51.

13. See, for example, *The Private Papers of Senator Vandenburg,* ed. A. H. Vandenburg, Jr., Boston, Houghton Mifflin, 1952, pp. 519–545; especially pp. 522–524 and 534–535.

14. For an excellent discussion of this factor in relation to the other forces which determined the outcome, see S. T. Possony, *A Century of Conflict,* Chicago, Henry Regnery, 1953, pp. 298–351.

15. For a discussion of such cyclical dynastic theories, see especially K. A. Wittfogel, "Theorie der orientalischen Gesellschaft," in *Zeitschrift für Sozialforschung,* 1937; John K. Fairbank, *The United States and China, op. cit.,* Ch. 5; also Owen Lattimore, *Inner Asian Frontiers of China,* New York, Capital Publishing Company, 1951, Ch. XVII.

PART

2

THE EVOLUTION OF
COMMUNIST POLICY: 1949–1954

THE REVOLUTIONARY ROOTS

At the time of its accession to full control of mainland China in 1949 the Chinese Communist Party was already seasoned by nearly thirty years' growth, a long war, and a degree of administrative experience. Moreover, it had survived the vicissitudes of intraparty struggles, and came to power with a hard-core veteran leadership of tested loyalty to Mao, whose top position had already been validated by eleven years of unchallenged supremacy.

The Chinese Communist Party, then, as a going concern, had a definable past; and it is important to recall the extent to which recent developments are rooted in that pre-1949 revolutionary past.

I. The Revolutionary Origins of Domestic Policy

Specifically, these were the major acts taken between 1940 and 1949 which have significantly affected the character of Chinese domestic policy since the takeover:

1. *The publication of Mao's "The New Democracy" in 1940.* Tactically a justification for the Popular Front line then being pursued within China, this pronouncement sketched an immediate national future designed to appeal to the widest number of Chinese. Mao stated that, in the first instance, the Communist China he sought would not be a proletarian dictatorship like the Soviet Union but a joint dictatorship of several revolutionary classes which would leave a considerable role for capitalism and for non-Communist parties and personages. Mao explicitly evoked Sun Yat-sen's Three People's Principles as the foundation for his proposed New China rather than the model of the Soviet Union as established by Lenin and developed by Stalin. Like Lenin and Hitler, Mao also stated overtly his ultimate purposes—which were complete socialization (including a collectivized

49

agriculture), and that mystical goal, the Communism which would come with the end of the class struggle and the withering away of the state. These were conventional Communist goals, but he worked on the assumptions that men generally make their political judgments on a short horizon and that his promise of tolerance over the short period at least would be effective. Many Chinese, and some Americans, ignored the fine print of Communist orthodoxy which Mao consistently included in his pronouncements.

2. *The Cheng Feng (Ideological Remolding) Movement, launched early in 1942*. Buried within Mao's short-period concept of the New Democracy was the principle of democratic centralism, the most fundamental of Leninist doctrines, which sanctioned the laying down of a single 'correct' line of policy from above through the instrument of a disciplined Communist Party, which in turn dominated the national structure. In ideological language, as opposed to organizational technique, democratic centralism in China was founded on the notion of the 'hegemony of the proletariat' within the four-class alliance of which the New Democracy was theoretically composed. The extension of this principle, basic to the creation of Soviet totalitarianism, is the core of Chinese Communist domestic policy. By the Cheng Feng Movement Mao sought to ensure that the highest degree of discipline and unity would be steadily maintained within the rapidly expanding Communist Party. It was evident that Mao regarded the indoctrination and especially the discipline of new recruits to the party as a matter of the highest priority—the key to continued Communist domination in a period when a surface of multiparty government would be tolerated.

3. *Wartime land reform*. Although the Agrarian Reform Law was not adopted until June 1950, the techniques of land reform were cultivated and developed throughout the war years wherever the Chinese Communists held control. Their purpose in the pre-1949 period was to give substance to the promise of rural reform and, especially, to win sufficient rural political support for the Communist armies to attract a flow of recruits, ensure supplies, and secure positive cooperation, chiefly in the fields of intelligence and supply, in rural areas through which they operated. When the Communists came to power they found themselves with a profound commitment to extend land reform throughout China. Although they have sought to make the land-reform process serve both their political and economic purposes, important clashes between the two sets of goals have emerged.

II. The Revolutionary Origins of Foreign Policy [1]

Judged by statement and performance, the Chinese Communists never questioned that their basic international orientation was toward the Soviet Union. But the peculiar exclusiveness of post-1949 relations between Communist China and the Soviet Union can be traced back to decisions taken in the years 1945–1949.

When Mao played the Popular Front game to the hilt in Yenan, that line was wholly in accord with Moscow's interest and policy. The Chinese Communist leadership never doubted that its Marxism was orthodox or that its views on imperialism were correctly Leninist and Stalinist. If anything, Mao's writings on imperialism were more consistent and more dogmatic than those of Stalin and other Soviet figures who had guided the Soviet Union through various 'hard' and 'soft' phases in Soviet external policy, leaving behind a convenient trail of ambiguities about 'co-existence.' It was natural that the Communist leader of a self-designated 'semi-colonial' area should lean heavily on Communist theories of imperialism. Within the strategic framework of a binding link to Moscow and international Communism there was still a range of tactical lines of policy that Communist China might pursue.

Mao's fundamental view of contemporary China has always emphasized its weakness as an independent power on the world scene. Contemplating his position in 1945, he could see clearly that the Communist effort to seize power in China would have to be worked out in relation to great-power politics. It was evident that the Soviet Union was not prepared to risk major war with the United States in order to install him in power in China. On the contrary, the evidence— notably Soviet dismantling of Manchurian industry—was that the Soviet Union expected a phase of Nationalist power with which Mao and the Soviet Union would have to contend.[2]

It seems likely that sometime in 1946 Moscow revised its estimate of Communist potentialities for expansion both in Europe and in China. In part this revision stemmed almost certainly from American policy after 1945. As it became evident that the United States was unwilling to back the Yalta Agreement on free elections in eastern Europe with the threat of force or its use, so it became clear that the United States was unwilling to maintain substantial numbers of troops on the Chinese mainland. The 50,000 U. S. Marines landed to assist in transferring Chiang's troops to the north were evidently limited in their somewhat unclear mission. The political pressure in the United States for rapid demobilization was overwhelming. These elements probably combined with progressive evidence of Nationalist political and military weakness to produce in Moscow as well as Yenan an upward revision of Mao's prospects.

The weakness and ambiguity with which the United States asserted its strategic interest on the Chinese scene may well have reinforced Mao in his instinctive ideological view that he would have to extend his power in association with the Soviet Union. If the United States was not prepared to regard the disposition of Manchuria as a matter of high strategic importance, he would have to find ways of ensuring Manchuria's attachment to China, rather than to Russia, by negotiating bilateral agreement with Moscow. It would be foolish to explain the Sino-Soviet alliance wholly or even mainly in these terms. Nevertheless, given China's intrinsic weakness in the face of Russia or Japan, it is a fact which applied then, and applies now, that, so long as the United States does not regard the integrity of China's borders as a matter of high American strategic interest, the American ability to influence the course of Chinese events is limited.

There were deep roots in Chinese Communism for the anti-American position it had adopted and maintained from its earliest days. On ideological grounds Chinese Communists had long regarded the United States as the key 'imperialist' enemy of Communist expansion, even when the American presence on the Chinese scene was limited and identifiable with 'imperialism' only by extraordinary strain on the facts. Communists sensed that, whereas in the long run Britain and France would be relatively weak in Asia, United States power would remain impressive over the foreseeable future. As Schwartz points out, this awareness led, as far back as 1929,[3] to a persistent, doctrinaire, and somewhat unpersuasive insistence among Chinese Communists that the United States was the key 'imperialist' enemy—a propaganda role from which the United States was relieved only during the years of American wartime alliance with the Soviet Union and of Chinese Communist Popular Front tactics.

In the immediate postwar years, United States' aid in moving Chiang Kai-shek's troops into North China and Manchuria and pressure for a political settlement between the Communists and the Nationalists made the United States the major western power in China—and, therefore, the major block, aside from Nationalist military strength, to the Communist seizure of power. Even at stages when superficially the negotiations between the Communists and Nationalists were going reasonably well, the Communists never flagged in their purposeful propaganda campaign against the United States.

They thought that they were bound to oppose American interests in the Far East. The United States was committed to the support of the Nationalist cause; and Nationalist China was the major immediate enemy. The United States had achieved virtually monopolistic powers in the occupation of Japan; and the Communists felt sure that they would sooner or later find themselves again in conflict with Japan in Asian power politics, a judgment clearly reflected in the published terms of the 1950 Sino-Soviet Treaty. The Chinese Communists had ambitions for extending Communist rule in Indo-China and elsewhere in southeast Asia. Such an extension, they knew, would run counter to American interests. Thus, in building the initial phase of their policy on anti-Americanism, the Chinese Communists were simply reflecting the inevitable clash between their own ambitions and the American interest as they understood it. The phase of relatively good behavior in the early stages of the Communist-Nationalist negotiations for unity under General Marshall can have been only a minor tactical deviation in their minds.

There was one major loss which the Communists accepted in building their policy on anti-Americanism; and this was frankly faced in certain of Mao's statements, notably *On the People's Democratic Dictatorship,* of July 1, 1949. Mao knew that his external policy implied the rejection of any possibility of American and western economic aid. Having taken steps which they knew would effectively deny them American economic aid, the Communists no doubt comforted themselves with the hope (and probably assurance) of Soviet assistance, as well as with the general Communist doctrine that economic development under Communism should proceed mainly by the effective exploitation of a region's own economic resources. A United States with abiding interests in the Asian balance of power as a whole, even though committed to minimizing its direct military commitments on the Asian mainland, could only be an enemy to a weak but ambitious Communist China. On the other hand, the Soviet Union was in a position both to deny the Chinese Communists certain important advantages and to assist Mao in the pursuit of major internal and external ambitions.

First, it was with the Soviet Union that the Chinese Communists would have to negotiate in order to settle the status of Manchuria, Inner Mongolia, and Sinkiang. Virtually surrounded by Soviet occupation in Outer Mongolia, Dairen, North Korea, and the Maritime

Provinces, Manchuria was in a precarious position if the Soviet Union were unfriendly and no countervailing force were available. In Sinkiang and elsewhere along China's interior borders there were other sensitive areas where, given China's fundamentally weak and dependent military status, a friendly Soviet Union would be important to China's interests, and where, under any circumstances, American pressure would be hard to exert.

Second, the Soviet Union might offer a measure of economic assistance and guidance in the process of industrialization. It is part of Asian Communist dogma that the example of Soviet industrialization is more relevant to Asia than that of the United States or other western countries. Whether or not this is so, the Chinese Communists, notably those without western experience, may have felt in 1949 that Soviet advice would be more relevant and helpful than that of Americans or western Europeans.

Finally, the Chinese Communists knew that it was fundamental to Moscow's long-run strategy to weaken the power of the West by eroding western political and economic strength in Asia. This was Lenin's strategic formula from the early 1920's; and it had never been wholly abandoned in Moscow. A joint policy in Asia as between Moscow and Peking commended itself as a logical outcome of converging Chinese and Soviet interests as long as a policy of Communist expansion was envisaged.

The argument of these pages is somewhat unconventional, and we would wish to avoid misunderstanding of it. It is our view that the Chinese Communists committed themselves to a basic international orientation to Moscow long before 1945 and probably never envisaged any other long-run strategic alternative. But we have more to explain in postwar history than that. We must explain why that alliance was virtually exclusive and, particularly, why Moscow and Peking launched a joint program of aggression in Asia immediately following the completion of Mao's seizure of power in China. Whether or not United States policy or action could have been any other than what it was—we are not attempting to describe alternative paths of history—we are convinced that two aspects of United States policy converged with Mao's instinctive posture toward Moscow. United States abstention from a strategic claim to interest in Manchuria left him face to face with Moscow; and, more important, United States demobilization and troop withdrawals from the mainland opened up, in the unstable state of postwar Asia, a wide range of possibilities for Communist expansion. These immediate possibilities of joint expansion made the Sino-

Soviet alliance extremely attractive to Peking, for it was in no position to exploit them without the backing of a major power.

In terms of Chinese Communist logic, then, there were important and precise reasons for entering an exclusive alliance with the Soviet Union in the postwar years. The partners could not then predict how far they might go together in extending Communist influence, or what the effective reaction of the United States and the West would be to their aggressive course. Remembering what potentialities for Communist expansion had existed after the First World War, and that they had been only partially exploited, it is likely that the Communist leaders intended after the Second World War to press their apparent advantages to the limit before the western world could stabilize itself.

In short, from some time in 1946 on, the fundamental strategy of international Communism was one of exploiting to the limit, short of major war, all possibilities for expansion which they perceived. An extreme version of the lean-to-one-side policy appears to have made good sense to top Chinese Communist leaders on grounds quite independent of but convergent with their profound ideological commitment to Moscow. It is, however, by no means clear that, in a phase where Communist expansion is effectively checked for a substantial period, and the primary concerns of Moscow and Peking are internal, the potential conflicts of interest between Moscow and Peking within the orbit of their alliance may not assume a greater importance.

In any case, to understand the Communists' total performance after their takeover in 1949, it is essential to understand that they got control of mainland China at a moment when they felt the time might well be ripe for a major further extension of Communist influence in Asia. As they sensed both their own strength in association with the Soviet Union and the apparent weakness of the western world, they judged that 1949–1950 was a time to strike and not to waste possibly transitory historical opportunities. They could not know how far they might go until the western reaction was revealed in June 1950; and their priority task was the assertion of sovereignty in Chinese territory, including Sinkiang, Tibet, and Formosa. But this hopeful and aggressive frame of mind profoundly affected domestic as well as foreign policy in the first years of Chinese Communist rule.

Summarizing, it is evident that the primary pre-1949 interests of the Chinese Communists centered on the seizure of power in China. From the Yenan period forward they sought to present such plans as would maximize popular support for the Communist cause. Although they were fully aware of China's need and aspiration for economic progress and industrialization, and although Mao, as a Marxist-Leninist expert on power, reiterated his view that a China which lacked a substantial industrial sector would remain militarily and politically dependent, most pre-1949 policy and action was directed toward the primary goals of achieving and consolidating domestic power rather than sustained Chinese economic growth.

Communist policy moved from victory in civil war directly into a period of the most acute military and political tension with the United States and the western world, accompanied by a military alliance with the Soviet Union. It was Chinese Communist attitudes and policies which purposefully eliminated the possibility of even exploring terms for relatively normal diplomatic relations with the non-Communist world. This break with the western world facilitated the task of consolidation of absolute internal power, including the elimination of symbols of western influence in China. It set what the Communist leadership evidently believed was the necessary framework for the national indoctrination which took place after 1949. It is our tentative judgment that this acute tension also arose from the inflated hopes of Moscow and Peking, as they came to define the possibilities for Communist expansion after 1946. The phase from late 1946 to mid-1951, from the launching of open civil war to the beginning of explorations looking to a Korean truce, is thus regarded as a single wave of Communist effort at expansion in Asia by military means short of major war. The exploitation of the Communist position in Indo-China and its diplomatic consolidation at Geneva in July 1954 rounded out this phase.

Against this general background the two following chapters seek to trace out in some detail how, by 1953, external problems had converged with internal difficulties to shift the focus of Communist attention, at least temporarily, toward the economic foundations for Chinese Communist power; and how, toward the end of 1953, basic decisions were taken decreeing that economic growth will be sought by a ruthless concentration of effort in the heavy-industry sector of the economy.

This new priority does not imply that the Chinese Communists have even temporarily abandoned efforts to expand their power in Asia. They will certainly press their advantages and exploit Free World weakness. It may well reflect a decision to avoid techniques of expansion which require important outlays of economic resources; that is, there may well be increased reliance on diplomatic, political, and subversive (as opposed to formal military) techniques.

Notes for Chapter 2

1. Sino-Soviet relations are examined at greater length in Ch. 9–11.

2. In addition to the persuasive evidence of 1945 Soviet reparations policy in Manchuria, and Moscow's negotiations with Chiang at the end of 1945, Vladimir Dedijer reports Stalin as follows in *Tito*, New York, Simon and Schuster, 1953, p. 332.

It is true, we have also made mistakes. For instance, after the war we invited the Chinese comrades to come to Moscow and we discussed the situation in China. We told them bluntly that we considered the development of the uprising in China had no prospect, and that the Chinese comrades should seek a *modus vivendi* with Chiang Kai-shek, that they should join the Chiang Kai-shek government and dissolve their army. The Chinese comrades agreed here with the views of the Soviet comrades, but went back to China and acted quite otherwise. They mustered their forces, organized their armies and now, as we see, they are beating the Chiang Kai-shek army. Now, in the case of China, we admit we were wrong. It proved that the Chinese comrades and not the Soviet comrades were right.

3. Benjamin I. Schwartz, *Chinese Communism and the Rise of Mao, op. cit.*, pp. 129–130.

CHAPTER

—— 3 ————————————————————————

THE SURGE ON ALL FRONTS: 1949–1950

I. DOMESTIC TASKS

The immediate coincidental domestic tasks facing Mao and his party in 1949 were the setting in operation of a new government for all China and establishing control over the people.

The People's Republic of China was set up by the Organic Law of September 27, 1949, following conclusions reached in a series of preparatory commissions which had operated over the previous seventeen months. In its beginning stages, especially at lower city and county levels, the creation of a new bureaucracy necessitated the employment of existing experienced personnel almost regardless of political background. As a part of calculated policy, prominent non-Communist collaborators and Kuomintang defectors—intellectuals, civil servants, and military leaders—were placed in ostensibly important positions. Thus the surface appearance of a coalition government, a major premise of Mao's *New Democracy,* was created with control and policy firmly in Communist hands from its inception.

The Organic Law defines superficially the structure of Communist China's government from the takeover down to the time when the new Draft Constitution succeeds it. In fact Communist China is governed not by the orderly table of organization provided in the Organic Law but by three chains of command unified by the triple functions of a small group of key Communist leaders whom Mao Tse-tung effectively dominates. There are the Communist Party, the Government of the People's Republic of China, and the People's Revolutionary Military Council, the last controlling the armed forces.[1] Although the People's Revolutionary Military Council is formally part of the government it is the chief authority in a separate chain of command unified in the hands of a few key Communist Party government leaders. The military bureaucracy is to be distinguished from the civil bureaucracy and from the horde of cadres who operate within the party chain of command. The employees of state and party number about 15 million, of whom perhaps 10 million are full-time military and people's militia. From the moment of coming to power (in a bad harvest year, marked by famine in Hopei and Anhwei), the Communist regime made a costly and purposeful effort to ensure special rations and privileges for this substantial group and their families, on whose disciplined loyalty all was judged to depend. By western standards these privileges are not great; and there is recent (1954) evidence that the lower-level cadres find themselves often in straitened circumstances. But there was no romantic egalitarianism in the China of 1949, as there was in the Soviet Union of 1917–1918.

The tripartite power structure operated initially through six area governments plus the Mongolia autonomous region and Tibet, which was brought definitively under Communist military control in May 1951. Each area had its own governmental structure headed by an administrative commission. The chairmen of the administrative commissions were Communist military figures, except in Manchuria and North China, where Kao Kang and Liu Lan-t'ao were chairmen. Below the area governments were provincial, county, and village administrations. Major cities linked directly to the area governments rather than to the provinces.

In June 1954 Peking announced that the regional administrations would be abolished in a gradual process, providing for a takeover of function by more highly centralized methods of administration. This announcement fits the general emphasis of the Draft Constitution of 1954, which is marked by a concentration of political power in Peking. The full meaning of the abolition of the regional administrations, notably for the relative power of Chinese Communist military leaders who have prominently figured in them, cannot yet be assessed.

The Chinese Communist government structure combines features of traditional China and the Soviet Union. Superficially, the regional layout originally differed little from the Nationalist system. As it has evolved, however, the Communist government has achieved a higher degree of effective power at the national level, and it has invaded local government at the village level to a degree unprecedented in Chinese history. Communist China resembles the Soviet Union in the interlocking of party and state functions (a feature also of Nationalist China), in the grouping of ministries under the Government Council (similar to the Presidium of the Supreme Soviet).[2] The People's Congress, now scheduled to convene for the first time in the latter part of 1954, will contain representatives of the mass organizations as well as representatives chosen by the People's Representatives Congresses (PRC). The PRC, like the Russian soviets on which they are modeled, run down from the national to the village level. These quasi-legislative bodies, whose membership is carefully controlled by the party at all levels, have extremely limited functions: as a source of information on popular attitudes; as sounding boards and transmission belts for officially determined policy; and as a façade of democratic procedures designed to give an illusion of popular participation in the deliberations of the state.

The national governmental structure was set in motion in 1949–1950. The major overt development in governmental structure since then has been a tendency, notable since 1952 and climaxed in the Draft Constitution of 1954, to tighten the control which the central administration at Peking exercises over the regional governments. It is evident that the Chinese Communists have been extremely sensitive to the problem which Chiang Kai-shek was never able to solve satisfactorily, that is, the powerful tendency for regional autonomy to persist.

It is extremely difficult to detect precisely the means by which government policy is implemented through the multiple chains of command. It is plain that the Communist Party, the armed forces, and the government operate in parallel but overlapping structures to apply policies created by a small group of men who manage the whole system; and that key positions at all levels in the governmental structures are held by members of the Communist Party. Nevertheless, the technique by which responsibility is split among these chains of command, the shifts in power as among the chains of command since 1949, and the methods of overlap are not yet wholly clear. On the whole, as in the early days of the Soviet Union, the Communist Party chain of command has evidently played a major role in the administration as well as formulation of national policy—although the military have assumed functions and powers for which there is no Soviet analogy. Efforts to clarify the respective areas of responsibility, possibly in favor of the governmental chain of command, may have been under way in the period 1952–1954.

Within this over-all structure, the system of control, already practiced in occupied areas, especially the Northeast, and eventually instituted in all China, followed Communist patterns familiar in the Soviet Union and eastern Europe: close observation and detailed reporting on individuals and families, regulation of all travel by permit, enlarged police forces and functions, the establishment of party-managed local peasant organizations and city neighborhood organizations, the rapid building-up of national mass organizations under party leadership, and the exploitation of expanded educational facilities for purposes of indoctrination.

From the beginning, the effort to get and to hold popular support was put on an institutional basis. The Communists made a special appeal to three groups in Chinese society which traditionally had held low status and whose advancement had long been an overt part of non-Communist as well as Communist revolutionary objectives: industrial workers, youth, and women. For each there was set up a major organization. The All China Federation of Trade Unions (known as All China Federation of Labor prior to 1953), the New Democratic Youth League of China, and the All China Federation of Democratic Women [3] were all organized by the end of April 1949. Their common purpose is to control and guide the opinion and action of these elevated social groups by tightly mobilizing their 'active elements.' Control by the Communist Party is exercised at high levels through the concentrated power of top groups which exercise the prerogatives of democratic centralism, and at intermediate and low levels by the presence of cadres whose task is to ensure that the policies laid down are executed. As in the Soviet Union, these 'transmission belt' organizations are designed also to impart some sense of participation in the policy of the state, and they administer certain welfare functions.

In addition to these three major mass organizations the All China Federation of Literature and Art, the All China Federation of Democratic Youth, the All China Students' Federation, and the Sino-Soviet Friendship Association were organized before the end of 1949.

This was the beginning of a process which, by the end of 1952, was to include also the preparation for the establishment of some twenty-one lesser organizations and the important All China Federation of Industry and Commerce, so that today there is virtually no segment of life in Communist China which is not organized by the Communist Party and controlled by its directives through the hierarchy of disciplined cadres.

The initial period of the Communist regime was one of effort at major transformation in Chinese society, designed both to guarantee in the short run full control by the Communist leaders and to bring about social and political changes which were believed to guarantee such control over the long pull.

This phase saw an important shift in formal party ideology. Starting in the early months of 1949, the party emphasized that henceforth the Chinese revolution would be built in much larger measure on urban workers. After two decades of tactical unorthodoxy, in which Mao had defined the poor peasants as the prime basis for Communist strength, the Chinese Communists moved verbally closer to the Moscow fold with hegemony-of-the-proletariat slogans of near (but not quite) Marxist purity.[4] This policy, begun in North China, spread throughout the country as the cities came under Communist control. It is to be interpreted as reflecting the fact of Communist power in urban areas rather than a basic change in ideology. The ideological shift in vocabulary was accompanied by the rapid transformation of the Chinese trade unions into a vital transmission belt for national policy and a major instrument for controlling industrial labor. There was no equivalent in China of the early post-revolutionary phase in Russia, when elements of real policy-making power were briefly allocated to the unions.

Side by side with this tactical shift, the principles of the New Democracy were applied. The New Democracy program had sought to rally the maximum number of social groups around the Communist cause and to minimize the groups who would be treated as implacable enemies of the new regime. In particular the intelligentsia and petty bourgeoisie were included along with the proletariat and the peasantry as legitimate participants in the Communist new order. In the first instance, only unregenerate KMT leaders, 'imperialists,' large landlords, and 'bureaucratic capitalists' (the more wealthy and powerful elements in the urban middle class) were to be excluded.

Within this framework of public commitments the regime followed a pattern of action which recalls Chinese Communist military strategy in the period of insurrection, although it does not differ greatly from Soviet strategy in taking over the East European satellites. As formulated in party slogans, Communist political-military strategy was the following: "To unite with the majority, to attack the minority, to divide the enemies and to destroy the enemies one by one."[5] Thus the Communists directly seized the real instruments of power in Chinese society while avoiding unnecessary overt clashes. The Red Army remained under a discipline rare in a conquering force and particularly impressive, in early takeover days, to a Chinese population which had deeply painful memories of armies, especially victorious armies. Secondary points where resistance might arise were bypassed. No immediate effort was made, for example, to replace the bulk of the civil service. Private businessmen were permitted to go about their work in a relatively normal manner; the university curricula were initially altered only by the addition of courses in Marxism and Revolution, although faculty confessions and brainwashing began early.

In North China and Manchuria land reform, pushed swiftly, was almost concluded by June 1950, with some 60 million acres redistributed. But in the North this was the culmination of a program begun in 1945. In Central and South China, which had to feed the cities, and where opposition to Communism was strong, land reform proceeded with comparative moderation, pending the land-reform legislation of June 1950.

The real sources of power and influence were rapidly taken in hand. Pockets of armed resistance were removed, and even the smallest stores of firearms were rounded up with almost pathological thoroughness. The police were brought firmly under Communist administration. The press and other means of mass communication became almost immediately a Communist monopoly.

Having seized the instruments of power, isolating potentially hostile elements and rendering them ineffective, the Communists simultaneously began to build what they believed were the popular foundations for their rule. There appears to be an element of distinct ideological faith reflected in this first phase of Chinese Communist policy. The leaders appeared to believe that a shift in social power among Chinese classes, combined with an intense and monopolistic flow of propaganda and re-education, would bring about a situation where, in some sense, the Communists might rule by consent. By 1949 Moscow had long since abandoned any serious effort to induce desired popular actions within the Soviet Union by propaganda devices which would make men act out of enthusiasm and by direct personal identification with the motives and purposes of the Communist state. Such efforts had been superseded by appeals to material advance, power, prestige, and nationalism, and by the threatening consequences of failure to conform. The Chinese Communists, at least briefly, sought to generate a mood of positive acceptance and enthusiasm, possibly as a cynical tactic to cover the period until full-scale machinery of control and coercion was installed, but possibly also in the hope that a measure of real persuasion could be achieved.

The core of authority in this process was the Chinese Communist Party. Its membership was 40,000 in 1937. It grew from 1,210,000 in 1945 to 5 million by the spring of 1951 and to 6 million in 1954— a growth which reflected both a purposeful policy of increasing the proportion of 'proletarians' in the Communist ranks and, in part, an opportunistic movement of Chinese to the winning side. Some certainly joined in all sincerity as the only realistic means they could perceive of contributing effectively to their nation's reconstruction. At the beginning of its exercise of total control, Communist Party membership was about 3 million. The key instruments of action were the cadres—the 'active element' chosen by the elite to lead 'the masses', along 'correct lines' determined from day to day by the top leadership. The cadres were usually members of the Communist Party and in all cases under close Communist Party control. In the armed forces, government, propaganda, industry, agriculture, and education they received their new instructions and busied themselves with the tasks of governing the country.

In the universities the cadres led the interminable meetings designed to remake the attitudes of teacher and student alike, by publicly confessing past misconceptions and embracing the new faith. They led the proliferating Marxist discussion groups, designed to inject a minimum ideological knowledge and conformity throughout the population. In the villages they stirred the antagonisms of poor peasants against the landowners and gentry, a process regarded as prerequisite to land reform. They led the way in the trade unions, youth movements, and the women's movements which were soon organized. They organized parades and demonstrations, plays and dances. All this had the triple purpose of winning over the Chinese population to the new regime; educating the Chinese people in its peculiar vocabulary and perspective; and defining the terms, concepts, and attitudes required of the citizen if he were safely to survive in the new order. In addition there was an unrelenting effort to educate and discipline the cadres themselves, for the old-guard Communists had a considerable and perhaps not wholly unjustified suspicion of their sincerity and understanding of Communism.

In explaining the Cheng Feng Movement in 1942 Mao thus indicated his view of how men could be persuaded to an appreciation of Communism: [6]

> If the reasoning is good, if it is to the point, it can be effective. The first method in reasoning is to give the patients a powerful stimulus, yell at them 'you're sick!' so the patients will have a fright and break out in an over-all sweat; then, they can be carefully treated.

This clinical approach was followed throughout China on a monumental scale in 1949–1950. Using every possible means of communication the Communists yelled; the patients were duly frightened; and, undoubtedly, they sweated to the point of confessing at length their past misconceptions and asserting their new-found understanding of the virtues of Communist rule. It is by no means evident, however, that Mao's therapy in itself had long-lasting results or that the subsequent 'careful treatment' could guarantee Communist control and popular support by even such energetic methods of 'persuasion.' At the minimum, however, the psychological exercise impressed one and all with the new government's intent to impose conformity in expressed thought; and the very act of public confession and acknowledgment of conformity had psychological consequences which made easier the problem of subsequent Communist control.

The extent of the effort at persuasion in this first phase is to be understood partly in terms of the prior experience and competence of the Communist leadership and the cadres.[7] For a generation and more the tasks of the Communists had been military and political. Communist politics in China meant agit-prop: agitation and propaganda. Here they knew all the tricks of the trade—at least for insurrectional politics. But, so far as civil government was concerned, their experience was derived from the Kiangsi, Yenan, and wartime operations. These operations, notably after 1937, often required civil administration in wide areas; but it was mainly rural administration, with limited communications and limited civil objectives governed largely by military requirements. And a substantial portion of such administration consisted of political indoctrination.

It should be noted here that one strand of policy was radical from the beginning. The official (not necessarily personal) attitude toward the western European countries and the United States, and toward their representatives and private citizens in China, was acutely hostile. Anti-Americanism was pressed with heightened force. Representatives of the West, as well as missionaries and businessmen, were progressively obstructed in pursuit of their work; cut off from any important connection with it; and sometimes jailed, expelled, or killed. At no time in this initial phase of total consolidation was there a serious suggestion that relations with the West might become easier as observers, especially British merchants, had predicted. It was the evident intent of the Chinese Communists promptly to remove any significant trace of direct western connection with Chinese life.

While the consolidation of total political and social domestic power was evidently a high priority in 1949–1950, the regime, nevertheless, confronted inescapable economic tasks which could not be ignored with impunity. Rail lines and other means of communication had been badly damaged in the course of the civil war, notably by Communist attacks on communications between Nationalist strong points. Track and roadbed sections were torn up over long stretches. The currency was in a state of roaring inflation, the third major inflationary phase in five years. Both domestic and foreign trade were disrupted. The industrial base in Manchuria had been severely damaged by Soviet reparation removals; and, although rehabilitation had begun there in 1948, a long road stretched ahead before industrial capacity could be brought back to the level at which the Japanese left it in 1945. In rural areas peasants had gone about raising their crops, civil war or no. But troops had confiscated seed grain; connections between rural areas and urban markets had been disrupted over considerable areas; drainage and irrigation and other water works had been somewhat neglected; and the movement of crops from surplus to deficit areas had been obstructed.

Aided by the end of hostilities on the mainland and by the installation of reasonably effective central government, the Chinese Communists made rapid progress in 1949–1950 in basic rehabilitation, that is, in bringing output back toward the limit of existing agricultural and industrial capabilities. In the classic Chinese manner, the government conscripted mass labor units to repair dikes and irrigation ditches as well as the railway system. In a vigorous series of measures, including especially the more effective collection of taxes, enforced purchase of government bonds, and the development of government production and marketing institutions, the new Communist currency was made reasonably stable. Inflation, the symbol and cause of so much KMT weakness, was brought under control by March 1950, as indicated in the accompanying table.[8] The meager harvest in the

MONTHLY AVERAGE VALUE OF STANDARD COMMODITY UNIT * IN SHANGHAI
(IN YUAN PEOPLE'S CURRENCY)

June 1949	341
September 1949	793
December 1949	2,861
March 1950	6,229
June 1950	5,238
September 1950	5,036
December 1950	4,982

* Each commodity unit consists of 1.56 catties of medium grade rice, 1 *chih* (0.4 yard) of cotton fabrics, 1 *liang* (1.33 ounces) of peanut oil, and 1 catty of coal briquettes.

North in 1949 was met by some shipments from surplus areas, but there was great suffering. Despite this, the regime pressed on with the expansion of acreage in industrial crops for domestic use and for export, notably cotton and peanuts; and foodstuffs, mostly from Manchuria, were included among China's exports in the first batch of trade agreements negotiated.

Despite a continuing Nationalist blockade, the grave economic situation inherited at the end of more than a decade of war, a bad harvest season, and land reform's initial deterrent effect on output, the Communist regime made rapid progress in rehabilitation in 1949–1950.

II. External Expansion

The effort to exploit possibilities for external expansion has evidently colored all aspects of domestic policy since 1949. Although we have no direct evidence, the only hypothesis which fits known facts is that the broad strategy for expansion was settled between Stalin and Mao at the meetings in Moscow from December 1949 to February 1950 which resulted in the publication of the Sino-Soviet Treaty of Alliance. Many issues were undoubtedly on the agenda. Among these were, almost certainly, Korea, Formosa, and Indo-China. And it was almost certainly agreed that, under Soviet guidance, the North Koreans would attempt their adventure of June 1950, while Communist China would seek to conquer Formosa, support Communist military efforts in Indo-China, and encourage and lead Communist efforts at subversion elsewhere in Southeast Asia.

Although it is debatable, lacking direct evidence, whether Communist China was fully apprised of Soviet plans in North Korea, it appears to us virtually inconceivable that this enterprise would or could have been undertaken without detailed and precise Chinese knowledge. Major Chinese interests were involved, and Mao's prestige in Moscow in 1949–1950 must have been very high indeed. It was not in Moscow's interest to deny him its confidence with respect to its plans in Asia. More than that, considerable preparations were required to arm the North Koreans for their offensive. Given the location of North Korean supply lines, these preparations could hardly have been undertaken without Chinese knowledge. Until there is evidence to the contrary, the only sensible assumption is that the top Soviet and Chinese leaders agreed on an offensive in Asia, short of risking major war; and that the Soviet Union undertook, in the first instance, the management of the North Korean enterprise. It was probably also agreed at this time that China would assume a major responsibility for guiding the Asian Communist parties, excepting those in Japan, North Korea, and, probably, India, where Moscow appears to have reserved special authority. Peking gave significant backing to the Communist enterprise in Indo-China; and the Chinese Communists took immediate steps to assume a public posture of leadership in the Asian Communist movement in general. It should be emphasized that this rise of Peking's role in relation to Asian Communism has at no point involved Moscow's withdrawal of a claim to major authority in Asia, a fact underlined by Molotov's active role in the Geneva Conference of 1954.

In the latter months of 1949 a force of some eighteen Communist armies was concentrated in the coastal areas of Kiangsu, Chekiang, and Fukien. Special measures of training were undertaken, including swimming lessons for assault troops. Roads and airfields were built; and invasion fleets of many small craft were mobilized from the large pool of China's coastal vessels. The total fleet was estimated by the Nationalist military on Formosa as comprising about 5,000 vessels, many of them capable of carrying 50 men each. No effort was made to hide these preparations for what was publicly announced as 'the greatest offensive in modern Chinese history.' It is not clear whether this enterprise was postponed because Communist capabilities were not judged sufficient to cope with Nationalist defenses as they developed on Formosa,[9] or whether the plan was disrupted by the difficulties which rapidly overtook the North Koreans in their adventure during the summer of 1950.

On September 15, 1950, the United Nations forces, having stemmed the North Korean onslaught short of Pusan, counterattacked with amphibious landings at Inchon which outflanked the bulk of the North Korean army. The consequent retreat and disorganization of the North Korean forces probably created a crisis in Moscow-Peking relations and certainly forced a radical reorganization in plans. Politically, Moscow's puppet structure was destroyed, raising as a fresh issue for the future the degree of relative Moscow and Peking influence in the sensitive North Korean area. As the United Nations forces proceeded vigorously towards the Manchurian frontier, in the autumn of 1950, after a clear warning delivered through the Indian government, the Chinese undertook to intervene in the Korean war. They secretly crossed into Korea on a large scale on about October 14, and launched a major offensive on November 25 from remarkably well-concealed troop concentrations. This intervention was probably accompanied by important new agreements with Moscow to supply the Chinese forces with artillery, tanks, aircraft, and the requisite technical advisers to ensure their effective employment.

It is possible only to speculate concerning the motives which led to Chinese acceptance of this major new commitment.[10] But three considerations almost certainly played an important role in the Sino-Soviet plans and the actions which followed the Inchon landings and the United Nations push to the north.

1. As leaders in the international Communist movement both Moscow and Peking faced a dangerous loss of worldwide prestige if the United Nations were permitted to consolidate a military position throughout Korea and to organize a unified Korea on a democratic basis. Initial plans were evidently based on the assumption that Communism was, in their own vocabulary, on a rising historical wave. A major purpose of the North Korean adventure was to dramatize, from one end of the world to the other, this triumphant conception of Communism and the futility of resistance to it.[11] A total defeat in Korea would have been a major setback; and it was judged unacceptable.

2. On a strictly national strategic basis both Russia and China would have lost in North Korea a buffer zone at a highly sensitive point. North Korea not only borders on Manchuria but is also less than 100 miles from Vladivostok, the major port of the Soviet Far East. Although in an age of air warfare Japan (let alone South Korea) is dangerously near these strategic points, the presence of United Nations ground forces at the very borders of Manchuria and the Soviet Far East was certainly judged a major security threat. It is doubtful that the Communists have yet achieved a fully unified and consistent merging of the strategic meaning of atomic warfare with older military concepts, a puzzlement fully shared by the western world.

3. Finally, China faced a special danger if it did not accept responsibility for turning back the United Nations troops in North Korea. In the Sino-Soviet negotiations of 1949–1950, Communist China had negotiated fairly thoroughgoing national control of Manchuria. Russia accepted at least formally China's claim to sovereignty. If, however, the Chinese Communists had accepted the North Korean defeat by the United Nations, their position *vis-à-vis* the Soviet Union in Manchuria would have been weakened. North Korean forces, intimately tied with the Soviet Union, would almost certainly have retreated into Manchuria as well as the Maritime Provinces, and the case for installing Soviet forces in Manchuria for defensive purposes, as well as to exercise control over the residual North Korean armies, would have been almost impossible to resist.

Thus, in urging Communist China to assume full responsibility in the field for the Korean War, the Soviet Union could appeal explicitly to a common interest in the international Communist movement, to Mao's claim for Communist leadership in Asia (partially granted in the Moscow Conference of early 1950), and to common national interests. Implicitly, Moscow could appeal as well to the Chinese national interest in maintaining Chinese sovereignty in the decisive

Manchurian area. Evidently the Chinese Communist regime, confronted with these converging lines of interest, felt called upon to accept whatever losses were required to avoid a major national and ideological setback.

This, as best we can reconstruct the story without direct evidence, is the setting for Peking's intervention in Korea. What we know is that on November 25, 1950, a major offensive by Chinese 'volunteers' was begun as United Nations troops set out, apparently without serious opposition, for the Yalu; and that by the end of 1950 the Chinese were at the 38th parallel, with the United Nations forces struggling to reorganize after a difficult, costly retreat.

NOTES FOR CHAPTER 3

1. We lack evidence on the size and importance of the Secret Police in the period 1949–1954. It well may be moving, as in the Soviet Union, toward status as a major quasi-independent chain of command; but we cannot confirm this trend with solid data. And, at the moment, as in the early days of the Soviet Union, it is probably still under reasonably effective control by the high levels of the Communist Party.

2. See Carsun Chang, *The Third Force in China*, New York, Bookman Associates, 1952, pp. 269–271, for a detailed comparison of the Chinese and Soviet governmental structures, emphasizing the many significant similarities. It will be recalled that as early as 1931, when the Chinese Soviet Republic was set up in Kiangsi, the Chinese Communists took the Soviet governmental system as a direct model.

3. K. C. Chao, *Mass Organizations in Communist China*, Cambridge, Mass., Massachusetts Institute of Technology, Center for International Studies, 1953. The account of mass organizations here is largely based on Mr. Chao's work.

4. For an examination of post-1949 differences in ideological vocabulary between Moscow and Peking and an evaluation of its limited possible significance, see Benjamin I. Schwartz, *Chinese Communism and the Rise of Mao, op. cit.* The 1954 Draft Constitution formally equates New Democracy with People's Democracy, thus reconciling Moscow's and Peking's vocabularies.

5. Quoted, Frederick T. C. Yu, *The Strategy and Tactics of Chinese Communist Propaganda*, October 15, 1952, p. 7. This strategy relates closely, of course, to the salami-slicing technique outlined in Rakosi's famous retrospect on Communist methods in Hungary (lecture delivered at the Party University of the Hungarian Workers' Party, February 29, 1952, reprinted by *Szikra*, Budapest, 1952, pp. 53–54).

6. C. Brandt, Benjamin I. Schwartz, and John K. Fairbank, *A Documentary History of Chinese Communism*, Cambridge, Mass., Harvard University Press, 1952, p. 396.

7. For the military and political training of Communist leaders see Robert C. North, *op. cit.*, p. 53.

8. R. Hsia, *Price Control in Communist China*, New York, Institute of Pacific Relations, 1953, p. 81.

9. There is well-attested evidence that some 60,000 assault troops came down with a serious liver disease in December 1949, as a result of swimming lessons undertaken in polluted waters. If correct, this may have postponed if not forestalled

the attack on Formosa. In June 1950 President Truman ordered the 7th Fleet to protect Formosa, drastically altering Peking's military problem of invasion.

10. For one reasonably persuasive version of the sequence of Sino-Soviet negotiations in 1950 see Carsun Chang, *op. cit.,* pp. 285–287.

11. In this connection Japan was almost certainly much in the minds of Moscow and Peking. Victory in South Korea by the Communists was probably judged one means of encouraging neutralist thought in Japan, making the Japanese reject an exclusive military alliance with the United States, and thus providing a political base for the ultimate subversion of Japan into the Communist bloc.

4

THE EMERGENCE OF
THE 'NEW GENERAL' LINE

I. THE POLICY OF INCREASED HARSHNESS: 1951–1952

(Violence was a familiar aspect of the Chinese Communist performance. In his report of 1927 on the peasant movement in Hunan Mao had defended violence as a political instrument, and it was a fully sanctioned Communist technique from Lenin forward.)Land reform in the Kiangsi days was a notoriously bloody operation; and it left a trail of bloodshed in the countryside in the 1948–1951 period. Nevertheless, the balance between persuasion and pressure on the one hand and violence on the other had generally been maintained in favor of the former down to 1951.

In the course of 1951–1952 the Chinese Communist government encountered a series of difficulties ranging over the whole spectrum of its activities, from land reform at the village level to the military front in Korea. The government found itself short of cash and confronted with the threat of inflation. The cadres in many areas proved inefficient and, apparently, corrupt as well; they were also evidently confused by the problem of balancing ideological objectives against efficiency as criteria for day-to-day action. The converging techniques of mass persuasion and social pressure were not yielding the expected long-term results. Signs of dissatisfaction and even of passive resistance appeared. Production, while undoubtedly rising from the abnormally low levels at the end of the civil war, was not meeting hopes or plans.

The retreat of the United Nations forces from the Yalu carried to a line some seventy miles south of the thirty-eighth parallel. By February 1951 effective United Nations counterattacks were under way, and Seoul was recaptured on March 14. In April and May the Chinese

Communists applied extreme mass assault techniques in a desperate effort to achieve a definitive victory. They proved unable to sustain offensive operations of sufficient momentum to crack United Nations defenses; and by the end of May 1951 it was clear that, short of a vast further increase in their forces, the Communists would not be able to proceed beyond the thirty-eighth parallel. On June 23 Jacob Malik, Soviet representative to the United Nations, suggested that an armistice was possible, and truce negotiations were opened on July 10, 1951, at Kaesong.

In addition to its indecisiveness and cost in casualties among first-class units, the Korean War was evidently proving expensive in real economic terms. The budget for 1950 (published late 1949) allocated 39 per cent of total government outlays to the military. This compared, for example, with an outlay of 24 per cent for investment in state enterprises and 21 per cent for administration. It is evident that, despite substantial aid from the Soviet Union in the form of heavy equipment and aircraft, the Korean War as it developed in 1950–1951 had significant effects on the Chinese economic position. The military budget increased at the expense of other categories. Some proportion of the limited Chinese heavy and engineering industries was diverted to the production and maintenance of military end items. Chinese foreign trade was increasingly diverted to the Communist bloc, as the West closed down trade in order to support the United Nations military effort in Korea.

The Chinese government sought to cover the costs of war at the expense of consumer income and accumulated savings rather than by cutting down government outlays for investment, administration, and other high-priority categories of public expenditure.

The compounding difficulties combined with the fact of effective consolidation of power to make a policy of terror useful and possible to Peking, and the regime launched the various mass movements undertaken in 1951–1952, designed in part to increase the effective political and social power of the regime over the Chinese people, and in most cases also designed to raise money and check inflation. The mass movements of this period include the following:

The Resist America, Aid Korea Campaign
The Suppression of Counterrevolutionaries
The Patriotic Pacts
The Donation for Purchase of Airplanes and Heavy Artillery
Relief and Aid to Military Personnel and Their Families
Campaign for Greater Production
The 3-Anti Campaign

The 5-Anti Campaign
Land Reform

As early as July 1950 there were indications that the Chinese Communists planned to alter their general policy of persuasion and pressure in favor of terror and bloodshed. In a proclamation of July 23 it was announced that the People's Republic of China "will suppress all counter-revolutionary activities, severely punish all Kuomintang counter-revolutionary war criminals and other leading incorrigible counter-revolutionary elements who collaborate with imperialism, commit treason against the fatherland, and oppose the cause of the People's Democracy." [1] It was not until the end of the year, however, that the full meaning of the program to suppress counterrevolutionaries became clear. The cadres, backed by the militia, began a general campaign of repression and terror at all levels.

On February 21, 1951, new legislation was adopted enumerating in some twenty-one articles crimes to be punished with death, life imprisonment, or confinement. Mutual spying to detect 'enemies of the regime' was encouraged. In a purposeful attack on the family, spying and denunciations within the family were explicitly encouraged. Large numbers of people were haled before the courts and publicly executed. It was at this stage also that large-scale mobilization in forced labor camps was instituted as a means of 'rehabilitation' for 'counterrevolutionaries.'

The Suppression of Counterrevolutionaries Campaign exploited a psychological device long associated with Soviet Communism. One of its features was the encouragement of violent action against alleged public enemies—a kind of officially sanctioned lynching. Citizens were urged to denounce subversive elements to the police and before the courts and to gather in the public squares for the executions. Thus the campaign, by inducing men to participate in acts of violence and bloodshed, drew them into association with the regime. There was another gain: since the money and property of counterrevolutionaries executed or sent to forced labor was confiscated by the state, and money was extorted by the state from prospective victims' families both in China and overseas, the Communist government was aided in concrete terms of labor supply and cash. But the real purpose is made evident by the fact that the regime made no attempt to hide the development of espionage, terror, imprisonment, and execution which marked this period: the entire Suppression of Counterrevolutionaries Campaign was evidently designed primarily to instill in the Chinese people what the regime regarded as a wholesome fear of its authority.

In October 1951 Chou En-lai indicated that this campaign had passed its peak; but the campaigns which followed were overlapping, and the techniques of espionage and terror have continued in Communist China down to the present. The total number of persons killed by the Communist regime has not been officially stated but some insight into the human cost of its program can be derived from local reports and from the impressions of foreigners who escaped or were expelled from China during and after the Counter-revolutionaries Campaign. Communist press reports, boasting of the accomplishments of the People's Liberation Army, set a total of 261,686 'bandits' killed in Kwangtung and Kwangsi in the first six months of 1951; a total for the Central-South regions of 1,060,000 by October 1951. Moraes set total executions by mid-1952 at nearly 2 million.[2] A priest, resident in China twenty-three years, basing his figures on the statements of Communist officials, estimated in 1953 that all-China executions numbered about 7 million—out of 20 million imprisoned in the same period. He points out that priests expelled from North China, and familiar with that area, consider 7 million to represent but a fraction of the total.[3] Obviously both figures represent purely personal estimates. Assistant Secretary of State Walter S. Robertson has set the four-year total of the regime's killing of its people at approximately 15 million.[4] A Nationalist summary of August 1, 1952, basing its estimates on such sources as the report made on October 28, 1951, by Fu Tso-yi, Minister of Water Conservancy in the Communist government, placed the number of forced laborers in China at 18 million,[5] but we have no verifiable figures.

We cannot establish scientifically the scale of political murder or political enslavement in Communist China, and in western societies, where these methods are not used, there is a natural reluctance to accept the reality and scale of the phenomena. What is undeniable, however, is that they exist and are regarded by Peking's leaders as a normal (and largely undisguised) part of the society they have erected since 1949.

The Resist America, Aid Korea Campaign was launched almost immediately after the outbreak of the Korean war in June 1950, developing with a new intensity the chronic Chinese Communist theme of anti-Americanism. The movement took the form of many meetings in which efforts were made to dramatize the Korean war as the great test of the 'imperialist' versus the Communist worlds and to persuade the Chinese people to identify themselves with the official view. The United States was presented as the aggressor. A defeat of the American 'paper tiger' was promised that would be as prompt and thorough as that administered to the KMT.

In the course of 1951 the Resist America, Aid Korea Movement proliferated into a series of campaigns designed to translate political sentiment and pressure into cash. The first of these was the Patriotic Pacts. The first pact, made by the merchants and trade unions of Peking on November 7, 1950, illustrates clearly the linkage of political and economic purposes in its five main articles:

1. Exert all energy to support the Resist America, Aid Korea Movement.
2. Do not listen to American-created rumors, and prevent the activities of bandits and special agents.
3. Promote the interflow of goods between city and country in order to meet the military needs.
4. Do not evade taxes; avoid speculation, going out of business, or upsetting financial stability.
5. Redouble efforts to study and propagandize current events.

The Patriotic Pacts were initiated by cadres all over the country. They were followed up by campaigns which aimed even more directly to translate the political leverage the regime was exerting on the people into funds for the treasury: the 1949 Famine Relief Campaign, the Victory Bond Drive, the Donations for the Liberation Army Drive, and the collection campaign for Chinese Volunteers in Korea of October 1950. A donation campaign for purchases of airplanes and heavy artillery was launched following the so-called June First Appeal of 1951. This appeal called in general for an increase in output and in savings. The airplane and heavy artillery contributions were supposed to be made from income earned by overtime or other special efforts.

The June First Appeal was also designed to mobilize political, social, and financial support for assistance to military personnel and their families. The social elevation of the Chinese soldiery (like that of the youth and women) ran counter to old cultural values in Chinese society. The relief drive was thus designed both to assist the government in providing aid and to persuade the Chinese people of their duty towards armed personnel.

The campaign for increased output through increased labor efficiency and effort began in Manchuria during the pre-takeover period. The technique adopted and maintained was based on the Soviet Stakhanovite system, with emphasis on locally defined 'quotas' rather than industry-wide norms. Steady pressure was applied to lift work quotas. Public acknowledgment and reward were given those individual workers or work teams who met those quotas. As far back as the winter of 1948 the Manchuria railways honored a locomotive called "The Iron Bull" and the leader of its crew, Tu Hsien-yung, who had kept the locomotive running for some hundred thousand miles without accident and without general overhaul.[6]

After the opening of the Korean War the productivity campaign was much accelerated in both industrial and agricultural areas. In the latter the newly formed Mutual-Aid Teams were the focus of cadre efforts. Following familiar Soviet practice, the Stakhanovite technique in China required 'activist' individuals and groups to formulate in fairly precise terms their production objectives. These were often published. Following is an example of an industrial team goal formulated in January 1951.[7]

1. Unify the workers to improve the working skills and methods so as to guarantee 99 per cent perfection of products.

2. Advance workers guarantee to bring up the working skill of the apprentices to at least 60 per cent, while the apprentices guarantee to love and to protect the machinery and to get necessary tools ready for the trainers to start out working promptly.

3. Obey the discipline, stay on the post, guarantee no decline in production during Chinese New Year.

4. Strengthen the work of 'four protections': protection of machinery, protection of human life, protection of public property, protection of public resources (anti-waste).

5. Study current events in earnest, heighten the political consciousness, and engage in propaganda.

The following sample 'letter of challenge,' which gained wide publicity throughout China, reflects typical Mutual-Aid team goals in agriculture: [8]

1. Precaution must be taken to prevent any damage to the autumn harvest. Damage could be done by autumn winds or frost or bad elements of the community. A system of night watch should be introduced to prevent any sabotage.

2. Guarantee to complete the job of harvesting and drying of corn and grain crops within 15 days.

3. Select 500 pounds of the best corn and grain seeds for our own use and to share with the neighboring Mutual-Aid Teams.

4. Critical evaluation of production process as well as the work of team members must take place right after the autumn harvest.

5. Guarantee to pay the tax on the first day of the assigned date. Only the best grain is used for taxation.

6. Plow the autumn fields while harvesting.

7. All the wheat fields (about 11 per cent of the total acreage) must be plowed and dug five times. The field must be properly fertilized and only the best bacteria-free seeds will be used.

8. Do a good job in farming for the dependents of martyrs and soldiers.

9. Determine to prune 30 *mow* of trees and plant 40 *mow* of new trees in the autumn.

10. Manufacture 2,940 pounds of fertilizer from the stalks of grain.

In October 1951 Mao threw his full weight behind the general effort to 'increase production and practice economy,' which was linked not only with the Communist goals in general but with the effort to 'carry on the holy war.'

Toward the end of 1951 this ardent political-economic phase of Chinese Communist policy reached a new high level in the 3-Anti and 5-Anti movements. The 3-Anti Movement was a drive within the Chinese Communist Party and state bureaucracy ostensibly to eliminate corruption, waste, and bureaucratism. It was launched, typically, in Manchuria at the end of August 1951. After developing appropriate techniques and experience in the Northeast, the regime conducted a purge throughout the country in 1952. The 5-Anti Movement was a general economic, social, and political attack on China's residual middle classes. It was designed ostensibly to eliminate bribery, tax evasion, fraud, theft of state assets, and leakage of state economic secrets. Although the urban Chinese industrial and commercial middle class in 1950–1951 was smaller in size than the landlord class in the pre-land-reform period, the 5-Anti Movement is in many ways to be regarded as an urban equivalent of land reform. It had similar mixed economic, social, and political purposes and similarly ambiguous results.

So far as the 3-Anti Movement is concerned, there seems little doubt that the Chinese Communist leaders felt some dissatisfaction with the efficiency and even honesty of many of the cadres and administrators who had taken control of the rapidly expanded governmental machinery and of state-operated industries and services during the first two years of Communist rule. Many of the cadres were ill-trained and inefficient, their enthusiasm an inadequate substitute for judgment and knowledge. Some of the administrators taken over from the Kuomintang rule were evidently opportunistic. Moreover, the tradition of corruption was old and strong in Chinese administration. There is no reason to doubt the stories of corruption, waste, and bureaucratic inefficiency which filled the mainland press during this substantial purge. But the leadership undoubtedly used the 3-Anti Movement for what it regarded as more important purposes; notably, to eliminate from their positions personnel who were unsatisfactory for political reasons and for a wide variety of reasons other than those formally indicated in the charges against them.

Among the converging motives which led to the 3-Anti Movement, three were almost certainly uppermost in the minds of the Communist leaders. (First, they desired to eliminate as many of the ex-Kuomintang personnel as they could afford to dispense with, given the rate at which adequate new cadres were coming forward.) The use of KMT and other collaborators of doubtful Communist sympathy is clearly an expedient from the perspective of the regime's leadership. Collaborators presumably will be replaced by new cadres as such recruits prove themselves. The 3-Anti Movement was, in part, a first phase in this probably long-drawn-out process, in which recruits from the Democratic Youth League move up to fill the places of unreliable, incompetent, or inappropriately trained older men. (Second, the top leadership wished to assert its overriding authority against the burgeoning bureaucracy and thus prevent the development of the notion that the bureaucracy could proceed in safety to gather to itself comfortable areas of limited authority.) It was no accident that this phase also saw a tightening of the regime's central control over regional administrations. (Third, the 3-Anti Movement was used as an occasion to reassert the unity of the Communist Party as a whole. There were open attacks on factionalism, a chronic disease in the history of Chinese Communism; and rumors spread of the removal of at least one highly trusted figure because of suspected 'Titoist thoughts.)

The 5-Anti campaign was officially launched November 1951 and continued until the end of May 1952. Like land reform, the 5-Anti Movement was organized with great care and in a set pattern. Like land reform, it also began with a whipped-up mobilization of class feelings, in this case against merchants and manufacturers.) The development of evidence against them was encouraged by open and secret denunciations. The cadres then moved in and ruled on the extent to which individuals had or had not committed one of the five sins. The extent of guilt was assessed both morally and in terms of a fine. The final stage involved payment of the fine and a decision on future status. Then committees were set up to restore 'normal' business conditions under increased surveillance and control by the state.

The scale of the 5-Anti operation and the categories applied are indicated in the accompanying data on decisions made concerning almost 100,000 small and medium-size Shanghai business firms. In addition it is to be noted that at least 2,000 large business firms were classified as serious offenders.

DECISIONS MADE CONCERNING SHANGHAI BUSINESS FIRMS

Classifications	Small-Size Business	Medium-Size Business
Law-abiding	59,471	7,782
Basically law-abiding	17,407	9,005
Semi-law-abiding and semi-law-breaking	736	1,529
Serious law-breaking	2	9
Completely law-breaking	0	0
Total number classified	77,616	18,325

The 5-Anti Movement signaled an end to the regime's uneasy tolerance of those middle-class elements prepared to work with them in the New Democracy. Many alleged offenders were sent off to labor camps; others fled or committed suicide. Those who remained found themselves not only virtually without cash reserves but permanently reduced to the status of virtual civil servants under government control. The 5-Anti Movement did not wipe out the private sector of the Chinese economy; but it fatally weakened or eliminated its foundation for independent action.

The considerable sums collected as a result of the 5-Anti Movement helped strengthen the government finances during 1952, permitting a retroactive balance of the 1950–1951 budgets. On the other hand, the immediate financial gain was at least in part offset by the output loss due to the profound upset and confusion caused in the private sector of the economy. The regime was obviously prepared to bear this loss not only in order to get cash quickly but also to increase middle-class subservience to the Communist state.

Reliable statistics on the funds diverted to the government by this whole series of campaigns are not available. Estimates based on official Chinese Communist information range from U. S. $850,000,000 to U. S. $1,275,000,000.[9] On all the evidence available to us—formed by adding partial and regional figures—we are inclined to place the figure at over $2 billion.

It is over this period also that the initial phase of land reform was completed and the Chinese Communists pressed on with their first efforts on the road to collectivization, which they envisage as developing in a progression from Mutual-Aid Teams and producers' cooperatives. In addition, a few model collective farms were set up in Manchuria and North China, where the availability and quality of land in relation to population made large-scale collective farming technically feasible. The rate at which land reform was carried out in this period is roughly indicated in the accompanying table.[10]

DEVELOPMENT OF LAND REDISTRIBUTION PROGRAM IN CHINA *

Period	Rural Population Affected (in millions)	Rural Population to Be Affected (in millions)
June 1950 †	145	264
February 1951 ‡	276	133
September 1951 §	319	90
September 1952 ‖	379	30
November 1952 ¶	420	5
Spring 1953 **	450	2

* Not including Sinkiang, Tibet, and Taiwan.

† Liu Shao-ch'i, "On the Problems of Agrarian Reform," June 14, 1950.

‡ Henry Lieberman, "Communist Land Reform Causes Social Ferment in Rural Districts," *NYT*, February 7, 1951, p. 4.

§ Tung Pi-wu, "Two Years of the People's Republic of China," *HY*, 4.6, October 1951, p. 1224.

‖ Liao Lu-yen, "The Great Victory in the Land Reform Movement in the Past Three Years," October 1, 1952, *HCJP*, October 20, 1952, p. 6.

¶ *HY*, December 1952, p. 121.

** Chou En-lai, Political Report, February 4, 1953, *HCJP*, February 12, 1953, p. 1.

About a third of the population had been already affected by land reform, on a piecemeal basis, before the Agrarian Reform Law was published in June 1950; and the job was virtually completed by the end of 1952. Manchuria led the way both in the initial land-reform stage and in developing subsequent measures designed to push the agricultural system toward the (not necessarily consistent) goals of collectivization and higher productivity.

Although there was variation in the character of the land-reform procedure from place to place, the fundamental method followed by the Communists is quite clear, and the variations stem from a centrally formulated model. The process would generally begin with the descent upon a village of a 'work team' made up of cadres led by a responsible Communist Party member. Their first task was to make sure that all the potentially hostile elements in the village were disarmed. With that preliminary business out of the way, the following stages were gone through:

1. *Political and psychological preparation.* The purposes of land reform were explained in a series of village meetings, posters, plays, dances, and other propaganda devices designed to mobilize the poorer peasants who ostensibly would be the chief beneficiaries of land reform.

2. *Selection of 'active elements.'* In this preparatory stage the work team selected men from the village to lead the way in carrying through the land reform both politically and technically. They were usually drawn from the 'active elements' among the poor peasants, although occasionally middle peasants were selected.

3. *Class struggle phase.* When the poor peasants were sufficiently excited by the prospects of land reform and when key local personnel had been selected to operate the scheme under cadre direction, a series of 'speak bitterness' meetings, 'settle account' meetings, or 'struggle' meetings were held, designed to bring out in the open the accumulated grievances of the poorer peasants against the richer. One maneuver during this preliminary stage often was to force landlords to repay the traditional rent deposits. It was in this phase also that local 'bullies,' 'despotic landlords,' or other unpopular characters were selected as human targets for the accumulated ill will which had been evoked. The scapegoats were publicly denounced, forced to flee, imprisoned, or killed.

4. *Definition of class status.* Families living in the village were then classified as landlords, rich peasants, middle peasants, and poor peasants. On this basis there was set up that strategic institution, the Peasants' Association, from which landlords and rich peasants were barred. The basic Communist political strategy was thus implemented: 'to unite with the majority, to attack the minority, to divide the enemies, and to destroy the enemies one by one.'

5. *Land redistribution.* The Peasants' Association, under the guidance of the cadres, made a definition of surplus land on the basis of class determination. The surplus land of the landlords, rich peasants, and middle peasants was then made available for distribution. Finally the surplus land was divided among the poor peasants, and a celebration meeting was held combined with the issuing of new titles to land.

The net effects of land distribution were to press acreage owned per family towards a common standard and to reduce drastically the proportion of land rented. Chinese agriculture is now conducted almost exclusively by middle peasants, who are barely above the minimum subsistence level, and poor peasants, at or occasionally below that level. Increased taxes draw off to the state the bulk of the income formerly available to the rich peasant and landlord, while cadres and other agents and institutions of the state perform the bulk of the local government and economic functions once performed by the gentry.

Land distribution was the decisive operation designed to destroy the political and social domination of the gentry over village life and to supplant that domination with Communist control. This control was exercised by Communists over the Peasants' Associations and over the two basic instruments of power at the village level: the People's Militia and the People's Tribunal—that is, the police and the courts.

Although ample care was taken to make sure that the militia and the courts as well as the Peasants' Association were sensitively under Communist Party control, there was probably a belief among some of the Communists that the social changes brought about by land distribution, accompanied by a continuing flow of propaganda, could transform the real locus of power from the gentry to a newly awakened poorer peasantry, who would throw their energies behind Communist purposes.

The enunciated long-term Communist goal, however, was not to create an enlarged group of very small landowners. It was, rather, to develop from this new equalized base a collective village society firmly run by the Communist state and a more productive collectivized agriculture, two goals which have proved incompatible in the Soviet Union and Eastern Europe and whose compatibility in Communist China has by no means been demonstrated.

The simple fact that land was cultivated largely by owners of small plots rather than by tenants of substantial landlords evidently could not bring about the increase in agricultural output that was desired. Therefore, almost immediately following the completion of land distribution, the second and third stages in the land-reform process were begun: setting up Mutual-Aid Teams, and, then, producers' cooperatives. These were designed both to move the social and political structure of the village toward collectivization and to bring about, if possible, the more efficient use of existing land, equipment, and labor. Although total collectivization was not contemplated or attempted at this time, the regime clearly looked in 1951–1952 to rapid movement by stages in the direction of collectivization. The evidence suggests that the pace attempted in 1951–1952 lay outside the regime's capabilities; and a period of respite and organizational planning in 1953 was required before the drive toward total state control of agriculture could be resumed—roughly from November 1, 1953.

In breaking the power of the landlords and richer peasants the Communists also damaged the source of local moneylending and the channels for marketing. These they attempted to supplant with cooperative institutions. But the government proved unable (or unwilling) to allocate the resources required to meet the needs for agricultural credit. Thus there was a prompt revival of private moneylending from those still above the subsistence margin; and the high rates of interest that characterize a capital-poor country persisted. Similarly, the other efforts in 1951–1952 to move beyond land redistribution toward new methods of economic organization and higher productivity yielded ambiguous results. The Mutual-Aid Teams were certainly organized on a massive scale: in August 1952 the government claimed that 35 million families (about 40 per cent of total rural families) belonged to the 6 million teams which had been organized. There is abundant official Communist evidence, however, that many of these produced only *pro forma* results. Groups of families cooperated on particular tasks at particular periods of the harvest year; but the individual family, not the Mutual-Aid Team, remained the basic production unit. And, when a serious team use of labor, tools, and farm animals was attempted, a variety of unsatisfactory results emerged: quarrels among the families interfered with efficient output; no one assumed responsibility for the upkeep of communal property; the claims of inefficient members violated the sense of equity of the more efficient; and when shares were fairly allocated, the less efficient lost economic ground and the beginnings of a potential 'rich' peasantry emerged. All in all, this reassertion, from the initial equalized base, of differences in wealth and income was probably the most pronounced of the post-land-reform trends down to the end of 1953. There is no reason to believe that the Mutual-Aid Teams, vigorously as they were pressed forward by the cadres during 1951–1952, took deep root as the production unit in the Chinese villages or have yet fulfilled Communist hopes as an instrument of social transition towards collective attitudes and institutions. China remained a country of small peasant landholders who looked to their family interests and in general eyed with suspicion the heavy apparatus of power that surrounded them. Evidence on all this filled the Chinese Communist press in 1951–1952.

The Producers' Cooperatives were in this period generally less successful than the Mutual-Aid Teams. The cooperatives require a serious pooling of land and equipment for which each family in turn receives a proportionate number of shares in the cooperatives' total output. In August 1952, 3,000 cooperatives were officially reported to be in existence. They obviously met serious resistance.

II. Tactical Retreat: 1953

Perhaps Mao's most famous maxim for guerrilla warfare is this:

When the enemy advances, we retreat.
When he escapes, we harass.

When he retreats, we pursue.
When he is tired, we attack.

This concept of flexible exploitation was carried over into Chinese Communist political strategy as it dealt with the KMT, and it has re-emerged in the performance of the Chinese Communist state.

The achievement of power in China altered the nature of the objective and, especially, the nature of the enemy. The triple objective is, now, the maximization of the Communist state's power in China, within the Communist bloc, and *vis-à-vis* the external world. The much simpler objective of overcoming the KMT has been superseded by these not necessarily compatible triple criteria for action. The enemy, too, is more complex. Internally, it is nothing less than the performance characteristics of the Chinese people, their physical and technical ability to perform the tasks set for them, their net performance in the face of incentives, restraints, threats, and propaganda with which they are confronted. Externally, 'the enemy' is, of course, the non-Communist world, and, in one sense also, the Soviet Union, whose actions are a source of constraint as well as assistance to the Chinese Communists.

In these terms the enemy advanced in 1951–1952, and the regime reacted in 1953 with a tactical retreat extending from the Korean front to the Chinese villages. The retreat was conducted in good order, against the background of a still maturing and tightening system of centralized totalitarian control within China. There was no overt crisis, no abandonment of strategic objectives.

The first advance of the 'enemy' occurred when the United Nations forces successfully contained the Chinese Communist attack in Korea during 1950–1951. By mid-year a stalemate resulted, roughly along the thirty-eighth parallel; and in July 1951 prolonged truce negotiations were begun. It is possible that the Chinese Communists were not clear for some time whether they wanted a clean truce or whether a continued situation of no-war-no-peace would better serve their purposes. This interval was certainly exploited for a rapid build-up of combat efficiency. It is also possible that, for some time, Moscow and Peking took somewhat different views of the matter. In any case, it is evident that the war in Korea proved more costly than its continuation was worth to the Chinese Communists; and they firmly decided to call it off, as Peking's failure to respond to Mr. Rhee's unilateral release of prisoners in June 1953 revealed.

Total military expenditures, as published officially by Peking, show an increase of 79 per cent between 1950 and 1951; and in 1950 the proportion of defense expenditures in the total budget was almost 40 per cent. Actual military expenditures were almost certainly higher than the official figures indicate. Since 1951 the government has been able to reduce the proportionate share of military outlays in the budget although the 1953 budget contained the highest absolute figure yet put forward.

MILITARY OUTLAYS IN THE BUDGET

	Proportion Defense Expenditure to Total Official Budget	Index of Size of Defense Budget (1950 = 100)
1950	39%	100
1951	40%	179
1952	24%	151
1953	28%	198

Although the Peking official budget figures are not inherently unreasonable, there is no reason to believe they are accurate, especially with respect to particular categories. On the other hand, it seems quite clear that the regime sought and obtained budget relief of the magnitude indicated, accepting stalemate in Korea in 1951–1952 and then ending the war. This permitted the approximate increase in the proportion and scale of outlays for 'National Economic Construction,' shown in the table.

OUTLAYS FOR 'NATIONAL ECONOMIC CONSTRUCTION' IN THE BUDGET

	Proportion Construction Expenditures to Total Official Budget	Index of Size of Construction Budget (1950 = 100)
1950	24%	100
1951	28%	202
1952	42%	421
1953 (planned)	42%	596

Roughly speaking, then, the virtual cessation of active hostilities in Korea in 1952 permitted a reversal of the proportionate outlays on defense and economic construction.

The retreat on the home front is less capable of even approximate measurement. It involved the following key elements:

1. A slackening in pressure at the village level toward the 'collective' stages in agriculture, and an effort to reassure the land-owning peasant that his private tenure was reasonably stable.[11]

2. An effort to reassure the residual middle classes that, since they had survived the 5-Anti Movement, their prospects were reasonably stable.

3. An effort in the 5-Too-Many Movement to concentrate the energy of the cadres on tasks of economic substance rather than on excessive meetings, propaganda, and bureaucratic exercises.

4. A slackening off of special fund-raising drives in favor of more regular devices for collecting revenue.

5. A focusing of attention in propaganda themes on the tasks of economic growth as opposed to external dangers and adventures, and public promises of an increased supply of consumers' goods.

This slackening in pressure on a hard-pressed people was accompanied by a hardening of central control over all branches of Chinese life. The national government asserted increased authority over the regional governments; the mass organizations were constricted into more tightly controlled institutions; there was, almost certainly, an expansion in the size and operations of the secret police; the forced labor sector of the Chinese economy almost certainly grew. In short, the lessening of pressure in 1953 was a tactic of retreat on certain fronts in order to achieve a greater concentration of effort and to plan the next forward movement. The focus of that effort is, clearly, the Chinese economy and its problems of industrialization.

III. SUMMARY: 1949–1953

From their own perspective, the Chinese Communist leaders faced five major and urgent tasks as they came to full power on the mainland in 1949:

1. To create and install a new national government structure under effective total Communist domination.

2. To bring the Chinese population immediately under full control.

3. To exploit promptly and to the limit compatible with avoiding major war the perceived potentialities for external expansion.

4. To alter permanently the balance of social power in rural and urban areas (by eliminating or weakening the landlords, rich peasants, and urban middle class), and to bring the newly elevated classes (poorer peasants, urban workers, youth, and women) under full Communist leadership and control.

5. To meet the requirements of government finance, to end inflation, and to reconstruct the economy in such a way as to provide a foundation for sustained and state-controlled economic growth.

They came to these tasks full of confidence born of easy victories in civil war. Moreover, elements in their experience and ideological heritage apparently made them believe that these tasks would prove not only mutually compatible but also mutually reinforcing. Certain of the tasks were, of course, judged to be of overriding importance, notably the creation of effective government and total control over the populace; and these, as the minimum conditions for the consolidation of Communist power, certainly enjoyed a priority in the leaders' allocation of scarce administrative resources. Nevertheless, there was in this first stage of Communist power a rather striking tendency to press on in all directions.

Evidence has emerged that this optimistic view was reconsidered during 1952, if not somewhat earlier, after there had arisen a variety of resistances and difficulties, both political and economic, which government measures had not fully overcome; and after the joint Moscow-Peking efforts to exploit potentialities for external expansion had resulted in a substantial war with the United Nations in Korea in which initial Communist purposes had been frustrated and the cost bore heavily on China. As of 1952, the Korean War promised to yield no decisive result, even if the Communists persisted; and any increase in its intensity carried the threat of perhaps unlimited reprisals. In December 1952, with Chinese Communist knowledge and backing, the Indians presented in the United Nations a prisoner-of-war resolution which fundamentally met United Nations terms for an armistice. This was promptly turned down by Vishinsky in New York, perhaps reflecting some Moscow-Peking differences, which were evidently resolved in Peking's favor after Stalin's death.

In the spring of 1953 it became apparent that, in general, the contradictions revealed among the five tasks had been at least partially faced by the Communist government, resulting in a new emphasis which gave priority to production, partly at the expense of alternative internal and external power goals.

The years 1949–1953 saw installed in China a structure of government and Communist Party control that permitted the Communist leaders to organize Chinese society under an unprecedented degree of central authority which reached down to each family in the villages and to the back streets of the cities.

Although some voices high in Chinese Communist councils may well have contested the view that consolidation and reconstruction could be made compatible with external adventures, they evidently did not prevail. Aside from such pressure as Moscow may have brought to bear during the negotiations leading to the Sino-Soviet treaty of February 1950, two particular considerations probably entered Mao's decision to support a general program of international Communist expansion, short of undertaking major war. First, for reasons of internal security, Mao was certainly not prepared to demobilize the Chinese armies substantially; and the additional real cost to China of an attack on Formosa, of aiding the Indo-Chinese Communists, and of backstopping the Korean gamble (as estimated in early 1950) were probably judged not to compromise seriously other Chinese Communist goals. Second, perhaps more important, Mao almost certainly believed that a state of military tension with the outside world, focusing on the United States as the 'paper tiger' external enemy, would assist in mobolizing and unifying China under Communist rule.

In particular the Communists certainly believed that a concentration of public attention on the alleged aggressive character of 'American imperialism' would impart a patriotic national basis to the domestic policies they sought to execute, and make more palatable to the Chinese people the virtually exclusive tie of China to the Soviet Union. It was essential to Mao's case for the seizure and maintenance of Communist power in China that no realistic third alternative should exist between total association with 'imperialists' on the one hand and complete association with the Soviet Union on the other. Similarly, the Communists had to assert that there was no realistic political alternative to dictatorship either by the KMT or by the Communist Party.

The Communists certainly believed that these related lines of argument on China's alternatives would be more persuasive if an atmosphere of national military siege could be created and maintained. The whole modern history of China, from the Boxer Rebellion forward through the May Fourth movement to the United Front against Japan, had demonstrated the unifying force of external aggression. Every conceivable device of persuasion and propaganda was steadily used by the Communists to gain this advantage for their new regime. While actual warfare with the West was not essential to sustain this propaganda offensive, and while the Communist aggressions in Asia were not determined by this factor alone, the heightening of the mood of national siege was certainly counted a major ancillary benefit. And, in this view, the Communist regime was not wholly mistaken. The Chinese Communist performance in Korea, whatever the grave military limitations it revealed, was a heartening national spectacle to a people long incapable of coping with modern armies. The surge of national pride extended outside of China to many anti-Communist Chinese; and, perhaps, even touched some on Formosa.

Further, the Chinese Communist leaders were in part certainly taken in by the magic of their own ideology and the propaganda based on it. The Marxist conception of the class struggle—an aspect of the old master's teaching which Mao and his associates fully accepted—emphasized the historical importance of mobilizing the energy of new and rising classes. Perhaps more persuasively, the Chinese Communists had found in the course of their insurrectional struggle that it was indeed possible to mobilize discontent among the poor peasants as a foundation for military operations. In a sense Mao had built the whole of his revolutionary success in China on the insights contained in his 1927 report on the Hunan peasantry.

It is also true, however, that Mao had some inkling that the Communists had much to learn about economic operations. In his famous statement *On the People's Democratic Dictatorship* (July 1, 1949), he said: [12]

> Some of the things with which we are familiar will soon be laid aside, and we are compelled to tackle things with which we are unfamiliar. This means difficulty. The imperialists are positive that we are incapable of tackling our economic work. They look on and wait for our failure. We must overcome difficulties, and master what we do not know. We must learn economic work from all who know the ropes (no matter who they are). We must acknowledge them as our teachers, and learn from them respectfully and earnestly. We must acknowledge our ignorance, and not pretend to know what we do not know, nor put on bureaucratic airs.

On balance, however, in the first days of the Chinese Communist effort the leadership appeared to believe that the land-reform measures in the countryside, coupled with the degrading of the old gentry, would release productive energies in agriculture and result in rapid increases in production, while, at the same time, the newly granted ideological status of the industrial worker, accompanied by inflamed exhortation, would yield rapid increases in industrial productivity. If, as the Chinese leaders professed, the Soviet Union was their model, it seems doubtful that they had studied profoundly and in technical detail the economic history of the Soviet Union, which long before had abandoned the class struggle and ideological motivation as the foundation for productive economic effort. This conclusion must be put forward with some reserve, since we lack solid evidence on the actual outlook in the top Communist leadership. There is, nevertheless, some tendency in the early days of Chinese Communist policy to identify actions that would result in revolutionary political and social change with those required to increase agricultural and industrial output; the regime certainly repeated certain aspects of Soviet policy that had failed and had been substantially abandoned at least fifteen years before its initial effort was undertaken.

In the course of 1952–1953 the Communist leaders appeared to recognize that they were confronted with two related conflicts:

1. A conflict between ambition for expansion in external power and ambition for the building of domestic strength.

2. A conflict between ambition for absolute domestic, political, and social authority and ambition for sustained increase in agricultural and industrial output.

These conflicts taken together apparently made them reassess their position. What began to emerge in 1953 was an increasingly technical and non-ideological approach to problems of production, in which a certain loss of faith in enthusiasm and exhortation could be detected. Through most of 1953 they accorded a new high priority to tasks of agricultural and industrial growth at the expense of movement towards collectivization and full socialization of private industry and trade, and at the expense of further external ventures which might prove costly in terms of economic resources.

The sequence of believed conflicts and shifts in priority described above is, we believe, a reasonably accurate reflection of the course of policy change in Peking over the period 1949–1953. There is, however, another way of looking at the evidence. One can take the view that Chinese Communist policy, based on Soviet experience, always envisaged a stage of political consolidation, of economic reconstruction, and of land reform, to be followed by a transition to collectivized agriculture, socialization of industry, and a sustained effort to expand the industrial base of the society. There is much in the formal statements of Chinese Communist leaders, as well as in Communist practice elsewhere—notably eastern Europe—to justify assuming a roughly foreseen strategic concept of successive stages.

The two views are, in our judgment, not incompatible. Governments, even Communist governments, must operate from day to day. They must make particular decisions in particular contexts to meet problems that have arisen. While the broad strategic framework of goals may be foreseen, the day-to-day decisions made to move toward them are taken in order to solve urgent problems—problems of allocating scarce resources, scarce administrative effort, and scarce energy to alternative possible uses. The evolution of Communist China, like that of the Soviet Union, can be described in terms of abstract stages which have an undoubted reality in the minds of Communist leaders. Looked at closely, however, these stages unfolded as an effort to meet *ad hoc* a series of particular problems where priorities among conflicting goals had to be set. This view takes on added force if one examines how, in fact, the concept of these stages emerged and became embedded in Communist doctrine. They sprang not from Marx or from the theories of Lenin before 1917. They emerged from the desperately practical experience of the Soviet Union, which, step by step, in its own historical context, faced a range of priority choices in the years after 1917 and resolved them *ad hoc,* creating the concept of stages, largely after the event, to rationalize a sequence of practical decisions.

IV. The New General Line: 1953–1954

The elevation of economic development in the priority schedule of the Communist regime did not in itself constitute a policy. It was one thing to decide to end active hostilities in Korea and conserve resources for building the domestic economic base; it was another matter to settle the pace, balance, and politics of the First Five Year Plan. Moreover, the issue of Indo-China, where Peking was committed to a flow of military equipment and perhaps some 'volunteers,' still hung fire. Although 1953 was, formally, the first year of the operation of the plan, it was in fact the period in which the shape of the plan was settled. In part at least the tactical retreat of 1953 was designed as a breathing spell to permit the task of operational planning to proceed, involving as it did matters of international negotiation as well as domestic decision.

These appear to have been the key interlocking issues requiring decision in 1953:

1. Clarification of the scale of exchanges, the terms of trade, and the scale of credits between Communist China and the rest of the Communist bloc.

2. Decision on the scale and composition of Free World trade required to fulfill the plan, in the light of 1, above, and decision on the measures required to achieve such trade.

3. Decision on the relative allocation of resources between military and economic purposes.

4. Decision on the relative allocation of resources between producers' and consumers' industries, and the partially consequent extent of reliance on positive economic incentives as opposed to force in achieving the First Five Year Plan.

5. Decision on the rate and technique of grain collection and on collectivization in agriculture.

6. Decision on the rate and technique of movement toward full socialization of industry and commerce.

7. The crystallization of political machinery and a constitution appropriate to the new phase of economic and social policy.

Although there is still (August 1954) no official Peking announcement of the Five Year Plan goals—we have only two rather imprecise *Pravda* articles—the sequence of events in 1953–1954 would appear to indicate that fundamental decisions were taken and are now being implemented.

The General Line of 'transition to socialism,' now being pumped into the cadres and the Chinese people, unfolded in a series of steps that can be at least partially traced out.

The story begins with the Sino-Soviet economic negotiations, which ran from late in 1952 to September 1953. These took place against a background of reductions in production targets for 1953—possibly related to the emerging modest level of Moscow's aid—and a relaxation of movement toward collectivization, decreed by the Central Committee in March 1953. The upshot of the negotiations appears to have been a detailed plan of Sino-Soviet economic cooperation and trade looking ahead to the period 1957–1959. The plan apparently included provision for:

1. Maintaining a substantial level of trade between China and the Communist bloc with some limited Soviet credits.

2. Maintaining a high level of Soviet technical assistance to Chinese industry.

3. A concentration of Soviet assistance around a specific group of 141 plants to be reconstructed or built.

4. Detailed scheduling of deliveries in both directions.

5. Detailed scheduling of Soviet deliveries of military equipment to China in exchange for Chinese exports to the Soviet Union.

Judging from the limited publicity that accompanied the announcement of the agreement and from the subsequent cast of Chinese Communist economic policy, it would appear that the results were disappointing to Peking. In particular it appears likely that very substantial Soviet credits were ruled out and that limits were set on the level at which the Communist bloc was prepared to import Chinese goods in exchange for scarce industrial and military equipment. In any case, a new note of austerity began to break into the NEP mood of relative relaxation that had dominated the earlier months of the year. By the end of September the theme of 'austerity' increasingly emerged in Communist propaganda. On the whole it seems likely that a reshaping of Chinese plans on a wide front followed upon an appreciation of where, in fact, Peking stood with respect to Moscow over the next years, 1953–1959.

⟨ The first substantial signs of change in policy came toward the end of the meeting of the All-China Federation of Industry and Commerce, the mass organization which politically controls the residual private sector of the Chinese Communist economy. The meeting opened on October 23 with speeches reaffirming the post-5-Anti line that private enterprise had a respectable and constructive role to play in the New Democracy; it closed with the flat announcement that the private sector would be increasingly nationalized. The transition to socialism was at hand.⟩

The leading editorials in the *People's Daily* throughout November underscored this decision and foreshadowed a parallel move toward agricultural collectivization. In January 1954 official announcement was made that a decision of the Central Committee of December 16, 1953, had decreed an increase in the number of producers' cooperatives from 14,000 to about 45,000 by the end of 1954 [13] and to 800,000 by the end of 1957. The intent of the government to continue to collect what food it needed for urban areas, the armed forces, government employees, forced labor, and exports was made clear; and it was plainly implied that, if output did not increase, the peasant's food supply would suffer. Whereas collectivization is proceeding at a moderate pace, grain collection at government-decreed prices has been urgently enforced, raising acute current difficulties on the rural scene.

⟨ In January 1954 the new General Line was defined at length to the Communist Party members, discussed in regional meetings, and presented to the Chinese people through the ample device of mass communication. Its rationale is 'transition to socialist industrialization' in order to modernize the armed forces and thus to secure the military defense and independence of China. The whole effort is cast explicitly on analogy to the Soviet effort during the Soviet First Five Year Plan. The cadres are instructed to read as a basic guide the relevant chapters (9–12) in Stalin's *History of the All-Union Communist Party (Bolshevik), A Short Course,* covering both the NEP and the First Five Year Plan. A mood of austerity and a style of 'bitter struggle' are being sedulously cultivated.⟩

In February a speech of Liu Shao-ch'i before the Central Committee, delivered between February 6 and 10, underlined with surprising force a theme recurrent over previous months: the need for a higher degree of discipline in the party. The terms of this speech implied that the General Line had not been adopted without some dissent within the party, and it carried into Chinese Communist Party politics a rare note of threat, subsequently sharpened in high pronouncements.

In March another systematic theme crept into high level editorials: 'collective leadership.' As far back as November 26, 1953, this phrase appeared in the *People's Daily.* Its context then, however, was medium- and low-level Communist Party decisions. Collective leadership was held up as a model opposed to individual 'subjective' decisions. The ultimate leadership of Chairman Mao continued to be proclaimed as the source of wisdom and decision for the nation, a line which had been sustained in Communist China after Stalin's death and which had, perhaps, even been presented with new emphasis. In March 1954, however, the Central Committee of the Communist Party, operating collectively, appeared to emerge as the source of decision. Mao was described as 'on leave' during the February Central Committee meetings and, in fact, made no further public appearance until late in March. This obscure development may have stemmed from Mao's chronic ill-health; or his absence may have been a political maneuver of substance. Whatever the basis for Mao's transient withdrawal from public view as the point of ultimate decision-making, it adds an extra dimension to the problems raised for the regime by the General Line. As of the moment, however, there is no reason to question Mao's effective primacy when he chooses to exercise it.

The reacceleration of movement toward collective agriculture brought with it the revival of large state loans. In December 1953 a loan of 6 trillion yuan, or U. S. $250,000,000, was announced, 70 per cent to be raised in urban areas and the other 30 per cent in the countryside. This anti-inflation measure is being supported by increased pressures to force deposits of even small cash holdings in government-owned banks. The peasant's grain collection receipts, for example, are held largely in banks, for withdrawal under controlled conditions. Thus the effort to supplement tax collection with other devices to minimize effective consumers' purchasing power will continue. There is nothing in the regime's pronouncements or in its policies to encourage the view that consumers can expect a rise in real income.

The crystallization of the General Line for the First Five Year Plan coincided with the problem of settling the war in Indo-China. From Peking's perspective that war had three major costs: it created a political atmosphere which obstructed the enlargement of East-West trade; it simplified the American problem of preventing Peking's entrance into the United Nations; and it involved some direct military costs in equipment and, possibly, trained personnel. On the other hand, the opportunities Indo-China continued to present to Peking were too great to ignore. France had signally failed to provide a political framework which would effectively rally the Indo-Chinese in the struggle against the local Communists. The United States limited its commitment in Indo-China by refusing to involve American units in combat. The French continued to conduct the war without the hope or purpose of bringing it to a decisive conclusion; and, in mid-1954, the cross-purposes among France, Great Britain, and the United States gave Peking ample opportunity to advance its position in Asia by offering France terms disagreeable to the United States but whose acceptance the United States could hardly prevent unless it assumed responsibility for the conduct of war and politics in Indo-China.

In this setting of Chinese Communist domestic strain and diplomatic opportunity the Indo-Chinese truce was negotiated, giving the northern half of the country to Viet Minh. In essence that settlement bears a family relation not only to the Korean settlement in 1945 but also to the kind of agreement General Marshall sought and failed to get in China in 1946: a military truce, leaving two armed forces within a single country, with the problem of political unity unsettled. Certainly that analogy is in the minds of Peking's rulers, with their strong sense of their own history. It is equally certain that they look on the Indo-Chinese truce as a tactical stage to creating, by whatever means they can afford and the weaknesses of the West permit, a '1949' in Indo-China.

While the negotiations at Geneva served as the main focus for international attention, at home Peking continued to implement the new middle-range policy incorporated in the General Line. The spring and early summer of 1954 saw these principal domestic public events:

1. Steady pressure on the cadres to improve the 'productive attitude' of the peasants, evidently reacting adversely to the grain collection and collectivization measures, the latter having proceeded more rapidly than plans announced earlier in 1954 had indicated.

2. Steady pressure to tighten discipline and central control in the party and administration, including gestures at limiting the scale of the burgeoning and costly bureaucracy and some actions which may reflect civil-military conflict for power.

3. Sporadic efforts of unknown efficacy to limit the 'blind flight' of impoverished peasants to the cities now taking place against an acknowledged rapid rise in total, and notably urban, population.

4. The circulation of a draft of the Constitution, to be passed at the People's Congress, scheduled for the fall of 1954, following the completion of the elections.

The Draft Constitution is, essentially, the political and institutional counterpart of the First Five Year Plan and the new General Line.[14] When it becomes law, it will supersede the Common Program which ostensibly governed Communist China from September 1949. Compared with the Common Program the Draft Constitution has the following features:

1. It emphasizes, rather than underplays, the authority of the Communist Party.

2. It focuses attention on the positive task of 'socialist transformation' rather than on the negative task of destroying imperialism, feudalism, and bureaucratic capitalism.

3. It emphasizes, rather than underplays, the tie of Communist China to the Soviet Union.

4. While maintaining still the notion of a united front of various acceptable social classes, the Draft Constitution elevates the industrial worker and leaves somewhat vague the constitutional status of the bourgeoisie and others to whom explicit appeal was made in the 1949 program.

5. While capitalism still has a formal place in the Constitution, the transition to socialism is forecast and the rights of private property are ominously hedged about by overriding state prerogatives.

6. The People's Congress is the formal seat of sovereignty; but power is in fact vested in the Chairman of the People's Republic, operating mainly through the State Council.

The Constitution makes provision for some three hundred minority areas, some of which border on neighboring states and are evidently centers for infiltration and the softening of frontier areas. On the whole the formal autonomy of these areas is likely to permit more rather than less central administration and control.

By and large the Chinese Communists have followed a pattern, begun in Kiangsi in 1931, of building on Soviet constitutional models, with minor modifications appropriate to their setting and problems. The People's Congress can be expected to play in Communist China the same minimal role as the Supreme Soviet. The guarantees for private property and civil rights can be expected to receive the same casual treatment as Moscow has accorded them. Power will remain where it has been—in the hands of those few men who dominate the Communist Party and governmental structures.

The Draft Constitution is mainly distinguished from its Soviet model by the timing of its promulgation in relation to Communist stages of history. The Soviet Constitution was put forward in 1936, when Stalin proclaimed that 'socialism' had been achieved: Peking, in 1954, regards itself as in transition to 'socialism.' Thus the old features of the Common Program are diluted, and their end is foreshadowed; but they do not wholly disappear. Communist China is judged not yet ready for full state ownership, full collectivization, full 'dictatorship of the proletariat.'

NOTES FOR CHAPTER 4

1. Wen-hui C. Chen, *"Mass Movements" in Communist China*, Series II, No. 4, advance edition, Studies in Chinese Communism under the direction of Theodore H. E. Chen, University of Southern California, Department of Asiatic Studies, October 15, 1952, Appendix A, p. 160. The account of the mass movements in 1951–1952 presented here owes much to Mr. Chen's excellent study.

2. Frank Moraes, *Report on Mao's China*, New York, The Macmillan Co., 1953, p. 50.

3. Mark Tennien, *No Secret Is Safe behind the Bamboo Curtain*, New York, Farrar, Straus & Young, 1952.

4. Testimony before the House Appropriations Committee, February 23, 1954.

5. *Mao's Slave Camps*, Free China Labor League, Taipei, Formosa, 1952.

6. Wen-hui C. Chen, *op. cit.*, p. 84.

7. *Ibid.*, pp. 85–86.

8. *Ibid.*, pp. 86–87.

9. *Papers on China*, Vol. 8, from the Regional Studies Seminars, Cambridge, Mass., Harvard University, February 1954.

10. K. C. Chao, "Land Policy of the Chinese Communist Party 1921–1953," unpublished doctoral dissertation, Cornell University, September 1953.

11. Despite this general slackening, the number of producers' cooperatives reached 14,000 by the end of 1953, according to official statements.

12. C. Brandt, B. Schwartz, and J. Fairbank, *A Documentary History of Chinese Communism, op. cit.*, p. 461.

13. In March 1954 the regime indicated that 90,000 cooperatives existed. It is not clear whether the cadres actually pushed the rate of collectivization at this unforeseen rate or whether the high figure includes forms of agricultural cooperatives (e.g., for credit, marketing, etc.) other than producers' cooperatives.

14. We are indebted to Mr. K. C. Chao for an unpublished paper analyzing the main features of the Draft Constitution, on which this passage draws.

PART
3

THE CHINESE COMMUNIST REGIME
AND THE PEOPLE IT RULES

FOREWORD

Like other societies, China under Communism contains elements of both cohesion and tension, both stability and instability—the people's reactions to the interplay between the conditions they confront and their human feelings. The regime helps determine those conditions, and, through education and propaganda, restraint and terror, it seeks to determine the human response to them.

Out of their life experience men develop a set of expectations concerning the prospects life will offer them. When these expectations conform to reality as they perceive it, men are, broadly speaking, satisfied. When expectations clash with perceived reality, they are dissatisfied. Dissatisfaction does not lead necessarily to revolt or to any other form of social instability. Men generally act to alter their environment when they believe that a more attractive alternative exists and, especially, if they believe that it lies within their ability to move toward or achieve it. When a realistic and attractive alternative is lacking, men generally lower their horizon of expectations. They make do with such gratifications as are available to them, and cultivate them sedulously; or they lapse into apathy.

Modern totalitarian societies are built on Lenin's perception that effective control of a society can be seized and held by a disciplined minority; and they operate on an understanding that the average individual among men takes a modest view of his ability to alter his environment, and that this innate modesty can be substantially enhanced by the threat of forceful reprisal.

The evidence permits us to reconstruct with reasonable accuracy the expectations of various Chinese groups in 1949, when the Communists came to power. It is vastly more difficult to state with confidence how the events of the past five years have conformed to those expectations or clashed with them; how expectations themselves have changed under the impact of events and the regime's unrelenting use of force, threat, and propaganda; and what currents have been set in motion making for change in the future. Nevertheless, it is our task here to attempt some such statement: to assess, in a sense, the impact on the Chinese people of the Communist policies and actions described in Part 2.

The evidence available for this assessment is, of course, inadequate by serious scholarly standards, its principal sources being the Communist press and official pronouncements. At its present stage the regime still relies mainly on some 6 million party and non-party cadres to administer civil policy. It has not yet developed a mature government bureaucracy by Soviet standards. Although the Communist Party and central government can communicate through confidential channels to the cadres, the main lines of their instructions and their accomplishments are widely reported and discussed in the press. Since it is the not always rewarding task of the cadres to execute policies down to the level of particular villages, factories, and city blocks, a good deal of the human interplay between the regime and those it rules can be surmised from the steady flow of press reports. Beyond this rich but ambiguous source there is the testimony of those non-Communists who have been in China since 1949 and have come out. Again it is difficult to evaluate their testimony: How much has the reporter seen; what are his biases and limitations of vision in reporting what he has seen?

Despite grave limitations in the evidence, we feel that certain useful observations can be made, notably if what we now can establish is set against the known history of the society and of the groups and classes which make it up; for the expectations the Chinese bring to their present situation are the product of a quite particular past—a past embedded in a culture which is perhaps the most persistent of which we have record, but which has been in the process of revolutionary change for a half-century or more. Our procedure here, therefore, is first to set the pattern of Communist society in an historical context and then to treat successively the apparent human response of various broad Chinese classes to their new environment.

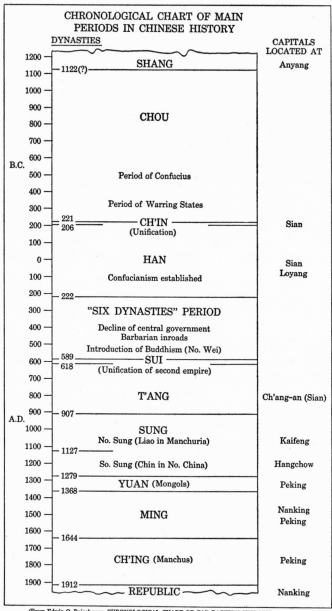

CHRONOLOGICAL CHART OF MAIN
PERIODS IN CHINESE HISTORY

DYNASTIES		CAPITALS LOCATED AT
1200	SHANG	
1100 — 1122(?)		Anyang
1000		
900		
800	CHOU	
700		
600		
B.C. 500	Period of Confucius	
400		
300	Period of Warring States	
221 200 — 206	CH'IN (Unification)	Sian
100		
0	HAN	Sian
100	Confucianism established	Loyang
200 — 222		
300	"SIX DYNASTIES" PERIOD	
400	Decline of central government Barbarian inroads	
500	Introduction of Buddhism (No. Wei)	
589 600 — 618	SUI (Unification of second empire)	
700		
800	T'ANG	Ch'ang-an (Sian)
A.D. 900 — 907		
1000	SUNG	
1100	No. Sung (Liao in Manchuria)	Kaifeng
— 1127		
1200	So. Sung (Chin in No. China)	Hangchow
— 1279 1300	YUAN (Mongols)	Peking
— 1368 1400		
1500	MING	Nanking Peking
1600		
— 1644 1700		
1800	CH'ING (Manchus)	Peking
1900 — 1912		
	REPUBLIC	Nanking

(From Edwin O. Reischauer, CHRONOLOGICAL CHART OF FAR EASTERN HISTORY, 1947)

THE CHINESE COMMUNISTS

IN THE LIGHT OF CHINESE HISTORY *

If we seek to understand contemporary China, we must answer a basic question: Will China, even under the Communists, cease to be the Middle Kingdom? Or, put another way, what relation does emerging Communist society bear to the long Chinese past?

I. The Traditional Shape of Chinese Society

Chinese society has always been perceived by western observers as differing in form and genesis from western society. Theorists vary in detail and interpretation, but they do not deny that Chinese society is a type apart, however differently they may view it. The most stimulating and satisfactory single theoretical picture of the autocratic framework of Oriental society which modern social science has produced is that of Karl A. Wittfogel, upon whose views the following description is largely based. †

Chinese society was vitally shaped by the necessity to control water, and Wittfogel suggests the sobriquet 'hydraulic society' for such social organizations. The agricultural pattern which furnishes the basis for Chinese society took shape in the river valleys of what is now Shensi, Shansi, and Honan, because the soft soil of that region is extraordi-

---

* This chapter is a condensation of a paper of the same title by Frank A. Kierman, Jr.

† Wittfogel's view is, of course, highly controversial among China experts. To an outside observer some of this controversy appears to hinge on a misunderstanding of its scope. It does not explain the full structure of traditional Chinese society. It does not explain the substance of China's unique and rich culture. It does appear to illuminate the evolution in China (and elsewhere in the Ancient World) of an autocratic state and a massive state bureaucracy.—W. W. R.

narily easy to till and dig, and, although the climate is semi-arid, with marginal rainfall, plentiful river water is immediately available. Through intensive irrigated agriculture the early Chinese were able both to support relatively dense populations and to produce enough surplus grain and wealth so that they could spread their power over neighboring tribes and Sinicize them. The institutionalization of dense populations close beside great streams introduced the other aspect of water control, the necessity of protection from floods.

Thus Chinese society was shaped by the urgent requirement that the ruling group have power to mobilize the individual's labor as needed, since the great mass tasks of irrigation and flood control could not be accomplished otherwise. As a consequence, Chinese society developed within an implacable control mechanism founded upon the proposition that the individual had to be forced to do what was necessary for his society and thus for himself.

The coercive forces of Chinese society could be diverted from accomplishing the fundamental tasks of water control and turned to mobilizing the populace for military defense or ventures, for great public works, or for other enterprises designed to further the central power, to symbolize it, or to satisfy its fancies. The pattern of Chinese political rule thus derived a sanction for utilizing the common man in the most brutal labor, upon enterprises infinitely remote from his concerns and often unjustifiable in terms of the public welfare. This was the framework of political despotism within which the complex forms of Chinese society took shape.

In its class structure Chinese society fell most simply into the two groups of rulers and ruled: the royal house plus its administrative extension, and the peasants. The ruling classes can be separated into two segments: the royal family and its favorites, and the gentry class from which the working bureaucracy was recruited. Even today estimates rarely calculate the peasants as less than 80 per cent of the Chinese total population.

The central government's direct control did not generally extend very far down into the body of traditional Chinese society. The nerve-end of authority was the *hsien* magistrate. The gentry class often functioned as a local extension of the bureaucracy, giving to the government's control devices far more intimate and far wider effect than the central officialdom could.[1] As the local gentry ordinarily had contacts in government outside their own area and above the *hsien* magistrate in the power hierarchy, their connections furnished a real check on his power.[2] They were in some respects adjuncts of the magistrate's power; but they were also objects of his control and his tax-gathering efforts. The gentry thus had two distinct and often conflicting functions: as the ultimate instruments of central authority, and as the leading elements in another whole level of society which included by far the majority of the Chinese people.

Within this great lower level Chinese society was intensely cellular, working by rules and techniques quite different from its autocratic framework. The agricultural working and ownership group was the family, which in times of prosperity expanded to become the extended family-group all living under a single roof. Prosperous or not, a village was often composed of a single clan, more frequently of a few major clans interlinked by marriage. Government within such a social unit logically becomes an extension of the family structure; and life within such villages demands much the same cooperation, forbearance, and mutual help as are necessary in the big family. This level of organization executed many serious functions: irrigation, self-defense, welfare, mutual aid, mediation in personal disputes.[3] The village was to some extent an independent entity, capable of retiring upon itself and surviving if disaster should render its ties to higher units disadvantageous or should cut them off.

It is conventional to ascribe to the scholar-gentry class the major role in preserving the shape of Chinese society; but the other element in the relationship, the peasant, was likewise a very powerful conservative force. The very intensity with which the peasant had to deal with such problems as flood, drought, and pests, with official demands for taxes and personal service, and with the economic crises caused by weddings or funerals, bred in him a great shrewdness and flexibility toward these problems; but ignorance, habit, and the fact that no alternative way of life was usually conceivable deterred him from the steady effort to smash his environment, except when it became unbearable and its control mechanisms weak.

The non-official strata of Chinese society executed these *de facto* functions of government at the village level. Significant extralegal organizations, often attaining more or less mass support, have also existed, at least since the Han dynasty and probably earlier. These secret societies, usually with a strong Taoist or Buddhist religious base, have been a persistent and widespread indigenous feature of Chinese society; and they are doubly important in that they offered alternative powers within the state potentially and often actively hostile to it. They are of special interest because their persistence indicated that the orthodox organizations of family and bureaucracy were only partially satisfactory; and because they also have proved repeatedly that the Chinese people, when real grievances and appropriate ideology converge, are capable of an extreme fanaticism quite opposed to the western stereotype of the Chinese character.

On its own level the scholar-official class was truly the vehicle of Chinese society. The ruler was of vital ritual importance; for, since the Mandate of Heaven had fallen upon him, he constituted the symbolic link between Heaven and Earth, whose conduct must placate Heaven and furnish a model for all below it. But he did not influence the people directly; by his example he influenced his chief administrators, who in turn conveyed the benign current to lesser bureaucrats and thus by stages to the local magistrates who affected the people.

Chinese society viewed from above has had not only a complex structural shape but also a temporal dimension: that interesting abstraction, the dynastic cycle. A dynasty came to the throne by defeating or outlasting all other contenders during a time of trouble. The literati gave it their allegiance; the closely supervised bureaucracy operated conscientiously; the empire's frontiers were pushed back as border barbarians were pacified; the water works were scrupulously maintained; a very high percentage of the taxes collected was used either locally for the public welfare or remitted to the central government; natural catastrophes were met with energetic measures to minimize their effect and restore equilibrium; and, generally for the first century of the dynasty, Chinese society worked well.

But, by apparently immutable laws which were effective everywhere and in all ages, so the theory goes, the bureaucracy expanded in size and deteriorated in efficiency. The greatly enlarged armies fought ever more distant and costly wars. The sovereign's entourage grew, and his demands upon the society became more capricious as his loosening control on the administrators left them increasing opportunity for personal profit. Palace favorites obtained undue influence at court, and ministers became corrupt; military expenditures to secure tribute for a court eager to express its own grandeur became increasingly costly; natural catastrophes or invasions occurred; the administrators lost the energy, flexibility, or control of their apparatus to minimize the consequences; the people, rebelling in their desperation, found able unemployed scholars as leaders to organize their energies; and the dynasty fell apart in another time of trouble.

This is the classic sequence of Chinese history.

The vital point differentiating this dynastic cycle from the alternations of prosperity and distress, advance and regression, energy and passivity which also characterize western society is that Chinese society itself changed very little as a result of it. This ultra-conservatism, the quality which has led social scientists to call Chinese society 'stagnant,' as opposed to the dynamic West, has been due partly to the lack of new challenges sufficiently energetic and respectable to force new accommodations, and partly to the crucial weight of traditional techniques and habits among the intelligentsia and the peasants.

Viewed from below, Chinese society also exhibited a cyclical character. Families showed energy, frugality, and shrewdness; they bought land and became well-to-do, or excursions into commerce gave an added boost to this rising curve; they began to divert their energies to consumption and enjoyment rather than production, and the purchase of land ceased; increased expenditure, often aggravated by political or meteorological disaster, forced the sale of land; and they fell back into poverty.⁴ The degree of social mobility involved in such changes might be minimal, or it might be great. The individual of greatest ability might be frustrated from the full realization of his capacities because he was born into a time of troubles which nobody could master.

Structurally, then, Chinese society was not single but double, two segments which not merely fitted together but interacted and intermingled. For the scholar-official had his roots in the village and was a senior member of a clan. He governed his family and his individual life after the model and the standards of other families. Yet the family, too, had not only its elements of compromise and moderation but also its elements of pressure and compulsion; members had to be supported however improvident they were. This consideration, however, takes us over into the realm of ideology, where again the two segments of Chinese society were interwoven.

II. The Ideology of Chinese Society

Probably well before Chou, but at any rate by that dynasty's beginning, c. 1000 B.C., China had created a philosophy which maintained essentially religious observances and served admirably to give sanction to the social system. Its precise content we do not know, since we have only the partial insights and personal distortions which constitute the 'Hundred Schools' of Warring States times (c. 475–221 B.C.). Of all the transmitters, Confucius probably did least violence to the tradition. We can infer this from the general respect in which he was held during the centuries which most immediately followed him; and indeed this is the justification for his high prestige. Confucius' sayings as we have them are too fragmentary and cryptic to let us reconstruct from them a full or unchallengeable picture of ancient Chinese philosophy. Some general characteristics of this primordial Confucianism can be guessed at, however.

First, it was predominantly dualistic and cyclical, on the analogy of day and night, the phases of the moon, the opposition and alternation of summer and winter, sowing and harvest, male and female. This doctrine is the rationale for the Golden Mean: 'When the sun is at the zenith, it declines; when the moon is at the full, it wanes.' Such a rubric would discourage extravagance of action, since success pushed too far would require, to maintain cyclical symmetry, an appropriately disastrous failure. The wisest course would be to keep one's desires and ambitions limited and one's efforts to satisfy them modest; thus with luck the inevitable oscillation of fortune would be minimal and, though prosperity would be unimpressive, neither would poverty go beyond endurance.

It would be wrong, however, to infer that this avoidance of extremes implies a tendency to seek stability, for the cycle is both the way of life and the engine of society. Second, human relationships were the foundation of society. These were all highly personal relationships. Third, a deep congruence was felt between society and family. Rites and ceremonies clearly showed this fact, which expressed itself on at least four levels: the relation of the Son of Heaven to Heaven, that of lords to the Son of Heaven as suzerain, that of subjects to their lord, and the system of hierarchical relationships within the family proper. Ancestor worship was a form of religious observance emphasizing the importance of the family; mourning for a father was a crucially important rite signalizing the apotheosis of the parent; investiture meant the acceptance of the overlord as symbolic father. There was a strong paternalistic strain in the entire relationship between rulers and ruled, whether as individuals or as classes, which emphasized subordination and inequality.

The attitudes adumbrated in these categories interacted in a most flexible, constant, and sophisticated fashion. Filial piety was incumbent upon the son, yet the father bore responsibility not only for producing proper attitudes in his offspring through education but also for inspiring reverence by his day-to-day conduct; the son was duty-bound to exhort his father where he detected fundamental obliquity in the paternal conduct, though he was also required to conceal such defects. The subject had not the mere right but the obligation to exhort his lord; and if expostulation failed and the master was irretrievably sunk in sin, the inviolability of his position vanished and he might be deposed. And just as son and father, subject and lord interacted, so Earth and Heaven affected one another: the virtues of the Son of Heaven, animating all his domain, compelled deity to favorable reaction, as the problems set by Heaven furnished the sovereign with the chance to exhibit his qualities. If a family were energetic and virtuous, it prospered, though trials might come later and bring misfortune.

In a society almost exclusively agricultural, with artisan and merchant classes still rudimentary and small, such an ideology furnished a comfortably loose, all-embracing, aesthetically satisfying framework for human life. It could spur or console a man according to his situation, but above all it reconciled him to the world about him.

A fundamental premise of such an ideology is that man is basically good: that he is susceptible to human feelings and that a restrained application of moral example will suffice to keep him in line—though it also hints at the penalties for extreme or inhuman action. Interdependence among men is stressed; and the whole ideology works to play down coercion and make cooperative co-existence easy, frictionless, and fruitful. Such an approach is comfortable and suitable for many aspects of a settled society, but it is bound to be less satisfactory in preparing populations for warfare or in furnishing techniques and sanctions for mass efforts upon public works.

In the rich Chinese philosophical tradition there are many strands concerned with governmental problems. In long-term influence, however, only one ideology can compare with the Mencian Confucianism: that is Legalism. Fundamentally, Legalism accepted the concept that man was by nature evil, contrary, and limited; and that his perverseness naturally required a social system of clear laws and severe punishments. Such a rigid control mechanism is the polar opposite of the loose aesthetic arrangement designed to give man's goodness free scope, to channel it through the five relationships, and to encourage it by the ruler's moral example. According to Han historians, the Legalist school originated with administrative officials, who "made promises of rewards trustworthy and penalties definite, in order thereby to give a support to rites and institutions." [5] This seems an acceptable origin, since the practical effort to accomplish or even plan the great tasks of irrigation, construction, and fighting, especially as states grow larger, would naturally demand some such philosophy as Legalism.

There seems no question that barbarians exerted a marked influence upon Chinese society during its formative stages as well as later. Wolfram Eberhard derives the concept of Heaven, the patrilineal family, and the rigid stratification into rulers and ruled from barbarian ideology or practice. Such contributions must remain conjectural unless further direct evidence is uncovered; but it is certain that barbarian influence was important during the pre-Han period as sponsoring or perhaps even originating the authoritarian, militaristic Legalist strain in Chinese thought. The Chou dynasty was founded by a tribe which, if not barbarian itself, was undoubtedly much influenced by barbarian institutions and by the exercise of combating the nomads.

Between the Mencian and the Legalist tendencies in Chinese ideology there went on a real dialectic. This appeared in the distinction between the 'kingly way' (*wang-tao*) and the 'tyrannical way' *(pa-tao)*. The outright appeal to force was conceived of as involving widespread practical penalties; the maintenance of leadership by moral influence was expected to bring a solid increment of practical advantage. The tyrant was such because he was fundamentally weak and inferior; the strong man ruled by moral example because his strength was great, and in its exercise that power was increased. During most of the Chou dynasty, despite the fact that public morality suffered steady and disastrous erosion, even the most unlikely sovereigns often demonstrated their belief in the truth of this perspective by turning away from final brutalities or aggressions even when such actions were the logical culmination of their whole past behavior. It remained for the essentially barbarian states of Ch'u and Ch'in to lead in showing that virtue did not necessarily entail any material reward. When Ch'in finally unified the empire in 221 b.c., it did so on Legalist lines and engaged in purposeful efforts to destroy the opposing tradition which we have styled Mencian. Thus was underlined the fundamental antagonism between the authoritarian and the humane, the administrative and the compromising, the Legalist and the Mencian strains in Chinese political thought.

Aside from these two central currents of governmental thought, there also existed strong individualistic currents. The Taoist tradition, for instance, was especially important in justifying the scholar who found himself debarred from participation in government. It is said that a Chinese is a Confucian in prosperity and a Taoist in adversity.

The traditional ideology of Chinese society was, then, capacious. It sanctioned a wide variety of conduct. An official could emerge into active public life or he could retire into studying the classics, writing poetry, drinking, and so on. A peasant could increase his holdings, become well-off, gather his clan about him in the county seat, even aspire to have his son become an official; or he could lose his land, become a hired laborer, even sell his wife and children, and become a beggar or a brigand. The prosperous upward phase was valued, but the downward curve was accorded a place. The central point is not merely that the Chinese could adjust his philosophy to changes of fortune but that his social and intellectual tradition possessed such roominess as to accommodate persons in the widest possible range of circumstances. A given dynasty often greatly diminished, for a period, the permissible range of behavior by its own peculiar emphases; but traditional Chinese society was so voluminous and multiform as to make outright deviation difficult if not impossible. The prospective deviant was all too likely to find that, far from having broken his lease, he was simply moving to another room in the same old mansion.

III. The Stages of Chinese Development

The pattern which the Chinese orthodox dynastic histories have imposed upon Chinese history is arbitrary. China's history did not, in fact, evolve in a fashion which can be effectively presented in terms of dynasties. If one talks only in terms of dynasties, the periods of division are left pretty much out of account, the currents of long-term change tend to be ignored, and even the mutual dissimilarities of the dynasties are underemphasized. It is necessary to keep the perspective that the essential power structure of Chinese society remained intact, while also recognizing the shifts of emphasis within and beneath the structure. For this purpose there seem to be several points in Chinese history which either constitute or symbolize watersheds in a continuing development.

One point in time which stands for a notable development was the period of Duke Huan and Kuan Chung Ch'i, roughly 685–643 B.C. Prior to this time Chinese society had developed from tribal to feudal form. But during the era of Ch'i's hegemony there emerged an administrative pattern which foreshadowed the unification of the empire and permitted steady progress toward it. The old proprieties of conduct were replaced by systematic codes of law. Patriotism was encouraged and focused upon the person of the ruler; a new type of bureaucrat emerged, owing his position chiefly to the sovereign's recognition of his merit rather than to connection with local noble families or to heredity. The territorial and social divisions of the state were meticulously subdivided into segments (*hsiang*) which made close supervision possible, permitting the central authority to assign responsibility and control the exercise of it. An inspectorate outside the direct chain of command was set up. A militia system, directly connected with the *hsiang* administration, formed the basis for Ch'i's army. Commerce was encouraged but taxed; and governmental monopolies upon salt and iron strengthened the administration's economic and military control. Thus within the confines of a single state were foreshadowed most of the techniques which would later enable Ch'in to control the entire empire. Owing chiefly to poor communications, control was less effective than it later became; but there can be no doubt of Kuan Chung's intention to create a system of implacable and everlasting preservatives for Ch'i's power.[6] Strength passed from Ch'i with the deaths of Duke Huan and Kuan Chung; but other sovereigns and ministers followed their example until, four centuries later, the First Emperor of Ch'in and Li Ssu used essentially the same techniques on the national scale.

Li Ssu and the First Emperor conquered, united, and administratively reorganized China; destroyed the remnants of the feudal order and, by destroying arms and transporting royal families, made reversion to it, or any lasting regionalism, impossible; gave employment to centuries of later scholars by destroying much of then recorded Chinese history and culture; and yet, by standardizing the written language, the laws, weights and measures, performed a set of services which were probably essential to the preservation of Chinese culture. Such a record of accomplishments would be remarkable however long they took; but they were completed probably within about two decades (Li Ssu was executed in 208 B.C.; the conventional date for the unification of China is 221 B.C., but Ch'in had acquired control over a large proportion of the empire several years before).

Such purposeful and rapid progress would have been unthinkable under the aegis of Mencian thought. It was made by a state which was felt to be outside the Chinese pale, and under a Legalist philosophy which made serious efforts to destroy the Mencian tradition, a fact of special significance if we again consider the political framework of Chinese society as Wittfogel describes it: a merciless despotism, a system of control designed to coerce its people irresistibly. One may argue that Confucianism, even the Mencian kind, contains in its suppressed premises the justification for Oriental despotism, but that it merely chooses to stress the allegedly benevolent character of such a society. But Confucianism was not cynical, however its premises may give that impression if clever modern dialecticians push them far enough. The Confucian ruler was a servant of the people who held office only conditionally and so long as he served the people; with the Legalists the state became an end in itself, with no checks upon the governing power.

After the unification one further step remained to be taken before the broad structure of Chinese society was complete: it had to have an ideology less stark than Legalism to soften the outlines and make it acceptable. This took shape during the Han dynasty. Essentially, Emperor Wu of Han took over intact the centralization of political, economic, military, and administrative power which had been inaugurated under Ch'in; but state Confucianism, an amalgam with a base of optimistic Mencian humanism mixed with soothsayers' superstitions and naive pseudo-historical sanctions, was installed as the official ideology. Sacrifices designed to emphasize the emperor's status as the Son of Heaven were instituted under Emperor Wu. The old Five Relationships were ostensibly the foundation of society, but that between sovereign and subject now received a disproportionate emphasis. The intrafamilial relationships were still vital to keep order in that sphere below the bureaucracy's direct reach. Thus, in one stroke, Chinese society acquired a palliative and a fiction of itself.[7]

After the Han development the basic power arrangements of Chinese society changed little, slowly, and inconspicuously. Upon the administrative level the scholars acquired a firm interest in maintaining the Legalist techniques by which they operated the government and the Mencian folkways by which they both ordered their own personal lives and sanctioned the system. The mass of peasants lived in the ancient Chinese way, concerned only with their agricultural problems and with the occasional manifestations of governmental requirements or failures which directly affected them as individuals. Between the conservatism of the scholar class and that of the peasants, Chinese society maintained its peculiarly stable character for nearly two millenniums.

It is easy to overemphasize the stark outlines of Chinese society and underemphasize the real pervasive significance of the ancient Chinese tradition. The system was intolerable or bearable, depending upon how it was administered; and here the real softening influence of the great old tradition generally had its effect. Most of the time the individual got along well enough. If the dynasty was new and vigorous, he got just treatment; if the dynasty was weak, he could usually manage to get justice or better with a well-placed bribe or because he was otherwise protected. One way or another, the genius for accommodation and the ancient principles which encouraged it combined to make life possible.

Although the Ch'in-Han developments essentially set the power structure of Chinese society, Han society proved vulnerable in itself and fell into an age of disunity and turmoil lasting more than four centuries. Only by the changes effected in T'ang (618–906) and Sung (907–1279) times was Chinese society finally established so securely that no further major dissolution of the national unit took place. The T'ang-Sung epoch must, therefore, be considered another watershed, the final one in producing traditional China.

Before this period the Chinese economy served the needs of centralized national government rather badly. By its end China had a nationally integrated economy based on a currency system rather than the old taxation in kind; the basis of taxation had been altered from the household as unit to the land; regional specialization and interdependence knit the nation together; and a vast expansion had taken place in both intramural and foreign trade.[8] The growth of commerce, signalized by the development of great cities and of urban classes to populate them, was of special importance. The fact that a rich new source of tax income existed meant that central authority could support itself beyond the period when the relatively inflexible land-tax would serve.

Before the T'ang-Sung developments there was an uneasy and shifting balance of power between the ruler and the gentry bureaucrats. Out of the pulling and hauling of T'ang and Sung times there emerged a real institutionalization of the scholar-gentry class, resolving its uncertain position. With the growth of cities, the artistic milieu acquired maturity; T'ang and Sung are in many ways the greatest of Chinese aesthetic eras. The examination system, focus of debates and reforms during this period, emerged from it confirmed and strengthened as the standard road to official position. Social control mechanisms were also perfected during T'ang and Sung times. Passports for internal travel were not only in use but indeed were the subject of typically bureaucratic evasion of responsibility. The *pao-chia* system of group responsibility was revived by Wang An-shih in the eleventh century. Within the civil service, administrative responsibility was encouraged by spreading the practice of sponsorship to cover most official positions.[9] By the end of the Sung dynasty (1279 A.D.) traditional China had thus attained very nearly her final administrative form.

One of the most interesting points of speculation raised by this maturing of Chinese society is its performance since the Sung dynasty. Perhaps the creative energies of the Chinese state or their favorable relation to the Chinese social context suffered a real weakening after the thirteenth century. At any rate, the modern history of China seems to have been most often a defensive battle against barbarian incursions which have posed a central, rather than a marginal, threat to the nation.

There has been a prevailing current of pressure and movement within the Chinese nation: under barbarian push from the north and northwest, Chinese influences, Chinese culture, and specific Chinese groups have moved south. The whole pattern of Chinese society, arising in Shensi and Shansi, moved out to the great plains of North China and thence southwards to the Yangtze and beyond. Barbarian incursions deeply influenced Chinese culture; and barbarian dynasties of conquest, coming from the north and northwest, have held Chinese society hardened in the mold.

The latest, and probably the greatest thaw in Chinese society commenced when a new group of barbarians struck from an entirely new quarter. The western impact upon China took many forms. Economically, it furnished new crops (corn, peanuts, sweet potatoes) which vitally affected the agricultural base of Chinese society, unsettled the currency (first by pouring in great quantities of precious metals from the New World and then through the direct impact of extensive western commerce), further increased the wealth and importance of the merchant class, and furnished the model and capital for industrialization. Militarily and politically, it decisively shook the Chinese complacent acceptance of their unique sovereignty and power, forcing them reluctantly to reconsider their entire system. As a result and concomitant of all these factors, it damaged Chinese self-confidence and contentment with tradition.

The effectiveness of the western impact in rending Chinese society is not to be understood merely in terms of how different was the western from the Chinese traditional approach, or in terms of how far the Ch'ing dynasty had gone beyond its peak, or even in terms of the purely economic disturbance which the European trade caused and which Chinese officialdom was unable to understand or contain.[10] All these factors contributed to the crisis, but there is another, perhaps more significant. Since very early in the development of Chinese society, merchant status had existed as an alternative to the status of the land-based scholar-gentry—a suppressed and despised alternative, to be sure, but an alternative nonetheless. At that very time in the T'ang and Sung dynasties when the scholar-gentry were finally institutionalizing their high status the merchant community was expanding tremendously also—an expansion which, in the nature of the case, was fated to be always open to the depredations of the bureaucracy. When the western impact came in the late eighteenth and early nineteenth centuries a class of energetic merchants existed throughout

China, used to living dangerously by bribery and trickery; and officialdom was habituated to connivance with them. Confucian ideology denigrated the merchant, but commerce furnished the food upon which the dynasty battened. The very existence of the dynamic merchant class directly challenged the position of the bureaucracy whose corruption it encouraged. Small wonder that the western impact, seeking to loosen up the old society and make it better for commercial endeavor, ruptured the entire fabric by destroying a delicate balance of power.

The western impact was all the greater since its maximum force was exerted at a time when Chinese society was well on the downward curve of the dynastic cycle. Thus it tended to deepen, confuse, and complicate the time of trouble which was due to occur within Chinese society even if the West had stayed home in Europe and America. Certainly the Chinese have suffered seriously for more than a century from foreign meddling and outright invasion. Western influence as exerted second-hand through the overseas Chinese and the merchants undoubtedly had a profoundly unsettling effect upon Chinese society, not least by permitting entrepreneurs to develop their economic and political power beyond the reach of the traditional bureaucracy. Whether the period of confusion and rebellion is ended or nearly ended now, nobody can possibly say. To what degree the Communist government represents, in effect, a new dynasty, and to what degree it is something brand-new in Chinese history, are for future historians to decide. But we shall do well to consider wherein Communist doctrine and practices derive from or resonate with the Chinese tradition, rather than simply to assume that Communism represents an outright and total victory of the West.

IV. Developments under the Communists

The Chinese Communists have had no need to alter the broad outlines of traditional Chinese society to make its political framework a centralized despotism. It was that already in theory, though the despotic power was in fact split between sovereign and gentry.

The real endeavor of the Chinese Communist regime has been along five lines: (1) deepening the direct control of the central government by reaching down far beyond the *hsien* level, and removing mitigating functions and attitudes which tend to dilute that control; (2) consolidating central control by interrelated economic, social, and political measures; (3) changing the old bureaucracy to a new one of its own training; (4) altering the entire social basis of the traditional polity by destroying old classes or removing their sources of power; and (5) seeking to change the old virtually circular dynastic development to a dynamic new concept of ceaseless linear progress.)

The effort to push central influence down completely through the texture of Chinese society is clearly based upon a philosophy which considers man limited, recalcitrant, and possible to socialize only under conditions of strict control: philosophy which in Chinese terms is Legalistic. The adoption of such a philosophy is a marked truncation of the Chinese tradition and indeed goes counter to the main current of Chinese ideology; it is not, however, wholly outside the Chinese tradition, but is a continuation of the perspectives through which the over-all framework of Chinese society was erected.

Most centrally, the Communists are endeavoring to remove from Chinese culture the spirit of Confucianism. Fundamentally, Confucianism rejected any pattern of action which approved violence and inhumanity, no matter what the ostensible purpose. It did not admit the distinction between ends and means.)

(One can hardly overemphasize how important sheer desperation was in preparing the way for this new Legalist phase, Communism. Over the course of a century rude shocks struck at China's understandably deep confidence in its basic viability as a form of social organization. In 1840 China was still, in its own eyes, the sole sovereignty in the world; by 1900 China had emerged into a world full of other aggressive sovereignties, where her attitudes were disastrously inappropriate and where she suffered repeated indignities.) Almost a half-century passed without any real solution, and thinking Chinese gradually came to fear that their country never would be able to take a dignified place among the nations. Inevitably they came to believe that only a radical operation would suffice. Other factors certainly contributed their weight. The Leninist vocabulary had virtually preempted the field of intellectual discourse by the middle twenties, so that when the time for decision arrived the appalling lines of choice were at least couched in familiar terms. (Communism, with its pseudoscientific shapeliness, proved as seductive to dissatisfied and unemployed Chinese intellectuals as it has to westerners in the same desperate condition; it offered guarantees that, after the night of darkness, the morn of song would really come;) it was a western ideology and, therefore, borrowed the aura of ruthless efficiency and uncomfortable logical rigor that had come to be associated with all things western; it had a peculiar attraction to an intelligentsia which nostalgically desired a link with the masses; and, on the personal level, it offered the twin satisfactions of self-flagellating submergence in a great cause and scientific assurance that the faith was correct—a combination which, in those special circumstances, was well-nigh irresistible.

The victory of Marxist thought and Leninist methods of organization derived not only from the pressures of China's immediate history and heritage and the energetic purposefulness with which the Soviets have spread their doctrines. The old Chinese derogation of the merchant class lent a traditional sanction to class struggle against the bourgeoisie. Dogma was not foreign to minds which had accepted Neo-Confucianism. The predominant dualistic habit of the Chinese mind is not the same as the Hegelian-Marxist dialectic; but it is not worlds away. The notion that the analysis of history can yield solid prediction and guidance for the future is strong in the Chinese mind; so the 'scientific' pretensions of Marxism get a sympathetic and to some degree a serious response. The sanction for revolution is old Chinese tradition: Mencius explicitly approves it if the regime is bad; and Chinese literature abounds in heroic bandits who live outside the fabric of conventional society. The idea of having a thoroughly despotic regime dress itself in a quite unrelated ideological cloak of humanitarianism is certainly not strange to the Chinese. And even among the detailed economic and social measures which the Communists have undertaken few are quite without precedent or precept in the capacious Chinese tradition.

Nevertheless, when all this is said, the major effort of the Communist regime has unquestionably been to strike at the foundations of traditional Chinese society. It has worked to break up the family in its old widespread functions. It has attempted to destroy the attitudes which inhibited extreme and determined action—by the lean-to-one-side policy, by mutual criticism and self-criticism going far beyond the limits that permit the conventional face-saving, by the individual examples of activists who are literally working themselves to death, and by involving the people in violence. It has wiped out certain classes, notably the landlords, the bigger capitalists, and the rich peasants.

The Communists have also tried, of course, to change the whole pace and purpose of production. Time has not hitherto been money in China. The western entrepreneur desires to get a given job done with the smallest investment of man-hours; the Chinese approach has been to discover a function that people will pay to have performed and then see how many persons it can be made to support.

This general effort at the destruction of traditional society must be understood as the renewal of an old antagonism. The Legalist

concept, which has been present, but generally muted, in Chinese society for almost two millenniums, is now again attempting to destroy
the age-old, generous, humane, moderate tradition.

The destructive achievements of the first few Communist years have
been impressive; but they have not accomplished so much as is generally thought. Despite the new General Line, the indications are that
the peasantry, still some 80 per cent of Chinese people, is pretty much
unreconstructed. Furthermore, the Communists have been riding,
since 1949, a high tide of achievement and optimism as a result of
their mainland victory, their sweeping reforms, their creditable Korean
showing, and, in July 1954, their diplomatic triumph at Geneva.
What will be the reaction of the Chinese people as the long painful
tasks of domestic transformation assert themselves, as the prevailing
mood changes, as it may well over coming years, to an indefinite extension of the 1954 style of 'bitter struggle'? The ordinary Chinese
expectation would be for a period of rest and recuperation to follow
this burst of energy. But this is contrary to the new progressive optimism: one drives always onwards and upwards, with only minor
tactical deviations.

The unrelenting pressure on society as a whole has its human
counterpart. The Communists have, in individual terms, largely destroyed not only the sanction for retirement but also the sphere into
which one could retreat. The large family, the study of the classics,
the wine-bottle—all these traditional havens are proscribed or limited
by some segment of the new orthodoxy. What will be the reaction
of the average Chinese in the face of this inescapable framework of
control and pressure? Moreover, by destroying the ambition of the
peasant masses, who see clearly that they cannot safely move toward
their old goal of rich peasant status, the Communists may have stifled
the motives of agricultural society. Capitalizing upon the violences
of peasant energies to seize power is not necessarily the same thing
as making the peasant work, produce, and supply capital for industrialization. Although Mao Tse-tung has proved that he understood
how to do the first, he has not demonstrated yet that he can execute
the second.

Despite the prevailing countertraditional current of their enterprise,
despite their imported doctrine, despite their ties to a foreign power
of a form unique in Chinese experience, the Communists have to be
viewed, in part, from the perspective of Chinese history. Shensi province, the Communists' base after the Long March, is the very area
from which China has been taken time and again; and it is close to
the seedpoint of Chinese culture. Vigorous, effective, rough con-

querors have emerged repeatedly from that territory to seize and invigorate Chinese society. The Communists are well cast in the role of semi-civilized barbarians, comparable to the Manchus when they took China; and the Soviets play the outer barbarian well—they are uncomfortable neighbors and a problem. In taking over China the Communists also appropriated to their own uses the tradition of Chinese imperialist expansion during energetic phases. All Asia has felt Chinese influence, either cultural or military; and precedents can certainly be found for strong Chinese interests in, for example, Indo-China, Korea, Burma, and Nepal.

The Communists might also consider certain precedents in Chinese history that ought to make them obscurely uneasy about their policies. Many dynasties have effectively seized power in part or all of China and then collapsed very rapidly. The Ch'in dynasty collapsed after only 15 years of general rule. The Sui dynasty (c. 589–618) expired exhausted after a disastrous expedition into Korea. The Yüan dynasty collapsed rapidly at about the point when a normal dynasty might have been entering upon its golden years of slightly decadent enjoyment. Such similitudes do not doom the Chinese Communist regime, certainly; but they cannot be dismissed as irrelevant, especially to a race with a strongly historical bent.

The really vital question is suggested by the entire background of Chinese history, and especially by these short-lived, highly energetic dynasties. Chinese society, with its characteristically tight-packed population occupying virtually every acre which it is possible to till through a sophisticated intensive irrigated agriculture, may be a marginal organism. Perhaps it can work well and sustain itself only in times of optimum administrative energy and rectitude, but cannot afford to support an increasingly large and parasitic ruling class, to sustain foreign ventures or great public works not directly contributory to the society, or even to progress beyond its basic condition. History has shown that Chinese society works when it is all efficiently geared together; but this working is simply maintaining itself, not developing in any direction. History has also shown that Chinese society firmly resists decided movement, and that it has on occasion reacted to severe stimulation by decomposition or rebellion. The question thus is: To what degree can Chinese society change even under tremendous new pressures and in the completely new circumstances of today?

The Chinese Communists expect to remodel the class structure of the land, to use mass suasion that will reach farther and deeper than any Chinese ideological pattern has before, to institute means of mass control comparably penetrating, to industrialize, to collectivize agri-

culture, and to unify China and give it a new national consciousness—
in short, to transform China from a culture into a national state, perhaps even an Asiatic empire in a twentieth-century world. The realization of all this—indeed, any of it—requires an impressive release of
popular energy as well as incisive use of it.

But Chinese society has many ways of dampening enthusiasm for
change. The population is maintained at virtually the Malthusian
limit by an ideology that demands descendants to till the fields and
to carry on the ancestral sacrifices; and this strongly inhibits basic
social change or even immediate capital formation for industrialization. The life of the family and the village is closely connected to
the means of agricultural production; and campaigns against the
'semi-feudal' organization and folkways are likely to have unforeseen
effects upon the harvest. The peasant knows but a little sphere, but
he knows that completely; and he operates very shrewdly within it.
There is some question whether Marxist cliches are any better preparation for dealing with this sophisticated peasant than Confucian homi-
lies were; but at least the old bureaucracy knew enough to protect
its composure and self-satisfaction by not delving too deeply or directly into village life.

Even if Chinese society is theoretically capable of change, it offers
stern and effective resistance to change. In China the Communists
have an extraordinarily aggravated form of the peasant problem, since
China lacks the surplus food production to provide a margin while
they try to bend the peasants to their plans. This is the basic line
upon which the Communists must fight; here they will win or lose.
What benefit will they have gained if they find themselves after five
years with a tremendous peasant population all producing just enough
to support themselves, and with a bureaucracy, frustrated but unable
to retreat, still in place but revolving uselessly like a gear without
teeth? This outcome cannot be predicted, but it is not ruled out on
present evidence.

It is clearly within the capacity of the Chinese Communists to replace the traditional bureaucracy with another; but what will they
do with that other and weightier element of Chinese society—the peasantry? Is Communist political and sociological sophistication adequate to the task of destroying the values which have led the peasantry
to till the land these many centuries without also suffering a disastrous
loss in production? The peasantry and the social forms in which they
move constitute the greatest problem the Communists must face; and
they symbolize the tremendous inertia of Chinese society, which the
Communists with all their energy will find it hard to affect.

In drawing this picture of relationship and conflict between Communist rule and traditional China, the special character of the modern situation cannot, of course, be overlooked. China is no longer isolated, but a nation among contending nations; and even within the Communist bloc China is not the leader. Industrialization and improved communications, both internal and external, give new dimensions to China's economic and political situation. Improved techniques and media for mass indoctrination, the new thoroughness in applying Leninist organizational patterns, and a tremendously widened base of political participation (however limited and false that participation may be) are all new and important factors.

On balance, nevertheless, it seems likely that the momentum of China's history and organization will in the end have greater influence upon the future of Chinese society than all the propaganda, all the dogma, and all the energy the Communists can bring to bear. The Soviet Union, avowed model of the Chinese Communists, fell back to a significant degree in the 1930's upon the cultural and social patterns of its czarist predecessors, with consequences still to be revealed. The Chinese Communists may be compelled to do likewise. If it is true that the old Confucian tradition was necessary to furnish real accommodations and reconciliations between traditional Chinese society and the people who made it up, the Chinese Communists by destroying that tradition may shake the social structure to pieces or confront the need for radical alterations in their own theory and practice.

Nothing in the current position encourages cheap optimism. The Chinese Communist regime is not likely to fall apart. Yet it is easy to give the Communists too much credit, overemphasizing their effectiveness and viability and overlooking their deep problems. At present they have probably done no more than furnish another proof of Fairbank's excellent statement: [11]

> The Confucian monarchy was a peculiarly non-national institution. It rested on a Confucian-Chinese social and cultural base but could be seized and manipulated by barbarian invaders quite as well as by Chinese rebels, sometimes indeed even more easily.

But it is one thing to seize a society's framework of political power; it is another thing to transform a society. The Chinese Communists face real difficulties, extraordinarily intertwined one with another. These problems demand ruthlessness—which they will undoubtedly provide. Chinese docility, high threshold of political pain, and age-old skill at evading or mitigating the impact of governmental exactions will undoubtedly work in two time-tested ways: to tolerate the virtually intolerable pressure, and to diffuse and alter it. The clash between the forces of rigor and accommodation, between the Chinese and the Communist, is being fought out in millions of tightly related skirmishes. We have no grounds for predicting the early overthrow of Communism by the deep resistances of Chinese culture; but the Communists have not yet won. Victory may not be clear-cut. What we can assert with confidence is that the elements of the Middle Kingdom, deeply embedded in the minds and hearts and habits of men and women, are still a vital factor in the equation of force which will determine the future of Chinese society.

NOTES FOR CHAPTER 5

1. Hsiao Kung-ch'uan, "Rural Control in Nineteenth Century China," paper presented at the Far Eastern Association Meeting, Boston, 1952.

2. Francis L. K. Hsü, *Americans and Chinese: Two Ways of Life*, New York, Henry Schuman, 1953, pp. 177–178.

3. Fei Hsiao-t'ung, *China's Gentry; Essays in Rural-Urban Relations*, Chicago, University of Chicago Press, 1953, p. 81.

4. Cf., Martin Yang, *A Chinese Village: Taitou, Shantung Province*, New York, Columbia University Press, 1946, p. 132. Tsao Hsueh-chin and Kao Ngoh, *The Dream of the Red Chamber*, trans., Chi-chen Yuang, London, G. Routledge & Sons, Ltd., 1929, illustrates this cycle; and *Chin P'ing Mei*, New York, G. P. Putnam's Sons, 1940, graphically describes its later phases.

5. Kung-sun Yang, *Book of Lord Shang*, trans. J. J. L. Duyvendak, London, A. Probstain, 1928, p. 68.

6. R. L. Walker, *The Multi-State System of Ancient China*, Hamden, Conn., Shoe String Press, 1953, pp. 31–35.

7. H. G. Creel, *Chinese Thought, from Confucius to Mao Tse-tung*, Chicago, University of Chicago Press, 1953, Ch. IX, "The Eclectics of Han," gives a lucid and persuasive detailed picture of developments during the Han dynasty.

8. E. A. Kracke, "Sung Society: Change Within Tradition," paper presented before the Far Eastern Association, New York, April 14, 1954.

9. E. A. Kracke, *Civil Service in Early Sung China, 960–1067*, Cambridge, Mass., Harvard University Press, 1953, *passim*.

10. John K. Fairbank, *Trade and Diplomacy on the China Coast: The Opening of the Treaty Ports 1842–1854*, Cambridge, Mass., Harvard University Press, Ch. IV–V.

11. *Ibid.*, p. 23.

CHAPTER

— 6 —

THE REGIME

I. The Top Leadership

The position of the top leadership in Communist China has features consistent with older Chinese tradition, features which are similar or identical to those of the top leadership position in the Soviet Union, and certain unique characteristics.

The Chinese Communist top leadership can be roughly said to include some fifty or more men who hold key overlapping positions high in the military and civil branches of the Chinese bureaucracy.[1] Within this group ultimate policy-making authority is effectively held by Mao and a few others who are his oldest and closest associates, notably Chou En-lai, Liu Shao-ch'i, Chu Teh, and, perhaps, Ch'en Yun.

In terms of formal organization the top leadership is headed by the Politburo:

Chang Wen-t'ien	Lin Tsu-han
Ch'en Yun	Liu Shao-ch'i
Chou En-lai	Mao Tse-tung
Chu Teh	P'eng Cheng
Kao Kang [2]	P'eng Te-huai

Tung Pi-wu

Following are the key characteristics of the leadership group in its wider context:

1. Although they have only recently come to full power in China, their common ties and experience go back at least to the early 1930's, when Mao Tse-tung rose to leadership in the Communist Party; and in many cases the personal ties among them are a decade older. The rulers of Communist China are thus middle-aged men, who after virtually a mature lifetime devoted to military and political insurrection,

124

have now acquired responsibility for exercising power in the Chinese state. The political and military background of the leadership is reflected in North's statistics on the professional careers of the Communist Party Central Committee, as of 1945: [3]

Party organization and administration	20	46%
Military	17	39
Labor	5	11
Education	1	2
Journalism	1	2
Total	44	100%

2. It has been characteristic of Mao's leadership that he has not felt called upon to conduct any substantial purge of the Chinese Communist Party membership at higher levels. There have been elevations and demotions within the ranks of the top leadership; but, like Lenin, Mao, observed from the outside, appears to have sought to maintain a spirit of comradeship and sense of security among his associates. Unlike Stalin, he does not appear to have kept his immediate subordinates under control primarily by overlapping responsibilities, surveillance, and mutual suspicion, but to have relied more largely upon his personal qualities of leadership and upon his unique prestige and authority. He is the symbol of successful authority both as the military leader and as the theoretical, or spiritual, leader of Chinese Communism. This, at least, is the view of Mao's method of leadership that emerges down through the years of his primacy in the Communist Party. Under the pressures and responsibilities of actual government, his method may have changed since 1949 in a Stalinesque direction: we simply do not know.

3. Following old Chinese tradition, there was in the growing period a strong regional bias within the top Chinese Communist leadership; and in general the strong men seem to have been recruited disproportionately from three provinces in the central interior: Hunan, Szechwan, and Hupei.[4] Although Communist ideology and principles of organization deprecate the importance of human and regional loyalties, it appears that Mao has used such ties as instruments of his personal power, and that they are still a significant, if declining and minor, element in his technique of rule.

4. As professional revolutionaries, the leadership group has not been seriously concerned with Marxist theory. Nevertheless, it is one of the well-established compulsions of Communism to articulate and rationalize courses of action in theoretical terms. As judges of the 'correct' course of history and action, even the most pragmatic and

anti-intellectual Communist leader must have theoretical pretensions; for this is his claim to legitimacy. Mao is no exception. He claims stature as a creative Marxist-Leninist theorist. Liu Shao-ch'i has similar if lesser pretensions as a theoretician.

It is quite evident that the Chinese Communist leaders think, or at least articulate, their views, in terms of a conventional Communist vocabulary. Their performance indicates clearly, however, a primary concern with the reality of power.[5] Such theoretical innovations as Mao's insurrection from a peasant rather than urban base and the notion of the New Democracy are practical formulae for seeking or manipulating power rather than creative theoretical elaborations. In fact, if there is any authentic bias in Chinese Communism it is somewhat anti-theoretical. In a manner consistent with certain persistent strands in Chinese philosophy Mao has argued for the tight linking of theory with practice, if necessary, at the expense of the former. This empirical theme has been emphasized in the instructions to Chinese Communist cadres over many years. Mao has underlined the equality of the situation confronted with the theoretical concept brought to it—if not the primacy of the former; and so far as the pursuit of power is concerned, the Chinese Communists have demonstrated a marked tactical flexibility.

Although the theoretical interests of the Chinese Communist leadership are extremely limited, it does not follow that their Communism is insincere. Since Lenin's creation of the Russian Communist Party, at about the turn of the twentieth century, the inner ideology of Communist leaders has not turned on a theory of society but rather on devotion to a particular institution, the party, and faith in particular methods of pursuing and maintaining power. Thus, while the Chinese Communist leadership's attachment to Marxism may be shallow, their attachment to the Chinese Communist Party is profound. They are thoroughly professional Communists; and they accept as a matter of course the conspiratorial procedures, the shifts in tactics, the bureaucratic infighting, the overriding discipline, and, above all, the notion of endless struggle to maintain and enlarge their power which is everywhere the effective ideology of contemporary Communism in action.

Although Mao's techniques of leadership are more Lenin's than Stalin's, on the whole the Chinese Communist top leadership is more unified than was the Soviet top leadership during the period of Lenin's primacy. Lenin, from April 1917 to his death, presided with success over an openly schismatic group. There had been disagreement on the timing and even the appropriateness of the November revolution;

on the degree of democracy in 'democratic centralism'; over the priority of international versus Russian revolution. There has been no Kronstadt in Chinese Communist history; no need to crush any large dissident group within the Chinese Communist Party by force. Superficially, then, one sees in Peking a high and practiced degree of unity around the figure of Mao Tse-tung: a unity based on the acceptance of Mao's leadership, the habits of common working, and twenty years of remarkable success since Mao took command of Chinese Communism.

There are, however, three potential sources of schism within the upper ranks of the Chinese Communist Party; and these elements may well interact with forces at work elsewhere in Chinese Communist society to produce important changes in the future.

First, there is the question of the succession to Mao. Like Lenin, Mao is virtually unchallengeable in his own lifetime. No one is in a position to claim the prestige and, in a sense, the legitimacy which he has accumulated on the basis of past success. This fact in itself poses a problem. It may well be that Mao's survivors can agree on a formal successor; but the passage of dictatorial power is more easily agreed than accomplished. The trend of governmental organization since 1949 has been, inevitably, toward the development of powerful arms of bureaucratic power. There are the Chinese armed forces, the apparatus of the Chinese Communist Party, and the state bureaucracy. Mao has been able to keep these instruments of policy firmly within his grasp. In this he has been aided by strong personal ties, especially those which ensure his effective control over the Chinese military. The Chinese armed forces played a role in the takeover in 1949, and in the early days of Chinese Communist administration of the mainland, quite different from that of the Red Army in the Soviet Union. They were the chief instrument for establishing Chinese administration on the mainland, and down to the present they play an extremely important role in administration since, as nearly as we know, the Chinese militia, which perform many functions assigned elsewhere in the Communist bloc to the secret police, are under their command.

Thus the first problem confronting a successor to Mao may well be to gain and hold an ascendency over the Chinese Communist military at a time when, almost inevitably, the relative civil authority of the military will be in a state of erosion. This is not an impossible task; but probably no other leader has anything like Mao's personal authority over the key military figures.

The alternative to a single successor is some form of collective leadership. Neither the experience after Lenin's death nor the somewhat uneasy evolution of events in the Soviet Union since Stalin's death makes it easy to believe that over the long pull Communist power can be effective unless it is centralized in the hands of one man. Engels' dictum—that conspiratorial practice demands dictatorship—is still to be disproved; and Communist regimes, even in full power, are engaged in conspiracy not only against the non-Communist world but also against those whom they rule at home. Nevertheless, notably if Mao dies soon, leaving a large group of his old colleagues alive, some form of collective rule with an agreed chairman is not unlikely on the Chinese Communist scene.

The basic succession issue is, then, how Mao's successor can maintain a unity in the sources of Peking's power—which Mao united through unique continuity of his personal authority stretching over two decades or more, and from the days of a small conspiratorial operation down to the present massive bureaucratic state structure. The problem comes to rest most sharply around the maintenance of effective political control over the Chinese Communist armed forces.

Next to the succession problem, the second divisive potential is one which can only be faintly detected in the Communist press,[6] but on the existence of which we can feel some confidence. There have almost certainly been considerable differences within the ranks of Chinese Communism as to whether or not, and especially at what pace and by what means, the regime should move toward agricultural collectivization, and, more broadly, on what degree of strain and oppression should be applied against the peasantry.

Several elements probably enter the issue. First, as already indicated, agricultural output is likely both to determine the ability of the Chinese Communist regime to achieve its first Five Year Plan and to determine how much hunger and perhaps starvation will accompany the effort to achieve it.

Second, the Chinese Communists have adopted their program of rapid movement towards producers' cooperatives at a peculiar moment in world Communist history. The post-Stalin leaders of Communism in Moscow have openly indicated that the course of output under Soviet collectivization has been distinctly discouraging; and throughout all other parts of the bloc they are putting forward a program which emphasizes the need for peasants' incentives on the one hand and increases of output in consumers' goods on the other. It is at just this moment—when past Communist failures are revealed and current pressure on the peasantry apparently relaxed—that the Chinese Communists appear to have decided to collectivize substantially in the course of the first Five Year Plan. The proposed method is not so rapid and need not be so brutal as that adopted by Stalin in the early years of the first Soviet Five Year Plan; but there is a distinct family resemblance. It is Chapters 9 to 12 in Stalin's *Short Course* that the cadres have been instructed to read—not Krushchev's August 1953 speech on the state of Soviet agriculture. The key editorial in the Peking *People's Daily* of November 25, 1953, is virtually a paraphrase of Stalin's language of the late 1920's:

> Socialism cannot be established on two entirely different and contradictory foundations, one of which is a great, progressive Socialist industry, the other being a backward economy of small peasants that frequently promotes capitalism . . . only agricultural cooperation can stop the spread of capitalism in agricultural enterprises and maintain a firm coordination with Socialist industry and business. To strengthen the workers' and peasants' alliance, it is absolutely necessary to fight the capitalists in the rural areas and curb the peasants' tendencies toward capitalism.

Starting with Russia in the 1920's, there has been no Communist Party in power which has escaped some form of controversy on the collectivization issue. And the present situation offers at least two additional reasons why doubts about the course adopted have been almost certainly raised within the higher ranks of Chinese Communism. First, Moscow has proclaimed the cost in agricultural output which accompanied its collectivization; and such costs, if projected on the Chinese scene, would endanger the Five Year Plan, since China lacks the margin of surplus agricultural resources available to Russia, and faces a more ominous population problem. Second, the current Chinese Communist line is distinctly at odds with the current line on agriculture throughout the Communist bloc. It may be that there are some within the Chinese Communist ranks who doubt the wisdom of this off-beat Chinese performance, notably if they judge it to offend Moscow or to endanger the needed Soviet alliance. If, as is possible, the rate and intensity of Peking's plan is not approved by Moscow, there may be some in the Chinese Communist leadership—like a group in Belgrade before 1948—who feel uneasy at this limited act of independence. But this is pure speculation.

A divisive factor centered on agricultural policy is without evidence, distinctly tenuous, but, in our judgment, probably real. Chinese Communism rose on the basis of peasant support. Many of its leaders, although not necessarily of peasant stock, are at least very close to the Chinese countryside. Having gained power by mobilizing a political base in the countryside for its armies, the Communists now aim to wring from the peasantry the resources necessary for the first Five

Year Plan, perhaps at the cost of widespread starvation, certainly at the cost of denying the peasant effective title to his land and to any substantial measure of material progress. One can assume that this policy is acceptable to most hardened top Communist Party members. It is not to be ruled out, however, that some will feel that the regime's austere collectivization policy is wrong. They may reason that the peasant's reaction will result in lower rather than higher output; or they may, in some obscure human way, regard it as wrong to betray the hopes and aspirations on which Chinese Communism was largely built. In one way or another they may wish to see policies pursued which, at the present stage, would bear less harshly on the peasant and which would require somewhat less compulsion. There may be, then, some Chinese Communist believers in an NEP.

It is to be strongly emphasized that as of the moment we have no firm evidence that such a controversy on domestic agricultural policy exists. The point is underlined because the *prima facie* case for its existence is strong, there is a suggestion of such controversy in official Peking pronouncements, and it may play an important part in the future.

The third major divisive potential concerns Communist China's relations with the Soviet Union. It is our view that Mao's lean-to-one-side policy is not based merely on a simple ideological association of Chinese Communists with Moscow. It did not originate as an act of ideological faith or conformity; and, in particular, the alliance does not appear to be conducted from day to day on such simple automatic ideological grounds. If this view is correct, Peking's acceptance of the Sino-Soviet alliance in the peculiar form it took in 1950 arose from a calculation of Chinese Communist domestic and external power interests as they were conceived at that time, set against a background which, of course, predisposed Peking to a Soviet alliance in one form or another.

There is a considerable body of discussion which centers around the possibility that a sharp difference of outlook towards the Soviet Union may exist in the leadership. It is conventional to try to identify 'national' and 'international' groups, oriented, respectively, to Chinese interests and to the interests of international Communism as defined by Moscow. The latter group is usually presumed more amenable, if not actually subservient, to Moscow's guidance and instruction. A division of this kind may exist. It seems important, however, to define the area within which such a difference in outlook is likely to operate. There is almost certainly no one within the upper Chinese Communist leadership who would now advocate a policy of Titoism:

that is, a clean break with the Soviet Union and an association for security purposes, if not ideologically, with the non-Communist world.[7] It can be taken as reasonably firm that top-level Communists are now all deeply committed to a program of national expansion of Chinese power in Asia, which requires that China associate itself with the other major aggressive power dedicated to diminishing the power of the common western (and Japanese) enemy. What is altogether likely, however, is that many Chinese Communists, within the framework of continued close relations with the Soviet Union, may press for these objectives: increased independence of the Chinese armed forces, with respect to Soviet supplies and advisers; diminished Soviet authority and bargaining leverage in Chinese border areas; diminished dependence of Chinese foreign trade on the Communist bloc; and, in general, a diminished Soviet ability to interfere directly with, control, or even observe the inner workings of the Chinese Communist regime.

The existence of this issue might very well lead to differences within the top leadership concerning the appropriate degree of resistance to Soviet pressure which Peking might exert on all manner of specific issues such as certainly arise in the course of the alliance's operation. It is almost certain that the issue of North Korea's future in the post-truce period raised this kind of question sharply. Similar conflicts may arise over trade, relations in the border areas, the direction of Asian Communist parties, and so on.

If this view of Sino-Soviet relations is correct, the existence within the Chinese Communist ranks of a group tactically hard *vis-à-vis* the Soviet Union and another tactically soft might take on strategic meaning in the circumstances of major crisis of the kind considered at the end of Chapter 11. Four conditions might lead to a definitive break between the two powers: major Soviet internal crisis; Soviet defeat or major setback in war; overextension of Soviet control efforts in China; or a gross failure of Peking's industrialization plan, leading to crisis in China.

It is our general conclusion, however, that the top leadership in Peking is now held together by cohesive forces of a rare and even unique power in the history of Communism. This cohesion centers around the person of Mao, and is founded in his success and in the personal relationships which have emerged from two decades of un-challenged command. Beneath the surface there are three major divisive forces, all likely to be contained so long as Mao is alive: first, the problem of distributing power among the emerging bureaucratic chains of command; second, the problem of domestic policy, notably policy towards the Chinese peasant; and third, Sino-Soviet relations.

It is altogether possible that these divisive potentials could be contained after Mao's death or incapacity either by some form of collective leadership or by an agreed successor. On the other hand, it is not to be ruled out that the power allocation problem posed by succession could merge with an eruption of accumulated dissatisfaction over domestic policy and Sino-Soviet relations and produce a serious crisis.

Our discussion has centered on the top echelon of Communist leadership because totalitarian systems are peculiarly dependent on unity at the apex of power. They can stand great strain so long as top-level unity is maintained, but only that long. In general, then, one finds in the top echelon a rare homogeneity of outlook even though certain strains and problems can be identified.

Proceeding down the hierarchy, one finds administrators and advisers whose basic dissidence is almost certain. The groups in the Chinese Communist regime likely to contain a substantial number of dissidents may be identified as follows:

1. Former KMT military leaders who defected to the Communists without any motivation other than the desire to preserve for themselves a preferred position within Chinese society and to avoid expatriation.

2. Leaders and members of non-Communist parties who with greater or lesser naïveté joined the popular-front façade of New Democracy.

3. Well-known scientists and other first-class technicians who went over to the Communists and who now serve as technical advisers and administrators. Many of these men are likely to be disappointed both with the policies of the regime and with their own diminishing prospects as the regime brings up more politically reliable, freshly trained replacements.

These groups are now virtually without political significance except as united-front symbols and will become even less important unless there is a split among the elements of top leadership and there emerges an alternative focus of power to which they can attach their loyalty.

II. The Military

Mao as a chief of state has apparently kept in mind the decisive lesson of his career as a revolutionary leader: namely, that the pursuit of power is a mixture of politics and war, in which the strictly military aspects of the problem cannot be underestimated or delegated simply to technicians.

Unlike Lenin, Mao came to power with a mature army in being. He has expanded this establishment since coming to power in 1949. From the beginning, the army has had assured rations; and a concerted effort has been made to raise the military from the traditional low place in the Chinese social value scale. The area governments have been largely in the hands of military men. Although their future in those roles is ambiguous since the decision to abolish area governments was announced in June 1954, the indication is that these military-political chieftains will be transferred to posts of nominally equal authority in Peking. Whatever their fate, however, the military chain of command still appears to control the horde of militia down to the village level, giving to the military a wholly different importance than that it has, for example, in the Soviet Union.

Thus, in power as in insurrection, the Chinese Communists have maintained a merging of civil and military authority at various levels in the hierarchy. Moreover the key military leaders remain those with whom Mao built up bonds of personal loyalty and intimacy in the period of insurrection; and it is on these more than on the infiltration of the military with party or police agents that the regime relies for its unity at the present stage of its evolution.

Both the character of China's economic program and the pattern of Sino-Soviet relations indicate Mao's current preoccupation with accelerating the build-up of the strictly military power of China, at the cost of other objectives if necessary; and there is every reason to believe that Mao regards military power and his control over it as the key to both the internal and external position of Communist China. Beneath Mao's level others almost certainly fear this role for the military and look to their ultimate effective subordination to the party; but there is as yet no evidence of a sharp reduction of military power and prestige.

Undoubtedly, however, there has been some relative rise in other elements of the Communist bureaucracy *vis-à-vis* the military since 1949. The running of a state is somewhat less a military operation than the making of insurrection. In particular, there has emerged a group of economic bureaucrats of importance at high levels. Their prestige, their claims on resources, and their influence on over-all policy have surely increased, perhaps markedly since the Korean and Indo-Chinese truces. There has probably been also an increase in the numbers of secret police. On the evidence thus far available to us, that organization does not appear to have attained the stature of the secret police under Stalin, or to be in a position to challenge independently the bureaucratic power either of the party chain of command or the military chain of command. But that evidence is scanty indeed; and it remains one of our most important tasks to establish the scale, mode of operation, and, especially, the source of ultimate authority of the secret police.

With such possible developments in mind, it still appears that the military has maintained its initial position of unique privilege and power in the Communist hierarchy; and it is our impression that so long as Mao remains in control the privileges and power of the military will not be successfully challenged by other elements in the bureaucracy. That the power of the old Mao-Chu Teh partnership remains strong is indicated by Chu Teh's recent appointment as vice-chairman of the People's Government—second only to Mao.

Moreover, so long as Mao is in control, the military is not likely to generate and press an independent political position at the highest levels of the government. On the other hand, the scale of the military, the number and quality of its leaders, and its historical position as the first effective arm of Chinese Communism make it a factor to reckon with in the aftermath of Mao's death in relation both to Chinese domestic policy and in the future of Sino-Soviet relations. In particular, the dynamics of Chinese Communist rule is likely to lead at some stage to a challenge of the present authority of the military in China by party (and/or, possibly, police) elements; and this issue of the apportionment of domestic power might easily interweave with issues of Sino-Soviet relations, notably after Mao's death.

III. The Intellectual

The intelligentsia in China, as elsewhere, is a complex group. Strictly speaking, this originally Russian term embraces all literate persons, although it is usually applied to a narrower, more highly educated segment of the literate. As of 1949 there were in China some 5 million college and middle-school graduates plus about 40 million with an elementary education. The literate formed about 10 per cent of the population; the intelligentsia, in the narrower sense, about 1 per cent. Since the takeover, education has been much expanded. As of the end of 1952 those undergoing education in some form were officially stated to be just under 60 million, as follows:

College and university students	203,000
Middle-school students	3,280,000
Primary-school students	55,000,000

Although the regime's drive to train a new generation of technicians and to reduce illiteracy has been allocated considerable resources, including materials for school construction, in the nature of the problem the proportions in the population will change only gradually. In particular, the intelligentsia in the narrower sense (those with middle-school training or better) will remain relatively a low proportion of the population.

This class has been important in China. The intellectual was a strategic figure in traditional China. He played a key role in the Chinese revolution of this century; and his attitudes and behavior are likely to affect the evolution of Chinese Communist society. But he has not been traditionally, nor is he now, the actual wielder of power. He has been and remains the generally acquiescent adviser and bureaucratic agent of a strong dynasty.

In the older tradition the literate man generally aimed for a place in the imperial civil service, whose examinations helped crystallize and preserve the Confucian heritage. Broadly speaking it was expected that he should serve the state even though its policies did not conform fully to his views; but withdrawal to the private world of gentry life was a permissible and respected response for the dissident. During the Mongol (Yüan) dynasty, and to some extent during the Ming dynasty, the conventional Chinese intellectual was rejected by the rulers; and in these periods he turned to creative literary and philosophical pursuits.

From the mid-nineteenth century the impact of the West was felt more directly and powerfully by the Chinese intellectual than by any other group in Chinese society. The West challenged the primacy of the deep-rooted slow-changing culture of which he was a part, and set in motion a long process of reappraisal of purposes and values which, in the end, led a high proportion of Chinese intellectuals to see some degree of relative national promise in the coming of Communism in 1949, as against the condition of disintegrating KMT rule.

Many elements converged to produce this phenomenon, of which the following were probably most important:

1. From the fall of the Manchu dynasty, the intellectual lacked an ordered structure of government within which to work and had been, in many cases, literally unemployed.

2. The Kuomintang, after 1927, as the result of mutually reinforcing suspicions and antagonisms, involving imprisonment and execution for some, had become progressively less attractive as a political base for the intellectuals.

3. Like the Russian intellectuals before 1917, and the intellectuals of eastern Europe, many Chinese felt strongly their divorce from the population in general and were attracted to the claim of Communism both to represent and to lead the peasant and industrial worker.

4. The attractiveness of the West and its ideas was associated with complex antagonisms rooted in a sense of western assumption of superiority, western racial attitudes, the believed betrayal of China at Yalta, etc. The Communists ably exploited this anti-western racial feeling, pitching their appeal predominantly around national symbols and aspirations.

5. The anti-middle class ideology of Communism appealed to many intellectuals and converged with old Chinese tradition, which rated the man of commerce low in the social hierarchy.

6. The Communist notion of elite rule, with a place for the intellectual within the elite, fell within the old Chinese tradition.

7. Finally, the Communists were winning in 1948–1949, and this very fact, combined with the long-sought possibility of internal peace and national unity, made many overcome reservations and second thoughts.

Among the older intellectuals especially these attractions were offset by misgivings. Whatever the degree of abstract harmony between Communism as an idea and certain elements in the Chinese tradition of political autocracy, many Chinese intellectuals were western trained and knew well that the Communists held to other values. After all, the Communists had been competing for the loyalty of the intellectuals for almost three decades. Their fate as persons and the fate of the basic values by which they had come to govern their lives were, evidently, in jeopardy; and so they viewed the coming of Communism with mixed feelings. Their mood, as of 1949, the choice they faced, and what was for so many the decisive factor in that choice, are movingly described by Han Suyin in her novel, *A Many Splendored Thing*, in which she writes: [8]

> When the New Order came in with benevolence and marvellous flags, with heart-stirring words and unity, with coherence and love of country; giving purpose to living, making death negligible, dazzling Today with the song of glorious Tomorrows, we had to choose.
> It is not easy to cut out great pieces of oneself. For whatever the West had done, some of us had loved it for one thing; that delicate reality, frail and hard to handle, gentle, and strong in tenderness: spiritual liberty. . . .
> And thus many of the best, the more honest among the westernized intellectuals of China, chose. They forsook individual, personal freedom for a larger self than their own, although it meant a

control and discipline stern and repugnant to a part of them. They chose what might overwhelm them, not through cowardice, nor through opportunism, but because they had a social conscience, they loved their people, and they had a deep need to be whole again, unfrustrated in service to a land so much in need of them.

They chose against themselves, renouncing the small liberty of one, so insignificant-seeming when faced with the spiritual challenge of communism in lands where freedom from hunger has never been known. They relinquished a difference which had made them alien among their own people for an oppression which would free their energies for the good of mankind. . . .

Our ardent nationalism, that foundation stone of the New Order everywhere in Asia, stimulated and irritated by contact with the West, pushed us headlong, making many of us choose, not a political creed, but our own land, China.

The younger intellectuals had fewer reservations and as a group were not subject to such an intense inner struggle. Many of them had been caught up in the Communist movement during the war against Japan and trained and disciplined by the Communist Party. And the very young, the youth of middle-school age, apparently were swept by a wave of patriotic, even fanatic, enthusiasm as the Communists rode to final victory. The Communists had addressed themselves with great purpose to Chinese youth, appearing to offer rapid and exciting advance, over the heads of their elders, to responsibility and leadership in the creation of a new great China. As the regime settled into place it enlisted youth in every kind of local reform campaign. It promised educational opportunities to the sons and daughters of poor peasants and workers—to youth who could not have aspired to intellectual status in the old society; and the emphasis on conformity and memorization of the Communist Party line as opposed to serious scholarship promised a short-cut to that status. The younger intellectual, especially the middle-school youth, had the motives and, in general, the high degree of enthusiasm in his initial commitment to serving the Communist regime which we associate with the new cadre. In many instances he became a new cadre. It is not strange that youth was caught up in the Communist victory, and that the reports of those who have come out are unanimous in ascribing a large measure of initial Communist popular success to the enthusiastic support of youth.

As of mid-1954 there is ample evidence that among older intellectuals the attitudes of acquiescence, hope, and positive support have significantly altered. Many of them, from all accounts, are disillusioned and feel trapped. Although the popular support of Communism has diminished the least perceptibly since 1949 in the very youthful student group, the younger intellectuals find their prospects distinctly different from what they expected—and less attractive than they appeared at the moment of Communist victory. What accounts for these changes?

The most important and general cause of disillusion is that Communist requirements for the holding and expansion of power are quite different from those for the insurrectional seizure of power. The regime now seeks to develop a corps of disciplined, technically competent, absolutely reliable bureaucrats. It is prepared to use the older men where they can be used. But it has made crystal clear the harsh terms of absolute conformity required; and it has not concealed its impatience to replace the older types as soon as possible with younger products of the new Communist technical training and indoctrination. Those with scientific and other directly usable skills have fared better than those with a more humanistic training; but all live and work under the tightest Party direction, evidently under suffrance, denied even the classic alternative of withdrawal to private realms.

Disillusion began for many with the initial reindoctrination and brainwashing, a process well described by Kierman: [9]

As the Chinese Communist took power in 1949 and 1950, the intelligentsia were in every way vulnerable to . . . persuasion and force; and they were few. . . . The Communist approach to the task of taking them over was very much like guerrilla warfare. . . .

The initial indoctrination gambit was a lengthy course in Ai Ssu-ch'i's twenty-page pamphlet, "The History of the Development of Society." . . . There gradually appeared a range of 'brainwashing' techniques which had something for everybody. Senior intellectuals, especially those technicians . . . who were in critically short supply, got individual . . . courses for their particular needs. If their abilities were much needed, the kid-glove treatment left them not much shaken, but still quite aware what verbal oblations were required for peaceful existence. . . . If they were prominent academicians with a more or less numerous intellectual following, they were often put through enough duress so that they either publicly forfeited the respect of their students or worked to swing those students towards blind conformity with the regime. If they were prominent and impossible to reconstruct adequately for public life, their retirement into obscurity was countenanced or forced. If they were run-of-the-mine bureaucrats or professors or students, they went through a harrowing low-level confession and self-criticism routine. This exerted a maximum but standard pressure on the individual. He was made terribly aware that his entire livelihood, even his continued existence, depended upon his being accepted by the Communists; and he was made to fear deeply that he might be rejected. . . .

The Chinese intelligentsia had a great range of vulnerabilities, and the Communists played skillfully upon them. They had no real hope of a career outside of government; so they stood to starve if they were intractable. . . . The Communists . . . invented the fascinating concept of an intellectual proletariat, and by qualifying for this category the 'mental workers' could acquire both jobs and absolution; most grasped at this like a drowning man for a straw. They loved China; and the Communists gave China an international stature far beyond anything the Kuomintang had been able to do. They wanted to help China; and the Communists wanted them to do it. . . . In the final analysis, the Chinese intelligentsia were unable to withstand these multifarious and omnipresent pressures; their tradition was not one of opposition to strong regimes, and they . . . made their peace with this one.

This initial treatment has been steadily reinforced by actions designed to maintain the mood of humiliation and subservience, including mutual spying, purges, further confession meetings, and reindoctrination often in the form of hard physical labor—this last a bitter dose for a group who traditionally have considered themselves above all work with the hands.

The disillusionment begun by their treatment as individuals was certainly increased in the older intellectuals by the drastic reshaping of the form and substance of college and university education to conform to Soviet practice. In the fall of 1953 the Communist press gave wide publicity to criticisms of the 'blind imitation' of Soviet courses [10] and to the assertion, made at a meeting called by the Ministry of Education, that "earnest study had become impossible." [11]

The peace the older intellectuals have made with the regime is awkward and sullen, although it undoubtedly has its areas of private rationalization and escape paralleling, as nearly as we can discern, those described by Milosz in his treatment of the eastern European intellectual under Communism.[12] These men will not make revolution against Communism; but they will react to alternative possibilities and leadership should these emerge from other sources.

IV. The Cadre

During insurrection the tasks of the young Communists were war and propaganda. Although discipline has always marked the Chinese Communist movement, there was wide scope for personal initiative and a real evocation of idealism. The young cadre worked hard for a Chinese future with indefinite horizons. He could fill in his vision of the future with all the good things he wanted for himself and for his country.

With Communist rule established, the tasks have altered, the horizons have lowered. They have become more definite. The regime requires a mass of technically competent, loyal, petty bureaucrats. And, as the social history of the Soviet Union amply demonstrates, the value standards of revolution and bureaucracy differ sharply.

In his initial training as a cadre the young Communist recruit is indoctrinated much like an officer recruit in the army, with an additional heavy overload of ideology. That training is designed to produce *esprit de corps,* discipline, an acceptance of the regime's vocabulary and its objectives. It generates a tremendous anxiety to conform. Most young Chinese Communist cadres, at the end of their initial indoctrination, have probably "internalized" the regime's values in high degree, although it should be remembered that there is no route to elevation in post-1949 China except through the Communist Party, and that there must be many who join the ranks of the cadres for pure careerist reasons. On the whole, however, the young cadre belongs, clearly, in the line of twentieth-century totalitarian enthusiasts, embracing Mussolini's Blackshirts of the early 1920's, Stalin's Party activists of the First Five Year Plan, and Hitler's Brownshirts of about the same period (1929–1934).

After indoctrination the cadre faces life. He goes out to a village or to a plant; he enters a propaganda organization or a ministry; he joins a military or a police unit. It is at this stage that he confronts conflicts between his training and older values that remain a living but submerged part of his life; or, equally important, he confronts conflicts between various parts of Communist doctrine when it is put into application. In general social science terms, clashes emerge between the expectations created by his indoctrination and reality as he perceives it. He may find the poor and middle peasants of his village—theoretically the core of the Peasants' Association—suspicious of him and the regime's intentions. He may find the workers in his factory exhausted and apathetic at propaganda meetings, lacking the elevation of spirit appropriate to a society moving towards a 'dictatorship of the proletariat.' He may find the Soviet adviser at his factory a more or less competent foreigner, doing his job as best he can, but by no means solving quickly the difficult and often unyielding problems of technique, equipment supply, and labor efficiency that must be confronted. He may find his superior in the hierarchy corrupt, stupid, or vacillating in his instructions, passing the buck upwards and downwards, and essentially baffled by the particular tasks he confronts: e.g., winning the confidence of the peasantry in steps towards collectivization, increasing industrial productivity, indoctrinating passive mass audiences, and so on.

Moreover, it is plain from the stream of official criticism of the cadres that even deeper sources of conflict may lie in the ignorance of the cadre confronted with the mental task of keeping up with, absorbing, and propagandizing correctly the current Communist Party line—for not all of the cadres are intellectuals or even intelligent.

Lastly there is the conflict between the new and old cadres—arising from youthful aggressiveness, jealousy, the sense on the part of the old cadres that they are being pushed out by youth whose brash zeal and ambition discount age and experience and, especially, prestige.

The atmosphere created by the cadre problem may explain what some observers have taken to be the failure of the Chinese Communist Party's 1952 recruiting campaign.[13]

We do not have to assume that the Chinese Communist regime is failing totally or about to collapse to be confident of the clash between the young cadre's initial postindoctrination perception of his task and the facts as they reveal themselves. It is inevitable that the cadre confront these realities and make one or another adjustment to them: he may turn into a hard-boiled efficient bureaucrat; he may escape the conflicts by developing the skills of the buck-passer, who keeps busy with the forms of bureaucratic action while avoiding the substance of action.

On the process set in motion when the cadre faces life we have an immense volume of evidence; for it is a kind of endless soap opera in the Communist press. The cadre poses difficulties for the regime which cannot be solved by simple intensive reindoctrination; for the question raised is not one of loyalty to the regime and its concepts but whether the regime's concepts and policies can yield the desired results when applied on the Chinese scene.

It is against this background that the Communist regime has faced one of its most difficult and persistent but not particularly dangerous problems: the problem of bureaucratizing the cadres. If the regime persists in power, one can expect that ideological indoctrination will diminish not so much in scale as in function. The regime will come to rely increasingly on competent technicians and tough administrators, disciplined in executing orders, without excessive concern for the relations of their actions to Communist theory or ideology. The slogans of Marx-Lenin-Stalin-Mao will undoubtedly be retained; but they are likely to become increasingly a *pro forma* background to actions and motives quite divorced from them.

V. Summary

Looking at the regime as a whole, we find almost no direct evidence of dissatisfaction or instability in the top levels of leadership; but there appear to be three major and general causes of tension and weakness in the Chinese Communist bureaucracy. First, there is uncertainty. The cadres operate on the basis of a general line laid down from the top, more or less well illustrated by example in their own particular field of operations. The 'correct' translation of this line in the complex circumstances of a particular village, factory, or organizational activity in which the cadre finds himself is no easy matter. The exact balance to be struck between hardness and softness, the extent to which ideological considerations can be safely sacrificed in favor of efficiency; the extent to which administrative regulations can be safely violated in the interests of performance—these are all difficult matters of judgment. This is particularly so because the balance of policy has shifted from time to time since 1949. In agriculture, for example, there have been successive stages of mass persuasion, terror, and concentration on productivity. Policy towards the residual middle class has similarly varied. The reaction of the Chinese Communist bureaucrat to this situation of uncertainty has followed age-old and universal patterns. He has taken refuge in avoiding dangerous decisions and in confining himself to bureaucratic routine, paper work, and other actions least likely to violate the current line as evaluated by his superiors.

The second pervasive cause of tension is suspicion. To some extent any man working in a Communist hierarchy is constantly aware that he is under surveillance, and that he is being weighed and judged on the basis of secret reports about him. There is some evidence that the consciousness of suspicious surveillance has increased in the Chinese Communist hierarchy. The 3-Anti movement of 1951–1952 brought home this lesson; and there has been a chronic slow purge in the bureaucracy proceeding more or less steadily ever since. What is to be noted is that the context in which the Chinese bureaucrat works has shifted. In the early days of the regime, there was an apparent free-and-easy acceptance of a variety of party members and hang-overs from the KMT administration. The process of weeding out and replacement from below, marked since 1951, has increasingly colored the atmosphere surrounding the bureaucrat with insecurity.

Third, there is increasing evidence that in the last year or so the criteria for success in the Chinese Communist bureaucracy have shifted away from the standards of earlier times. In particular, technical efficiency rather than effective agit-prop appears to be coming to the fore as a criterion for success. For many Chinese Communist bureaucrats, long experienced in political and propaganda work but ill-accustomed to technical and production tasks, this alteration in the qualities most esteemed by the regime must be unsettling. There is official Communist evidence, for example, that technically qualified non-party cadres have been promoted over the heads of party members. This tendency became marked in Soviet society in the 1930's, leading to a sea-change in the function of the party apparatus.

In addition to these general causes of tension and instability there are certain categories of Chinese Communist bureaucrats who appear to be rising at the expense of others. In particular, it is now evident to many former KMT officials and older intellectuals, who placed themselves at the service of the Chinese Communists in 1949, that their days are numbered unless they are unusually competent technicians or have particularly scarce skills. The weight of the 3-Anti movement and later purges has borne heavily on former KMT personnel. It is evident that the regime intends to replace this older group as rapidly as younger men come forward from the New Democratic Youth League. Some 500,000 recruits from the Communist Youth League entered the Chinese Communist Party over the period 1949–1953.

The period 1949–1953 saw an ostensible effort to recruit Communist Party members from 'proletarian' rather than 'peasant' stock—although official evidence as late as May 1954 indicates that the technical requirements for effective administration give a *de facto* priority to better educated recruits of middle-class origin. The undoubted changes in composition of party personnel, and, even more, the increasingly subordinate role of the peasant in the thought of the regime, may be disturbing to older cadres whose mature experience consisted almost wholly in political and military operations in the countryside.

These shifts in atmosphere, personnel, and policy, which have moved the Communist Party structure and the state's bureaucracy rapidly towards the norms of totalitarian practice elsewhere, have undoubtedly affected sharply those who joined the Communist movement, or collaborated with it, in a mood of humanistic idealism. There are undoubtedly many disappointed men in the Chinese Communist hierarchy. The operative significance of this kind of disappointment can, however, easily be overestimated. There is an old and powerful Chinese tradition which dictates that literate men should serve a strong national regime even if they disagree with certain of its purposes and with its methods. The Chinese intelligentsia have generally been revolutionaries only when the weakness of a regime has been demonstrated. There is a tradition of mannered conformity which governs those occasions when men serve as efficient bureaucrats a regime with which they feel no emotional or ideological identity.

In a realistic view of the tensions and instabilities in the bureaucracy, there may be a limited number of men prepared to defect to the West if there is an attractive alternative social and political structure outside of China within which they might play a useful part—and if the means of escape can be worked out. There may even be an increasing number of men prepared to undertake acts of defiance or subversion inside China if such acts are linked to a political program for the future which commands their loyalty. But we cannot equate dissatisfaction itself—even acute dissatisfaction—with effective resistance; and it should be strongly emphasized that, so long as the instruments of force in China are effectively centralized in a unified Chinese Communist top leadership, the dissatisfactions we have noted are not likely to result in any effective action directed against the regime. They may well affect the efficiency of the bureaucracy; and, in the long run, they may determine the behavior of Chinese Communist bureaucrats under circumstances where the regime's unity is violated; but, as of the present, they are not to be equated with action by the bureaucrats which would effectively weaken the unity or destroy the stability of the regime.

A second general proposition which should be strongly emphasized is that, from 1949 forward, the Chinese Communist regime has placed the bureaucrat in a favored position. After the November Revolution the Communist functionary in Russia operated for about a decade in an atmosphere of egalitarian austerity. From 1949 forward Mao has made sure that, relatively speaking, the income of the Chinese Communist bureaucrat and soldier is high and, especially, that the food supply for himself and his family is assured. This sense of relative material privilege has historic Chinese (as well as Stalinist) overtones, and may be an important solvent for other dissatisfactions. Mao has understood the power of the principle immortalized on the American scene as "Tammany looks after its own."

Thus, what we can see now is not effective opposition or sabotage but a widespread retreat of the bureaucrat, under the pressures that beset him, into empty forms of action which keep him safe while avoiding responsibility to the maximum possible, and a powerful regime striving against his confusion and inertia to make him an effective instrument by stick and carrot.

Notes for Chapter 6

1. The lack of substantial verifiable information about the Chinese Communist leaders and their relative power positions makes the setting down of any inclusive listing largely a matter of personal opinion and inference. Among the more interesting exercises in this field are: Frederick T. C. Yu, *Key Leaders in Communist China* (unpublished), Los Angeles, University of Southern California, 1953; Robert S. Elegant, *China's Red Masters; Political Biographies of Chinese Communist Leaders,* New York, Twayne Publishers, 1951; Nym Wales, *Red Dust,* Stanford, California, Stanford University Press, 1952.

2. Kao Kang has been considered by many observers to be a member of the smallest top policy-making group. A Shensi guerrilla leader and outstanding organizer and administrator who joined Mao in Shensi at the end of the Long March, he has been the symbol of Communist power in Manchuria since 1945 and Chairman of the powerful State Planning Commission since its organization in November 1952. The absence of frequent or systematic references to him in the Communist press over the recent period has been noted by many observers—evidence from which it is too early to draw any positive conclusions, but interpreted by some to indicate that he no longer exerts significant influence even though he nominally holds his former positions.

3. Robert C. North, *op. cit.,* p. 53.

4. *Ibid.,* p. 70.

5. The relation between 'power' and 'ideology' in modern Communism is a subject of debate, with some analysts emphasizing one as opposed to the other motivation. It is our view that the debate hinges on a failure to distinguish among the various diverse elements lumped together under the wide and ambiguous concept of ideology. Specifically, we would hold that the priority accorded to the pursuit of power arises from one aspect of Communist ideology: namely, its claim to reveal the 'correct' course of history. It follows that Communism's leaders have the right to impose 'correct' history by force. On the other hand, Communism's ideology ostensibly embraces a wide range of welfare and other social goals. The attainment of these goals often clashes with the imperatives of pursuing and maintaining power. Both Soviet and Chinese Communist leaders have exhibited an ability to maintain the priority of the former over the latter element in their 'ideology.' For further discussion of these and other elements in the power-ideology problem, see W. W. Rostow and others, *Dynamics of Soviet Society, op. cit.*

6. For possible reflections of intra-Party struggle, in connection with policy decisions taken toward the end of 1953, see: *People's Daily,* Peking, November 1953; references to Liu Shao-ch'i's Central Committee speech, *NYT,* News of the Week in Review, February 28, 1954; and *NYT,* "Hongkong disputes on collective leadership," March 6, 1954.

7. A third alternative is conceivable: namely, an association of China with a group of Asian powers in turn linked neither to Moscow nor to the West. At the moment Peking's gestures in this direction are to be regarded as a tactic for expanding its power within the framework of alliance with Moscow. And in the foreseeable future it is doubtful that the hard facts of military power in the modern world make this a real alternative.

8. Han Suyin, *A Many Splendored Thing*, Boston, Little, Brown & Co., 1952, pp. 298–299.

9. Frank A. Kierman, Jr., *The Chinese Intelligentsia and the Communists*, Cambridge, Mass., Massachusetts Institute of Technology, Center for International Studies, 1954, pp. 17–19.

10. *People's Daily*, Peking, September 11, 1953, and New China News Agency, September 25, 1953, citing the report of the Vice President of Tientsin University.

11. *Ibid.* Report of meeting of September 10, 1953.

12. Czeslaw Milosz, *The Captive Mind*, New York, Alfred A. Knopf, 1953.

13. Fang Shu, "The Campaign of Party Expansion of the Chinese Communist Party in 1952," *Communist China Problem Research Series*, No. 1, Hong Kong, Union Research Institute, 1953.

THE PEASANT, THE URBAN WORKER,

AND THE RESIDUAL MIDDLE CLASS

I. THE PEASANT

Although Chinese industrialization efforts date at least from the turn of the century and have been intensified by the Communists, 80 per cent or more of the Chinese mainland population still lives in villages and is primarily engaged in or directly dependent upon agriculture. In considering Chinese life at the village level under Communism, then, we are dealing with the impact of Communism on almost 500 million people. Since the planned increase in industrial working force is likely to be matched by a rise in rural population, even complete success in the present Five Year Plan for industrialization is unlikely to change significantly the primarily rural pattern of Chinese society in the near future.

The Communist regime's policies of land redistribution, grain collection, and collectivization have been applied against a deeply rooted economic, social, and political village structure. Although a discontented peasantry is in a poor position to revolt against a totalitarian control system, the future of Chinese Communism may well be determined indirectly by the forces set in motion in the last five years in the Chinese villages. For Asia's problem is fundamentally the problem of an impoverished and overpopulated agricultural sector; and the Chinese Communists propose to solve the problem by industrialization. But Chinese industrialization as now planned hinges on an increase in agricultural output, both to feed a rising population and to finance requisite machinery imports; and other Communist efforts at collectivization, in the Soviet Union and eastern Europe, have yielded sluggish or even declining output, a result of the human response of the peasant to collectivization. A similar result in China may yield mass

147

starvation on a scale dwarfing Soviet experience of the early 1930's.

Chinese Communist success in the present collectivization effort—success in terms of rising output—would go far to make good Mao's claim to leadership in the solution of Asia's problems. Failure might be the decisive setback to Communism's claim as the wave of the future, especially in Asia but also throughout the world. It is in this large strategic setting that the human attitudes generated at China's village level since 1949 must be viewed.

In 1949 China was a country of small farms, averaging under five acres in wheat areas, under three acres in the more intensively cultivated rice areas. As the accompanying tables from the Buck survey indicate, land distribution resulted in about 80 per cent of the farms being medium or small in size.[1]

Land was held and cultivated by individual families; and the families were often linked in clan structures. Substantial amounts of land were allotted to communal family or clan, religious, or educational

MEDIAN SIZE FOR FARMS IN EACH SIZE GROUP

(16,786 farms, 168 localities, 154 *hsien*, 22 provinces)

(China: 1929–1933)

Regions and Areas	No. of Localities	Median Farm Area in Acres for Specified Size Groups						Most Usual Size of Farm (acres)
		Small	Medium	Medium-Large	Large	Very Large	Average	
China	168	1.46	2.79	4.79	6.92	11.56	3.16	4.27
Wheat region	71	1.83	3.56	6.01	9.09	14.95	4.05	7.80
Rice region	97	1.19	2.25	3.90	5.16	8.61	2.52	1.86
Wheat region area								
Spring wheat	13	2.82	5.29	8.48	13.66	15.20	5.98	7.25
Winter wheat-millet	20	1.53	2.89	4.79	6.89	10.03	3.34	
Winter wheat-kaoliang	38	1.66	3.31	5.73	8.80	17.47	3.81	12.80
Rice region areas								
Yangtze rice-wheat	38	1.41	2.77	5.09	6.15	11.17	3.04	3.38
Rice-tea	27	0.99	1.80	3.11	1.75	6.25	2.08	1.77
Szechwan rice	8	1.21	2.30	3.95	6.10	3.68	2.69	1.90
Double-cropping rice	12	1.06	1.80	2.84	3.93	6.94	2.00	0.96
Southwestern rice	12	0.99	2.03	2.31	5.02	9.59	2.22	1.02

PER CENT OF FARMS IN EACH CLASS

(16,786 farms, 168 localities, 154 *hsien*, 22 provinces)

(China: 1929–1933)

Regions and Areas	No. of Local- ities	Very Small	Small	Me- dium	Me- dium- Large	Large	Very Large
China	168	1	23	37	20	11	8
Wheat region	71	2	24	34	17	12	11
Rice region	97	1	22	39	22	10	6
Wheat region areas							
Spring wheat	13	4	22	32	20	10	12
Winter wheat-millet	20	...	24	38	16	12	10
Winter wheat- kaoliang	38	2	24	33	17	12	12
Rice region areas							
Yangtze rice-wheat	38	1	24	40	19	10	6
Rice-tea	27	1	22	38	23	10	6
Szechwan rice	8	1	21	36	21	13	8
Double-cropping rice	12	1	19	40	25	10	5
Southwestern rice	12	1	21	44	23	7	4

purposes. The largest landowning families formed the gentry and exercised important economic, social, and political powers at the village level.

Although the village presented at any particular period of time an hierarchical structure, there was opportunity for the individual family to acquire more land. Martin Yang, in his study of a Chinese village, noted that "no family in our village has been able to hold the same amount of land for as long as three or four generations," [2] a condition probably typical of Chinese village life. A rich family had important possibilities for perpetuating its position—for example, by money-lending; but over long periods there was a marked rise and fall of family fortunes. More than that, private land ownership among middle and even poor peasants furnished a strong incentive to wring the last pound of food out of the soil. In China, this is no figure of speech. The western world knows little of the intensity of effort required for subsistence in Asiatic agriculture in overpopulated areas—notably India, China, and Japan. The required intensity of effort was forth-coming in China when the system was based on private holdings rooted in the family. Chinese agriculture has thus been based in a peculiarly direct way on private family incentive; and in no meaningful sense can it be described as feudal—a fact which has given some difficulty to Communist theorists.

The poor Chinese peasant lived a life of bare subsistence. He could easily be pushed into starvation or near-starvation—by a bad crop year, by a sequence of such expensive family occasions as marriages and funerals, by arbitrary additional tax levies of war lord or government, by the compounding of his debt burden. If he did not starve at time of crisis, he might surrender all but a minimum of his land and become a hired farm worker; or he might go to the city. The middle peasant was usually just above the margin of subsistence, but by any objective standards he lived an austere life. The landlord and rich peasant had a margin of comfort: in housing, food supply, and leisure. The very rich Chinese was more likely to be found in the city, living in part on land rents and rural moneylending but principally engaged in commerce and banking.

Generally speaking, there has been some tendency toward a deterioration of Chinese agricultural life over the past century, caused principally, as nearly as one can make out, not only by a rise in population, leading to a decrease in the average size of holdings,[3] but also by other factors such as war, banditry, and floods. It is argued by some that the coming of manufactured foreign imports, notably textiles, caused the decay of village handicraft industries which had formed an important supplement to agricultural income; and that the cheaper machine-manufactured commodities available were an inadequate compensation for this loss in non-agricultural revenue to the village.

Although the whole structure of village life—political and social, as well as economic—was remarkably self-contained, and capable of maintaining its viability under conditions of national upheaval and disintegration, the period of war against Japan, followed by civil war, undoubtedly accentuated the difficulties of village life. Urban markets for handicraft output, vegetables, and fruit were sometimes blocked off; the currency was unstable and, at times, meaningless; taxes were high, and supplementary arbitrary levies numerous; irrigation installations were poorly maintained; sons were drafted into armies; and the armies fought over wide areas, interfering with the harvests. Nevertheless, output in Chinese agriculture revived briskly after 1945; and the old structure survived in most of China.

The Chinese Communists imposed land reform in the areas they controlled; but until 1948 this often took the form of rent reductions rather than drastic land redistribution.[4] In general, then, the first phase of Communist land redistribution had its impact on the familiar old system.

Although the village structure emerged more or less intact down to 1949–1950, the peasant attitudes, hopes, and expectations had to some extent been altered by the events of the previous decade. The unsettlement of protracted war, the promises of Communism, and the counterpromises of the KMT had all stirred the peasant—in some areas and to some extent—to expect that his age-old usually muted demands might somehow be met: his demand for more land, for cheaper credit, and, in some dim way, perhaps, for better status in the structure of rule.

The Chinese revolutionary mood, at least a half-century old, had penetrated the countryside to a degree. The exact extent and character of this feeling is extremely hard to judge. The peasant's life is generally so hard and exhausting that he has little margin of energy to devote to matters outside his labor and family. National governments have always been distant uncontrollable agencies outside his orbit, to be coped with and fended off, especially at tax-collection time or army recruitment periods. The Communists during the period of their insurrection had succeeded in gaining some peasant cooperation in the areas they controlled and in avoiding serious peasant hostility—a great achievement in China for an armed establishment. It is difficult to weigh the pre-1949 impact of Communism outside its own areas; but it is probably fair to say that the Chinese peasantry accepted the coming of the new regime without great opposition, with definite hope in certain regions, but mainly with an attitude of wait and see.

The land redistribution phase of the regime's policy produced a wide range of human reactions. For the rich peasant and landlord families, representing some 10–15 per cent of the total, it was unmitigated disaster. The extent of violence in 1948–1950 varied from village to village; but the Counterrevolutionary campaign in the countryside in 1951 was a bloody affair. At worst the landlord lost his life; at best he lost the bulk of his land and became a poor or middle peasant.

At the other extreme, perhaps 50–55 per cent of the peasant families received some small increment of land. Given the deep land hunger of the Chinese peasant, this was on the whole gratefully received—although there is some evidence that the arbitrary transfer of land was felt by some to violate morality; and the whole process stirred a sense of insecurity about the future.

Some 35 per cent of the farm families, mainly middle peasants, were untouched so far as land-holding was concerned and watched the process of land redistribution with mixed feelings. The equalization of land-holdings was an impressive phenomenon on the village scene, but the evident danger of proceeding beyond middle peasant status was lost on no one.

The redistribution of land previously allocated to communal purposes both symbolized and completed the destruction of one part of the old structure of village life. When land reform was completed, however, powerful forces resumed their operation; and what emerged was, again, a private agricultural system based on family ownership and family incentives. There was a distinct tendency for the more able and industrious to improve their positions, acquiring increased land and lending money at the usual high interest rates of a capital-poor country. As late as February 15, 1954, the Peking *People's Daily* could still argue, "the spontaneous tendency of small peasant farming toward capitalism has increased rich peasant farming; though constituting a small sector of rural economy, [it] still exercises a certain influence and power of attraction among the peasants."

Considerable numbers of peasants who found that, with current tax rates, their holdings were too small resumed hired labor status or headed for the cities. Meanwhile the mood of the peasant was colored by two uncertainties: Was it safe to move towards rich peasant status? Would the government collectivize the land?

As we have already noted, there have been three distinct phases in government policy since land redistribution: the encouragement of steps towards collectivization in 1951–1952; the temporary drawing back and encouragement of private enterprise through most of 1953; and the grain collection program (November 1, 1953) followed by the announcement, on January 11, 1954, of a determination to create 800,000 producers' cooperatives by the end of the First Five Year Plan.

This last decision is momentous if carried through; and the grain collection program is a profound current reality. There is ample evidence that the Chinese peasant, however grateful he may have initially been for land redistribution, does not wish to enter collective arrangements, and feels trapped by the grain collection system. In this respect he fully shares the outlook of Russian and eastern European peasants; and the peculiar intimacy of intensive Asiatic agriculture may well heighten his reluctance. Typical of the mountain of official evidence on this point is the following evaluation from the *Kwangsi Daily* of October 29, 1953:

> These districts may be classified into three types of villages. First, come the villages which are basically stable. There, the leadership backbone is comparatively strong, the policies of publicity and thorough implementation have been better carried out, the salient problems have been solved and the production sentiment of the

peasants is high. But there remain a number of minor concrete problems which have not been solved. About 30 per cent of all the villages comes under this type.

Under the second type are villages which are, generally speaking, unstable. In these villages, the organizations of *hsiang* level are capable of functioning, but certain cadres are backward. The policies of publicity and thorough implementation have in a general sense been carried out, but the salient major problems remain to be solved. Part of the masses are not free from worries in the development of production, but on the surface, everything looks placid and calm.

Under the third type are the villages which are seriously unstable. There, the organizations of the *hsiang* level are in a mess. The cadres are passive and their relations with the masses are far from good. The publicity policy is only for show and disputes are either in existence or in the brewing. Things evil are on the ascent, and the solution of the problem is urgently needed.

About 70 per cent of the villages come under the second and third types and their ratio varies according to the conditions of the various places, but the number of villages under the third type is smaller. . . .

But because the fundamental solution of certain concrete problems left over by land reform is pending, coupled with the shock of the land reform struggle and the influence of the agricultural socialist ideologies, certain peasants have engendered suspicions over the protection of private ownership rights and worries over the development of production. As a result, their production sentiment has become unstable. This unstable production sentiment has become the chief obstacle and contradiction to the development of production.

On the other hand, so long as the Communist control apparatus remains unified the peasant has no opportunity for active resistance; and there is little doubt that, if the regime so wishes, it can continue to collect its grain and move Chinese agriculture into producers' cooperatives. It can do so by force or the threat of force. It can do so by differential taxes and other devices which would make it costly or even economically impossible to remain outside. It cannot, however, guarantee higher output by such devices.

In general the issues of land ownership and grain sale have determined, more than any other factors, the attitude of the peasant toward the regime. On land ownership he firmly demonstrated passive dissidence from 1951 forward; and in 1954 there is abundant evidence that the government's grain collection program is widely resented, and resisted where possible.[5] There is no reason to believe that he regards in any favorable light the current accelerated effort to move into producers' cooperatives.

What of the other aspects of the regime's impact on the village? On the whole, the substitution of efficiently collected taxes for rents was at first popular among the middle and poor peasants who rented land. There is, however, no evidence that the total real income left to the village after taxes is higher than its real income after rent payment if additional special taxes and levies, including state loans, are taken into account. On the contrary it is our impression that the upshot of Communist agricultural policy has been a downward leveling of individual family incomes, leaving the poorer peasants at their old marginal level, and reducing the total real income left in the village. Lacking direct evidence, this is a surmise; but it is a surmise wholly consistent with reiterated official statements that the requirements of industrialization make it impossible to satisfy the people's current and daily-growing needs and wants.[6]

The regime appeared to appreciate this situation in 1953, when rural taxes were slightly relaxed and no large bond drives were launched; but the resumption of movement towards collectivization has been accompanied by a new bond drive launched at the end of 1953, one-third of which is to be drawn from the countryside. More than that, the regime has made clear that, whatever the course of agricultural output, it intends to make its tax collections. An editorial from the Peking *People's Daily* broadcast on November 9, 1953, exhorted the cadres to explain to the peasants their allotted role in China's economic construction during the period of transition to socialism:

> If the peasants do not carry out large-scale production, they will be unable to meet the needs of the nation and those of the peasants themselves, and will also cause difficulties for national industrial construction and for a portion of the peasants who are desirous of making a living from agricultural production . . . if the peasants do not unite to carry out large-scale production, not only will it be impossible for the rural living standards to keep up with those of the cities, but owing to the inherent weakness of the "small-farmer" economy and expansion of capitalist fleecing, there will surely be many poverty-stricken peasants.

As of early 1954 the regime was deeply committed to making good the First Five Year Plan for industrialization, and was prepared to make the peasant forego what is required for that purpose even, apparently, at the cost of starvation. Since any margin above subsistence is required to feed the cities, the armies, the forced labor contingents, the bureaucracy, and the cadres, and to finance industrial imports, the peasant has no current prospect of a substantial improvement in welfare. What the peasant sees, at best, is that the regime intends to freeze his real income and social status, at a minimum level, by grain control and, ultimately, by collectivization.

These are the foundations for his prevailing mood of passive dissidence and his occasional flashes of active resistance.

The regime has sought to soften the impact of its land and real income policy by political and propaganda devices which appear to elevate the status of the peasant and to give him a sense of participation in the process of government. The seat of village power is now ostensibly the Peasants' Association rather than the gentry and the larger clans. Elections of a type have been proceeding throughout the countryside, looking to a National Congress in 1954. The Communist Party has brought its propaganda machine to work in the villages, purveying the current themes. Although there is little direct evidence of his views, the peasant probably regards all these goings-on as the manipulation of a distant ruler personified by the local cadres and other administrators.

The performance of the Communist regime on the whole would tend to reinforce the peasant's traditional view that central governments are dedicated to the damage of his interests; and so he is likely to feel that the present regime is unique not in its concern for his welfare but in its ability to penetrate the subtle and flexible wall with which the village traditionally insulated itself. There are fewer opportunities now for evading rent or tax payments; lower horizons of possibility for improving the family fortune by the family's own effort. The peasant may see one or another of the village's bright boys or even girls join the Communist Party and become a part of the state's machinery, for such elevation is now available to nearly all. But this is a variation on an old theme, since the state's service and banditry were classic Chinese channels of vertical mobility, as the sociologists say; and present possibilities are unlikely, in the face of the brute facts which surround him, to make the average peasant identify himself and his family with the regime and its destiny.

The peasant's dissatisfactions in themselves are not likely to bring on open sustained revolt unless there are divisions and conflict within the higher levels of the regime. On the other hand, the peasant problem in the widest sense may enter into high-level conflict and at some stage help to detonate it; and the peasants' resentments and still frustrated aspirations will certainly play a part in China's future should the powerful system of control be loosened or broken by other forces.

II. THE URBAN WORKER [7]

Some 20 per cent of China's labor force is engaged in non-agricultural pursuits; but those who earn their living from modern industry number only about 3 million and with their families comprise less than three per cent of the total population. The remaining urban population consists of families dependent for their livelihood on small-scale handicraft industries, construction work, internal trade and commerce, coolie labor, national and regional government administration, office work, teaching, and providing professional and personal services.

Broadly speaking, there were two phases of labor policy under KMT rule after 1927. Before 1937 the KMT mainly sought to repress union organizations, bringing those that survived under strict control. Even in this phase unions connected with stable or skilled activities such as transport, public utilities, and the engineering industries maintained themselves reasonably well and were able to exert a certain pressure in the face of KMT domination. And, despite the elements of control, and considerable corruption in union leadership, the so-called Yellow Unions resisted Communist infiltration with considerable success, partly due to KMT counter-measures, partly due to rank-and-file resistance to Communist blandishments. After the Japanese invasion of China in 1937, the KMT shifted to a policy of 'controlled promotion' of unions, a direct result of war mobilization, and, in particular, of both the need to shift factories to the interior and the rise in government ownership of industry during the war years. The nature and quality of the unions which emerged varied greatly. In general, despite government control and a policy of keeping union organizations fractionalized, labor enjoyed a degree of autonomy in the sense that its demands were transmitted into pressures on policy, notably, for higher wages to match inflationary price increases. There was, further, a remarkable wartime growth in industrial cooperatives, which often had effective social welfare functions. The history of labor under the KMT is by no means wholly black from labor's point of view. Habits of organization and the orderly formulation and negotiation of demands grew, notably among the more skilled workers, whose bargaining position was good despite the general surplus of labor in the cities.

In the chaos after 1945, when the unions were distinctly assertive, the KMT leadership was too weak and preoccupied to bring them under disciplined control. And the poor quality of KMT urban administration after the war, combined with uncontrolled inflation, destroyed the possibility of building active and positive loyalty of the worker to the KMT.

In the period of struggle in the 1920's the worker exhibited not only a concern with his own impoverished condition of life but also an awareness of wider national political goals; and union organization and political experience did not end with the workers' defeats of 1927 and afterwards. The post-1927 vitality of the unions is roughly reflected in the number of strikes and lockouts in Greater Shanghai over the period 1918–1932.[8]

1918	21	1926	257
1919	56	1927	117
1920	33	1928	118
1921	19	1929	108
1922	29	1930	87
1923	14	1931	122
1924	16	1932	82
1925	175		

Moreover, the urban worker, along with the students, gave weight to the revolutionary movement in the 1920's. The workers in the coastal cities joined the students in the famous Nationalist protest of May 1919; under Communist leadership (with the Communists still inside the KMT) they were central to the famous Shanghai insurrection of 1925; they had backed Chiang Kai-shek's Northern Expedition and rose to welcome him in Shanghai in 1927—only to be crushed. They responded to the orders of their Communist leaders, derived directly from Moscow, to attempt further urban insurrection after Chiang had achieved his 1927 victory. They were thoroughly beaten and their leaders fled or were executed.

Thus the Communists, having seized inner direction of the unions in the early 1920's, had led them to defeat; and, although the Communists never wholly abandoned contact with urban workers' organizations, the success of Mao's strategy of building insurrectional strength in the countryside had an important corollary in 1949: namely, that the Chinese industrial worker was a virtually passive observer of the Communist takeover. There was no spontaneous working-class revolt in the cities; and apparently little authentic identification by the Chinese worker himself of the Communist victory with the workers' interests. In a somewhat comic sequence the worker found himself elevated to status as the leading social class—the proletariat—exercising an alleged 'hegemony' in the New Democracy. He did not seek this 'hegemony'; and he has been hard put to discover its advantages—

apart from the verbal elevation accorded in speeches of Communist leaders and the agitation of the ubiquitous cadres.

As for actual union membership, by June 1944 the KMT had brought more than a million workers into somewhat over 3,000 unions registered with the Ministry of Social Affairs.[9] The Communists meanwhile maintained a rival union structure, the All-China Federation of Labor (ACFL), which claimed to represent 2,830,000 workers when it held its Sixth Congress in Harbin in August 1948.

Whatever its actual membership position in 1948, the ACFL became the labor organization instrument of the regime during and after the takeover period; and in May 1953 it was transformed into the All-China Federation of Trade Unions (ACFTU), a 'democratically centralized' instrument of labor organization and control based in detail on the Soviet model. The honorary chairman of the ACFTU is Liu Shao-ch'i; and its other key officials in the presidium and strategic secretariat of eight are high Communist Party officials. It touches intimately the life of virtually all Chinese urban workers.

The primary functions of the ACFTU are labor control and propaganda. The administration of employment, wage-scales, transfers, training, promotion, and welfare is in the hands of the union bureaucracy; and the unions sponsor endless indoctrination meetings designed to drive home the party line. The increase in productivity through higher work quotas along modified Stakhanovite lines has been the union's first priority task in 1953–1954.

At present, then, the industrial worker under the Communist regime finds his union membership fees entitling him to such benefits as 'cultural and educational' activities, 'training of cadres,' and 'international activities'; while the government has established a system of pensions and health and disability insurance, largely paid for by management, and stands ready to assist the worker in getting further training. He sees widespread official notices of nurseries, rest homes, and sanatoria being built for his benefit—perhaps a symbol of status even though still mostly in the stage of promise.

But the most insistent meaning of his position as a union member lies in the unceasing urge to do more work, to increase productivity—a constant pressure brought directly home to him by the overorganization of the unions. The Communist press, in a general criticism of union organization early this year, noted one union of some thirty members which had ten work committees and another of only three members which had a work committee.[10] And, so far as the organization of the regime is concerned, he finds himself caught up in a vast and powerful machine, whose leadership and policy lines are outside his control, which sets the terms of his work and livelihood, and which tries endlessly to convince him that its purposes are good and that, as a member of the proletariat, he is, or will be, its prime beneficiary.

One noticeable feature of the present labor scene is the 'new' status of women. From its earliest days a dominant theme of Chinese Communist promises has been the liberation of women from their traditionally inferior position in marriage and in property and other rights established by law and custom. The principal effective result of Communist policy since 1949 apparently is that freedom for women is essentially freedom to work. Recent official Communist figures reveal that 60 per cent of textile workers and 20 per cent of workers in the new tubing mill at the Ashan steel center are women, and that more than 20,000 are employed on the railways.[11] In this connection the regime has pointed to the increase during 1953 of nurseries for workers' children, for instance, from 86 to 227 in Tientsin and from 45 to 104 in Canton,[12] obviously not a charitable undertaking but part of the creation of a functional system to make possible the use of female labor.

The Marriage Law of the People's Republic, passed April 13, 1950, is probably the outstanding example of Communist fulfillment of promises made in the revolutionary period. Designed to open the new era of women's freedom from all the faults of traditional and legal marriage and divorce procedures, it was given the widest publicity. Apparently the expected dramatic change has not taken place. Two years after the passage of the law, Shih Liang, Minister of Justice, stated that it had been successfully implemented in only three of the 2,086 counties in China;[13] and an official estimate at the end of 1953 was that only 15 per cent of Chinese women had accepted the law.[14] We would conclude that, despite apparent reluctance on the part of Chinese women to accept the benefits of the Marriage Law, there still continues the slow pre-Communist trend toward greater independence for women, a steady erosion of old custom, which Communist rule is likely to accelerate more by measures which increase the degree of urbanization in China than by formal law and propaganda.

Membership in trade unions was officially given as 10,200,000 as of the spring of 1953.[15] In this figure are included many of the non-agricultural workers in addition to nearly all industrial workers for whom union membership is virtually compulsory. If the First Five Year Plan is wholly successful, the Chinese industrial working force might rise by a few million by 1957, but this figure would still represent a minor proportion of the population. Given the strategic importance of industrialization in Communist plans, however, and the location of industrial workers in key areas, the urban worker is of evident importance for China's future.

What does he make of all this? The question is exceedingly difficult to answer—more difficult for the industrial worker than for the peasant or intellectual. For the latter two groups there has been a sharp break between the expectations held in 1949 and the reality which has emerged. For the industrial worker there is no shift in prospect as sharp as that from land redistribution to collectivization, or from humanistic idealism to brainwashing. There are, nevertheless, certain brute facts which shape his life and which undoubtedly represent conscious dissatisfaction:

1. As a matter of high and explicit policy the regime has sought to avoid a rise in real wages. From 1947 down to the present, high wages have been denounced by the Communists as dangerous 'ultra-left, erroneous' policy.[16] So the worker remains essentially as poor as he was; and the increased effort evoked from him, barring a rise in skill more rapid than the increase in work quotas, is not to be compensated for in material welfare.

2. There has been chronic urban unemployment, in part due to the altered structure of the new Communist economy, in part due to the influx of rural workers. The existence of this rural labor army is a threat to the stability of employment of the less skilled worker and a direct source of dissatisfaction to the unemployed.

3. The worker has been under the most extreme direct and indirect pressure to increase his output—through disciplined organization, emulation drives, and propaganda. In 1951–1952 this resulted in a sharp rise in sickness and accident rates,[17] a rise which continued throughout 1953 according to the Chinese Communists' own reports. The Peking *People's Daily* reported on September 1, 1953:

> During the first half of the year, accidents were not only not reduced, but actually more serious compared with the same period in 1952. Particularly in the Northeast and North China regions, accidents in the state owned coal mines greatly increased.

The pressure on the worker is likely to persist, since such forced draft devices as the 'storm attack' operations practiced in China in late 1953 are the classic Soviet technique in the early stage of industrialization.

4. Such margins of time as have been available to the worker have been disproportionately absorbed in propaganda meetings, openly referred to as 'fatigue meetings.' The apparent imperviousness of the industrial worker to ideological indoctrination as a rationale and sub-

stitute for improvement in real income and welfare is a subject of chronic discussion in the official press.

What does the urban worker see by way of compensation for this life of exhausting poverty dominated at every point by an implacable organization? Since 1951 the price-level has been steady, a favorable contrast with the pretakeover inflation with which the worker had to contend. The more able and ambitious can rise into the Communist Party structure, the party being anxious to recruit men from an urban background and to diminish the proportion of party cadres with rural ties. In general, the cities have been relatively clean and orderly as compared with the past; and it is certain that the regime is effectively in control of the nation. There is an enormous industrial effort by past Chinese standards, and the worker lives in the midst of the most rapidly expanding segment of Chinese Communist society. He may feel a sense of association with such constructive activity, on patriotic grounds, even though the round of life is no less difficult or even more difficult than it was. For a while, the repetition of 'proletariat hegemony' may have some meaning which softens the harsh realities.

On balance, the most probable mood of the Chinese urban worker is one of fatigue. There is little energy left to him—given his workload, his compulsory meetings, and his diet. He is certainly not likely to detonate revolt on his own. Even if he formulates his dissatisfactions clearly to himself, he understands the regime well enough to know the risks run in sharing them with others. And one of the purposes of such mass organizations as the trade unions under Communism is to isolate men by ensuring that they forgather only in large numbers under Communist surveillance, guidance, and control. So long as the control apparatus of the regime continues to be unified, the Chinese worker will not undertake serious revolt.

Nevertheless, it should not be forgotten that he is a revolutionary who has never had the chance to play out his revolutionary role. In the 1920's he stirred with an awareness of dissatisfaction—personal, class, and national; and his acts shook China and the world's relations to China, notably in 1925. In the 1927 struggle he was caught between the contending elites, Communist and KMT, each of which sought to exploit him for its special power purposes. Under the KMT he developed a measure of quasi-independent experience; but his unions were controlled, sometimes corruptly led, and, above all, China itself was so torn by war and civil strife that his aspirations for human and national dignity were certainly not satisfied. Now again he is being used by men he has not chosen and for purposes he has not determined.

But it is one of the ironies of totalitarian rule that it must present its purposes in terms of humanistic goals—the classic tribute of hypocrisy to virtue. In the long run, by processes which cannot now be discerned, this will certainly have its consequence in China as it will in the Soviet Union and eastern Europe; for the Chinese worker's aspirations will be kept alive by the very system which imprisons him. In the meanwhile he bows his head, earns his bread, looks after his family, and is intermittently stirred but generally frustrated and exhausted by the power machine which now holds him in its grip.

III. THE RESIDUAL MIDDLE CLASS

The tragic story of the Chinese middle class under Communism can be briefly told. Pre-Communist modern Chinese society contained a substantial class of small merchants and manufacturers in addition to the large-scale banking, commercial, and manufacturing interests of the coastal cities. In absolute terms this group was large, although a minute fraction of the Chinese population. They represented an essential element, handling the flows of food to the cities, arranging the manufacture, distribution, and sale of the textiles, salt, utensils, etc., which constituted the non-food segment of the population's living standard.

Mainly excepting the modern and relatively efficient Chinese textile industry, large-scale manufacturing and banking enterprise quickly came under Communist control after 1949. The Common Program explicitly envisaged, however, that in the first instance the myriad small commercial and manufacturing enterprises of China would remain in private hands. Pre-1949 Communist propaganda sought to allay the fears of the bulk of the middle class and make them accept, at least passively, the takeover.

Although high taxes, forced loans, and 'contributions,' in addition to a measure of state competition and direct interference, immediately bore heavily on the middle class, in 1949–1950 its members probably felt that by and large the bargain had been kept; and the containment of inflation, civil order, and rapid rehabilitation probably gained their respect. Land reform largely wiped out the absentee ownership of land which characterized the urban middle class, but an area for action remained in the cities.

The turning point in middle-class experience under Chinese Communism was the 5-Anti Movement of 1952. Although the intrusion of the state into its affairs had gradually grown, and the Korean War had brought increased exactions of various kinds, the great squeeze of the 5-Anti program brought a definitive change in status and prospects—and in attitudes toward the regime. The 5-Anti Campaign brought arrest and arraignment, widespread fines, public humiliation, and, for many, forced labor, execution, ruin, or suicide. Knowledge of the Communist concept of stages, and especially the transitory character of the New Democracy, was vividly impressed on the middle class of China.

In terms of numbers the bulk of the middle class has survived. Its functions have been narrowed, however, and its economic operations are now so hedged about with government control and surveillance that it is to be regarded as a more or less willing arm of the state rather than as a class engaging in private enterprise. Specifically, the area of state manufacture and trading has been vastly enlarged, notably the grain trade and village cooperative stores. The government monopoly in the grain trade set up in November 1953 virtually wiped out a major segment of surviving merchants. The state has moved into joint public-private enterprise on a substantial scale. And for those who remain, the requirements of depositing all cash in government banks and withdrawing only on explanation and sufferance minimizes freedom of action and enterprise as well as the making of profit. They are even frequently forbidden the ultimate businessman's freedom: the freedom to withdraw from profitless enterprise.

All this reflects not only the regime's doctrinal commitment to socialism but also its determination to mobilize resources in its hands by controlling the margin between costs and prices and drawing to itself turnover profit.

In general, the residual middle class is dissident, but effectively controlled and cowed.

To this general characterization a footnote is required. The Chinese merchant and small manufacturer did not rate high in traditional Chinese society. He had to make his way, even in pre-Communist times, in a maze of state controls and influences, many requiring appeasement in cash. The members of the middle class have never enjoyed the climate of social approbation and freedom familiar in the West. They are a hardy, resilient, resourceful breed. Communism has been, of course, a staggering blow. Many have been killed or forced back to the land or to labor. A few have escaped through Hong Kong. Nevertheless, many are carrying on, despite the tight limits and controls imposed by the state, and with the transition to socialism and the extinction of private enterprise the proximate public goal of the regime. Some can be counted on to continue to operate until the day of their individual takeover; others will merge into the regime's administrative machine; others will drop to working class or peasant status. But the enterprising acquisitive spirit of the Chinese middle class will be hard to kill.

Notes for Chapter 7

1. J. L. Buck, *op. cit.*, pp. 271, 273. Buck's figures are roughly confirmed by evidence that 10–15 per cent of village families have generally been classified as 'landlords and rich peasants' in the process of land redistribution.

2. Martin C. Yang, *A Chinese Village: Taitou, Shantung Province, op. cit.*, p. 132.

3. J. L. Buck, *op. cit.*, pp. 269–271. The decline in acreage per family can be traced in both wheat and rice areas, taken over-all, from 1890 to 1933. It was not, however, universal to all regions. In some areas, the opening of new lands and regional emigration permitted a rise in acreage per family.

4. In earlier days, however, before the Long March and the Popular Front phase of Communist policy, land reform was a bloody egalitarian affair in Communist areas.

5. For official discussion of efforts to sabotage food policy, see *People's Daily*, Peking, March 7, 1954; for grain sale evasion by bootleg manufacture of assorted alcoholic beverages, *Ta Kung Pao* (Impartiality Daily), Tientsin, February 20, 1954.

6. *Shansi Daily*, Taiwan, September 23, 1953. (Article on convening of a Rural Propaganda Work Conference by the Shansi Provincial Committee of the CCP.)

7. For a basic analysis of the regime's labor policy, see especially R. L. Walker, "The Working Class in Communist China," *Problems of Communism: China*, Vol. II, U. S. Information Agency, Combined Issues No. 3–4. Also, Shao-er Ong, "Labor Problems in Communist China," *Studies in Chinese Communism, op. cit.*, Series III, No. 5, February 1953.

8. William Ayers, "Shanghai Labor and the May 30th Movement," *Papers on China*, Vol. 5, from the Regional Studies Seminars, Harvard University, Cambridge, Mass, May 1951. Figures adapted from *Strikes and Lockouts in Shanghai since 1918*, Bureau of Social Affairs, The City Government of Greater Shanghai, 1933, p. 47.

9. *China Handbook*, Calcutta, 1944, p. 298.

10. *Workers' Daily*, Peking, February 9, 1954.

11. New China News Agency, Peking, March 6, 1954.

12. *Ibid.*

13. *People's Daily*, Peking, July 4, 1952.

14. *Ibid.*, November 19, 1953. Report of Liu Ching-fan, Vice Chairman of Committee for Regulation of the Marriage Law Movement.

15. K. C. Chao, *The Mass Organizations in Communist China, op. cit.*, p. 5.

16. Shao-er Ong, *op. cit.*, pp. 57–59.

17. R. L. Walker, *op. cit.*

THE REGIME AND THE PEOPLE: 1954

It is difficult to assess firmly the current attitude of the Chinese people toward the regime. Human motive and attitude are the most complex of subjects with which the social sciences pretend to deal. Human beings in themselves are so wonderfully complex that men can carry in their heads and hearts extraordinarily divergent and even conflicting reactions to the situation they confront at any moment.

We are acutely aware not only that the subject matter of this part of our essay is difficult but also that our information is limited and unsatisfactory. Nevertheless, we have a clear if rough picture of Chinese attitudes. We trust that its errors will be corrected in time and that its inadequacies will be made good. But we feel that the broad position at which we have arrived should be firmly set down, if only as an unambiguous target for later research. The purpose of this chapter is to put the position we hold in its widest context.

The top Chinese Communist leaders are now a unified, mature, determined, disciplined ruling group. From what we know of their early lives—and we know a good deal—their original motivation was often good, both in their own eyes and by western standards, if one is prepared to accept the distinction between ends and means. They sought an effectively unified China capable of overcoming the economic and social consequences of its deepening agrarian poverty and taking its place in the twentieth-century world with dignity, a goal which they came to believe only a disciplined, militarily competent, purposeful, conspiratorial group could achieve. They committed themselves as young men to the pursuit of power, and have long since ceased to question their moral right to rule.

In Chiang Kai-shek they fought an opponent who shared their sense of private destiny and right to rule; for the top KMT leaders and the top Communist leaders understood each other fully, as indeed they do today. The two contending leadership groups accepted almost to the same degree both Leninist concepts of elite party organization and Leninist concepts of imperialism—although by western standards, the KMT contained saving political cross-purposes, and it was weakened as an organization by the old-fashioned, personal, and dilute character of Chiang Kai-shek's rule. And so the Communists came to power in 1949 in reasonably clear conscience. They regarded the National Assembly of 1946, set up by the KMT, as a façade for the reality of power. They almost certainly felt less of a twinge at its interment than did Lenin and his clique three decades earlier when they broke up the duly elected Russian Constituent Assembly—for the simple reason that they had never accepted the presuppositions of democratic government. The Russian Communists were bedeviled by persistent but secondary democratic strands in European Marxism, which never gained much hold on the Chinese movement, launched as it was only after Lenin's *coup d'état* of November 1917. There is a sense in which the Chinese Communists were uninhibited Stalinists before Stalin showed his hand after 1929.

When seeking power as an insurrectional party, the Communists had confronted men and women who had choices open to them: they could join or not join the party; in Communist areas they could provision the Communist armies more or less voluntarily, or only under a duress costly in Communist troop allocations; they could provide or not provide intelligence on Japanese and KMT troop dispositions; they could express political views over a wide range, for it was the erratic and not wholly efficient secret police of the KMT who were responsible in most of the country, and there was, in any case, considerable latitude for expression within Nationalist China. Thus peasant and worker, intellectual and soldier, had to be won over or neutralized individually and authentically before the military victory of 1948–1949.

To the top Communist leadership this had been simply a fact of insurrectional life; and, without hypocrisy from their point of view, they had adjusted their methods, their tactics, and even their human behavior to this fact. Further down the line, in and out of the Communist Party, they had stirred hopes for a humanistic future in China quite different from that which has emerged; but to the top leadership such hopes were the product of a 'bourgeois immaturity' which they might exploit but for which they felt no responsibility.

When power was seized, the Communist goals changed. They became the full consolidation of power, economic growth for military potential, and enlarged external authority. The human materials to be dealt with were in a new situation, where their choices were or could be sharply narrowed by the regime's control system. And so, with new historic goals, and new opportunities for manipulating 'the masses'—by stick as well as by carrot—the regime went about its business.

As in the Soviet Union after 1917, we have seen a phase in post-1949 China when the leaders appeared to believe that a continuation of intensive propaganda would produce positive, individually motivated support. But now that power is fully consolidated, the humanistic propaganda which played an important part in the first months after takeover, although it continues on a massive scale, seems intended mainly to confuse and exhaust rather than to persuade. The main reliance has shifted clearly to discipline, intimate control over movement by such devices as peasant and neighborhood associations, force and threat of force, and appeal to the desire for status and relative material advantage. The Chinese people are regarded individually and collectively as instruments to be manipulated for larger purposes: they are merely the raw material of a history the regime intends to make.

This general view must be tempered in four main directions. First, for some, idealism may still burn bright despite disappointments, notably if they are engaged personally in a constructive enterprise where positive results can be observed. There has been no purge in Chinese Communist ranks equivalent to that of the Soviet Union of the 1930's; and in certain areas and activities there is likely to be some satisfaction for those who struggled successfully for power and are now engaged in directing the repair of irrigation and railway installations, building factories, erecting schools, and so on. Second, there are those who find congenial the struggle for survival and power in a totalitarian bureaucracy, cheerfully accepting the pressures, surveillance, and risks. There are apparently those in every society so constituted as to enjoy this rugged game. Third, there are many in China—for example, landless peasants and unemployed urban workers—whose lives have been so impoverished and whose influence on the society is so negligible that neither politics nor totalitarian politicians have significantly concerned them or altered the terms of their existence. But here we must be cautious. To this list one would have added the average Chinese soldier but for the remarkable evidence of the choice made by the Chinese prisoners of war in Korea. It may well be that if the landless peasant and marginal urban worker were confronted similarly with a real choice—with living alternatives—they would act with a similar lack of ambiguity.

Fourth, to some unknown extent the effective power generated by Peking, at home but especially abroad, meets powerful nationalist feelings which may mitigate other negative sentiments.

A Hong Kong observer summarizes the mainland mood as follows: [1]

> On one point all reports agree. The 'People's Government' has enslaved the people to a point where fear is the spirit of the times. No one dares speak in public for fear that it will be reported. No one dares laugh or even smile, lest it be reported and investigated. No one dares associate with others, lest by that association reasons for accusations and persecution be begotten. In fact, no one dares think freely, for one's thoughts might filter through one's eyes and be discovered by the Government. It is said that the people of the 'People's Government' have become cold, silent, and filled with fear. They are a people who have forgotten to laugh.

An Indian observer, Raja Hutheesing, thus records a visit to a Shanghai nursery school early in 1952: [2]

> In the classroom [the children] were being taught the five loves: love of fatherland, love of the people, love of labor, love of science, and care of public property. There was no love for parents or family, and these little children sorely missed it. They clung to the visitors and wanted to be fondled and kissed. Some had tears in their eyes as they were picked up and patted. I knew then what cruelty meant. I saw it again and again elsewhere, in the clusters of small children that flocked around us, in the faces of men and women who wanted a little affection. There are no friendly faces in the New China. Those who had lived for years in China spoke repeatedly of the Chinese smiling in the midst of poverty. But now the faces are set and grim.

This is a familiar enough story in the Soviet Union and in western totalitarian states; but it has Chinese philosophical roots as well. The Communist leaders long ago accepted one of the two main lines of thought which run through Chinese culture. There is the complex line of Confucian thought which, despite its ambiguities and variations, is profoundly concerned with the destiny of the individual, and, in particular, relates good and evil in public life to criteria of private morality; and there are the Legalists, who regarded human beings as difficult material to be molded to higher public purposes by known and reliable punishments and rewards. Thus the Chinese tradition posed the universal problems of men in organized society: Do public ends justify bad means? Should societies be organized so as to appeal to the best or worst in human beings? The Chinese tradition has reflected both conceptions. The Legalists and the Communists after them opted starkly for the primacy of ends over means, fear over idealism. And, more important, the Communists seek to drive the Legalist view to its logical limits, destroying the balances, restraints, and escapes that have made Chinese life tolerable in human terms despite the autocratic political theories which have pervaded its organization.

The Chinese dialogue on the theme of the individual and the state is unique in its terms and, especially, in its continuity over centuries; but it has its close western analogy. There is the view, Greek, Roman, and Hebrew, then strengthened by Christianity and woven into our tradition, that each man is unique and responsible, and that his private destiny matters—a view which limits the conception of the state and the moral right of society to infringe upon the individual; and there is the view, with diverse western roots, but associated in modern times with Hegel's view of history, that the individual is essentially meaningless except in his relation to the society of which he is a part.

Just as the Chinese conception of the social problem is universal, so also there is little unique about the basic human response of the Chinese people to totalitarian rule. The Chinese peasant dislikes collectivization and the violation of the roots of his traditional life which it entails; the urban worker dislikes his life of purposefully directed exhaustion and poverty; the intellectual dislikes the ready-made bureaucratic formulae for truth; the lower party member is worried, anxious to conform, seeking to secure his safety by guessing what those above desire. The dispossessed landlord or businessman, harnessed into the state bureaucracy, impotently hates those who have violated his status. At every level there is some degree of awareness that the regime has wrung from Chinese life its complex human retreats and graces, destroyed its balance, and that it presses its people incessantly along the paths it decrees.

The reactions of the Chinese people to the emergent pattern of life under Communism are easily documented in their broad outlines. Indeed, in their essentials they can be read in the Communist press. Nor is it difficult to detect the mutual suspicion, caution, and fear which are in the very air of the Chinese mainland.

To translate this assessment of mood into prediction raises two searching questions which we cannot answer at this time.

The first concerns the viability of a modern Communist totalitarian regime. From the western view, that is, in the context of an open society, men's aspirations, both individual and collective, find public expression. They are openly shared; and they are openly debated when in conflict. Men's aspirations also have a direct bearing on both the actions and survival of the government which rules them. But does a regime such as the present Chinese Communist regime have to satisfy certain basic popular aspirations in order to consolidate its power—in order to survive? The history of modern totalitarianism is comparatively young. We do not know yet the extent to which it can rely indefinitely on the extraordinary coercive techniques available to it, in combination with the satisfaction of the aspirations of certain very limited groups given a central strategic position in the society. The Soviet regime under Stalin put a special group, including what we might call a Soviet managerial class, in a position where it has a vested interest in the survival of the regime; and frustrated popular aspirations have been effectively controlled thus far by totalitarian techniques. The course of internal events in the Soviet Union since Stalin's death raises many questions concerning the long-term viability of his method. But it is, nevertheless, clear that the fact that the Chinese Communist Party appealed successfully to Chinese popular aspirations in the course of its long rise to power is no *prima facie* proof that it must satisfy those aspirations now that the regime has forged its instruments of coercive control.

The other, and closely related, question is: How do we determine and give relative weight to Chinese aspirations? The collective aspiration toward a status of national dignity is palpable throughout Asia, as is the desire for improvement in material welfare. But beyond that, when we come to the individual Chinese in the widely diversified settings of the various regions and classes of China, there arise serious questions we are as yet unprepared to answer with any degree of certainty. The individual Chinese appears not only to be trapped by the system's strength, but also without either a clear conception of an alternative or a method of altering his environment without intolerable risk. Action to remove dissatisfaction requires an alternative and the realistic possibility of achieving it. Neither condition now exists on the mainland.

There are various quite arbitrary ways in which a regime can be assessed. Its military capabilities may be examined or its capabilities to foster economic growth. Its performance may be measured against that of its predecessors or against the observer's (quite arbitrary) judgment as to what is good for the country in question. Its performance may be measured against the regime's own objectives and intentions. All of these forms of assessment may serve useful purposes, notably if the observer is clear about the standards of judgment he is applying.

In this portion of our analysis we have been considering the interplay between the Chinese people and the Communist regime. Confronted with this problem, some western observers, living outside a
totalitarian framework, compare the present with the recent past in
terms of what the western world believes is good for China. In
terms of such arbitrary standards of good and bad a balance sheet
can be drawn up. Unity, order, cleaner streets, more public health,
reasonably honest tax collection, a relatively high level of investment,
enlightened laws on the statute books governing the position of
women, tasks for the unemployed and rootless intellectual, a decrease
in illiteracy—all these are placed on the positive side. An increased
reliance on force and fear, enlarged forced labor camps, a lying propaganda, a wastage of resources to maintain instruments of control, a
swollen army, an aggressive foreign policy, brainwashing for the intellectual, an exploited peasantry, a loss of individual freedom for all—
these go on the negative side. Thus, in our time, similar moral
balance-sheets have been struck for Mussolini and Hitler, Lenin and
Stalin.

This form of judgment does not illuminate Communist capabilities,
nor does it match Peking's own assessment of its successes or failures.
More specifically, it misses what may well be the central human fact
of contemporary China. That central fact, as nearly as it can be perceived by us, is that the attitude of the top leadership towards the
human beings it rules, and the means it has chosen to effect its rule,
have largely turned to ashes such advantages as it may offer, yielding
for most of China's citizens a life of fearful apathy.

NOTES FOR CHAPTER 8

1. Rev. Albert O'Hara, S.J., "Phony Progress in Red China," *America,* June 13,
1953, pp. 298–299.
2. *The Great Peace,* New York, Harper & Bros., 1953, p. 174.

PART

—————— 4 ——————

SINO–SOVIET RELATIONS

SINO-SOVIET RELATIONS TO 1949

I. The Principal Elements

In official Communist doctrine the relations between Moscow and
Peking since 1949 have been exceedingly simple: in a virtually exclusive alliance the Soviet Union is senior partner, Communist China the
'creative' junior partner; the Soviet Union is assisting China on the
road to industrialization, socialism, and communism, while, with a
common ideological approach to both domestic and foreign affairs
and with a common view of modern history and its destined course,
together they lead the world struggle against 'imperialism.'

There may be some temptation to accept such an easy explanation
of current Sino-Soviet relations. For, if their development since 1949
is taken exclusively as a logical sequence in Russian Communist and
Chinese Communist history, then, it would appear, they can be
summed up in a clear alternative: either the Sino-Soviet alliance is
indissolubly knit by the common ideology and goals of international
Communism—or that alliance is inevitably doomed to rupture by a
struggle between the parties for the unequivocal leadership of Asian,
if not world, Communism.

This would be a very misleading oversimplification. Granting a
real if partial convergence of interests between Moscow and Peking
over the years of rapid Communist expansion in Asia, 1946–1951, based
on Chinese Communist ambitions and continuing substantially down
to the present, the nature of that convergence, and of the frictions
between Peking and Moscow as well, is more complex than overt
statements of Soviet and Chinese Communist leaders would indicate.
Communism and Communist history make but one of several strands
in a relationship which is anything but simple; they must be placed

in a longer and broader historical perspective, centering the persistent power interests of Moscow and Peking.

The regimes in both Moscow and Peking are obsessively concerned with maintaining and enlarging their power over both their own peoples and the external world. They operate with only two significant internal restraints to the pursuit of power: the only partially controllable response of the Russian and Chinese peoples to their policies and actions; and the nature of the resources and geographical areas they control. Internally, their limitations lie in the range of human and material factors which even efficient totalitarian states must take as given or as subject only to slow change. Externally, they face the capabilities of the non-Communist world. Sino-Soviet relations are thus to be judged primarily in terms of their consequences for the internal and external power of each participant.

The respective power of Moscow and Peking as affected by the Sino-Soviet alliance hinges on several elements which enter this relationship; and the perspective of Moscow and Peking on these elements is somewhat different. Six principal areas and issues on which Sino-Soviet relations now depend can be distinguished:

1. *The Military Balance:* the nature and extent of the military dependence of the Soviet Union and Communist China on one another.

2. *The Border Areas:* the relative power of Moscow and Peking in Manchuria, Mongolia, and Sinkiang (Chinese Turkestan).

3. *Regional Power Politics in Asia:* notably the relative influence in Northeast Asia of Japan and Japan's allies and the relative role of Moscow and Peking in determining Communist policy in Asia as a whole.

4. *World Power Politics:* the influence of powers other than China and Russia in Asia and the relation of Communist power in Asia to the world power position of Communism and the Communist bloc.

5. *Ideology:* the role of Moscow and Peking in Communist dogma, a factor operationally related to 3 and 4, above, and mainly an index of power relations and attitudes.

6. *Economic Relations:* the direct significance of Sino-Soviet trade and technical assistance for their respective rates of economic development and the indirect relation of their trade to their relative power positions.

Sino-Soviet relations now consist in a complex interweaving of these elements. Each side has applied to them its own criteria of power. Thus far the results have probably been judged favorable to both parties; but each side has made commitments so profound that any break or serious dilution of the alliance is likely to be a most serious matter. For an area of conflict as well as convergence of interest has resulted, the roots of which are longer than Communist history. Sino-Soviet diplomacy is thus conducted in great secrecy beneath a surface of concord; and any substantial cracks that appear in public are likely to be deep. It will be recalled that the rupture between Stalin and Tito, although it had a long secret history, emerged only when it was virtually definitive.

This line of approach to Sino-Soviet relations in terms of the balance sheet of power interests would not deny the part that ideology and the habit of lifelong connection between Chinese Communists and Moscow have played in the alliance. There is more to the alliance than wholly rational motives, as in any action undertaken by human beings; and, with this generation of top Chinese Communist leaders, the balance could become very unequal without endangering the alliance as a whole. But the realities of power have played a large part in shaping this alliance and will do so, perhaps increasingly, in the future.

II. Sino-Russian Relations pre-1917

The long historical prologue to formal Sino-Russian diplomatic and commercial relations included the drama of the Asiatic invasion of Russia, climaxed by the Mongol occupation of the thirteenth and fourteenth centuries; the emergence of Moscow as the center of a Russian national state; and the long slow Russian expansion in the sixteenth and seventeenth centuries into Siberia, an area of ambiguous sovereignty to which China had never laid effective claim.

As Russia emerged in the early seventeenth century as a united nation under the Romanov dynasty, China was being reunified by the Manchus after the civil wars which ended the Ming dynasty. The limited trade which had existed between Russia and China since Mongol times expanded spontaneously as the two empires made contact in the Amur area in the seventeenth century, and frontier troops stumbled across each other along the borders. After considerable awkwardness, formal diplomatic relations were established between Russia and China which led to the Treaty of Nerchinsk (1689). This treaty defined the frontier and forbade the settlement of Russian colonists beyond that line; but it also provided for the opening of China to organized Russian trade and asserted the intent of both powers to maintain peaceful relations.

This was the first treaty signed by China with a European power. Despite occasional difficulties along the border, it successfully governed Sino-Russian relations down to 1858.

Sino-Russian relations after the middle of the nineteenth century were characterized by steady Russian pressure and China's reactions, limited by her power position at the time, to that pressure, in three border areas: Sinkiang, Mongolia, and Manchuria.

Sinkiang

By 1850 the Russians had slowly pushed into Central Asia down towards the borders of Persia and Afghanistan. In that year the Russian government requested China to open Kashgar in Sinkiang to Russian trade. Sinkiang had for centuries been formally at least part of the Chinese Empire. Its distance from imperial headquarters and its mainly non-Chinese population combined, however, to give the province quasi-independent status, varying with the internal strength of the dynasty and especially with the ability and energy of the local governor.

In the course of the 1850's agreements were made permitting Russian trade in Sinkiang; and in 1862 the Sino-Russian Overland Trade Regulations were signed in Peking. These gave Russia preferential customs treatment and confirmed a border area between Sinkiang and Russian Central Asia within which trade was to be duty-free.

There followed chronic disputes between Russia and China in Sinkiang. Russian pressure was generally attuned to moments of dynastic weakness, notably during the Taiping Rebellion and the Islamic Revolt of the 1860's. The success of General Tso Tsung-t'ang in suppressing the Islamic revolt by 1878 temporarily consolidated China's position. During the Moslem uprising, however, Russians occupied the Ili area, partly to block the possibility of the British developing a foothold in this disorganized region. Extremely complex and difficult negotiations were required between China and Russia to bring about Russia's removal, which was finally accomplished by the 1881 Treaty of St. Petersburg, in which an indemnity of 9 million rubles was paid to Russia to cover the costs of defending Ili ostensibly on Chinese behalf. The treaty confirmed Russia's special trading privileges in Sinkiang (and in Mongolia), and governed Sino-Russian relations in Sinkiang down to the Russian Revolution of 1917.

Mongolia

Russia's ties to Mongolia stemmed from the push to the east which began to assume importance in the seventeenth and eighteenth centuries.

The Mongols had a long history of racial independence, complicated by their attachment to Lamaism and by the memory of a brief, remarkable period in the thirteenth century when they threatened to dominate all of Eurasia. The Mongol (Yüan) dynasty in China fell in the fourteenth century; but not until the end of the seventeenth century was Mongolia tied effectively into Peking's domain.

In the early eighteenth century, when Russian colonization impinged on the Mongolian borders, the difficulties which arose between Russia and China were settled in the Treaty of Kiakhta in 1727, which defined the frontiers and made special provision for Sino-Russian trade. The treaty further forbade the settlement of rebel Mongols in Russian territory.

But the persistent cultural and racial autonomy of Mongolia, the weakness of the Manchu dynasty's control over that region, and the links to Outer Mongolia provided by Cossack infiltration proved too substantial a temptation for Russia. After the turn of the nineteenth century Russia systematically built up its position in Outer Mongolia, exploiting the region's desire for a greater degree of autonomy *vis-à-vis* Peking. In 1907, when Russia and Japan were agreeably dividing the spoils of empire in China, Japan recognized Russia's special position in Outer Mongolia and agreed not to interfere with it. This was confirmed in the Russian-Japanese agreement of 1910. The Chinese countered with a plan for encouraging Chinese immigration into the area, although, as with Sinkiang, the terrain and the existing racial and cultural strains proved resistant to effective Chinese penetration. They also increased their Outer Mongolia garrison.

These Chinese protective measures were disrupted by the outbreak of the Chinese revolution in 1911, during which the Mongolian government made terms with Russia which, in effect, detached Mongolia from China and made it a Russian protectorate.

During the First World War a Chinese-Russian-Mongolian agreement was signed (1915). This tripartite agreement, undertaken at a time when Russia was at war against the Central Powers and Yüan Shih-kai appeared reasonably effective in China, defined a subtle balance of interests: Outer Mongolia abandoned its claim to sovereignty, and recognized Chinese suzerainty; but Russian special interests in Outer Mongolia were formally recognized. This agreement held until the Russian Revolution of 1917.

Manchuria

After the Crimean War the defeated and frustrated Russian government gave increased support to Muraviev, governor general of eastern Siberia from 1847, and founder of the modern Russian Empire in Asia. Muraviev pushed Russia's border to the Pacific—across the inhospitable land China had never claimed formally because it was not suitable to the agricultural society and culture which were the substance of the Middle Kingdom. He forced a modification of the Chinese-Russian border permitting unobstructed Russian use of the Amur River, the Chinese acceptance of this modification being dictated by the dynasty's weakness in the face of pressure from the Taiping rebels on the one hand and from Britain and France on the other. The 1858 Treaty of Aigun, surrendering the left bank of the Amur to Russia, was confirmed in 1860 by the Treaty of Peking. The Russian General Ignatiev, who pushed Russian power through to the Maritime Provinces, strengthened the czarist negotiating hand with promises of arms for the suppression of the Taiping Rebellion, then in its final stage.

China's partly instinctive and partly planned reaction to Russian pressure in the northeast was a flow of peasant migration from the south into Manchuria (north of Mukden), notably after 1900. The *de facto* presence of Chinese in Manchuria has, ever since, constituted a major force limiting the manner and extent to which Manchuria could be dominated by more powerful nations.

Like Muraviev's mid-century drive to Vladivostok, the building of the Chinese Eastern Railway was related to Russian frustration in Europe. After the Berlin conference of 1878 the Russians, encouraged by Bismarck, turned to the problem of constructing a Trans-Siberian railroad which would permit more effective colonization, trade, and communications between Moscow and the eastern portions of the empire. Construction was started at both ends in 1891; and by 1901 the railway was completed as far as Chita, virtually connecting Moscow with the Manchurian border. There then arose the issue of where the route from Chita to Vladivostok should run: along the circuitous arc of the Amur River, or straight across Manchuria. Exploiting a bargaining position earned in Peking by its role in mitigating the terms of peace after the Japanese War of 1895, in which Russian and other pressure had salvaged the Liaotung Peninsula for China, the Russians negotiated the right to build the Trans-Siberian Railway across Manchurian territory, saving many miles and an estimated 35 million rubles and simultaneously staking a strong claim of interest in Manchuria. Although the original agreement on the Chinese Eastern Railway envisaged a substantial financial responsibility for China and the cession of the whole line to China free of charge after 80 years (with the right of redemption after 36 years), the financial weakness of Peking left immediate responsibility and authority largely in Russian hands. It was about this time that, in general, major power interests in China turned from a simple interest in trade concessions to the deeper incursions that went with a foreign interest in railroads, mines, and, later, factories.

The whole of this enterprise was carried out within the framework of a general policy enunciated by Russia after the Sino-Japanese War of 1895, which declared the principle of China's territorial integrity.

The Chinese Eastern Railway thus became a major Russian interest in Manchuria and an occasion for asserting further interests. Russia asserted a claim to Port Arthur and Dairen, thus helping detonate the Boxer uprising and then the Russian-Japanese War of 1904–1905, since emergent Japan regarded the Liaotung Peninsula as within its sphere of influence on the mainland.

The Yalta agreement of 1945 and the Chinese Treaties of 1945 and 1950 confirmed a Russian position on the Liaotung Peninsula. It is worth recalling that this deep penetration of China represented a high point of czarist imperialist aggression in the face of Chinese weakness, about which the Russian statesman Count Witte wrote: [1]

> . . . we had declared (1895) the principle of China's territorial integrity and . . . on the strength of that principle we forced Japan to withdraw from the Liaotung Peninsula. . . . The Chinese Eastern Railway was designed exclusively for cultural and peaceful purposes, but jingoist adventurers turned it into a means of political aggression involving the violation of treaties, the breaking of freely given promises, and the disregard of the elementary interests of other nationalities.

These passages might well have been quoted by western statesmen to Stalin in 1945 as he made his bid for Russian position in the Far East based upon 1904 status. The irony of the 1945 Soviet argument was heightened by Russian Communist opposition to czarist imperial ambitions in the Far East in the early years of the century.

In 1907, checked in their expansion by the Japanese, Moscow altered its approach and agreed with Tokyo to share their Manchurian interests at China's expense. This was a low point in China's internal strength; and the secret agreements of Japan and Russia to maintain their special interests in Manchuria both reflected and accentuated that weakness. In these years Russia and Japan united to oppose American diplomatic and financial efforts to establish an open-door policy in Manchuria by creating a major power consortium to operate the Manchurian railroads. During the First World War, the preoccupations of Russia and the European powers permitted Japan to make important further incursions on the mainland, in the Shantung

Peninsula and Manchuria, deeply stirring Chinese nationalism in the process.

Summarizing this history down to 1917, we observe along China's borders a process of limited Russian aggression. After the Chinese defeat by Japan in 1895, Count Witte, sensing that on the world scene Russia's balance of interests lay in strengthening China, the weaker power area, against the incursions of Japan and other more substantial powers, enunciated Russia's interest in a policy of Chinese territorial integrity. But this long-term policy, attuned to a world power perspective, was rejected in favor of Russian unilateral pressure on China. The collision with Japan resulted, and, with it, Russian defeat. Russia responded to its setback and the increasing energy of the United States and western powers in Manchuria by collaborating with Japan, from about 1907, in a joint exploitation of China's weakness designed to exclude other powers from influence in Northeast Asia. In all this period China's fundamental weakness and the limited force Russia was prepared to apply to achieve its objectives were recognized on both sides. There were fluctuations in the degree of Russian penetration, as in the internal power of Chinese regimes. The net result was enlarged formal recognition by China of Russia's special interests in Sinkiang, Outer Mongolia, and Manchuria.

III. Sino-Soviet Relations: 1917–1949

During and after the Russian Revolution of 1917, China, swept along by the efforts of its wartime allies to organize resistance to Bolshevik rule, supported various insurrectional groups in Manchuria and Siberia and became involved in unsystematic efforts to retrieve positions previously lost to Russia in the border areas. In the same period, Japan sought to extract from the postrevolutionary confusion and China's weakness large positions on the Chinese mainland.

The various anti-Bolshevik efforts in Sinkiang, Mongolia, and Siberia were gradually defeated by the Soviet regime. China's major allies largely withdrew from the scene, and, by about 1923, Sino-Soviet diplomacy along the frontier resumed its pre-1917 shape. In fact, Russia had gained in relative strength, for the process of defeating the counterrevolutionary efforts along its eastern borders had given the Soviet Union occasion to redefine and extend Russian positions.

As with the preceding period, the history of Sino-Russian, now Sino-Soviet, relations in the years following the consolidation of Bolshevik power in Russia is most readily understood in terms of the border areas of Sinkiang, Mongolia, and Manchuria.

Sinkiang

When Soviet forces defeated the White Russian Baron Ungern Sternberg in Mongolia, September 1921, many of the baron's troops fell back on Sinkiang. Alarmed by the possibilities of Soviet entry, the Chinese undertook to avoid involvement. The retreating White Russian soldiers were interned, and a strict policy of neutrality was maintained in Sinkiang. The adventitious presence of a strong governor, Yang Tseng-hsin, was an effective check on the Soviets, the *de facto* strength of the Chinese position resulting in a trade agreement in 1920, revised in 1923, which did not extend, and perhaps even limited, the pre-1914 Russian privileges in Sinkiang.

The Chinese position could not be sustained. The Islamic Revolt of 1930–1934, a regional uprising in Sinkiang staged while the central government was weak, led to a reestablishment there of monopolistic Soviet trading rights.[2] In exchange for the Soviet promise of arms to deal with the revolting General Ma Chung-yin, the local governor, Chin Shu-jen, without the knowledge of the Chinese central government, negotiated a new provisional trade agreement with Soviet authorities. This *ad hoc* arrangement permitted the establishment of Soviet financial bureaus in Sinkiang, led to the formation of the Sinkiang-Soviet Trading Company, and was followed by the steady increase of Soviet influence in the 1930's.

From the signing of the Soviet-Japanese Non-Aggression Pact, April 1941, the weight of authority in Sinkiang shifted back to the central government, which a heavily engaged Soviet Union did not immediately contest. The wartime preoccupations of both Moscow and Chungking permitted, however, the persistent underlying sentiment for autonomy to assert itself, notably in 1944–1946; and from the end of 1943 Moscow resumed the active pursuit of its imperial interests in the area. In 1949 the autonomous tendencies and the underlying Russian strength in Sinkiang facilitated Communist takeover; native forces did not welcome or support Communism, but they did not lift a finger in support of the isolated KMT garrison.

Mongolia

During the postrevolutionary period the Russian position in Outer Mongolia was distinctly strengthened beyond the point where czarist imperialism had left off. Soviet forces had the excuse of marching into Mongolia to defeat the forces of the erratic Baron Sternberg. In a series of stages which now strongly and precisely recall the techniques used by the Soviet Union in eastern Europe after the Second World

War, this military occasion was used as a pretext for complete political sovietization of Outer Mongolia. It is no accident that the Soviet theorists invoked Mongolia as the historic model for the eastern European peoples' democracies after 1945. The takeover process included an early stage in which the living Buddha was maintained as a symbol of the Mongolian independence which was never really granted. Between 1921 and 1924 the political subversion of Outer Mongolia was completed, in thorough-going imitation of then current Soviet domestic practice. The Chinese government was forced to accept this state of affairs, with the provision that Soviet troops be withdrawn—an act which at this stage did not endanger the Soviet grip. A Mongolian Army had been created which was (and is) a part of the Red Army. From 1924 down to the present, despite the maintenance of the diplomatic fiction that Outer Mongolia is 'an integral part of the Chinese Republic and respects Chinese sovereignty,' it has been effectively a part of the Soviet Union: a position confirmed by Mao in 1950. Unlike Tannu-Tuva, however, Outer Mongolia has never been incorporated into the Soviet Union.

Manchuria

As early as July 1918 the hard-pressed Soviet government bid for popular support in China by announcing that '. . . we relinquish the conquests of the Tsarist Government in Manchuria.' In particular Moscow offered to permit China to acquire the Chinese Eastern Railway at a date earlier than that contemplated in the original treaty.

In 1924, when Soviet Russia and China attempted to settle formally the outstanding differences between them, the government in Peking was so feeble that Moscow concluded a separate agreement with the northern war lord Chang Tso-lin, covering the Chinese Eastern Railway. The Peking government reluctantly accepted this agreement. The period for the return to China of the Chinese Eastern Railway was reduced from 80 to 60 years; but, beyond that, Soviet powers over the railroad were formally in no way reduced, and, in fact, were exercised with increased vigor. Despite the fact that these negotiations took place while the Soviet Union was making a considerable propaganda effort to pose as an enemy of imperialism, and Comintern agents were assisting Dr. Sun Yat-sen in the reorganization of the KMT, the Sino-Soviet negotiations were conducted strictly on the basis of old and well-established Russian national interests, in which, among other things, the threat of a Russo-Japanese agreement was held over the head of the Chinese government in the classic manner of pre-1917 imperialism in Asia.

When the KMT split in 1926–1927, the lines of formal Soviet diplomacy to Peking and of Comintern activities within the KMT became entangled. In the period 1923–1927 the Soviet Union had operated, in effect, with two missions in China: one headed by Karakhan, to the declining and weak government at Peking; the other, headed by Borodin, with the KMT at Canton. Borodin master-minded plans for the Northern Expedition and, in general, for the effective military and political organization of the KMT. In 1927 not only did Chiang Kai-shek disrupt the power of the Communists both inside and outside of the KMT, but the Chinese government at Peking also raided the Soviet embassy on the well-founded suspicion that it was the base for extensive covert operations in China. Both Karakhan and Borodin departed from the scene, and, except for the presence of Soviet consuls in Manchuria, Sino-Soviet relations were effectively cut off.

The hostility between the Soviet Union and China caused a crisis in 1929 over the Chinese Eastern Railway. The Chinese tried to diminish Soviet administrative power in the railroad by a series of unilateral measures. Their actions resulted in a brief Soviet invasion of Manchuria in August 1929, with which neither Nationalist forces nor Chang Tso-lin could contend. The result was the Khabarovsk Convention, which confirmed Moscow's monopolistic control over the railway.

Despite its interest in the Chinese Eastern Railway, the Soviet government in no way interfered with the Japanese aggression in Manchuria, which began in September 1931. In fact, confronted with the complications which arose from the Japanese takeover in Manchuria, the Soviet government, despite Chinese protests, in 1933 offered to sell the railway to the Japanese; and, after considerable haggling over the price to be paid by Japan, the railway was sold in 1935. This tactical move was designed primarily to extract some cash from a situation of no profit to the Soviet Union and, simultaneously, to avoid unnecessary complications with the Japanese. Moscow completed the deal by recognizing Manchukuo.

This Soviet tactical withdrawal from Manchuria, at a period of greater potential menace from Germany, did not represent the whole of Soviet policy. In this same period Moscow moved towards an understanding with Nationalist China. Sino-Soviet relations were resumed as early as 1932, and ambassadors were appointed in the following year. Beneath the surface of diplomacy Moscow used its powerful influence over the Chinese Communists to press on Chiang Kai-shek a policy of resistance against Japan, and persuaded the Communists to grant various short-term concessions to the KMT designed to encourage this result. In 1936 the dramatic kidnaping of Chiang and the subsequent agreement between the KMT and the Communists created a limited national front against Japan.

In 1937, when Japan launched a full-scale invasion of China, the Soviet government followed a policy designed to increase Chinese resistance while avoiding direct difficulty with Japan. A Sino-Soviet non-aggression pact was concluded as early as August 1937, some six weeks after the Japanese invasion of China had begun. In the following years the Soviet Union made several substantial loans to Nationalist China and furnished important amounts of military assistance in the form of ammunition, equipment, technical advice, planes, and pilots who, for a time, flew against the Japanese. Several substantial military engagements between Japanese and Soviet troops occurred in 1937–1939. These were almost certainly initiated by Japan to test the possibilities of expansion on the mainland at Soviet expense. Sharp and effective Soviet response firmly defined for Tokyo Moscow's view of their respective spheres of influence in the Far East; and Japanese strategic planning looked elsewhere for expansion.

Soviet Far Eastern policy remained one of limited liability. Trade relations with Japan and the agreements concerning Japanese fishing in Russian waters were maintained. Moreover, in April 1941, when there were ample signs of degeneration in German-Soviet relations, a Soviet-Japanese neutrality pact was signed—undoubtedly designed by both Tokyo and Moscow to minimize the possibility of war on two fronts.

It seems evident, as noted earlier, that as the Second World War came to an end the Soviet Union counted on a phase of more or less effective domination of China by the Nationalist government and the KMT, while continuing to strengthen the Chinese Communists for the long-haul struggle for power. When, in early 1945, the outline of a postwar settlement was negotiated among Roosevelt, Churchill, and Stalin at Yalta, the Soviet Union appeared willing to trade its continued recognition of the Nationalist government of China, and restraint in exploiting its considerable trouble-making capabilities, for a set of specific national advantages in the Far East. So far as China was concerned, the pattern of Soviet demands followed the lines of the position which had emerged by about 1927, with one important exception covering the Liaotung Peninsula.

The puppet status of Outer Mongolia was confirmed; and the Chinese Eastern Railway (already paid for by the Japanese) reverted to joint Sino-Soviet operation, with the 'pre-eminent interests' of the Soviet Union preserved, including the right to transport troops and supplies through Manchuria to Port Arthur. In the Liaotung Peninsula, however, the Soviet Union insisted on pre-1904 Russian rights: the commercial port of Dairen was to be internationalized, the pre-eminent interest of the Soviet Union in this port safeguarded, and the lease of Port Arthur as a naval base of the Soviet Union was to be granted. So far as Japan was concerned, again the Soviet Union claimed the *status quo ante*-1904, insisting also on the return of the southern part of Sakhalin and the Kurile Islands to the Soviet Union. In reasserting this classic imperialist position in the Far East, Soviet diplomacy behaved in complete continuity with a Russian tradition which went back a century to Muraviev, if not to earlier times. In 1945 Stalin made no reference to Chicherin's 1918 statement relinquishing czarist rights in China. The terms of the Yalta agreement were confirmed and elaborated further in the Sino-Soviet agreement of August 1945. This agreement was negotiated before the war against Japan had come to an end and was signed on August 14, a few days after the Japanese capitulation. Thus the Soviet Union derived the full measure of diplomatic gain from its promise to enter the war against Japan.

The Chinese Nationalists received from the 1945 agreement a positive Soviet commitment to friendship, including recognition of both their major power status and their authority in China. Discounting the professions of assistance and friendship, the KMT hoped that the Soviet would honor its other commitments: to avoid interference in China's internal affairs and to deny military supplies to the Chinese Communists; to respect China's full sovereignty in Manchuria, and to forego interference with the internal affairs of Sinkiang; to return the Chinese Eastern Railway to China after thirty years, without compensation; and to withdraw Soviet troops from Manchuria within three months after Japan's capitulation.

The course of Soviet behavior between 1945–1949 has been earlier described and analyzed. There is no doubt that the spirit and, to some extent, the letter of the 1945 agreement between the Nationalist government and the Soviet Union were violated in the postwar years by various forms of Soviet aid to the Communists and obstruction to the Nationalist government. In no sense did the Soviet Union behave as 'friend and ally,' as the 1945 Treaty required.

NOTES FOR CHAPTER 9

1. Quoted, A. K. Wu, *China and the Soviet Union*, London, Methuen & Co., Ltd., 1950, pp. 87–88. (New York, John Day, 1950.)

2. For a detailed account of Soviet penetration of Sinkiang from 1928 forward, see Li Chang, "The Soviet Grip on Sinkiang," *Foreign Affairs*, April 1954.

CHAPTER

—— 10 ——————————————————

SINO-SOVIET RELATIONS:

THE PRESENT STRUCTURE AND ITS

IMPLICATIONS

I. THE SINO-SOVIET TREATY OF 1950

In view of their historical background, the first postwar arrangements between Russia and China (negotiated at Yalta by the Big Three with China absent and confirmed in the 1945 Sino-Soviet treaty) must have seemed in Chinese eyes a formal international confirmation of advantages Russia had only tentatively achieved at the peak of her imperialist power and when China had been at a nadir of weakness, in the last days of the Manchu dynasty. Nationalist China had to accept this humiliation: Soviet troops were in Manchuria; the overriding purpose of the allies was to erect a structure of organized peace based on major power agreement, including Moscow; and Chiang Kai-shek's only hope in 1945 was that the Soviet Union could be negotiated into a denial of assistance to the Chinese Communists. At this cost, the Nationalists hoped to clear the way to national unity and to confirm the major-power diplomatic status they had been granted, at United States insistence, during the war years.

When Mao Tse-tung came to power in 1949 it was extremely desirable for him to be able to present to the Chinese people a pattern of Sino-Soviet relations more favorable to China than those negotiated by the Nationalists. The Soviet leaders recognized this need, and in the period December 1949–February 1950 the thirty-year Sino-Soviet treaty of friendship, alliance, and mutual assistance was negotiated. This treaty laid the foundation of contemporary Sino-Soviet relations and provides us the best clues to their general structure.

In terms of historic Sino-Russian issues, the 1950 treaty made two concessions to China: transfer of the Chinese Eastern Railway to China was to be effected upon the conclusion of the peace treaty with Japan and not later than the end of 1952; the base at Port Arthur was to be transferred to Communist China under the same conditions. But these concessions (only the former of which has been implemented) were offset by Soviet retention of a foothold in the Liaotung Peninsula: in case of "aggression on the part of Japan or any State which should unite with Japan, and as a result of this being involved in military operations, China and the Soviet Union may, on the proposal of the Government of the People's Republic of China and with the agreement of the Soviet Government, jointly use the naval base of Port Arthur in the interests of conducting joint military operations against the aggressor." Also, the issue of Dairen's port was left open. In effect, then, the Soviet government gave the Chinese Eastern Railway to the Communists as part of the price for close association with the Soviet Union and to assist them in justifying Mao's lean-to-one-side policy to the Chinese people. More than that, the agreement made provision for military, economic, political, and cultural ties of a peculiar intimacy between the two powers.

There is no doubt that the Sino-Soviet agreement of 1950 was regarded as meager and disappointing in China. Soviet credits of $300 million for five years were granted. Although substantial by Moscow's standards, they were a disappointment to many Chinese who noted that they were hardly on the scale of American aid to South Korea. The Russian grip on China at strategic points was not significantly loosened. To the literate Chinese the agreement helped begin a process of disillusionment which has drastically altered the mood of China since 1949.

As yet the full meaning of the Sino-Soviet ties is still not wholly clear, although their main lines can be discerned. The following parts of this chapter consider the apparent form and some of the implications as they can be discerned from the outside both in the context of the 1950 Sino-Soviet treaty and in the light of subsequent developments.

II. DOMESTIC IMPLICATIONS
Military

We do not know the precise terms of the Sino-Soviet military alliance. Given the basic military weakness of the Chinese Communists in relation to the United States and the western allies, and the fact that over at least the next decade China will not have an industrial base capable of fully equipping its armed forces, we can infer an arrangement which increases current Chinese Communist military strength beyond China's own capabilities.

It is our basic judgment that Chinese Communist strategy is to exploit the association with Soviet military strength in order to pursue both a current policy of expansion in Asia and the long-term goal of increased security independence from Moscow without envisaging at any point a break with the Soviet Union. We take it that Peking's aim is a progressive increase in stature within a close alliance to Moscow.

The Chinese Communists seek to expand in Asia at the maximum rate compatible with their internal objectives and the avoidance of major war. They are aware that, alone, they are not in a position to cope with the military capabilities of Japan, especially a Japan allied with the United States. The tie to the Soviet Union permits them to pursue an aggressive external policy to the extent that Moscow agrees; and it limits the risks of such an aggressive policy, since any opponent of China must consider the possibility of war with the Soviet Union.

The Soviet tie also commends itself to the Chinese Communists on immediate tactical grounds, since it provides a means of training the Chinese Communist armed forces in the strategy, tactics, and staff work of modern warfare. The Chinese Communists are aware that their armed forces had limited capabilities against the Japanese; and that their victory over the KMT in 1946–1949 was against an enemy of meager capabilities as compared with those of other armies that the Chinese Communists have had to face in Korea and may have to face in the future. Against United Nations and South Korean forces, on a fixed front, the Chinese exhibited extremely limited offensive capabilities despite willingness to accept massive casualties. The stalemate in Korea certainly had propaganda advantages to the Chinese, but it must have given Peking's military leaders a sharp sense of their limitations against a western force of even modest size. They are undoubtedly anxious to modernize the organization, training, and equipment of their armed forces; and the present tie with the Soviet Union makes this possible.

Although the number of Soviet military advisers now in China is not precisely known to us, it is certainly high.[1] Soviet military are stationed in Chinese training schools, and Asian Soviet troops (e.g., Mongols, Turks, Uigurs) have been reported in ostensibly Chinese units using aircraft, anti-aircraft equipment, tanks, and other modern weapons.

From the Soviet point of view, modernization of the Chinese Communist armed forces, although an undoubted short-run advantage, may well create certain problems for the future. In the short run the increased military capabilities of the Chinese Communists make the enemies of the Sino-Soviet alliance count on diverting increased resources to deal with the Chinese in any major war. More than that, the use of the Chinese armies in Korea and their threat to Formosa, Indo-China, and Southeast Asia generally have forced a significant allocation of Free World resources to that part of the world, which, from the Soviet point of view, represents a diversion of resources away from the Soviet Union itself and from the primary theater of western Eurasia. Although some countervailing Soviet resource investment is required to produce this result, the returns have evidently been judged satisfactory up to the present.

In the longer run the problem raised with respect to the increasing strength of the Chinese Communist armed forces is simply one facet of the general problem which Communist China poses for the Soviet Union: How can the Soviet Union guarantee that Communist China will continue to act in the Soviet interest? It is evident that Moscow has thus far behaved in terms of its immediate interests while doing what is possible to diminish such long-run risks as may be involved. It will be many years before the Chinese are able to produce a full replacement flow of modern weapons; and the Soviet Union is not likely to accelerate the day when the Chinese Communists can manufacture atomic weapons on their own—a possible source of conflict in the alliance, since for economic as well as military reasons the Chinese are likely to be exceedingly eager to discover and to apply the mysteries of atomic energy. Further, the Soviet Union is in a position to exert considerable pressure on China in Manchuria, Inner Mongolia, and Sinkiang, which might well make it difficult for the Chinese Communists, or any future Chinese regime, to withdraw from the present ties with the Soviet Union unless massive external pressures are exerted on the Soviet Union or it is seriously weakened by internal strife. In general, then, the Soviet Union has chosen to take such risks as may be involved in the future from increasing the military strength of the Chinese Communists, counting on its ability to maintain by other means their dependence on Moscow. It would, nevertheless, be surprising if the Soviet Union were encouraging the Chinese Communists to press ahead as a matter of first priority with domestic production of military end items for which the Chinese Communists are now heavily dependent on the Soviet Union. Common prudence in Moscow would dictate that an important degree of Chinese military dependence be maintained as long as it is feasible.

It is on this longer-run issue of the degree of Chinese Communist military independence, and especially the manner in which Moscow exploits its powerful security leverage over Peking, that the stability of the Sino-Soviet alliance may hinge. And, given the explicit link between Peking's First Five Year Plan and armed forces modernization, this issue may come to a head in the reasonably near future.

Economic

Sino-Soviet economic arrangements since the 1950 treaty are clear in their broad outlines although somewhat obscure in detail. They have involved the following key elements:

1. The grant of Moscow to Peking of a line of credit at the rate of $60–100 million per annum carrying only 1 per cent interest. This relates to total Chinese Communist investment outlays of about $4 billion in 1953. Soviet assistance thus does not exceed 2½ per cent of Chinese capital formation in aggregate terms.

2. The sending to China of perhaps 15,000 Russian military, engineering, and administrative advisers. Since the salaries and living costs of advisers are almost certainly met by the Chinese, and they probably receive substantial payment in rubles deposited in Russian banks, some proportion of the foreign exchange afforded by the Soviet loan and a high proportion of its real value may be offset by the cost of Soviet advisers to Peking. On the other hand, Moscow may finance, in addition to its formal credits, the period of production of complex equipment, tying up working capital in the course of construction.

3. The volume of Chinese trade with the Soviet Union and its European satellites has increased to about 75 per cent of total Chinese exports and imports. This compares with a prewar figure of 8 per cent in 1931. This trade furnishes a decisive margin of industrial equipment needed by Peking for its Five Year Plan.

4. In Sinkiang two joint Sino-Soviet companies have been set up for the exploitation of oil and minerals; in addition a Sino-Soviet civil air line operates between North China and the Soviet Union, and there is a joint Sino-Soviet shipbuilding company in Dairen.

Although direct evidence is not available, Sino-Soviet trade appears to have had two key characteristics. First, Moscow has probably conducted this trade on a businesslike basis, setting prices for Soviet and satellite products and for Chinese products by conventional methods, affording reasonable terms of trade to Peking. Second, Moscow may well have set a ceiling on the level of Chinese products it is willing to accept. This was indicated in one major Peking pronouncement; [2] and is suggested by the fact that Chinese products, notably hog bristles and tung oil, have been resold, via the Soviet Union and eastern Europe, at low prices in western Europe. Chinese exports in certain categories may overfulfill the Communist bloc's import requirements. Further, Peking has made positive efforts to revive trade with the non-Communist world in the post-Korea period, most notably at Geneva in 1954, where detailed trade discussions were initiated with the British.

In short, as nearly as we can make out, Moscow-Peking trade has not involved a Soviet effort at direct economic exploitation, but it has raised problems of the scale on which it can be economically conducted. The upshot appears to be a serious interest in Peking to enlarge its margin of East-West trade without diminishing significantly the present level of its trade inside the Soviet bloc.

One aspect of Sino-Soviet economic arrangements may prove of long-run importance: namely, the tendency of both powers to develop new industry in the Asian interior. Peking is evidently planning eventually to locate new developments south and west of the existing industrial center in Manchuria, although at the moment the Japanese-constructed base maintains its primacy. In North China the rich coal deposits centered on Taiyuan are evidently to be linked to new steel installations. The population of Taiyuan is reported to have been increased from 240,000 in 1949 to more than 500,000 at the end of 1951. In Northwest China an oil, chemical, and engineering center may be building up around Lanchow, the population of which is rumored to have expanded from about 200,000 in 1947 to 700,000 in 1952. In Sinkiang important transport developments, oil production, and mineral surveys and exploitations are under way. It is altogether possible that uranium is being mined for shipment to the Soviet Union, probably to plants in nearby Central Asia. Remote and primitive Sinkiang is, however, still some decades from full development, even if its basic resources prove rich.

Although more extensive industrial development may be envisaged for Southwest China, current activity there appears confined to planning an expansion of the rail network, part of the substantial effort to expand rail communications between interior bases and between China and the Soviet Union.

The planned center of gravity of the Chinese economy is thus being slowly shifted away from the coast to North and West China. This tendency in long-run objective reflects three converging factors: the known and believed location of unexploited Chinese mineral deposits;

the desire to develop an interior strategic base for military operations in case of invasion of Southeast China; and the Soviet, if not Chinese, interest in locating Chinese industry in areas accessible to the Russian borders and, perhaps, in a relation of dependence on Soviet supplies. In the latter connection it should be recalled that, under Soviet pressure, Poland's new steel installations have been built near Cracow and thus made dependent on Ukrainian rather than Swedish ore.

It is important not to overestimate the scale of this effort and the rate of movement of China's actual industrial center of gravity. The tendency and the policy are reasonably clear, as is the eastward industrial movement in the Soviet Union. Nevertheless, for the foreseeable future Manchuria, given its initial headstart, its natural resources, and the heavy overhead outlays required to create new industrial centers, is likely to remain the most important of China's industrial areas, and its industries will continue to expand more rapidly than those elsewhere.

The increased dependence of China on the Soviet Union resulting from industrial location, joint ownership, and trade patterns is measurably increased by the large-scale use of Soviet advisers in Chinese industry. An official announcement of October 4, 1953, indicates that Soviet advisers are present in at least the following sectors of the Chinese economy: metallurgy, coal, oil, chemicals, power, machinery, geology, water conservation, agriculture, forestry, communications, transport, finance, trade, and cooperatives. Their functions are officially described as embracing: "The selection of construction sites, the collection of basic data on designing, the preparation of designing layout, the supply of equipment, and the directing of construction and installation . . . the manufacturing of new products and the supply of technique and material in the production of these new products . . ."

The bulk of these advisers operate simply as technicians. Evidently they are under instructions to avoid offending Chinese sensibilities. They enjoy the best living conditions and amenities available in China, but their status is not a flagrant element on the Chinese scene. They are certainly paid at a much higher rate than either their Chinese opposite numbers or their fellow technicians in the Soviet Union; but this margin is largely siphoned into bank accounts in the Soviet Union. Although some incidents of profligate expenditure were reported in the early post-takeover days, the present arrangements apparently do not lead to unseemly purchasing power on the Chinese scene by Soviet advisers.

The presence of these advisers serves several Soviet purposes:

1. It permits exact and detailed intelligence on Chinese economic development.

2. It encourages the use of Soviet machines and techniques, which increases the long-run dependence of China on the Soviet Union.

3. It puts Moscow in a position to interfere in Chinese affairs at strategic points when it so desires.

All available evidence appears to indicate that the Soviet Union is conducting its relations with Communist China on a formal quasi-diplomatic basis. The profound influence of Moscow on Peking has taken the form mainly of high-level intergovernmental agreements rather than piecemeal Soviet intervention. The immense bargaining power of the Soviet Union over China, as well as the convergence of their interests, has ensured that Chinese behavior generally meets Moscow's interests. Moreover, under Mao, Peking has firmly embraced the lean-to-one-side policy—its costs as well as its benefits; and Mao is in effective control. Thus, while the advisers undoubtedly report back in detail and their reports may well influence Moscow's decisions, they are not likely to be the operating agents of Moscow's policy in China.

From Moscow's point of view the strict economics of Sino-Soviet relations are decidedly a matter of tertiary importance, although Moscow will watch closely the effects of its own trade policy on Peking political attitudes and behavior. Russian imports of Chinese grain, soy beans, and other foodstuffs are helpful; and Chinese tungsten is a valuable supplement to Soviet supplies of steel-hardening alloys. On their present scale, these imports probably justify, on strict economic grounds, the sale of advanced industrial equipment to China. Soviet credits and the related allocation of specialists to China are, however, a real if modest cost to Moscow, compensated for by their military and political value. The strengthening of the Chinese military is evidently an asset to Moscow so long as China is held firmly within the Communist bloc; and the success of Chinese Communist industrialization is, in the long run, essential to Moscow's ideological purposes in Asia.

From Peking's point of view, Sino-Soviet economic relations are a matter of major importance to Communist China. Although Chinese foreign trade represents a small proportion of the Chinese gross national product (say, 5 per cent), the imports it permits supply a high and indispensable proportion of equipment and raw material required for Chinese industrialization. Anywhere up to 20 per cent of Chinese industrial capital formation may hinge directly on foreign trade; and the whole industrialization effort is dependent on it indirectly to a degree never paralleled in the experience of the Soviet Union. Thus Mao's lean-to-one-side policy and the break with the non-Communist world caused by the Korean war had different economic impacts on the Russians and the Chinese. The Russian pattern of trade with the external world remained much as it was, with perhaps some accentuation of the steady postwar decline in East-West trade—a matter of relatively minor significance to the Soviet Union, and one which was probably judged a political advantage. On the other hand, the proportion of China's trade going to the Soviet Union and the European satellites increased sharply. With this increase there came an increase of Chinese dependence on the Soviet Union at a strategic point in Communist China's domestic development—that is, on the eve of the Chinese first Five Year Plan. The economic costs to Communist China of the quasi-monopolistic trade position of the Soviet Union are of two kinds:

1. Chinese capital imports are limited to those the Soviets are prepared to grant, and are probably less than could be generated if the lean-to-one-side policy were not applied.

2. Chinese medium- and long-term plans must be made within the confining framework of the Sino-Soviet tie, including that special form of dependence which derives from a single source of industrial equipment and spare parts.

From the Soviet point of view the major interest in this set of trade and credit relations is not economic but political. The dependence of China on trade with the Communist bloc is a major device for holding China within that bloc and for exercising over-all pressure on Chinese Communist policy, ends for which the price of, say, $60 million per year in credits is obviously not high—notably since it may well take substantially the form of technicians' services, and since their presence in China also serves Soviet intelligence and control interests.

From the Chinese Communist point of view the trade and credit relations with the Communist world are not ideal; but, on balance, Communist China has received adequate if not optimum technical assistance; considerable but possibly constraining opportunities for trade and the acquisition of industrial equipment; and limited amounts of capital in the form of foreign exchange credits and Soviet contribution to joint enterprises. Although China may well make an effort to better its terms of trade and to enlarge its supply of equipment by enlarging commerce with the Free World, this move—if it, in fact, results in enlarged trade—represents at the moment a minor modification in the basic ties with Moscow, not an effort to break away. The basic interests of Peking in the Sino-Soviet tie are power interests; that is, they center on military and political issues. The economics of Sino-Soviet relations are increasingly important to Peking at the present cooler phase of the cold war in Asia, and in the early phase of the First Five Year Plan. Sino-Soviet trade must roughly meet certain requirements; but, in themselves, the economic aspects of the alliance are unlikely to be judged decisive. Put another way, Peking is likely to accept some downward modification in its economic plans rather than fracture its alliance to Moscow on economic grounds alone.

Cultural and Ideological

Moscow and Peking have made elaborate mass propaganda efforts to orient the Chinese people sympathetically toward the Soviet Union. Cultural relations have been a major channel for this policy. There is some reciprocity in Sino-Soviet cultural relations, but the weight of the effort is directed towards the Chinese people. From Peking's point of view this effort was judged necessary to give a popular basis to the lean-to-one-side policy. From Moscow's point of view it is a re-assuring symbol of Mao's long-run concept of the alliance and, perhaps, a device for attracting the authentic loyalty of Chinese youth to Moscow, irrespective of the policies and outlook of the party leaders.

The operative problem confronted by Communist propagandists was dual: to fill the gap left in Chinese life by the total rupture of previous extensive relations with western cultural life; and to persuade the Chinese people of the richness and vitality of the Soviet cultural offering. The notion of close contact with another culture is not intrinsically foreign or offensive to the modern Chinese intellectual or to the Chinese people in general, although perhaps the peak period of eagerness to explore and absorb passed with the 1920's.

The general instrument chosen for the effort is the Sino-Soviet Friendship Association, organized as an early order of business after the Communist takeover in October 1949. It rapidly developed the heavy bureaucratic structure that characterizes Communist organizations.[3] In two years there were offices at the level of administrative region, province, city, county, and some 26,000 subcounty units. Membership was stated to be 17 million in October 1951, including the armed forces and security troops.

The Association disseminates Russian films, literature, music, and, notably, middle-school and college text books. It organizes pro-Soviet meetings and disseminates propaganda, publishes newspapers and periodicals devoted to the theme of Sino-Soviet friendship. It arranges tours for Soviet artists, visiting professorships for Soviet scholars, and technical assistance in cultural fields, especially moving pictures and educational method.

An unknown number of advanced Chinese students go to Soviet universities for study, perhaps several thousand each year. In addition, short-term visits of Chinese youth to the Soviet Union are arranged. There is some reciprocal flow of Chinese culture to the Soviet Union—for example, nation-wide tours of a Chinese vaudeville troupe and of an exhibit of Chinese art objects; but it is clear that the primary purpose of the exercise is to establish among the Chinese peoples, and notably the literate population, a foundation of acceptance in depth for the peculiarly intimate and dependent ties which Mao has created between Moscow and Peking.

As to the real nature of the ideological bond between the Soviet Union and Communist China, it is our view that neither the Soviet Union nor Communist China is devoted to the development of international Communism in the abstract; that is, as an ideological crusade independent of the extension of effective military and political authority. The Soviet and Chinese Communist leaders look on the extension of Communist ideology as a potential instrument for their exercising enlarged power on the world scene. Since the formation of the Russian Communist Party by Lenin just after the turn of the century the purposeful pursuit of power by a self-appointed elite has been at the core of Communist ideology. It is this link between ideology and the exercise of power which gives a certain importance to differences in ideological formulation as between Moscow and Peking.

The strict ideological differences between Russian and Chinese Communism have always been minor. They share a view of history which promises ultimate power to Communism; they share the Leninist concept of a Communist dictatorship as the decisive instrument for bringing about this historical development; and they share an elitist concept of the Communist Party as history's chosen instrument for bringing about the 'dictatorship of the proletariat' (Moscow) or the 'proletarian hegemony' (Peking). They share the concept of 'democratic centralism'—that is, of dictatorial disciplined rule from the top; a view of class hostility as a device for mobilizing support for the seizure of power; and the concept of endless struggle on the world scene between polarized Communist and anti-Communist camps. Their principal formal difference at the present time is hardly detectable to the western mind: Moscow holds to a standard 'dictatorship of the proletariat' model for the transition to Socialism and Communism, once power has been seized by Communists; while Peking puts forward, for Asia, its own concept of 'proletarian hegemony' among revolutionary classes or classes prepared to participate positively in the revolution. This difference conceals no conflict in belief discernible to the western mind in either the writings or the operating performance of the two groups of leaders; but it does reflect an unresolved conflicting claim for ultimate Communist authority in Asia, thus far kept perfectly under control by the two partners.[4] For example, the performance of Molotov and Chou En-lai at Geneva in 1954 appears to have been a model of coordination, with all differences settled behind the scenes, and tactics pre-planned with precision.

There was, of course, one famous passage of difference between the two Communist movements, concerning the development of the Chinese revolution: Mao believed that he could generate sufficient political and military strength in the Chinese countryside to capture the cities; whereas Moscow believed that the primary center for insurrectional power was likely to be in the cities. Mao proved correct under the special conditions of modern Chinese history. Again, from a western observer's point of view this is a minor tactical matter.

Nevertheless, this difference in tactical view and in ideological history may play a significant though ancillary role in Moscow-Peking relations. As noted above, the interests of the two power centers are not wholly identical with respect to the Asian Communist parties. They share an interest in the expansion of Asian Communism; but they may well clash over the degree of orientation of the Asian movements as between Moscow and Peking. One aspect of this contrapuntal power struggle may be the manner in which Mao's triumph in China is proclaimed. While both Moscow and Peking recognize it as a general operational model, Moscow tends to call it an application of Leninism and Stalinism; and Peking calls it a creative adaptation of Leninism for Asia.

It should be strongly emphasized that the relative power of Moscow and Peking among the Asiatic Communist parties will not be primarily determined by this question of ideological formulation. It will be determined proximately by the structure of the international and national party machinery and the relative ability of Moscow and Peking to maintain control at strategic points in that machinery; and, in turn, this ability to intervene and to control will be determined by the whole balance of power in Sino-Soviet relations.

In short, in this aspect of the ideological question we have merely an index of deeper convergences of interest or clashes of interest between Moscow and Peking. It seems improbable, for example, that

Moscow will surrender to Peking complete direction of the Japanese or Indian Communist parties or the making of Communist policy toward these areas, although Peking almost certainly has received some voice in the matter. Russia's power interests there are direct and significant. Despite Peking's salvage of North Korea with Chinese blood, a distinct Soviet line of authority persists there. At Geneva in 1954 Molotov was an active diplomat, not a benevolent observer of Chou En-lai's performance. And in the long run Japan and India are vastly more important than Korea and Indo-China. The surface of Communist ideological discourse is likely, at least occasionally, to reflect this fact of dual national Communist interests rather than a simple unified international conspiracy.

It is our view, then, that Sino-Soviet relations are basically determined by real power factors as they are perceived by the top leadership in the two centers; and that their obsession with power criteria is not distinct from their common Leninist ideology but is an integral part of that ideology.

It would be a mistake, however, not to recognize two further influences, not wholly rational in character, which affect the contours of the alliance.

First, there is the force of common habits of mind, and especially of a history of association, now some thirty years old, between the Soviet Union and the Chinese Communist Party. The major relationships in the past and at present between the Chinese Communists and the Soviet Union have not been determined by sentiments grounded in a common adherence to the doctrines of Marx and Lenin. On the other hand, the existence of the historic tie is a significant independent force in this sense: it sets up a strong predisposition for the Chinese Communists and the Soviet Union to settle by compromise such differences as they may have. Put another way, by strictly objective power criteria the balance-sheet of the Sino-Soviet alliance may show considerable imbalance, item by item, without producing a clean break in the relationship. The historical, emotional, and ideological tie of the Chinese Communists to Moscow goes so deep that only the most drastic violation of their own interests is likely to produce a rupture between the two power centers.

Second, within these bonds of habit and personal commitment the Chinese Communists are not likely to defer to Moscow's judgment without question. While the example of Lenin and Stalin in Russia has undoubtedly been suggestive to the Chinese Communists, Moscow's record of advice and guidance on the Chinese scene has not been wholly fortunate. Moscow led the Chinese Communists into the booby-trap of association with the KMT from 1923 to 1927; it only reluctantly accepted Mao's strategy of building military strength in the countryside on the peasantry; and it accepted Mao himself as the Chinese Communist leader only after appointing a series of ineffectual stooges; it misjudged the relative military potential of the Chinese Communists and the KMT after 1945; and it bore what must have been primary responsibility for the 1950 misjudgment of prospects in Korea, for which error the Chinese Communists paid substantially. On their own Asian ground Mao and his close colleagues have reason to form their own appreciations in making 'correct' interpretations of the current 'historical stage.' This sense of at least tactical ideological independence merges, of course, with a strong personal sense of confidence and with deep undercurrents of raw nationalism to set distinct limits within which Moscow can control Peking without risking serious rupture.

III. EXTERNAL IMPLICATIONS: MOSCOW, PEKING, AND THE ASIAN COMMUNIST PARTIES, 1945–1954 *

Although we have little enough knowledge of the specific form and workings of the Sino-Soviet alliance in terms of the domestic Chinese Communist scene, we have even less concrete evidence of its application to Chinese Communist external interests—especially to the whole issue of Asian Communism, in which the Chinese Communists have staked out repeated claims to leadership, and in which Chinese Communist external interests are explicitly centered. To the western observer Mao's asserted position in Asian Communism now, and, in the longer run, the possible potentials of the Chinese Communists' numbers, native pride, and strategic geographical position suggest at least a chance of conflict between Moscow's and Peking's interests in Asian Communism—depending, of course, on such presently incalculable factors as the relative strength of future Soviet and Chinese leadership, the success or failure of Chinese Communist domestic policies, the long-pull influence in Asia of the United States and its allies, and so on.

By the very nature of what it is given the outside world to know about the ostensibly harmonious Sino-Soviet relationship, no possibility of such a conflict now appears in Sino-Soviet dealings either with each other or with other nations; and yet we would be ignoring

* This section incorporates a contribution by John H. Kautsky and Toshio Tsukahira.

a vital element in the total Chinese Communist scene if we did not at least briefly examine the recent course of Asian Communist tactics and policies for such light as they throw on the Moscow-Peking relationship.

In the immediate postwar period (1945–1947) the Soviet Union sought to attain its objectives by a policy of ostensibly peaceful cooperation with the western powers and by having Communist parties participate in coalition governments or work together with other parties. Following a similar policy, the Asian Communist parties sought to cooperate with all 'anti-reactionary' forces within their respective countries. At least throughout 1945 they tended to be less strongly opposed to the colonial powers than were the nationalists in India and in the colonial or dependent areas of Southeast Asia, while in Japan the Communists hailed the United States occupation forces as a 'liberation army.' On the whole, little specific day-to-day direction or guidance seemed to be forthcoming from Moscow to the Asian Communist parties in this period. The worldwide Communist line was simply developed by each national party in its own context.

During 1947 Soviet relations with the West sharply deteriorated, and open civil war was under way in China after the failure of the Marshall mission. The attendant shift of Soviet policy found its ultimate expression in Zhdanov's speech at the founding meeting of the Cominform in September 1947, in which he set forth the theory of a world divided into a Soviet-led and an American-led camp. In a few months this view was reflected in Communist policy around the world. The line of the various Communist parties shifted away from cooperation with their erstwhile local political allies to attacks on them as servants of foreign imperialism. The change in line resulted in a more militant attitude everywhere. Guerrilla warfare on the Chinese Communist pattern broke out in rural areas in Burma in April 1948 and in Malaya in June; and it was resumed in the Philippines when the Huks broke their truce with the government in the fall of the same year. In Viet Nam fighting had already begun in November 1946. In Indonesia the Communists seized the city of Madiun in Eastern Java in September 1948, but were crushed by the Indonesian government. In India, from March 1948, two main factions of the Communist Party followed a policy of violence and terrorism in rural and urban areas respectively. The official Indian party line, however, became one of 'ultra-leftist' and 'anti-bourgeois' urban struggle, culminating in 1949 in a specific attack on Mao Tse-tung for his 'pro-capitalist' stand. The Japanese Communist Party, too, adopted a more militant attitude, abandoned its attempts to form an alliance with the

Socialist Party, and, at the end of 1947, began to attack—though as yet not directly—the United States as the would-be colonizer of Japan.

In 1949 the rise of the Chinese Communists to power was accompanied by a gradual acceptance in Moscow of the 'correctness' of the Maoist strategy for Asia: that is, the inclusion of the 'national capitalists' in the 'united front from below,' and, 'wherever and whenever possible,' the use of armed struggle. Hitherto potential appeals to the bourgeoisie had been made only in the framework of the 'united front from above,' i.e., of alliances with bourgeois parties.

This position was made formally clear at the Peking WFTU Conference of November 1949. In all the countries where guerrilla warfare was already in progress—Viet Nam, Burma, Malaya, and the Philippines—reliance on the Chinese military strategy was now openly acknowledged. The use of the Maoist four-class appeal now became general among the Asian Communist parties even in those areas where no significant capitalist element existed. Only in the Indian Party did this change in policy require a drastic readjustment, shifting power from the urban anti-bourgeois faction in the party to the rural pro-Maoist faction. In Japan, where the four-class appeal had already been followed for some time, the Communist Party was suddenly in January 1950 ordered to abandon its peaceful tactics and engage in direct action against the American occupation. The move was probably a direct result of the decision to strike in Korea six months later. On the other hand, by the end of 1950 Moscow made clear to the Indian Communist Party that armed struggle, even such as the new leadership had carried on in the countryside, was not, like the four-class appeal, a necessary part of the recommended strategy and was to be abandoned.

Since 1951, and the Korean stalemate, the Communist emphasis throughout Asia, excepting Indo-China, has definitely shifted to propaganda for 'peace' and an appreciation of the potentialities of neutralism in these countries. Though the Indian Communists have not relaxed their opposition to the Nehru government, they have applauded some of its positions on international issues which favored 'peace.' The Communist Party in India has been concentrating on the Soviet-sponsored peace movement, participating in elections and parliamentary activities, and seeking to form a broad united front of all elements and factions opposed to the Congress and the Socialist Party leadership. In Indonesia, too, the Communists are concentrating on parliamentary politics and are now in a position of lending vital support to the nationalist parties forming the government. The Japanese Communist Party, with most of its key personnel driven underground since mid-1950, has been using its overt apparatus and network of front organizations to conduct a broad campaign of agitation and propaganda designed to focus the grievances of all classes and groups against the United States. The current Japanese Communist Party line defines Japan as a 'colonial dependency' of the United States and calls for the mobilization of a 'national liberation democratic united front' which is to embrace all elements opposed to the United States-sponsored Peace Treaty and Mutual Security Pact. At the same time the party adopted in the fall of 1951, and has since been reported to be following, a so-called military program envisaging the systematic organization of armed partisan or guerrilla-type units.

In spite of the prominence given to the peace offensive, fighting continued in Indo-China and there were some further military operations in Malaya, Burma, and the Philippines. In the latter three countries, where the Communist insurrections have been gradually reduced in effectiveness by government action, the Communists seem to be receiving little direct support or even attention from either the Soviet Union or Communist China and are continuing largely on their own momentum. The Indo-Chinese Communists, on the other hand, have been given substantial material support and encouragement by both Peking and Moscow up to the point where it proved possible to translate Viet Minh military power into accession of northern Viet Nam by diplomacy.

The foregoing summary demonstrates that, broadly speaking, in each period since the end of the war certain common tendencies have been in evidence in the policies pursued by the Asian Communist parties. These have been geared to the high level policies and objectives of Russian and, since 1949, Chinese Communists, which have largely overlapped. So far as tactics were concerned, two aspects of Mao's methods were commended by Moscow to Asian Communists: armed insurrection based in the countryside for some; and united front politics—the so-called four-class appeal—for all. This does not mean that policy control of Asian Communism passed in this period to Peking. It is believed that in the Communist parties of India, Indonesia, and Japan the influence of Moscow is substantial and probably primary, whereas the Communists of Indo-China, Thailand, and Malaya seem oriented somewhat more directly to Peking, while acknowledging steadily the ultimate source of strength and wisdom in Moscow. The Philippine and Burmese parties appear to have operated on lines from Moscow, transmitted through the Indian Communist Party down to 1950. Since that time links with Peking appear to have developed.

It should be emphasized that the Asian Communist parties claim to be indebted to both the Soviet and the Chinese Communists for valuable lessons; and the Chinese Communist Party itself recognizes the Soviet Union as the parent and center of world Communism. It is our judgment that the question of loyalty to one as opposed to the other of the two Communist powers has not yet been posed to the Asian Communists; and that it may not have even arisen in the minds of many of the rank and file, especially since thus far there has been apparent agreement on current action between Moscow's and Peking's leadership.

If we postulate a break between Moscow and Peking, then indeed a split along the lines just mentioned among the Asian Communist parties might occur for the following reasons:

1. The Japanese, Indian, and Indonesian parties owe their origins historically to the Comintern and have always maintained ties with Moscow either directly, as in Japan, or indirectly through the British and Dutch parties, as in India and Indonesia respectively, but always independently of the Chinese Communists. In Indo-China and Malaya, on the other hand, the Communist movements were organized from China and remained in the prewar period virtually branches of the Chinese Communist Party. The Thai and Burmese parties grew only out of the anti-Japanese resistance movement during World War II and thus had few if any connections with the Comintern. The Philippine Communist Party, although organized in the early thirties, also gained its main strength from the anti-Japanese movement.

2. In most of these countries the Communist movements originated as and still are to a large extent movements led by intellectuals. In countries like Japan, India, and Indonesia the intellectuals, especially those with left-wing tendencies, have looked to the West rather than to China for inspiration. On the other hand, in Indo-China, for example, Chinese influence has been much more significant.

3. In Malaya and Thailand Communist interest has always been largely confined to the sizeable Chinese minorities in these countries—minorities which have tended to maintain some loyalty to the government in power in China. There are smaller Chinese minorities also in Indonesia, Burma, and the Philippines which play some part in their respective Communist movements; but these latter are largely led by and composed of indigenous elements. The ethnic tie of the Communist parties with China is, of course, absent in Japan and India.

4. Finally, Japan and India traditionally have been areas of interest to Russia since czarist times. It is, therefore, unlikely that Soviet Russia would voluntarily relinquish to China any positions of strength

it holds in these countries, including authority over their Communist parties. On the other hand, Russian interest has never been direct in Southeast Asia, and the areas adjacent to China in this region have been in China's sphere of influence for centuries.

So far as we can make out, there is little or no direct and explicit guidance from day to day in the form of Moscow directives addressed to the various Asian Communist parties which are not engaged in active major hostilities directly involving the high level interests of Moscow and Peking. Nevertheless, substantial guidance is provided. Lines are explicitly laid out and presumably agreed upon at high Moscow-Peking levels. These are transmitted in general terms by the Soviet and Cominform press. Having been given the international line, the local Communist parties have then faced the not always simple task of translating it into local political terms and possibilities.

In general Moscow and Peking have thus far resolved any differences that may have arisen in connection with current Communist tactics in Asia, subordinating all such issues to their common over-all interest in enlarging Communist strength in Asia and in presenting a solid front to the West—while unshaped but potentially divisive issues are swept under the rug.

Moscow, Peking, and Japan

The primary power interest of the Soviet Union has been and still remains western Eurasia. On the whole this bias has persisted despite three major new factors: first, the emergence of the United States as a major world power with interests in the Pacific as well as the Atlantic; second, the emergence of air warfare with atomic weapons, which makes the world a single theater of operations at a time of major war; and third, Moscow's acceptance of Lenin's strategy of attacking the West through current and former colonial areas. There is no doubt that, as compared with the period before 1914, Russia now looks to Asia with more hope than fear. It is the principal current area of opportunity, short of major war, for the extension of Soviet power. Substantially frustrated in Europe, the Soviet Union may devote an increasing proportion of its attention to developing its power in Asia. Measured in terms of military strength and potential, Asia remains over the foreseeable future a secondary theater of power. Nevertheless, it is at the moment the primary theater of cold war hostilities; for it may be judged in Moscow as in Peking the most promising area for Communist expansion, and the appropriate locus of concentrated attack on the West as a whole.

For China, of course, Asia is the primary arena of power for the foreseeable future; and its interest in power elsewhere is determined mainly by the Chinese estimate of how it is judged likely to affect China's position in Asia.

Since 1868 the story of Sino-Russian relations has interwoven with the rise of Japan. The appearance of Japanese military strength in Northeast Asia, dramatized by its victories over China in 1895 and over Russia in 1905, altered the entire pattern of international politics in this area. At times Japanese strength has brought Russia and China together, notably in the years 1937–1941. But Russia in the past has been also prepared to secure its limited objectives in the area in association with Japan at the expense of China, notably from 1907 to 1914. And the threat of Russo-Japanese collaboration at China's expense, never far below the surface of Sino-Soviet relations, undoubtedly persists implicitly down to the present.

The clash between the Japanese and Chinese objectives in Northeast Asia has been direct. It has given China virtually no opportunities to work with Japan against Russia; although in the period after the 1917 revolution there was some obscure intertwining of Chinese and Japanese activities against Russian interests in Northeast Asia, as well as major Sino-Japanese conflicts of purpose. Beneath the surface of Chinese thought the possibility of a Sino-Japanese association against Russia may still lurk just as in eastern Europe the view of Germany—despite awful memories—has somewhat altered in the face of current Soviet dominance.

Looking ahead, we cannot wholly rule out the possibilities of a Russian flirtation with Japan at China's expense or an association of China with Japan to reduce the weight of Russian power in Northeast Asia, although both possibilities appear at the moment to be remote in the extreme. The fundamental interplay of the three powers recalls somewhat that among Germany, Russia, and eastern Europe. It is not impossible to conceive of the Soviet Union's offering Japan important concessions, even at China's expense, to ensure its detachment from the United States, just as the Soviet Union might well be prepared in Europe to offer western Germany important concessions, at eastern European expense, to the same end. It is also possible to conceive of China's seeking to expand its relations with Japan, notably trade relations, as a way of diminishing the pressure of Soviet bargaining power on China, just as some eastern European Communists have looked to East-West trade as a limited mode of relief from Soviet trading pressure. But given the strength of anti-Communist forces in both western Germany and Japan, it is likely that such bargaining strength as Moscow and Peking can exert will be used to dilute German and Japanese ties to the West rather than to seek their attachment to the Communist world by political and economic blandishments. And on this matter the interests of Moscow and Peking fully converge. Only a drastic weakening in Free World strength and cohesion would make realistic a thoroughgoing detachment, and bring into play a potential Sino-Soviet rivalry over Japan.

NOTES FOR CHAPTER 10

1. An unpublished study by M. X. Hsieh gives the following figures:

Estimates of the number of the advisers vary greatly, ranging from 3,000 * to more than 20,000 † and even to 150,000 ‡. The most reasonable figures seem to be those given by a Japanese report that provides the following table regarding the officers the Soviet Union has sent and will send to Communist China: §

Advisers—from the spring of 1950 to the summer of 1952		Numbers to be increased in the future to
Army	5,000	10,000
Navy	1,000	2,500
Air Force	1,000	2,500

This 'future' estimate may be approximately correct for mid-1954.

2. *People's Daily*, Peking, December 16, 1953.

3. For an account of the Sino-Soviet Friendship Association, see Henry Wei, Mao Tse-tung's 'Lean-to-one-side' Policy, *Studies in Chinese Communism*, Series II, No. 1, Los Angeles, University of Southern California, October 1952.

4. See, notably, Benjamin I. Schwartz, *China and the Soviet Theory of Peoples' Democracy*, Cambridge, Mass., Massachusetts Institute of Technology, Center for International Studies, 1954.

* R. B. Rigg, *Red China's Fighting Hordes,* Harrisburg, Pa., Military Service Publishing Co., 1951.

† K. Liu, *Analysis of the Chinese Communist Regime,* Hong Kong, 1952 (in Chinese).

‡ K. Fan, "The Soviet Controlled Chinese Communist Military Forces," *National Renaissance,* Vol. 3, No. 9, February 1952.

§ Institute for Studying Continental Problems, "Analysis of the Strength of the Chinese Communist Military Forces," *Continental Problems,* Tokyo, August 1952 (in Japanese).

SINO-SOVIET RELATIONS:

SUMMARY AND CONCLUSIONS

I. SUMMARY

In recent decades Moscow has judged its interests best served by an effectively united China antagonistic to the 'imperialist' world but friendly with the Soviet Union. For a quarter of a century before 1949 this was the overriding goal of Russian policy in China, to which even the Chinese Communists had to bow; for Moscow made its ideological interest in China systematically subservient to its security interest when the two were in conflict. The Soviet policy represented one formula for meeting the major Russian objectives of blocking Japan and other powers in Asia while at the same time weakening the over-all position of the United States and the western European countries on the world scene. Both the security and ideological objectives of Moscow were achieved by the Chinese Communist victory of 1949; and it was this convergence which was crystallized in the subsequent negotiation of the Mutual-Aid Pact of 1950, the foundation of the present Sino-Soviet relationship.

The more important meanings of this relationship in terms of the interests of the Soviet Union can be outlined as follows:

1. In security terms the Soviet interest in diverting Free World military resources from the Soviet Union and the primary locus of world power in the West is accomplished; and Chinese military dependence on the Soviet Union is a powerful instrument for maintaining Moscow's bargaining position over Peking. The Chinese Communists, on the other hand, are permitted by the military alliance to press harder their expansionist ambitions in Asia; to acquire modern military equipment and the skills to employ it; and to move in the direction of greater long-run freedom of action.

2. In the border areas the persistent historic Russian interest in maintaining a position in Manchuria, Mongolia, and Sinkiang has taken on, since 1949, a special importance as a means of implicit threat, control, and bargaining advantage over China.

3. Since the alliance makes Communist China a partner of the Soviet Union in Northeast Asia, it is a Soviet interest to keep Japan as weak and ineffective as possible so long as it is outside the Communist bloc, and to subvert Japan into the bloc, if possible, as a member subservient to Moscow.

4. In terms of world power politics it is in the Soviet interest:

(*a*) To maintain the integrity of a dependent China in order to prevent any other power from developing positions on the mainland of Northeast Asia beyond that in South Korea.

(*b*) To use the ideological and military power of Communist China further to harass the United States and the western powers in Asia, to weaken their positions there, and to force a maximum dissipation of western resources in political and military theaters judged secondary by both Moscow and the West.

(*c*) To use the ideological force of the Communist example in Asia to spread the doctrines of Communism at the cost of the United States and Western Europe.

(*d*) To minimize Communist Chinese independent participation in the world arena of power, in order to prevent the dilution of its ties with the Soviet Union which might come about if China progressively developed relations with bargaining partners other than the Soviet Union.

(*e*) To maintain a surface of maximum ideological conformity between China and the Soviet Union and, within that ideological alliance, to maintain the primacy of the Soviet over the Chinese Communist examples.

On the other side of the alliance, since in general it is the Chinese Communists' intent to exploit all aspects of the Soviet tie to expand the foundation for their own power and increasing independence of action, there are embraced in the present relationship particular Chinese interests which may be outlined as follows:

1. To maximize the rate of build-up of Chinese military strength.

2. To maximize over time the relative power of China in the border areas: Manchuria, Mongolia, and Sinkiang.

3. To minimize the effective power of Japan and of other powers in Northeast Asia.

4. To extend Chinese Communist power in Asia at the expense of the United States and the western European countries.

5. To seek ideological and political primacy in the Asian Communist movements and in Asia generally as a purported leader of 'anti-
imperialist' sentiment.

6. To acquire the best possible terms of trade and the maximum
capital imports from the Soviet Union.

It is evident that within the complex of Soviet and Chinese interests there is sufficient overlap to justify the leaders in both Moscow
and Peking in maintaining a close alliance at the present time.

Broadly speaking, Soviet power interests can be safeguarded by
either a united friendly China or a weak China incapable of interfering with those interests. The major danger to Moscow is that a
united and strong China might seek to make itself independent of the
Soviet Union at some future stage, and, in particular, that China
might come actually to dominate Asia. Peking acts admirably for
Moscow when it engages western resources indecisively. Peking's
power could raise real problems for Moscow if it were to achieve the
degree of authority in Asia that the Chinese Communists now evidently seek. For Moscow, therefore, Sino-Soviet relations take on the
character of a problem of balance between objectives which conflict if
pushed too far. Since Chinese unity and strength are an immediate
advantage but a potential long-run threat, Moscow seeks to exploit
the Sino-Soviet tie in order to pursue immediate power objectives
while minimizing the risks that China might be ultimately in a position to break away from the Soviet Union; and so Moscow has sought
systematically to create an important degree of Chinese dependence
on the Soviet Union. Therefore, to hold a series of strategic positions
vis-à-vis China would promise to maintain such dependence. These
situations of implicit threat and control for the longer pull now include the following:

1. Soviet positions—of greater or lesser directness and strength—in
Sinkiang, Mongolia, Manchuria, and North Korea which, in effect,
hold as a hostage for good behavior areas vital for China's future economic development.

2. Dependence of the Chinese armed forces on Soviet equipment and
spare parts.

3. Dependence of China on trade with the Communist bloc and on
a flow of spare parts for Soviet machinery.

4. Education and indoctrination in the Soviet Union of key younger
cadres.

5. Possible (but not well-substantiated) infiltration of key points in
the Chinese Communist structure with Soviet personnel or agents.

6. Maintenance of an important, if variable, degree of direct Soviet control over the Asian Communist parties as a hedge on independent Chinese political strength in Asia.

It follows from this longer-term Soviet interest that Moscow will interest itself greatly in the problem of the succession to Mao and the subsequent inevitable reorganization of the Chinese Communist power structure and possible reassessment of Peking's policy.

One massive offset to China's weakness should be noted in the Sino-Soviet tie. Although on any given issue Moscow's bargaining position is likely to be the stronger, the threat by Peking of defection or attempted defection from Moscow would be a serious matter indeed to the Kremlin. The ideological and subversive struggle for Asia is a major active front in the cold war. The victory of the Communists in China was a mighty advance for the Soviet Union. The loss of Communist China, or gross failure in its domestic or foreign performance, however, would be an even greater loss than its attachment to the Communist bloc was a gain.

Although it increased the strength of Asian Communism, Mao's victory did not make all Asians believe that Communism was Asia's wave of the future. The defection of China from the Soviet bloc, or a definitive failure of Communism in China, might well be taken as firm evidence in Asia that the path of Communism under Soviet tutelage is inappropriate to Asia's aspirations. The Chinese Communists, trained to exploit every possible advantage, almost certainly are aware of this threat they wield from weakness; and they have probably found ways of making Moscow conscious of it.

II. Conclusions

Within the frame set by common history and ideology the Sino-Soviet tie in its concrete current form is a product of Soviet power interests on the one hand and the mixture of Chinese Communist ambitions and weakness on the other. It has resulted in a situation where Peking maintains the mechanisms of national sovereignty profoundly hedged about by Soviet power; while Moscow, with greater apparent freedom of action, has given hostages to fortune such as to make the future of its international status hinge in good part on the continued success of the alliance and even on a creditable domestic performance of the Communists in China.

At every strategic point Moscow is in a position to observe in detail the Chinese performance. Moscow wields a tremendous bargaining power over China: China's armed forces depend on Soviet supplies;

China's industry depends on Soviet machines and spare parts; China's sovereignty in the border areas is dependent on Soviet restraint, these regions being either infiltrated with Soviet strength, as is Sinkiang, or militarily vulnerable, as are Manchuria, Inner Mongolia, and North China. Given its expansionist ambitions, Peking requires the Soviet alliance to ensure its defense; and the top leadership has made the deepest public commitments to the Sino-Soviet tie.

The Sino-Soviet alliance was formed in a period of military expansion, on a believed rising tide of Communist strength in Asia. Under the circumstances of Communist engagement in civil war, after 1946, and, later, in the context of Communist ventures in Korea and Indo-China, the alliance made great good sense in both Communist capitals. The combination of Soviet backing in military supplies and Chinese ground force and political power served the related but not identical interests of the partners: to the Chinese Communists the period 1947–1951 was a phase of staking out their authority in China and of probing outward into Asia; to Moscow the rise of the Communists in China and the Korean and Indo-Chinese ventures were major moves in the process of weakening the western allies at vulnerable secondary points.

With the stalemate in Korea, the pushing back of the guerrillas in Malay and the Huks in the Philippines, and the translation of the Communist offensive in Viet Nam to a political stage after the truce of July 1954, the non-military aspects of the Sino-Soviet tie have risen in importance. As of mid-1954 Communist China had shifted its priorities to the problem of generating sustained economic growth. This does not imply that the urge for external expansion is spent. It may well imply a decision to pursue external expansion for the time being only where it is not likely to divert substantial resources from domestic development; i.e., by diplomacy, propaganda, local politics, and subversion.

With the forward surge of Communism in Asia shifting to non-military techniques, the Sino-Soviet balance sheet may alter in its composition. In a stalemated cold war the immediate advantage of the alliance to both Moscow and Peking may somewhat diminish if the Free World can prevent further disintegration in Asia. In Moscow, Peking's claims to substantial loans could not be set off against the prospect of major damage to the Free World in the immediate future. Peking's claim for equality, if not primacy, in North Korea—earned when Chinese soldiers filled the gap left by the military collapse of Moscow's North Korean puppet—was hard to meet; but it has, apparently, now been satisfied. It was one thing for Moscow to talk to

Mao of a joint Sino-Soviet policy in 1950 following a successful North
Korean coup engineered by Soviet-created and controlled agents; for
a North Korean quick success would have left Moscow in undisputed
control of Korea, with, perhaps, a *pro forma* voice for Peking. It was
another matter to confront this issue after a failure in which Peking
retrieved stalemate from disaster at a heavy cost in casualties and a
considerable strain on scarce resources not wholly mitigated by Soviet
lend-lease and loans. The sharing of spoils between allies may be
difficult; but it is less difficult than allocating the costs of failure. And
the costs of minimum reconstruction in North Korea are likely to be
substantial. Although Peking has significantly buttressed its position
vis-à-vis Russia in Northeast Asia, and notably in Manchuria, this
was not, after all, the point of the Korean adventure when Stalin and
Mao considered it in 1950.

In Peking also the immediate advantages of the Sino-Soviet tie
may somewhat diminish—again on the assumption of a successful Free
World containment of Communist advance at present limits. With
the Communist offensive stalemated and major military hostilities
with the West at an end, Peking does not need, for the time being,
the threat of Soviet involvement to protect it from the full weight of
Free World military power.

A similar shift may occur on the diplomatic front. While the
Korean War was in progress it mattered little in Peking whether its
very limited diplomacy with the West was conducted through Moscow
or Peking had independent diplomatic access to other powers. In a
period of cold war, when Chinese Communist aggression must be pursued by less violent means, the cost to Peking of its virtual isolation
within the Communist bloc has undoubtedly become irksome. It
would certainly wish, for example, to play the game of leader of Asian
nationalism within the United Nations, and to enhance the image of
China as the Asian wave of the future by eliminating Formosa from
diplomatic status. It would enjoy the freedom to exploit the economic and political uneasiness of Japan with formal economic and
even political overtures. It would wish to play its game in the Economic Commission for Asia and the Far East. All of these minor
gambits were well worth sacrificing or postponing when there floated
in the minds of Stalin and Mao the larger expansionist visions of
early 1950: a unified Communist Korea; a Communist Formosa and
Indo-China; progressive Communist undermining of the Philippines,
Malaya, and Indonesia. But these have not come to pass. Despite
its serious consequences for the West the Geneva truce essentially recognized old facts of life—military facts—in Viet Nam, which neither

side was prepared to force to total military victory. The pace of Communist subversion has perceptibly slowed down. The unsatisfactory long-run features of the 1950 arrangement may be more acutely felt than they were when the alliance was formed.

Economically also Peking has had to re-examine the balance-sheet. When the 1950 concept of the joint offensive dominated the Sino-Soviet relationship, the strict economics of the alliance were secondary. Both in post-Stalin Moscow and in Peking of the new General Line these economic margins may have become more important. There is an evident desire in Peking to expand its machinery imports from the non-Communist world, and the suggestion of a limit to Sino-Soviet trade set by Moscow.

There is a more general suggestion—no more than that—of cross-purposes in the propaganda lines emanating from the two capitals in the spring and summer of 1954. Moscow has come to underline the role of Communist China as 'guarantor of peace' in Asia, meanwhile deprecating a little Peking's pretensions to being in 'transition to socialism.' By Moscow's calculus Peking is in a pre-1929 phase; that is, 'pre-transition to socialism.' Peking, with great symmetry, presses on with the older Moscow line that the Sino-Soviet alliance is the 'reliable foundation for peace in Asia and the world,' while pushing on with industrialization at a pace and with pretensions of which Moscow may not approve. We know that the new General Line was launched at the close of economic negotiations in Moscow which yielded results clearly disappointing to Peking. It may well be that the General Line is, in part, an act of limited defiance to Malenkov's Moscow, harking back as it does to an older Soviet pattern of Stalin at his ruthless peak after 1929.

What this all suggests is that Moscow would be content to see Peking continue with more vigorous and costly aggression in Asia, even at the expense of Peking's domestic program; and that Peking has opted for a different distribution of its effort and resources.

The power balance sheet may, then, have altered, and short-run interests may be at work making for some slight dilution of the Sino-Soviet alliance. Those short-run interests are real, and conflicts among them may well be reflected in the current and future behavior of the two governments. Nevertheless, the men at the top of the two regimes did not make their mutual commitments merely on a short-run basis. They looked to a long future of joint struggle against the non-Communist world, and to the mutually reinforcing role of the two powers in that struggle. To them the long-run advantages of the alliance persist. It is our judgment that, at the moment, the most that is to be expected is a modest shift in the intensity of the Sino-Soviet alliance, not a definitive violation of it. We see no signs of incipient Titoism; we see much that makes it most unlikely in the foreseeable future.

Under what circumstances, if any, is a break-up of the alliance to be foreseen? In a technical sense the essence of the alliance lies in the relative weakness of China *vis-à-vis* the Soviet Union. This means that three conditions are probably required to effect a Chinese withdrawal from the Sino-Soviet alliance:

1. Acute dissatisfaction among an effective group of Chinese leaders with the workings of the Soviet alliance, and, probably, with the consequences of applying Soviet techniques to the problem of China's economic growth.

2. Assurance that withdrawal would be met by more favorable terms of association with the West.

3. The neutralization of potential Soviet strength *vis-à-vis* China either by severe internal Soviet difficulties or by some third power.

In the light of this basic situation there are several conditions, now beyond the horizon of immediate possibility, under which the Sino-Soviet tie might be definitively altered.

1. *Major Soviet internal crisis.* If the uneasy process of adjustment to the situation in the Soviet Union created by Stalin's death should break into open conflict, resulting in either a drastic weakening of Moscow's power on the world scene or a drastic shift in its internal and external political orientation, even the present Chinese Communist rulers might be prepared to rethink their present relationship to Moscow and move towards a greater degree of independence or association with the non-Communist world. Their precise course of action would depend on many factors, notably the character and probable duration of changes in the Soviet Union and the terms the Free World might offer for a change in orientation. The essential point here is that it is Moscow's relative strength combined with its presently aggressive intentions towards non-Communist Asia which helps make the Sino-Soviet tie attractive to Mao; and any alteration in those characteristics of Moscow's position would strike at the foundations of the alliance.

2. *Soviet defeat or major setback in war.* A similar result might be induced by a weakening of Moscow's position brought about by external military force. Communist China's present leaders are likely to be loyal allies to Moscow in the early stages of a major war. Should such a war go badly, however, they are likely to consider terms involving a different orientation to the external world. Despite their

evident confidence in themselves and in the long future of Communism in China, they are conscious of their current basic weakness as an independent military and economic power. Their present position is built on assumptions of Soviet strength. Evidence of Soviet weakness *vis-à-vis* the Free World would lead them to examine alternatives. Their exact behavior under these hypothetical circumstances would hinge, again, on the alternatives held out to them by the Free World. Given the difficulties of conquering China with external ground forces, and the profound nationalism to which the Communist leaders might appeal, the Communist structure might well hold together on its own if faced simply with unconditional surrender. Confronted with positive terms which would offer China a way of seeking its national objectives (short of aggressive extension of national power), the present structure of power might well break down.

3. *An overextension of Soviet control in China.* Despite its reserve bargaining strength *vis-à-vis* Peking, Moscow has taken great care to avoid overplaying its hand. So far as we know, it has dealt with Peking as a government, building the intimate relations described above through high-level diplomatic agreements. It has not exercised its power unilaterally and piecemeal through direct control over internal chains of command as it has done in other Communist countries and as it sought to do without success in Belgrade. This unaccustomed behavior reflects a simple major fact: there are limits in subservience to Moscow beyond which the present leaders of Chinese Communism are not prepared to go. It is Moscow's understanding that Mao might envisage a sharp break in the alliance if the condition of the alliance were direct Soviet control over the instruments of Chinese national power. As noted earlier, the threat of Chinese withdrawal thus serves to check Soviet application of the full weight of its potential bargaining position.

The Sino-Soviet alliance is a curious and not necessarily stable relationship. One can envisage a self-reinforcing chain of circumstances which might upset it in the future. It is possible, for example, that some Chinese Communist assertion of independence on a relatively minor issue (e.g., trade with the West, Asian Communist policy, or North Korea) might lead to application of increased Soviet pressure (e.g., via trade, credit, or border relations). Such pressure might lead to some act of further defiance by the Chinese Communists which, in turn, might lead Moscow to apply still further its potential bargaining weight. In short, given the obsessive concern of both parties with the realities of power, it is not to be ruled out that a crisis involving some sort of test of will and strength might spiral out of the power balance which exists.

It should be strongly emphasized that, with Mao in control of Peking and with a stable situation in Moscow, strong forces exist which would contain such power frictions short of a test of relative strength. The Chinese Communists have so heavily committed their domestic prestige on the alleged benefits to China of the Soviet tie that while a break with Moscow would not be intrinsically unpopular in China it would be a costly affair to the Chinese Communist leadership and would demand a staggering re-orientation in the outlook of the cadres. And Moscow has given even greater hostages to fortune in building the Sino-Soviet relation. Thus, in the short run and under foreseeable circumstances, these large ultimate interests are likely to contain pressures set up on lesser matters—especially so long as the cold war continues at a high level of intensity, and, by their own aggressive intent and aggressive action, the two regimes confront a hostile external world. The sense of overriding common cause was peculiarly strong so long as active hostilities were being pursued in Korea and envisaged elsewhere; and at present, despite some reduction in the intensity of hostilities, the two regimes remain closely allied. It is under conditions of sustained stalemate—still to be created by an effective Free World policy—that the tie is most likely to be weakened.

Looking further ahead, we see two more distant circumstances that might provide a favorable framework for a fracture in the Sino-Soviet tie. First, there might be a change in Chinese leadership to hands less competent than Mao's. It is his combination of internal strength and external eminence in the Communist world which both helps hold Soviet pressure at bay and assures those beneath him that the national integrity of the regime will be maintained. The sustaining of a Chinese Communist leadership at once sufficiently strong to cope with Moscow and sufficiently in accord with Moscow's interests is a major problem for the future. It will enter strongly into both Moscow's and Peking's behavior at the time of Mao's succession and thereafter.

4. *A failure of the general line.* A fracture in the Sino-Soviet alliance might be detonated out of internal as well as external situations. It is our judgment, developed in subsequent chapters, that the success of Peking's First Five Year Plan is not assured. In the face of a rapidly rising population, concentrating in the cities, with enormous overhead commitments to feed the armed forces, cadres, and forced labor, with a requirement to maintain agricultural exports as a means of acquiring necessary industrial equipment, tremendous pressure comes

to rest on Chinese agricultural output. It is not impossible that the regime can bring about the requisite increase to fulfill its plan (say, 10 per cent over 1952 by 1957–1959). Its control system is surely capable of collecting the supplies needed—even in the face of considerable peasant hunger or starvation. But a sharp and sustained fall in output of say 10 per cent below 1952—not wholly to be ruled out—could force a drastic change in the whole of Peking's policy, internal and external. Such a crisis cannot be firmly predicted; but it belongs in this array of speculative possibilities.

Our general conclusion, then, is that it is unlikely that a crisis in Sino-Soviet relations will arise so long as Mao remains alive and in command; so long as Moscow avoids either a major internal Soviet crisis or major war; so long as Moscow maintains its present degree of restraint in applying its leverage over Peking; and so long as the application of Stalin's techniques for industrialization do not lead China to palpable crisis.

It seems unlikely, given the complex of interests which now hold the alliance together, that the Sino-Soviet tie can be broken by seductive offers from the West taken alone. In fact, a partial accommodation to the West, brought about while maintaining the present Sino-Soviet tie, would tend to give Peking the best of both worlds and diminish the pressure for serious alteration in the links which now bind Peking to Moscow.

If our view is correct, the well-meant efforts to alter Peking's attitude by urging a place for it in the UN and by seeking an expansion of trade in no important respect increase the chance of a break in the Sino-Soviet alliance; on the contrary, they may make it a more acceptable foundation for Peking's conduct of external affairs, by diminishing some of its costs. The probability of a crisis in Sino-Soviet affairs will be maximized if Communist expansion is halted for a sustained period and Peking is forced to live with the consequences of the Sino-Soviet Alliance of 1950 and the new General Line of 1953–1954.

It is, of course, important that China's current and potential leaders understand that the Free World offers to China an alternative relationship consistent with the nation's dignity. We suspect this is now fully understood. Peking's leaders are not hostile out of fear but out of hope for further expansion. Nevertheless it is worth emphasizing that, even in a major crisis or hot war, the Free World's objective cannot be unconditional surrender or military liberation. There must be a clear Free World concept of a Chinese future that would meet the basic, continuing, still unsatisfied aspirations of modern China.

A long-run western policy toward Communist China must be erected, therefore, on a double awareness: an awareness of China's underlying weakness and the extent of its present enmeshment with a stronger partner; and an awareness of the power in China of its historic aspirations for national dignity, cultural modernization, and material progress.

PART
5

COMMUNIST POWER

AND THE CHINESE ECONOMY

FOREWORD

It may be taken as axiomatic that the Chinese Communist leaders regard the economy they control as a means to the larger ends which constitute their policy objectives. Over the foreseeable future they will not be concerned directly with the goals of economic welfare except as welfare factors may affect the efficiency of the working force or the stability of the regime. The regime's welfare goal is the minimum level of consumption compatible with ultimate Communist purposes. The regime proclaims the need for industrialization as a foundation for Chinese national independence, military strength, and international status.

Industrialization had come to represent one of the deep-seated national aspirations of modern China long before the Communists came to power in 1949. This was reflected in Sun Yat-sen's Three People's Principles as well as in his Industrial Plan; it also constitutes one of the central themes of Chiang Kai-shek's *China's Destiny:* "If we desire to replace our hundred-year-old, restricted, unbalanced, semicolonial economy with a free and independent economy that will satisfy the requirements of national defense, we must employ political power to guide economic development."

Although the objectives of the Chinese Communist regime are not in themselves economic objectives, but, rather, objectives of enlarged domestic and international power, tactically all its policies have an economic dimension. This is so because all its actions require the mobilization of resources; and China's resources are acutely scarce in relation to the regime's purposes. Thus an analysis of the Chinese economy from this perspective is calculated to throw some light on the fundamental questions of choice which beset Peking at the present juncture.

The scale and composition of Chinese output will help determine whether Communist policies succeed or fail. The performance of the Chinese economy will determine the degree of independent military strength enjoyed by the regime *vis-à-vis* both Moscow and the external world. It will determine in substantial part the extent of popular dissidence which the regime must confront and contain. It will in substantial part determine whether Asia will regard Communist China as a model to be imitated. In a sense, the Chinese economy and the somewhat intractable human beings who constitute its working force and determine its performance constitute the most challenging opponent that the regime confronts at this stage of its history. The following four chapters analyze the nature of this challenge.*

* These four chapters have been extensively discussed in their entirety between Mr. Alexander Eckstein and myself. Chapter 12 is our joint work; Chapters 13 and 14 are wholly Mr. Eckstein's. W. W. R.

THE CHINESE ECONOMY PRE-1949

I. THE INHERITED ECONOMY

With their conquest of the Chinese mainland in 1949 the Communists inherited an economy that can best be envisaged as made up of three sectors: a vast, largely self-sufficient agricultural sector; a modern sector, located in the coastal cities, largely devoted to the management of foreign trade and the manufacture of textiles and other light industry products; a heavy industry sector in Manchuria, built mainly under Japanese occupation after 1931 and not linked to the rest of the Chinese economy until after 1949. The relations between the coastal cities and the agricultural sector were limited but important. The import and later the Chinese manufacture of factory-made textiles had eroded the handicraft textile industry in the countryside; and there is some question as to whether advantages accruing from the resultant cheap textiles available were not more than outweighed by the failure of the village economy to find alternative productive uses for the margin of labor and time left to the peasant beyond his tasks of cultivation. The rise of the cities also increased the degree of agricultural production for export as well as to supply urban needs. The interaction of the cities and rural China was, however, limited and fluctuating. Due to poor transport facilities, vast areas remained 'earth-bound,' with the area of commercial exchange limited to a radius of a few miles; and thus in times of trouble, with the urban link broken, even regions close by the cities returned to virtual self-sufficiency. Viewed in these terms, one of the key long-term economic tasks of the Communist regime is to link the still largely autarchic rural economy to the modern sector in such a way as to induce a widely diffused and sustained process of economic growth—by devices consistent with the regime's compulsion to totalitarian power and in directions determined by its power goals.

As of 1949 all segments of the Chinese economy (agriculture, industry, transport, and foreign trade) and the institutional framework within which they operated were damaged by war and civil conflict. Therefore, the most urgent short-term task of the regime was to restore the basic capacity to produce and to exchange goods and services, preparing the way for a long-term program of industrialization. Linked to this was the task of remaking China's institutions so as to guarantee a maximum degree of detailed Communist authority over the disposition of resources.

In essence, these recovery and institutional targets were attained by 1952 despite the Chinese intervention in the Korean War. The existence of large military operations in 1950–1951 cut both ways: it drained off resources from reconstruction, but it also provided a suitable political setting for a drastic transfer of economic powers and resources to the Communist state. Basically, recovery was rapid because labor and developed resources were underemployed during this stage. Therefore the 1949–1952 period provided primarily a test of the new regime's capabilities in the field of economic organization and control rather than its capacity to launch and carry through successfully a program of industrialization and economic development. The latter issue began to assume paramount importance in 1953, as resources began to be more or less fully employed and as the regime was increasingly confronted with basic limitations imposed by the interacting forces of physical environment, population pressure, past inheritance, and the human responses to the character of Communist rule.

To understand the logistics of the economic development problem in Communist China it is necessary to examine briefly these limiting factors in terms of the economy which the Communists inherited in 1949.

II. AGRICULTURE

The structure of China's mainland economy prior to 1949 was typical of a pre-industrial society. Agriculture, accounting for 75 per cent of the population, contributed 40 per cent to national product, while the urban sector, with only 15 per cent of the population, made roughly the same contribution. At least an additional 10 per cent of China's people lived in rural areas, engaged mostly in non-farm tasks and producing about 20 per cent of total national output.[1] Thus it took three out of four Chinese workers to feed the country (and supply a modest margin of agricultural exports) as opposed to one out of seven in the United States, and one out of two in Japan and the Soviet Union.

These conditions are essentially unchanged today. Chinese agriculture is a classic example of intensive cultivation with high yields per acre, low output per man. The result is a vast population kept at or barely above subsistence only by the most arduous, subtle, personalized cultivation of the soil. The Chinese farmer is caught in a familiar *cul-de-sac* with its self-reinforcing interaction of overpopulation, intensive low per-man yields, illiteracy, and poverty, with practically no margin left for saving and investment.

The pattern of mainland China's population growth constitutes one of the most confusing chapters in the country's long history. However, sinologists are fairly well agreed that, paralleling the rise and decline of dynasties, China's population may have followed a cyclical pattern for about fifteen centuries.[2] Expanding food production, brought about by an extension of the cultivated area and by the introduction of corn, sweet potatoes, and peanuts, and a long period of dynastic peace apparently led to a doubling of the population between the seventeenth and nineteenth centuries. As a result, population is believed to have been around 340 million in 1850, rising further thereafter possibly to 450–500 million in the twentieth century. Figures in this range were conventional for several decades until the 1954 Peking announcement of census results, which put the mainland population at 582 million.[3] This rapid increase in population so outstripped the expansion in acreage that the cultivated area per capita may have been almost halved between 1685 and 1930.[4]

Inefficiencies inherent in small-size farms were greatly aggravated by the continuous fragmentation of landholding which resulted from population pressure, lack of non-farm employment opportunities, and China's age-old inheritance practices of splitting up land among all surviving sons.[5] Surveys conducted in the early 1930's indicate that the average farm of approximately 3.2 to 3.3 acres, or 21 mou, was broken up into about 6 distinctly separated parcels with an average distance of 0.4 mile between farmsteads and parcels. However, these averages conceal very marked inequalities in farm size inasmuch as 36 per cent of farms were under 10 mou (1.5 acres) and 25 per cent were between 10 and 20 mou.[6]

Such small and highly fragmented holdings could maintain a densely settled population only by exceedingly intensive land use and double cropping on nearly two-thirds of the cultivated land area. Double cropping is particularly widespread in the irrigated rice area of the South, where two or more crops are planted on about 75 per cent of the farm area as compared to only 7 per cent in the wheat region of the North. The high intensity of land use in China is illustrated further by the fact that in all regions about 90 per cent of the farm area is in crops, while only about 1 per cent is in pastures as compared to 40 per cent or more in the United States. Yet livestock density per acre is higher than in Japan or the United States. Most of the farm animals are used for draft power, only about one-fourth being available for human consumption or for industrial raw materials; and, owing to the small size of the farms, parcels, and fields, animal draft power is underemployed. Therefore, some of the livestock on China's farms represents a net drain on food resources.

The same can be said of farm labor. It has been estimated that on China's farms the able-bodied men (15–60) are idle for an average of almost two months a year. Were one to include women in the labor force, this underemployment would be even greater. While much of it is of a seasonal character, there is no question that in China just as in other underdeveloped agrarian countries moderate and gradual withdrawals of labor from agriculture without change in technology need not affect total farm production.

With high intensity of land use, and age-old soil conservation and irrigation practices, crop yields per acre are quite high. They are somewhat above the levels attained in Meiji Japan, but lag considerably behind the yields attained in present-day Japan. This fact suggests that crop productivity in China has been pushed about as far as traditional practices and methods will permit, and that large improvements in farm productivity can be attained, as in Japan, only through improved practices and notably by the application of chemical fertilizers to the soil.

All of these factors combined have traditionally pressed the Chinese peasant close to the margin of subsistence. However, his situation probably deteriorated over the disordered century after 1840, mainly in response to the rise in population, but also reflecting civil disturbance and the decay of handicraft industry, notably textiles, in competition with manufactured products. Just as in earlier periods of dynastic decline, the impact of natural disasters such as droughts and floods may have been aggravated during this period of civil disorder and weak central rule, resulting as they did in a failure to maintain flood control and irrigation works on which Chinese agriculture depends. Thus Buck's investigations show that within the memory of his informants there was an average of close to 4 famines in the northern wheat region and about 2.5 in the rice areas of the south, caused for the most part by droughts and floods.

During the Nanking government period, 1928–1937, considerable efforts were made to reverse this situation by improvement in farm and irrigation practices and in flood control. However, these modest beginnings were interrupted by the Japanese War, which led to a decline of perhaps 20 per cent in agricultural output, from a peak in 1936 to a low point in 1945. Excepting 1949, a year of acute drought, Chinese agriculture recovered steadily after 1945 to, roughly, the 1936 level by 1952. There was, however, a considerable backlog of repair and maintenance to be done on river control and irrigation installations.

All this may be said in general. But China is an enormous country with a variety of climates, soils, and agricultural products, the most important distinction being between the northern wheat region and the southern rice areas. Moreover, Manchuria and Inner Mongolia are much less densely populated than the rest of China. There are limited opportunities for mechanized farming and the opening up of new land, notably in Manchuria. The impact of the weather varies from season to season, and the fortunes of war and civil disturbance have had highly differentiated effects in various parts of the country. Broadly speaking, it appears that the Chinese population has concentrated at the points of highest soil productivity, and that there is a crude economic rationality in the present density distribution on the land.

III. INDUSTRY

State entrepreneurship provided the initial impetus to the establishment of factory industry in China, confined for most part to government arsenals and armament works in the 1860's and 1870's. The development of modern industry was not really launched until the 1890's, when the Treaty of Shimonoseki opened the way for the construction and operation of foreign-owned factories in the Treaty Ports and was followed by the granting to the Treaty Powers of such differential advantages as the right of inland water navigation exempt from native charges. The interests of the imperial powers consequently shifted from trade to railroads, mines, and industrial concessions, a shift accompanied by heightened competition for strategic power in China as opposed to merely commercial profit.

In the meantime, cotton textile imports increased appreciably with the cheapening of overseas transport and the low-cost production of factory-made cotton-yarn in India, developments which served to undermine the position of rural handicrafts, particularly the hand spinning of yarn, and to create a market for manufactured textile products.[7] The next natural step was the development of a cotton textile industry in China, which, as in many other industrializing societies, took the lead. There followed the rise of other consumer-goods industries which developed as a by-product of foreign trade and urbanization; i.e., flour mills, cigarette and match factories, etc. At the same time, power plants and light engineering works had to be developed to service the new industries and railroads. All of this industrial development was accompanied by the institution of other external economies such as banking and trading facilities.

Industrial expansion was greatly stimulated during World War I, when China was cut off from the world market and her infant industries temporarily enjoyed the benefits of protection with but a nominal tariff. The wartime protectionist effects continued to prevail after the war, first, because the terms of trade moved against China under the impact of the falling gold price of silver,[8] and second, owing to the introduction of the 1929 tariff. As a result, textile and other industries grew in China proper, with some interruptions, up to 1937. In the latter stages of this period the initiative passed largely from western to Japanese and Chinese capital and enterprise. By 1937 not much less than half of China's cotton spindles and looms were under Japanese management; and, of course, Japan controlled virtually all of China's industry as World War II ended.

During this half century of growth there developed a modest, largely light-consumer-goods industry on the periphery of the Chinese economy. It was confined to the Treaty Ports, where there was established a western institutional and legal framework conducive to its growth. An entirely different pattern emerged in Manchuria, where the population-resource balance was more favorable and the institutional environment less resistant to industrialization than in China proper. However, the decisive factor in Manchuria was the injection of the Japanese, who from 1931 on were determined to develop Manchuria into a heavy-industry and war base. This decision involved them in a program of comprehensive and planned economic development with an accent upon expansion of communications and producers'-goods industries, reinforced by agricultural development.

The upshot of this complex and erratic evolution was that the Communists inherited a basic industrial capacity roughly indicated by the accompanying production figures (Table 1), which combine 1943 Japanese-controlled output in Manchuria and the 1936 figures for the rest of China.

This modern sector operating at its peak employed about 3 million workers and produced about 10 per cent of national output.

TABLE 1. ESTIMATED PRE-1949 PEAK PRODUCTION OF SELECTED INDUSTRIAL PRODUCTS IN MAINLAND CHINA *

Product	Unit	China Proper	Manchuria
Pig iron	Metric tons	290,640	1,700,000
Crude steel	Metric tons	50,000	843,000
Rolled steel	Metric tons	Negligible	485,700
Coal	Metric tons	33,000,000 †	25,630,000
Crude oil	Metric tons	n.a.	214,300
Cement	Metric tons	608,000	1,532,000
Paper	Metric tons	n.a.	76,000
Flour	Metric tons	1,800,000	650,000 ‡
Sugar	Metric tons	392,000	17,600 §
Cotton yarn	Bales	2,100,000	n.a.
Cotton cloth	Bolts	30,000,000	n.a.
Cigarettes	Billions of sticks	57	25
Electric power:			
Capacity	Thousands of kw	893	1,786
Output	Millions of kw-hr	2,425	4,475

* Sources: Edwin W. Pauley, *Report on Japanese Assets in Manchuria to the President of the United States*, July 1946; *Report by Kao Kang at the First Conference of Representatives of the Chinese Communist Party in the Northeast*, Mukden, March 13, 1950; *Manchukuo Yearbook, 1942*, Mukden, Manchukuo Government official publication; *China Yearbook* (in Chinese), Nanking, China Yearbook Committee of the Chinese Nationalist Government, September 1948, Vol. I, 830 pp., Vol. II, pp. 831–2080, used as translated by K. C. Chao; *The Chinese Yearbook, 1944–1945*, Shanghai, Commercial Press, 1948, pp. 654–655; T. H. Shen, *Agricultural Resources of China*, Ithaca, New York, Cornell University Press, 1951; *Statistical Year-Book of the League of Nations, 1942–1944*, Geneva, 1945; Kate Mitchell, *Industrialization of the Western Pacific*, New York, Institute of Pacific Relations, 1942; W. S. Woytinsky and E. S. Woytinsky, *World Population and Production*, New York, The Twentieth Century Fund, 1953.

† Estimates range from 22,000,000 to 40,000,000; the figure used here is based on Woytinsky and represents a 1940–1944 average.

‡ 1937.

§ 1940.

The Communists did not inherit Chinese industry intact. In 1945, operating on the likelihood that the KMT would re-establish its authority in China, Moscow had ordered the dismantling of many key installations in Manchuria and their removal to Russia as Japanese reparations. In addition, there had been important war damage to industrial installations elsewhere in China.

The Japanese never operated Manchurian industry at full capacity; and it is likely that in certain areas capacity may not have been fully restored even now, despite the achievement of peak output figures; for the Communists have undoubtedly used available capacity at a high degree of intensity. When restored, the Chinese industrial sector inherited by the Communists was roughly of the same order of magnitude as that of postwar India, Japan in 1920–1925, Russia in 1913, the United States in 1870.[9]

IV. Distribution

Primitive, inadequate, and costly transport has been one of the key factors limiting China's economic development. In 1949 mainland China (excluding Outer Mongolia and Tibet), with territory roughly the size of the United States, had only 15,000 miles of railway, as compared to approximately 400,000 in the United States. With such a small network, only East China and southern Manchuria were well served, while South and West China were barely touched.

As a result, a very large share of trade was carried by traditional methods, i.e., coastal shipping, inland water transport, pack animals, carts, and the backs of men. Such modes of transport appear cheap per day, but are expensive per mile; so that farmers seldom took their produce more than thirty miles to market.[10] According to one investigator, the transport cost of grain from Shensi to Shanghai would have exceeded the total cost of grain imported from the West Coast of the United States.[11]

These high transport costs were among the principal factors hampering the commercialization of agriculture and narrowing the market for industrial products. But rural self-sufficiency, so far as the family or village was concerned, was by far not so complete as is frequently supposed. Probably agricultural families purchased over a quarter of the goods they consumed. In turn they sold about half of their total output; but the bulk of farm products marketed involved exchange within the same *hsien,* and only an estimated 8 per cent was shipped to distant urban markets.[12]

Consequently, China exhibited a highly cellular marketing pattern with varying and fluctuating scarcity relationships and price tendencies in different areas. Frequent local famines were a reflection of this high degree of fragmentation. All of these problems were greatly aggravated by civil strife and a lack of central administrative unity. As the civil war spread between 1945 and 1949, the Communists took over a system of distribution and urban-rural interchange which had been further corroded under the impact of hyperinflation and repeated disruption of railway transport.

V. FOREIGN TRADE

In aggregate terms, foreign trade has never been of major importance for the Chinese economy. Thus, in 1936, for example, per capita imports and exports, including Manchuria, were smaller than in any other country.[18] Moreover, probably at no time did total trade exceed 10 per cent of national product. At the same time, however, foreign trade played a major role in bringing the closed traditional economy of China within the purview of the world economy, thereby providing the impetus for the rise of a small modern industry.

Broadly speaking, China's imports and exports evolved along lines typical of a generally underdeveloped and slowly growing economy. This is best illustrated by the course of cotton textile trade. At first, China was a net exporter of hand-woven cotton goods. With the opening of the Suez Canal and the decline in overseas transport costs, manufactured cotton textiles began to compete successfully with native cloth, as a result of which cotton goods imports grew rapidly until the turn of the century, when they constituted 40 per cent of total imports. During this same period China was a small net exporter of raw cotton. With an expanding domestic market for manufactured cotton textiles, the development of a cotton textile industry led to a gradual decline in the import of textile products. This change was accompanied by growing net imports of raw cotton; but, with expanding domestic cotton production, this trend was reversed, so that by the time of the Sino-Japanese War in 1937 production had just about caught up with requirements.

A number of other import products such as cigarettes, matches, and flour followed a similar course. Thus manufactured and semi-manufactured consumers' goods, which dominated total import figures at the turn of the century, gave way slowly but steadily to industrial equipment and raw materials. On the other hand, the rise in urban population combined with a lag in internal transport development led to an increasing food import requirement.

Chinese exports, initially confined mainly to silk and tea, broadened out over the years to embrace a wider range of natural resource products: beans and bean products, eggs, hog bristles, hides, soybeans, tungsten, tung oil, and, later, iron ore and coal for Japan. Manufactures derived from household and handicraft industries declined as the market process drew labor on to activities with higher monetary rate of return.

The structural changes in China's foreign trade and economy were reflected in her balance of payments. Early in the nineteenth century China had a favorable balance of trade and a surplus on current account. As trade expanded and opium imports grew, this surplus diminished, while the trade and current-account balance became consistently unfavorable.[14] From then on, China's balance of payments, as shown in the accompanying table, exhibited characteristics typical for most underdeveloped areas.

TABLE 2. BALANCE OF CHINA'S INTERNATIONAL PAYMENTS, 1841–1935 *
(in millions of Chinese dollars)

	1841 (Sargent)	1903 (Morse)	1930 (Remer)	1935 (Bank of China)
Current outpayments:				
Merchandise imports	25 †	492	1,965	1,129
Specie imports	...	58	101	...
Service of foreign loans	...	69	111	108
Chinese expenditures abroad	...	7	13	55
Remittance of foreign enterprises and other profits	...	35	227	55
Total	25	661	2,417	1,347
Current inpayments:				
Merchandise exports	13.3	374	1,476	662
Specie exports	11.2	51	48	357
Foreign expenditures in China	0.5	81	218	150
Overseas remittances	...	114	316	260
Total	25.0	620	2,058	1,429
Capital inpayments:				
New foreign investments in China		42	202	140
Unaccounted for		−1	−157	222

* Li Choh-ming, *op. cit.*, p. 501.
† Including treasure imports.

The key features revealed in the table are the following:

1. The expansion of China's total foreign trade as it became part of the world trading framework. Including Japanese trade with Manchuria, Chinese exports may have reached a pre-1949 peak of about U. S. $1 billion at 1952 prices.

2. The large excess of new foreign investments and foreign expenditures combined over outpayments of interest and profit.

3. The extremely important role of remittances from overseas Chinese in sustaining China's balance of payments.

4. The resultant ability of Chinese consistently to sustain merchandise imports in excess of merchandise exports.

5. The decline in China's level of trade (see 1935 figures) caused by the loss of Manchuria after 1931—despite considerable efforts to increase production for export in the rest of China.

China's balance of payments followed a rather different pattern during the highly disturbed postwar years. Balance of payment deficits, financed largely by various forms of foreign aid, were constantly growing, while the flow of private foreign investment declined appreciably. Trade recovered to about half its peak prewar level by 1948.

After their victory, between 1949 and 1952, the Communists reestablished roughly the prewar level. But the direction and composition of foreign trade since the inception of the Communist regime has been drastically altered as compared with the prewar pattern, with Soviet bloc countries fulfilling the predominant role formerly held by Japan and the West with respect to both imports and exports—a shift accomplished substantially during the period of the Korean War.

VI. The Institutional Framework

In agriculture the system of organization inherited by the Communists was essentially that of traditional China. Land was privately held and unequally distributed; thus 10 to 15 per cent of the farm population owned 53 to 63 per cent of the land.[15] According to a 1934–1935 Nationalist government survey of 1,545 big landlord families and 752,865 peasant families in 87 districts scattered throughout 11 provinces, landlord holdings ranged from 300 to 20,000 mou and averaged around 2,030 mou as compared to an average peasant holding of 15.8 mou.[16] This concentration of land ownership was most pronounced in the Yangtze and Pearl River valleys and in recently settled provinces of Manchuria and Inner Mongolia.

In general, outright tenancy, even though it was increasing in recent decades, was not so prevalent as it is generally believed. In 1947 only about one-third of the farm population were tenants, one-quarter were part owners, and about 40 to 45 per cent were full owners.[17] Therefore agrarian unrest in China was primarily compounded of interacting influences generated by the pressure of population and low productivity rather than the extent of tenancy. High population densities, particularly pronounced in South China, led to an intense competition for land; this land hunger of the peasants—based on scarcity—opened the way for exploitation and abuse as illustrated by insecurity of tenure, high rents varying from 40 to 70 per cent of the crop, and, for Szechwan at least, collections of rent for years ahead.

The negative features of the tenancy system were greatly aggravated by very onerous terms of credit imposed upon the farmer. His margin over subsistence was low even in a normal year; as a result of poor communications a local scarcity could push up food prices and so diminish the real value of a money loan. When to these conditions there is added a 30 to 35 per cent rate of interest per annum,[18] the economic forces which tended to pauperize the peasant become clear. The situation was further complicated by the fact that it was the landlord who frequently performed the moneylending and marketing function. Through the complex structure of secret society, clan, and family organization the landlords dominated the social life of the villages; and, politically, they remained the villages' chief intermediaries with the central political authorities on the strategic issues of taxation, army recruitment, and the mobilization of labor for public works.

There had, of course, been changes in the traditional pattern over the first half of this century. The classically trained scholar-gentry had declined, giving way to a variety of more contemporary village leaders, oriented often to the life of the growing cities.[19] The KMT had attempted with limited success to penetrate below the traditional high-water mark of central authority, the *hsien,* and link the villages to national life through the *pao chia* system; and there had been a slow spread of peasant cooperatives, institutes to improve cultivation methods, and other government and private efforts to increase the efficiency and equity of life in Chinese agriculture. And, in the North, the Communists had already begun their restructuring of village life by land redistribution and rent reductions in the areas they held. By and large, however, the old system of agricultural life was still intact during the process of takeover in 1948–1949.

The private enterprise structure of Chinese banking, commercial, and industrial life, with its large component of foreign interest, had, by 1945, been broken or seriously damaged by the Japanese war and occupation. Under the pressures of war and the immediate postwar situation the Nationalist government had assumed an enlarged place in the economy. The scope of government participation increased particularly after 1945, when the Nationalist government confiscated as war booty all Japanese-owned and operated enterprises on the Chinese mainland. Although the trend in Nationalist China to increased governmental direction and participation in the economy is clear, there was, nevertheless, a rapid revival of private enterprise after 1945 in the great coastal cities in trade, banking, and light industry. The Communists thus inherited a completely nationalized industry in Manchuria, and a partially nationalized manufacturing sector in China proper.

Since the post-1945 Chinese economy was in a state of chronic inflation, the Communists inherited an unstable monetary setting which posed for them their first major challenge in economic policy. Gaping budget deficits primarily financed by new note issues had been a major source of inflationary pressure in China ever since the beginning of the Sino-Japanese War in 1937; and this situation was getting progressively worse with actual government expenditures invariably exceeding budgeted amounts. This condition contributed to further currency depreciation; while, in turn, the very speed of hyperinflation made it even more difficult to balance the budget or to estimate expenditures in advance. Although large-scale barter arrangements of some subtlety tended to emerge in the face of rapidly rising prices, inflation nevertheless bore heavily on the urban population, complicated internal and foreign trade, and transmitted itself as a symbol of the Nationalist government's weakness and inadequacy throughout the country.

NOTES FOR CHAPTER 12

1. These as well as all national income estimates throughout this paper are based on preliminary findings emerging from a detailed study of Communist China's gross national product, which Mr. A. Eckstein is in the process of preparing.

2. Ta Chen, *Population in Modern China,* Chicago, University of Chicago Press, 1946, p. 1.

3. New China News Agency, Peking, June 20, 1954, *New China News Agency Daily Bulletin,* No. 1073, London, June 21, 1954.

4. A. K. Chiu, "Agriculture," *China, op. cit.,* Ch. XXXII, p. 469.

5. This seems to have been the practice at least as far back as the Han dynasty.

6. J. L. Buck, *op. cit.,* pp. 181–185 and 267–273; C. C. Chang, *An Estimate of China's Farms and Crops,* Nanking, University of Nanking Press, 1932. It should be noted that some of the smallest farm units represented part-time employment for families deriving a part of their subsistence from farm labor or other sources.

7. H. D. Fong, "Rural Industries in China," *Problems of the Pacific,* Fifth Conference of the Institute of Pacific Relations, 1933.

8. Li Choh-ming, "International Trade," *China, op. cit.,* p. 498.

9. These comparisons are made in terms of estimated aggregate net industrial product. It is interesting to note that if these intercountry comparisons are based on steel production and cotton textile spindleage, the dates for Japan and the United States are approximately the same; but for Russia one must go back to 1890–1895. Of course, were one to make all of these comparisons in per capita terms, one would have to go much further back in Japanese, Russian, and United

States history to reach levels corresponding to current Chinese output or capacity.

10. G. B. Cressey, *China's Geographic Foundations, A Survey of the Land and Its People,* New York, McGraw-Hill, 1934, p. 26.

11. Julean Arnold, "Modern Industry in China," *Chinese Economic Journal,* October 1930, p. 1069.

12. J. L. Buck, *op. cit.,* p. 349.

13. U. S. Department of Commerce, *Foreign Commerce Yearbook, 1937,* Washington, 1938.

14. C. F. Remer, *The Foreign Trade of China,* Shanghai, The Commercial Press, Ltd., 1926, pp. 222–223.

15. A. K. Chiu, *op. cit.,* pp. 473–474.

16. *Ibid.,* p. 474.

17. *China Handbook, 1950,* New York, Rockport Press, pp. 581–583.

18. J. L. Buck, *op. cit.,* Table 18, p. 462. See also, D. N. Rowe, *China among the Powers,* New York, Harcourt, Brace and Company, 1945, p. 47.

19. See the vivid account by Fei Hsiao-tung, *op. cit.*

RECONSTRUCTION AND CONTROL: 1949–1952

I. The General Setting

The purpose of Chinese Communist economic policy in the first three years of the Communist regime was to prepare the way for a sustained process of industrialization. The technical task of the regime over this period was to restore agricultural output, industry, and trade to the maximum levels consistent with the existing framework of China's resources. Its institutional task was to reorganize economic institutions under intimate and sensitive state control.

The Communists inherited an economy in which productive capacity was appreciably curtailed: first by the Sino-Japanese War, and, later, by Soviet occupation and civil war. Manufacturing capacity was impaired—particularly in Manchuria, where over half of the capital stock in industry had been dismantled and carried off by the Soviets in 1945.[1] Industrial capacity was shrinking in China proper, though to a much lesser extent, owing to depreciation and obsolescence and to the flight of some movable facilities to Hong Kong and Formosa. The situation was aggravated by a constant shortage of raw materials throughout 1949, particularly in Shanghai, where many industries depended on imported materials cut off by the Nationalist blockade of the port. At the same time, owing to the disruption of internal trade and transport, domestic supply difficulties were multiplied. Industrial output was further curtailed by a gradual demoralization of labor under the impact of hyperinflation and a breakdown of plant discipline following the Communist conquest of large cities. Urban labor tended to interpret the Communist victory as a signal for asserting its rights and placing its accumulated grievances and demands before industrial management. Several months elapsed after their accession to power before the new authorities were in a position to consolidate fully their control over the trade unions and disabuse them of their misconception that major improvements in welfare would accompany the ideological elevation of the industrial worker to a position of 'hegemony.'

All of these factors combined to reduce industrial production to 56 per cent of its pre-1949 peak.[2] According to this index, the production of investment goods had dropped to 30 per cent of peak, while consumer goods fell only to 70 per cent. The much sharper curtailment in the heavy industries was primarily a reflection of the marked contraction in Manchuria's manufacturing capacity.

On the whole, the rural sector of the economy had been less affected by the vicissitudes of the civil conflict. Civil war brought to the countryside more disorganization and disruption than devastation. Owing to the great importance of the subsistence, non-monetized sector in the rural economy, agriculture could much more easily fall back on its own resources than industry. As a result, food production had declined only by about 20 to 25 per cent below the pre-1949 peak.[3] Unfavorable weather and floods, rather than civil war, were the most important factors accounting for the drop. According to Chinese Communist sources, in 1949 mainland China had its worst flood since 1931: 120 million mou of land, constituting about 10 per cent of the total cultivated area, were affected.[4] It must be borne in mind that under more peaceful conditions the same weather conditions would have created less havoc.

II. Recovery in Production

In this situation, the regime set itself the task of restoring by 1952 industrial and farm production to pre-1949 peak levels. The extent to which this goal was attained may be gauged by the data in Table 3.

Table 3 shows that while recovery in industrial and agricultural production was quite rapid the degree to which past production records were surpassed is appreciably less than that commonly claimed by Chinese Communist officials. In reality, contrary to official claims, output of pig iron, coal, electric power, sugar, soybeans, and wheat actually lagged behind past peak levels.[5]

The decline in pig iron production primarily reflects changed market relationships. Under Japanese tutelage at least half of Manchuria's pig iron production had been exported to Japan. With changed trading conditions, this market was lost and current output was governed by rates of domestic steel production. On the other hand, reduction in electric power production may have been due to

TABLE 3. ESTIMATED PRODUCTION OF SELECTED COMMODITIES IN
MAINLAND CHINA *

Product	Unit	Peak	1949	1950	1952
Pig iron	000 metric tons	2,000	210	827	1,589
Crude steel	000 metric tons	900	144	551	1,215
Rolled steel	000 metric tons	500	90	259	740
Coal	000 metric tons	59,000	26,000	35,000	53,000
Crude oil	000 metric tons	330	125	207	389
Cement	000 metric tons	2,140	663	1,412	2,311
Paper	000 metric tons	120	108	101	264
Flour	000 metric tons	2,450	1,911	1,200	3,087
Sugar	000 metric tons	410	164	198	328
Cotton yarn	000 bales	2,400	1,728	2,040	2,784
Cotton cloth	000 bolts	41,000	29,930	3,230	56,580
Cigarettes	000,000 sticks	82,000	47,000	54,520	102,500
Electric power	000,000 kw-hr	6,900	3,600	3,800	5,700
Rice	000 metric tons	48,600		46,900	55,890
Wheat	000 metric tons	24,000		19,300	22,800
Soybeans	000 metric tons	10,000		5,890	8,900
Cotton	000 metric tons	1,115			1,290

* Based on Table 1 and Appendix 1.

the fact that power generating capacity dismantled by the Soviets in
Manchuria had not been fully restored by 1952. However, as most
of this curtailment in production was apparently borne by household
consumption, industrial power consumption may have been greater
than before.[6]

The lag in coal recovery may be partly accounted for by a marked
drop in output of the Kailan mine, the largest in China proper, apparently related to obsolescence and lack of replacement in equipment.
Strenuous efforts, thus far only partially successful, are still being made
to compensate for this loss through expansion of the Manchurian deposits. The need to restore and expand coal and power production
is assigned a particularly high priority, since failure in these fields
limits growth in the other industrial sectors.

As against these shortfalls, substantial gains were made in steel,
cotton cloth, paper, flour, and cigarette production. An expansion
in steel production, despite Soviet removals of equipment in 1945, is
not as surprising as it may seem at first sight. Since even at its peak
the Japanese iron and steel industry in Manchuria had operated at
only about 60 per cent of capacity, full restoration was not necessary
in order to produce the 1952 output. To maintain the plant that was
left and to replace as much of the dismantled equipment as was needed
to produce the 1952 output, an estimated investment of about U. S.

$160 million (in terms of 1952 U. S. investment costs) would have been required. This is an amount which, allowing for competing investment requirements, was certainly within Communist China's capacity to invest and import.

The arithmetic behind this estimate is as follows:

Peak Manchurian finished steel capacity	910,000 metric tons
Finished steel capacity after dismantling	325,000 metric tons
Capacity which must be reinstalled to produce 1952 output	475,000 metric tons
Capital requirement per ton of finished steel	U. S. $400
Total capital requirement for reinstallation of capacity	U. S. $190,000,000
However, about half of this capital investment was for structures, which had been left more or less intact, so that one should count only equipment costs, which may be estimated as	U. S. $95,000,000
Add to this a replacement allowance of 10 per cent per year on old capital which was not removed. For 2 years	U. S. $65,000,000
Total cost of replacement and reinstallation	U. S. $160,000,000

Recognizing the crucial role of textiles as barter and incentive goods in the Chinese rural setting, the new regime placed particular emphasis upon increasing raw cotton and cotton textile production. This effort was motivated also by the Chinese Communist drive for self-sufficiency. In both these respects the Chinese Communists have had a fair measure of success; they expanded output, and by 1953 reduced imports to negligible proportions. However, they have tended to exaggerate their achievements in this field more than in any other. For instance, by using a low (860,000 metric tons) prewar peak figure they claimed that 1952 raw cotton production was about 50 per cent above prewar. In reality, 1936 output was substantially higher (1,100,000 metric tons),[7] and the increase was only 15 per cent. Similarly, increases in cotton cloth production may be more apparent than real. Unlike cotton spinning, weaving was still a preponderantly handicraft industry before the Sino-Japanese War. Thus the apparent post-1949 rapid growth in output of cotton cloth may represent essentially a displacement of handicraft by factory production. The same may be true for flour.

While the pace of recovery was quite rapid, it apparently lagged behind Chinese Communist expectations, as evidenced by the fact that 1952 industrial production targets, with the exception of coal and flour, were not met. In this respect, as in so many others, Chinese Communists seem to follow the Soviet and satellite statistical practice of camouflaging failures and exaggerating accomplishments.[8]

Mainland China's economic recovery in all fields was greatly facilitated by the succession of three favorable harvests in 1950, 1951, and 1952. As a result, 1952 farm production attained or possibly even exceeded prewar record levels, despite land redistribution and the subsequent beginnings of the collectivization process. It is impossible to ascertain accurately the net effect of the regime's agricultural policies upon output. There is no question that during the period of agitation, land redistribution, and transfer of title there was a great deal of unrest which could not help but disrupt output in the areas affected each year. However, since the process of reform was spread over a three-year period, the total impact upon the country's production as a whole was probably not great—despite the fact that land redistribution also seriously disrupted the system of farm credit. Land redistribution may have had a positive short-term incentive effect upon those farmers who received land; but this effect may be gradually dissipated as the collectivization campaign gathers steam—a development which could not yet have been a major factor affecting farm output during the 1949–1952 period.

Therefore, the favorable crop conditions must be ascribed to other factors than land reform, most important of which was weather. However, there were other less transient factors at work, foremost of which were absence of civil conflict, improved transport and distribution, and efforts to rehabilitate and develop flood control and irrigation facilities.

III. THE NATIONALIZATION OF THE ECONOMY

The Chinese Communist economic program has essentially two dimensions. On the one hand it aims at rapid recovery and growth in production, most particularly in heavy industry; on the other hand, it is bent upon bringing an increasing share of output under government control—for broad political purposes as well as for planning, and for specific investment and military uses. These objectives required a restructuring of the institutional framework, a task in which nationalization, land, fiscal, monetary, and distribution policies have been blended into an instrument for resource mobilization and allocation. Consequently, the sizable state enterprise sector which the Chinese Communists inherited from the Nationalist government has been, since 1949, consistently enlarged, partly at the expense of the private sector. However, there has been little additional outright nationalization of private trade and industry thus far, although it has been explicitly foreshadowed since the end of October 1953. In this field Chinese Communist tactics have consisted in squeezing out private enterprise through tax pressures, credit rationing, capital levies, establishment of joint state-private enterprises, state competition, and union demands rather than through outright expropriation. In effect, without yet assuming the full responsibilities of state ownership, the regime has reduced the private capitalist to performing a bureaucrat's function.

Under the impact of these policies the government increased its share in industrial production from 44 per cent to 67 per cent between 1949 and 1952.[9] It was officially reported that by October 1952 all the railways, 80 per cent of the heavy and 60 per cent of the light industries, and 60 per cent of the steamships plying in home waters were state operated. At the same time, the government controlled over 90 per cent of all loans and deposits through the People's Bank; and state trading companies were responsible for about 90 per cent of foreign trade, for about half of wholesale trade, and for about 30 per cent of retail trade.[10]

The area of effective government control is actually even greater than indicated by these figures. Through allocations of raw materials and credit, through introduction of "cash and currency control," and through monopoly of trade in key agricultural and industrial commodities the regime placed itself in a position to manipulate directly most of the strategic levers in the economy.[11]

The same general pattern is evident in Chinese Communist land policy which, through a series of intermediate stages, aims at gradual step-by-step expropriation of the Chinese peasant's land. The first stage, land redistribution, was designed to harness land hunger and agrarian unrest into a politically potent weapon and to break the political and economic power of the landlord. While land distribution created a mass of middle and poor peasants, an effort was begun (but not completed by 1952) to supplant the traditional institutions with state-controlled organs: cooperative institutions for moneylending and marketing; mutual-aid teams and producers' cooperatives as the basic production unit; and Communist-dominated peasant associations as the center of local power.

In the strategy and tactics of Chinese Communism land redistribution performed a triple function: it helped to pave the road to power; it helped to extend and consolidate that power at the village level; and it served to transfer the wealth-accumulating function from the landlord to the state. In effect, it provided a vehicle by which the land rent could be appropriated by the state for its own use. Inasmuch as land rent in China was mostly dissipated in consumption, conspicuous and otherwise, in hoarding, and after 1936 also in capital flight, expropriation of this rent furnished a means for raising the level of investment in the economy. The outstanding economic achievement of the regime has certainly been its ability to mobilize and to allocate higher proportions of China's national income to investment and military purposes than ever before.

IV. The Quest for Price Stability

As the regime consolidated its control, it felt ready to launch a comprehensive attack upon fiscal and financial instability. This attack was based upon the following elements:

1. *Balancing the budget.* This involved an initial curtailment, in early 1950, of government expenditure and a reorganization of the tax system based on increased rates of urban taxation. At the same time fiscal management was greatly centralized, many local government functions being transferred to the central government. After the outbreak of the Korean War, government outlays began to increase once more, but most of this rise was covered by regular income or by extraordinary levies and campaigns [12] which served both to raise revenue and to mop up liquid purchasing power.

2. *Restoring confidence in the monetary medium.* In the face of continuing monetary devaluation, the regime decided to guarantee the purchasing power of certain types of transactions. Accordingly, wage and salary payments, bank deposits, some government expenditures, and bond issues were expressed in commodity basket values termed wage, parity deposit, and victory bond units respectively.[13] This action was designed to discourage the flight from money into goods, and to foster the accumulation of savings and bank deposits.

3. *Controlling money and credit.* In accord with the series of stabilization moves of January to April 1950, the People's Bank began to pursue a tight deflationary credit policy. In combination with other anti-inflationary devices the Bank finally succeeded in curbing speculation and black market credit and in controlling the interest rate. Thus monthly interest rates for loans to Shanghai traders rose from 24–30 per cent in June 1949 to a peak of 70–80 per cent in December, and then declined continuously to 18 per cent in April 1950 and to 3 per cent a year later.[14]

4. *Reactivation of exchange and distribution.* The success of the whole stabilization experiment depended upon the government's capacity to mop up liquid purchasing power, its ability to guarantee a supply of consumer necessities to match residual effective demand, and the faith of the public in such a guarantee. The latter condition is

clearly recognized by the regime, as illustrated by the following statement of a Bank of China manager: [15]

> The reserve for the issuance of JMP is not gold, but the supplies under the control of the government in the liberated areas. . . . The reserve is not kept in the vaults of the bank but is being continuously dumped on the market through the government-run trading companies. The duty of these companies is to stabilize the commodity prices, prevent sudden rises or declines, regulate supply and demand, and prevent speculative activities.

However, the state trading mechanism could perform the function assigned to it only if the volume of goods entering distributive channels could be greatly expanded. In turn, such expansion required not only a recovery in agricultural and industrial production but also restoration of the badly disrupted transport network. For this reason, rehabilitation and expansion of transport was one of the regime's high priority targets; and a high proportion of government investment in 1950 and 1951 was devoted to railroad reconstruction. As a result, while in October 1949 less than half of China's total railway trackage was in operation, by mid-1951 all lines were restored and the intensity of their use greatly stepped up. New railroad construction was vigorously pushed also; for instance, the 320-mile Chungking-Chengtu railway, the roadbed for which was prepared by the Nationalist government before the war, was completed in 1952, thus bringing the Szechwan rice basin into closer proximity to East and North China.

During the whole recovery period, 1949–1952, the regime placed great reliance upon indirect controls and market forces as instruments for stabilization, resource mobilization, and resource allocation. Chinese Communist policymakers apparently realized that at the very outset price-fixing would not be practicable, since direct price-control would place tremendous administrative burdens upon the bureaucratic apparatus and would be difficult to enforce. Moreover, as the Nationalist government had been unsuccessful in attempting direct price-control on several occasions during the 1945–1949 period, the device was in such disrepute that an attempt to introduce it would probably have been viewed by the population as a repetition of the past—an impression the Communists tried assiduously to avoid. Indirect price-control based upon state trading as a manipulative device in combination with monetary and fiscal tools was likely to prove more flexible and better suited to China's present stage of economic and bureaucratic development.

On the whole, Communist policies proved rather effective in arresting inflation and gradually instituting price stability. The inflationary spiral was broken in March 1950. However, under the impact of the rather drastic deflationary policies there ensued a temporary crisis marked by bank failures, business bankruptcies, accumulation of unsold inventories in the cities, and large-scale urban unemployment. This trend was reversed with the outbreak of the Korean War, after which wholesale prices rose very rapidly once more, so that by the end of 1950 they approached the March peak. Thus 1950 was a year of violent price fluctuations, during which the regime had only partial control over price formation. This was much less true in 1951, as illustrated by the fact that, although prices of producers' goods increased much more rapidly under the competing pressures of Korean War requirements and of domestic reconstruction, the average price level rose only by about 20 per cent.

By 1952, with virtual price stability attained, open inflation was beginning to be replaced by suppressed inflation—a characteristic of almost all full-employment economies operating within a framework of economic controls. Comparatively high rates of investment and military expenditure became in China, as elsewhere, a constant source of imbalance between the stream of consumer income and the supply of consumer products. Therefore, as in the Soviet Union and the satellites, occasional bond campaigns or other extraordinary levies have been employed to mop up liquid purchasing power. Similarly, in late 1953, the regime was forced to introduce formal rationing at the retail level for the first time, not merely because of an indifferent harvest but because of the pressure of effective money demand.

V. Mobilization and Allocation of Resources

Economic controls were developed during the 1949–1952 period not only to attain fiscal and financial stability but also to step up the rate of resource mobilization. While state participation in industry and trade was growing, changes were taking place in the nature and scope of the government budget, which gradually evolved from a traditional instrument for financing standard government operations into an economic budget of the Soviet type, controlling the contours of the whole economy. In this context one of the functions of government fiscal operations is to keep consumption in check through high taxation and the maintenance of wide state-enterprise profit margins.[16] In particular, price and distribution policy serves as a means for raising the level and rate of forced saving. As the volume of domestic trade expands, state revenues are automatically augmented through commodity taxation levied at the wholesale stage. At the same time, state trading companies are encouraged to use their market power to buy cheap and sell dear. Thus the state appropriates resources through trade in two ways: through the pricing process and through the taxing mechanism.

The growing importance of the budget is clearly illustrated by the data in Table 4. It may also be gauged by the increasing share of the

TABLE 4. CHINESE COMMUNIST GOVERNMENT BUDGETS, 1950–1953 *

(in trillion JMP)

	1950		1951	1952	
	Budget	Actual	Actual	Budget	Actual
Expenditures:					
Military	23.2	28.3	50.6	44.4	42.8
Government administration	12.8	13.1	17.5	22.7	19.3
Economic construction	14.3	17.4	35.1	58.6	73.1
Cultural construction	2.4	7.6	13.4	20.2	22.3
Other	1.4	1.8	2.4	6.8	5.7
Total	54.1	68.2	119.0	152.7	163.2
Revenues:					
Agricultural tax	20.1	19.1	21.7	n.a.	25.6
Industrial and commercial taxes	18.9	29.9	58.5	n.a.	69.0
Other taxes	....	....	1.0	....	1.6
Total taxes	39.0	49.0	81.2	91.7	96.2
Revenue from government enterprises	8.3	8.7	30.5	37.0	46.6
Income from credit and insurance	....	3.3	5.7	4.4	2.5
Total	47.3	61.0	117.4	n.a.	145.3
Deficit	6.8	7.2	1.6	n.a.	17.9
Proceeds of deficit financing †	12.4	8.5	23.3	2.6	20.9
Carry-over	....	....	1.3	23.0	23.0
"Surplus"	5.6	1.3	23.0	n.a.	26.0

* The data in this table are based on Po I-po's "Report on the 1953 State Budget of the People's Republic of China," Supplement to *People's China*, March 16, 1953.

† Listed in Chinese Communist sources as 'other' revenue.

budget in the gross national expenditure, which rose from about 15 per cent in 1950 to roughly 27 per cent in 1952.

The annual budget figures given in Table 4 are not comparable from year to year since they reflect a continuing extension in the scope of government fiscal operations. On the one hand, the government sector has been growing at the expense of the private sector so that more and more new enterprises and functions are brought within the purview of the government budget. On the other hand, the central government has been adopting more and more of the local government functions every year.

If these qualifications are kept in mind, it is evident from the data that government expenditures rose very rapidly between 1950 and 1952, and particularly between 1950 and 1951. Officially stated military expenditures were almost doubled during 1951 in response to increasing Korean War requirements. As the Korean fighting subsided in 1952, increasing emphasis was placed upon modernization of the army, weapons development, and military investment. Actually, the dividing line between military expenditures and investment is rather blurred. For instance, military expenditures include the accumulation of military stockpiles which could legitimately be viewed as an item of investment. On the other hand, investment outlays embrace those for the Second Ministry of Machine Building, which is in charge of arsenal and other types of military construction.

The Korean War undoubtedly imposed a serious drain upon the Chinese mainland economy even though much military hardware was provided by the Soviet Union on lend-lease terms. The war, particularly in its more active fighting stage, diverted scarce industrial and transport resources from 'economic construction,' i.e., from investment. This is illustrated by the fact that between 1951 and 1952, as fighting in Korea slackened off, the proportion of total government expenditure channeled into investment rose from about 30 per cent to 45 per cent, while the actual amount was doubled. Thus the Korean War interfered increasingly with the internal program of reconstruction and development.

Owing to this resource drain and greatly curtailed production, investment may have constituted only about 4 per cent of gross national product in 1950; by 1952 its share rose to approximately 12 per cent. While the exact allocation of these investment resources is known officially only for 1953 and 1954, there is no question that from the very outset industry and transport were accorded the highest priority. Agriculture was kept on a short investment ration, with major reliance placed upon mass applications of seasonally underemployed labor in water conservancy.

Chinese Communist budgets differ so radically in their scope and character from the budgets of the Nationalist government that they are not comparable. First of all, the Communist budgets are based on a much more tightly knit and centralized system of fiscal management in which the scope of local government functions is minimized and local government finance is closely integrated into central government fiscal operations. As a matter of fact, in this system fiscal management provides one of the principal tools for developing a more highly centralized administrative apparatus through which the tentacles of government control reach down to the local levels. Secondly, Chinese Communist budgets include Manchuria, which was excluded from Nationalist accounts after 1931. Finally, current budgets reflect a much greater government participation in the economy.

One of the salient features of the 1950–1953 budgets is the relatively small deficits; [17] apparently they did not exceed 11 per cent of total expenditure during any one year—a reflection of the new regime's much greater fiscal capacity, resulting from its larger and more effective controls and pressure mechanisms. Contrary to earlier Chinese Communist statements, Po I-po's report, on which Table 4 is based, indicates that there have never been any deficits, only surpluses. This extraordinary feat has apparently been accomplished through accounting manipulations. For instance, in Chinese Communist budget practice, proceeds from deficit financing such as bond and note issues, bank overdrafts, and special levies are treated as 'other' revenue. Special campaigns were launched every year: in 1950 there was a bond campaign; in 1951 the drive on 'counterrevolutionaries' netted important sums by way of confiscation; and there was the 'donations' drive for guns and planes for Korea that netted about 5 trillion JMP; in 1952 there was the 5-Anti Movement, which netted a much larger but unknown sum, perhaps over $2 billion. These facts still leave the 1951 and 1952 surpluses unexplained, since it is rather puzzling why there should be such levies if the sums collected are not to be spent. Initially these 'surpluses' may have been unintended to the extent that they reflected higher proceeds from capital and other levies than were anticipated. Since 1952, however, these 'surpluses' seem to be actually budgeted in advance to serve as revolving capital and operating reserve funds for the government apparatus and the state enterprise system.

While government expenditures were rapidly rising between 1950 and 1952, the revenue base was constantly widened. In 1949 the agricultural tax in kind provided the principal source of revenue, but in 1950 it was gradually displaced by industrial and commercial taxes, which grew in importance thereafter. However, it is important to note that by pricing tax grain throughout at its 1950 price, which was below the market price, the budget grossly understates income from agricultural taxation.

Taxation in the rural sector is generally direct, while in the urban sector indirect sales and turnover taxes predominate. Indirect taxes and customs duties have traditionally provided the principal sources of revenue in China. While customs duties are of only minor importance in Communist China, indirect taxes have been constantly gaining, with a gradual approach to the Soviet system of turnover taxation. At the same time, profits of state enterprises have constituted a major and growing source of revenue.

As the scope of the government budget and the area of economic controls spread, the regime increased its capacity to allocate resources and plan their use. During the 1949–1952 period, the Chinese Communist economy operated within a framework of certain general objectives and partial rather than comprehensive and integrated economic plans. Partial plans were mostly confined to specific annual targets for individual industries without a serious effort to interrelate them. In Manchuria, where the regime was longer in power and where a great deal of experience had accumulated under the Japanese, planning was in a much more advanced stage; and this region served as something of a planning laboratory and training ground for the mainland as a whole. It was not surprising, therefore, that Kao Kang (Chairman of the regional government in the Northeast) was made Chairman of the State Planning Commission formed in late 1952 to prepare the Five Year Plan.

During this period credit and price policy served as the principal instruments of planning. Through discriminatory pricing and favorable or unfavorable rates of interest and credit terms, resources were diverted from industries accorded a low priority to lines of production which the state wished to encourage. Cotton provides a good case in point: in order to encourage an extension in cotton acreage, Chinese Communist planners increased the cotton-grain exchange ratio as is shown in the accompanying table.[18]

RATIO OF EXCHANGE FOR 0.5 KG. OF ⅞-IN. COTTON LINT

	1950	1951	1952
		in kg.	
North China millet	4.0	4.5	4.5
Northwest China wheat	3.5	4.0	4.75
Central South China wheat	3.25	4.0	4.25

The general scope and character of planning were considerably broadened in 1952. A more integrated annual plan was formulated at least for the state enterprise and urban sector, and increased reliance was placed upon more direct methods of resource allocation. These measures were designed to prepare the way for longer-range planning of the Five Year Plan type.

VI. CHANGES IN FOREIGN ECONOMIC RELATIONS

China traditionally maintained very close economic relations with Great Britain, the United States, Germany, and Japan. Trade with these countries was based on an exchange of coarse grains, foodstuffs, raw materials of agricultural origin, and minerals for wheat flour, rice, sugar, tobacco, raw cotton, textiles, other manufactured consumer goods, mineral oils, chemicals, and capital goods. In contrast, China's contact with Russia and eastern Europe was of negligible importance.

This pattern has been radically altered since the Communist capture of the mainland. Western enterprise and economic influences have been gradually pushed out while intimate ties have been established with the Soviet Union and the Communist bloc as a whole. On the one hand, this process was accelerated by Free World trade controls which compelled mainland China to divert an increasing share of its trade to the Communist bloc. On the other hand, it may be assumed that, given the 'lean-to-one-side' policy, China's relative trade with the bloc would in any case have expanded to a degree, even in the absence of western trade restrictions. The impact of western trade controls apparently began to be fully felt only in the second half of 1951. While Free World exports to China were at U. S. $314 million in the first half of 1951, they dropped to about $130 million in the second half. The nature of this push and pull in China's trade orientation is illustrated by the data in Table 5.

Several facts emerge from an examination of this table. Foreign trade recovered so rapidly from its abnormally low 1950 level that by 1951 it had more or less attained its prewar peak level. Practically all of this expansion was confined to the Communist bloc, more specifically to the Soviet Union, since trade with eastern Europe was still very small. In 1952 China's trade with the bloc increased even further, most of the expansion being in trade with eastern Europe rather than with the Soviet Union itself, while total trade actually declined somewhat. It is interesting to note that mainland China maintained an export surplus in trade with the Free World; this may have been

TABLE 5. MAINLAND CHINA'S FOREIGN TRADE, 1950–1952 *

(in millions of dollars)

Year	Trade with the Free World			As Per Cent of Total Mainland Trade	Estimated Total Mainland Trade	Estimated Soviet Bloc Trade		
	Ex-ports	Im-ports	Total			U.S.S.R.	Eastern Europe	Total
1950	476	409	885	74	1,200	285	30	315
1951	433	440	873	39	2,240	n.a.	n.a.	1,367
1952	345	257	602	28	2,150	1,148	400	1,548

* Sources: United Nations *World Economic Report, 1951–1952*, New York, April 1953; U. S. Foreign Operations Administration, *World-Wide Enforcement of Strategic Trade Controls*, Mutual Defense Assistance Control, October Third Report to Congress, Washington, D. C., November 1953; Yeh Chi-chuang, "Three Years of China's Foreign Trade," *New China's Economic Achievements, op. cit.,* pp. 237–244; Pei Hsiang-yin, "Sino-Soviet Trade," *People's China,* June 16, 1953. *People's China,* October 16, 1951.

more than counterbalanced by an import surplus with the Communist bloc, financed out of the net earnings in trade with the West and the Soviet loan of U. S. $60 million per annum.

Close economic relations with the Soviet Union involve not only intimate trade ties but also joint stock companies, credits, and technical assistance. Three Sino-Soviet companies were organized: for civil aviation and for the exploitation of oil and non-ferrous mineral resources in Sinkiang. Given their location and scale, these companies do not provide leverage over the Chinese economy as a whole equivalent to that exercised by joint companies in eastern Europe. The character of technical assistance also differs greatly from that suggested by the role of Soviet advisers in eastern Europe. All available evidence tends to indicate that Soviet advisers do not perform management or control functions in the Chinese setting.[19] However, their effective influence appears to be growing, as Chinese Communist planners run into organization, managerial, planning, and technical bottlenecks. For instance, Soviet-type economic policies, particularly in the fields of fiscal and monetary management, gained in importance during 1952 and 1953.

Apart from technical advice, Soviet material assistance, exclusive of shipments of war material to Korea, was on a modest scale during this period, i.e., at a rate of about U. S. $60 million per annum. It may have been less, since it is probable that the ruble costs of technical assistance were charged against the annual proceeds of the loan. On the other hand, by combining the proceeds of the Soviet loan with the net foreign exchange earned in her trade with the West, Communist China could maintain an import surplus with the Soviet Union of about U. S. $100–150 million. Since the bulk of Communist bloc imports, possibly about 75 per cent,[20] consists of capital goods, the Soviet Union in effect helps China to maximize the import of those goods which come within the purview of Free World trade controls. Within this context, Soviet credits, even though small, have played an important role in the rehabilitation of transport and of Manchurian industry; but in this sense Soviet credit has, in effect, made possible the replacement of only some of the equipment dismantled and removed by Moscow in 1945.

The radical shift in mainland China's economic orientation was necessarily accompanied by marked shifts in the commodity composition of foreign trade, particularly in respect to imports. In line with the economic objectives of the new regime, imports of consumer goods were drastically curtailed, while capital goods imports were significantly stepped up. More specifically, imports of food and textiles were largely displaced by machinery and metals, mineral oils, chemicals, and industrial raw materials, particularly rubber and raw cotton. The latter constituted close to one-fifth of total import value in 1950. As domestic raw cotton production increased, however, imports declined. By 1953 the country was self-sufficient in this commodity.

These shifts in the character of import demand have far-reaching implications for the direction of trade. For instance, since Japan's prewar trading position in China was to a large extent based upon exports of cotton textiles, the disappearance of this market inevitably narrows the potential scope of exchange between the two countries. Of course, Communist China would be interested in replacing the textile imports with imports of capital goods; but Japan faces a much more acute marketing problem for textiles than for machinery or industrial equipment; and, like the United Kingdom in recent decades, Japan may require a structural shift from textile to engineering exports in order to meet the changing pattern of world demand.

Changes in the structure of Chinese exports have been much less marked. Communist China continues to base export trade upon foodstuffs, raw materials of agricultural origin, and mineral products. Most important among these are soybeans with other vegetable oils and products, tung oil, hog bristles, and grains. Grains seem to have grown in importance as compared to the prewar period, mainland China having become a net exporter in recent years. There were shipments of 66,000 tons of rice and 450,000 tons of kaoliang to India, as well as substantial amounts of wheat to the Soviet Far East, in 1951.

These net exports are not as surprising as they might appear at first sight. Known net shipments constituted only about 1 per cent of total mainland grain production and not more than 2 per cent of grain entering market channels. Similarly, prewar net imports were a very small proportion of production and marketings, being primarily a function of high costs of inland transport and inefficient domestic distribution. Thus the margin between net grain imports and exports is quite narrow.[21] It still remains to be seen whether Communist China can build up and sustain a substantial net export position in foodstuffs.

In a static sense exports are of comparatively small importance for mainland China's economy. In 1952 they constituted only about 3 per cent of gross national product. But in dynamic terms they are of great economic importance, as illustrated by the fact that the direct foreign trade component in capital formation was close to 20 per cent in 1952. Its indirect importance is much greater than this figure would suggest. Given its industrialization objective and its limited current capabilities for manufacturing complex capital goods, one of the regime's principal tasks is to find ways and means for translating internal savings (largely in the form of agricultural output) into expanding capital goods imports. The pace of industrialization and the rate of economic growth will in large measure depend upon the extent to which this transformation of resources is successfully carried out.

The conditions and terms on which mainland exports can be transformed into capital goods imports will, however, depend not only upon the extent to which the regime can mobilize agricultural surpluses but also upon the terms of trade between China and the Communist bloc. While there is no quantitative information concerning these terms, some of the factors that are likely to affect Sino-Soviet trade relations are quite clear.

In a technical economic sense there is a substantial basis for trade between China and the bloc. This is the case with soybeans, oilseeds and their products, tea, tungsten, tin, and antimony, which have been traditional import products for the Soviet Union. Also, under the impact of the post-Stalin policies, Soviet import demand for livestock products has risen considerably—a development that broadens the scope for Sino-Soviet trade. At the same time, the Soviet Union and the satellites undoubtedly have the capacity to provide China with capital goods and industrial raw materials up to the level that she can afford within the limits of her export proceeds and credits. In this connection, it may be worth noting that the Soviet Union industrial exports to China may have amounted to 1–2 per cent of Soviet industrial output in 1952.

The relative bargaining position of the partners—again in technical economic terms—is evidently unequal. China's demand for Soviet imports is likely to be much more inelastic than the Soviet demand for Chinese products. On the one hand, China's imports are absolutely essential for its industrialization program, while Soviet imports of Chinese products are more or less peripheral for the economy of the Soviet Union. Further, owing to Free World trade controls, China is completely dependent upon the Communist bloc for its imports of capital goods and certain industrial raw materials, while the Soviet Union can obtain livestock products, tea, oilseeds, etc., from other countries in exchange for gold or those raw materials that are in surplus in the Soviet Union; that is, she can obtain these products without exporting capital goods at the expense of Communist bloc development. For all of these reasons, in the Sino-Soviet bilateral trade relationship the Soviet Union is bound to enjoy superior bargaining powers, at least in economic terms.

This Soviet advantage may well be countered by wider considerations of the alliance. In fact, scattered evidence seems to suggest that the Soviets have thus far not fully exploited their bargaining advantage; i.e., prices of goods imported from the Soviet Union seem to correspond roughly to world market prices, and so also with prices paid for Chinese exports.

NOTES FOR CHAPTER 13

1. Edwin W. Pauley, *Report on Japanese Assets in Manchuria to the President of the United States,* July 1946, p. 37.
2. This figure is based on the official index compiled by the Central Committee on Financial and Economic Affairs. See "Economic Development in Mainland China, 1949–53," *Economic Bulletin for Asia and the Far East,* United Nations Economic Commission for Asia and the Far East, Bangkok, November 1953.
3. Li Shu-cheng, "New China's Achievements in Agricultural Production During the Past Three Years," *New China's Economic Achievements, 1949–1952,* Peking, Foreign Language Press, 1952, p. 188.
4. Chen Yun, "The Financial and Food Situation," *ibid.,* pp. 53–54.
5. For coal, official statements admit a shortfall.
6. Power for household use is strictly rationed, particularly in Manchuria.
7. T. H. Shen, *op. cit.,* p. 308.
8. Indices of plan fulfillment were calculated by cross-checking available Chinese Communist data and then comparing this with the official statement of plan-fulfillment. See Appendix 1.
9. Po I-po, "Three Years of Achievement of the People's Republic of China," *New China's Economic Achievements, 1949–1952, op. cit.,* p. 158.

10. Hsueh Mu-chiao, "China's Great Victories on the Economic Front During the Past Three Years," *ibid.,* p. 281.

11. The "cash and currency control" plan placed the People's Bank in the position of a central clearing house for all transactions and a repository of all capital, including current working capital, for the state enterprise system.

12. See budgets in Table 4.

13. The victory bond units, known as 'fen,' are composed of 6 catties of rice (millet in Tientsin), 1.5 catties of flour, 4 feet of white shirting, and 16 catties of coal. The 'fen' is quoted nationally every ten days with the value based on the wholesale prices of these items in Shanghai, Tientsin, Hankow, Sian, Canton, and Chungking; in computing the 'fen,' the commodity basket values in these cities are given the following weights: Shanghai, 45; Tientsin, 20; Hankow, Canton, and Chungking, 10 each; Sian, 5.

Unlike the 'fen,' parity deposit and wage units are separately quoted for all large cities. The exact composition of these varies from city to city, but they all include some grain, staple cloth, vegetable oil, and coal.

14. Chung Kan-en, "The Success of the State Bank's Policy on Interest Rate," *Economic Weekly,* Shanghai, July 3, 1952, as summarized in *Source Materials from Communist China,* compiled by K. C. Chao, Cambridge, Mass., Harvard University, Russian Research Center, October 1952, Vol. 3, p. 62.

15. *Ta Kung Pao* (Impartiality Daily), Shanghai, June 10, 1949.

16. F. D. Holzman, "The Burden of Soviet Taxation," *The American Economic Review,* September 1953, pp. 548–571.

17. Following western fiscal practice, we treated all expenditures not covered by regular revenues as deficits which had to be covered by extrabudgetary levies, bond issues, or bank overdrafts.

18. "Economic Development in Mainland China, 1949–1953," *op. cit.,* p. 22.

19. This was not true prior to 1953, when the Manchurian transport system was under joint Sino-Soviet management.

20. Based on Hsu Hsueh-han, "China's Trade with the European People's Democracies," *People's China,* Peking, September 1, 1953. This figure may include, however, substantial military equipment paid for by Peking.

21. This observation applies of course only to small net imports or exports.

CHAPTER

—— 14 ————————————————————————————————

CONDITIONS AND PROSPECTS

FOR ECONOMIC GROWTH

I. THE CHINESE COMMUNIST MODEL

In general terms, by the end of 1952 mainland China's productive capacity was reactivated and its institutional framework transformed to such an extent that the regime considered the time ripe for launching an ambitious and comprehensive program of economic development. However, the announcement of a Five Year Plan for China was not preceded by a major public debate on issues, methods, and problems of industrialization such as occurred in Russia in the 1920's.[1] It would seem that Chinese Communist thinking and the policy which has emerged are almost completely dominated by the Stalinist model of economic development, with Preobrazhenski's and Bukharin's absent from the scene.

Proceeding on this basis, the regime envisages a development focused on the rapid expansion of producers' goods and defense industries, to be accompanied by a more modest rate of growth in the manufacture of textiles needed for barter with the countryside. Agriculture is to be developed primarily through better organization rather than capital investment; specifically this is to be based upon creation of capital by underemployed labor in mass water conservancy and other labor-intensive projects. Finally, the process of industrialization is to be financed partly through net resource transfers out of agriculture to be assured by collectivization of the peasantry gradually and in such a way as not to disrupt output drastically or damage farm capital. Chinese Communist leaders would like to avoid the costly Soviet one-sweep collectivization experience.

The financing of industrialization through net resource transfers out of agriculture has, of course, been a feature of economic develop-

256

ment in many countries, even though in a much less extreme and deliberate form than in the Soviet case. Perhaps the most notable of these, from a Chinese point of view, is the Japanese experience. Japan's evolution differs from that of the Sino-Soviet model in several respects, particularly in the early stages, when the Japanese placed great emphasis upon agricultural development, which was largely attained through introduction of western technology but most especially through large applications of imported fertilizer.[2] By all indications, Chinese Communist policymakers are not prepared to sacrifice domestic industrial capacity or imports of industrial capital for agricultural requisites, except possibly for some imports of seed and livestock for breeding, which would absorb only a small share of export proceeds. The impact of these improvements is generally much slower and less dramatic than is the case with commercial fertilizer.

In essence, the Chinese Communist model is one which involves industrial development at the expense of agricultural development. Industrialization is accelerated at the outset by virtue of the very fact that, since agriculture is kept on a short investment ration, a larger share of investment resources can be concentrated in industry. This policy, in turn, sets up its own vicious circles: just because agricultural development is sluggish while the demand for farm products grows—owing to an increasing population, urbanization, and exports—the regime is forced to extract a rising proportion of farm output if this demand is to be met. This very process further interferes with agricultural development, so that the screw must be applied even tighter; under such circumstances, increases in farm output are sacrificed for control over current farm output, and strong compulsions are set in force which drive the system toward collectivization.

Thus, given their economic objectives and the nature of their program, the Chinese Communists are caught in a series of dilemmas, of which the agricultural problem is the most fundamental. These dilemmas, and the ways in which they are likely to affect the character and rate of economic growth within the confines of mainland China's economy, will be analyzed below. Before proceeding on this path, it may be well to examine where the Chinese economy stands today in relation to that of Japan, the Soviet Union, and India.

II. Mainland China's Stage of Economic Development on the Eve of the Five Year Plan

Employing figures for 1952, the Chinese Communist economy on the eve of the Five Year Plan can be said to be at a stage of development

TABLE 6. INDICATORS OF COMPARATIVE LEVELS OF DEVELOPMENT

| | | U.S.S.R. | | | |
| | | Approximately 1928 | | Approximately 1950 | |
	Units	Amount	Year	Amount	Year
Gross National Product	Billions of 1952 U. S. Dollars	$ 35.00	1928	$100.00(a)	1952
GNP per head(b)	1952 U. S. Dollars	$240.00	1928	$490.00	1952
Population	Millions	147.00	1926	198.00	1950
Crude birth rate	Per 1,000	43.50(d)	1926	25.00 to 34.00	1950/51
Crude death rate	Per 1,000	19.90(d)	1926	10.00 to 16.00	1950/51
Proportion in agriculture and fishing	Per 1,000	76.50(h)	1926	49.00 to 53.00(i)	1950
Agriculture					
Number of persons dependent on agriculture per acre of cultivated land	Persons per acre	0.20	1926	0.20	1950
Paddy rice yield	Metric quintals per hectare	21.50	1934–38		
Wheat yield	Metric quintals per hectare	7.90	1934–38		
Industry					
Coal	Total in million metric tons	40.10	1929	281.00	1951
	Kilograms per capita	273.00	1929	1,419.00	1951
Pig iron	Total in million metric tons	3.30	1927–28	19.40	1950
	Kilograms per capita	22.00	1927–28	98.00	1950
Crude steel	Total in million metric tons	4.30	1927–28	24.80	1950
	Kilograms per capita	29.00	1927–28	125.00	1950
Finished steel	Total in million metric tons				
	Kilograms per capita				
Generating capacity	Total in thousand kilowatts	1,900.00	1928	16,000.00	1949
of electric power	Kilowatts per capita	0.01	1928	0.08	1949
Cotton spindleage in	Total in thousands	7,465.00	1929	10,000.00	1949
industry	Units per capita	0.05	1929	0.05	1949
Cement	Total in million metric tons	1.90	1928	19.40	1950
	Kilograms per capita	13.00	1928	98.00	1950

* Compiled by Alexander Eckstein.
(a) 1950 GNP was $87 billions, or $440 per head.
(b) To nearest $5.00.
(c) 1938 GNP was $24.6 billions, or $355 per head.
(d) European Russia.
(e) Taeuber and Notestein interpretation (cf. *Population Studies*, I, 1, June 1947, p. 10), not the official statistics.
(f) Official statistics (implying some understatement of both).
(g) Estimated from the official returns by applying the Kingsley Davis figures. Estimates by Kingsley Davis for 1931–41 are 45 per 1,000 birth rate and 31.2 per 1,000 death rate.

roughly comparable to that of Meiji Japan and present day India—but much more underdeveloped than the Soviet economy on the eve of its First Five Year Plan in 1928.

The data in Table 6 show that the Soviet Union embarked upon its drive for industrialization in a much more favorable economic set-

IN MAINLAND CHINA, THE SOVIET UNION, JAPAN, AND INDIA *

Japan				India		China	
Meiji		1930's					
Amount	Year	Amount	Year	Amount	Year	Amount	Year
$ 2.20	1878–82	$ 22.60(c)	1936	$22.00	1950	$30.00	1952
$65.00	1878–82	$325.00	1936	$60.00	1950	$60.00	1952
35.56	1875	69.25(f)	1935	358.00	1950	582.00	1953
39.00(e)	1885	31.20	1931–37	38.00(g)	1949	40.00	1930–35
32.00(e)		17.90	1931–37	24.00(g)	1949	34.00	1930–35
84.80	1872	42.10(k)	1940	68.00(l)	1931	80.00	1952
2.00	1872	1.60	1936–40	0.60	1931	1.90	1953
21.60	1880–84	36.30	1934–38	13.30	1934–38	25.30	1931–37
		18.80	1934–38	6.80	1937–39	10.80	1931–37
0.60	1875	41.80	1936	34.90	1951	53.00	1952
17.00	1875	604.00	1936	97.00	1951	91.00	1952
0.01	1877	2.00	1936	1.90	1951	1.60	1952
0.20	1877	29.00	1936	5.00	1951	2.75	1952
None				1.50	1951	1.20	1952
None				4.00	1951	2.00	1952
None		4.50	1936			0.70	1952
None		66.00	1936			1.20	1952
None		6,777.00	1936	2,409.00	1951	2,850.00	1952
None		0.10	1936	0.01	1951	0.005	1952
8.00	1877	11,823.00	1936	10,144.00	1952	5,000.00	1952
Negligible		0.17	1936	0.03	1952	0.01	1952
Negligible		4.30	1929	3.20	1951	2.30	1952
Negligible		63.00	1929	9.00	1951	4.00	1952

(h) Distribution of the male labor force. The figure is 77.6% for the distribution of the population and 81.8% for the distribution of the total labor force.

(i) Distribution of the male labor force. The figure is 53–57% for the 1950 distribution of the total labor force. It was 53.8% for 1939.

(j) Distribution of the total occupied population, including females. Some estimates place the 1872 percentage at 77.1%.

(k) Distribution of the total occupied population, including females. The 1936 figure for the occupied population excluding women in agriculture is 30.1%.

(l) Distribution of the total population.

ting than confronts the policymakers of Communist China. Low density per unit of cultivated land area, a per capita product four times as high as that of present-day China, large tracts of arable but uncultivated land, and vast and high-quality mineral resources were all factors that facilitated the Soviet take-off. As a result, starting from an aggregate economic and industrial base which in 1928 was not appreciably above that of China today, the Soviet Union found it possible to treble its gross national product in twenty-five years.

Moreover, the Soviet Union launched its program of deliberate industrialization in a much more favorable international setting. The Soviet Union could devote ten to twelve years of undivided effort to building up its industrial and military potential without involving itself in Korea-like interruptions which would drain resources away from internal construction and investment; and, as strategic trade controls were absent from the interwar landscape, the Soviet Union could import capital goods, technology, and know-how from the West without restrictions.

In contrast to the Soviet case, the Japanese experience is much more encouraging from a Chinese Communist point of view. In terms of all major indicators, Meiji Japan was at about the same level as or lagged behind present-day China. Per capita product, degree of population pressure, and birth and death rates were about the same as in China. On the other hand, Japan possessed practically no factory industry and a much poorer mineral resource base. However, Meiji Japan, to an even greater extent than the Soviet Union, launched its take-off in a favorable international climate. The world economy was expanding, the volume of international trade was increasing, and the impediments to trade were minimal as compared to the post-World War II era. In such a setting it was relatively easy for Japan to find foreign markets for its products and thus earn foreign exchange with which to import the technology and wherewithal of economic development. Because of the paucity of Japan's natural resources, foreign trade was absolutely central and vital for Japan's economic growth. Since foreign trade is probably a less critical factor for Chinese economic growth, export marketing difficulties and trade restrictions may slow down but not necessarily frustrate Chinese Communist economic development.

Despite the stage of development in which Meiji Japan found itself, and its poor resource base, gross national product was raised about tenfold in about sixty years, between 1880 and 1940.[3] Were Communist China's economy to grow at about the same rate, its gross national product would attain the 1952 Soviet level around 1980, while the 1952 United States level would be reached around 2010. On a per capita basis, China's output would still lag behind current United States levels. On the other hand, should China grow at the Soviet rate (though this seems most unlikely), current Soviet gross product levels would be attained around 1970, while current United States output would be approached around 1990.

Several references have been made above to the comparative resource endowments of China, the Soviet Union, and Japan. The following data may serve to illustrate these differences: [4]

	Mainland China	Soviet Union	Japan
Coal reserves, millions of metric tons	265,000	1,200,000	16,218
Iron ore reserves, millions of metric tons	2,504	10,900	38

China is particularly well endowed with coal and non-ferrous metals
but is comparatively poor in iron ore and petroleum. However, quantitative resource limitations do not present a serious problem at this
stage; much more immediate and pressing are the questions of accessi-
bility and quality. Many of the deposits are not reached either by
inland water or railroad transport. At the same time, while aggregate coal reserves are abundant, China is quite short of coking coal,
and much of what they have is of inferior quality. Similarly, most
of the known iron ore deposits are low in iron content, the principal
exceptions being the Tayeh mines near Hankow, where one of the
new steel mills is to be located, and the high quality ore of Hainan
island. The latter, owing to its strategically vulnerable location, is
apparently not fully exploited at present.

Since the bulk of the Manchurian ore deposits has an iron content
of less than 40 per cent, they have to be concentrated before they can
be charged into a blast furnace. Moreover, whereas the lean ores are
massive and can be mined by surface and open-cut equipment, rich
ores occur in veins or dykes which require underground mining
methods,[5] which raises investment and current operating costs in the
iron and steel industry.

Probably the two most critical bottlenecks and immediately limiting
factors in mainland China's economic development are power and
transport. While current generating capacity exceeds that of the
Soviet Union in 1928, this capacity is taxed to the limit. On the
other hand, transport is an even more critical factor than it was in
the Soviet Union on the eve of the First Five Year Plan, since the
density of the Soviet rail network was almost twice as great as that
of China today, a factor of particular importance because the Chinese
rural economy is much less commercialized and more fragmented
than was Russia's in 1928. Given China's geographic configuration,
she is just as dependent as Russia upon inland railroad transport,
while Japan, with her comparatively small inland distances, could rely
to a much greater extent upon more economical coastal shipping.

The Chinese Communists have recognized the problem of transport, and have devoted a great deal of attention to railroad rehabilitation and development; and they plan to continue this effort in the future. However, while transport is an absolutely essential prerequisite of economic growth in the long run, its development draws away resources from industrial investment, despite the lavish substitution of labor for capital, and thus slows down the process of industrial expansion in the short run. The Soviets under Stalin, recognizing this fact, did not do much more than replace and maintain the railroad plant they inherited. Obviously the Chinese cannot afford to do this. The Chinese dilemma is aggravated by the fact that the new regime seems to have embarked upon an extensive rather than intensive type of railroad development; that is, primary emphasis is placed upon the construction of a railroad line that will eventually run from Chungking to Tihua in Sinkiang and then connect up with the Trans-Siberian, thus linking West China simultaneously with the Soviet Union and with the rest of China. Since most of this railroad will run through underdeveloped dead space which can have only long-run economic significance,[6] it would have been more logical from a purely developmental point of view to extend the network in South China and build feeder lines in other regions of population concentration so as to tap more effectively agricultural resources and output.

This brief review of some of the salient factors affecting the take-off in China as compared to the Soviet Union and Japan would not be complete without a consideration of China's population dynamics. The data in Table 6 show that population pressure in China is close to the level of that in Meiji Japan, and exceeds that of modern Japan, India, and the Soviet Union. Mainland China's preponderantly rural population is pressed down close to the bare margin of subsistence with very little room left for saving and capital formation.

However, on the basis of the available evidence, most of it poor and incomplete, rates of natural increase have been low in China. Birth, death, and infant mortality rates are among the highest in the world.[7] They exhibit characteristics typical of countries in which population movements are close to the biological limit and in which the Malthusian checks are still more or less fully operative. This fact is also illustrated by the very large annual fluctuations in the rates in China in response to famines, floods, epidemics, and civil war.

The character of the Chinese population dynamics is bound to be changed by the impact of Communist power. Under the Communist regime all of mainland China has been administratively unified and put under effective control, probably for the first time in decades. The injection of a centralized authority with its tentacles of control extending down to the village level, and the maintenance of political stability as a prerequisite for survival of the regime, are likely to have a direct or indirect effect upon the death rate. While the termination of civil conflict must have had the most immediate effect upon the death rate, there are other forces at work which tend to reinforce the downward pressures. Administrative unity and the rehabilitation of transport have combined to extend the scope of food distribution so that local famines can be kept within narrower bounds than heretofore. Moreover, the Chinese Communist regime has devoted a great deal of attention to flood control, which, to the extent that it proves successful, is likely to contribute to famine control. Such factors may be counterbalanced to some extent by rising rates of extraction from agriculture and by the increase in tuberculosis rates caused by harder work, long meetings, and long hours for the urban labor force.

The very character of the regime, its goals, and its commitments to effective and comprehensive control of all segments of the population, to military prowess, and to industrialization compel it to institute a public health program of some dimensions. Under conditions such as prevail in China even rudimentary and inexpensive measures can go far in checking epidemics and disease. The regime embarked promptly on a series of nationwide campaigns for cleanliness and disease control, while the anti-American bacterial-warfare hoax has been effectively utilized to propagate domestic bacteria controls. People were induced to enter fly-catching competitions, with prizes being awarded to those bringing in the largest number of flies.

It is most probable that there has already been some decline in the death rate, and that, barring a civil conflict or external ventures of major proportions, the reduction in death rates is likely to be accelerated. This conclusion is reinforced by the experience of other countries: the death rate is estimated to have declined by about 30 per cent in India between 1920 and 1940; by 20 per cent in Egypt between 1940 and 1949; by 26 per cent in Mexico between 1940 and 1950; and by 45 per cent in Ceylon between 1939 and 1951.[8]

At the same time, birth rates in all of these countries remained approximately stationary at a very high level. One may expect the same general relationship to prevail, at least for the decade ahead, in China also, since the complex of cultural, social, and economic forces which influence the birth rates are much more resistant to change.

Proceeding on the basis of the considerations outlined above, one may expect the death rate to decline appreciably within a decade, possibly yielding a rate of natural increase of about 1.0 to 1.5 per cent a year.[9] This rate would still be substantially below the Soviet rate of the 1920's and would roughly correspond to current Indian rates.

III. The Role of Agriculture in the Economic Development of Mainland China

Chinese agriculture, and for that matter agriculture in most underdeveloped areas, is called upon to foster the process of economic growth in three principal ways: to serve as a reservoir for an expanding urban labor force; to provide for food consumption standards (urban and rural) at levels designed to foster an increasing productivity of labor and the maintenance of political stability; and to furnish a source of foreign exchange and needed imports.

The first function can be discharged without too much difficulty under China mainland conditions. At this juncture there is considerable underemployment in both the rural and urban sectors. Urban unemployment and underemployment have been aggravated in recent years by what the Chinese Communist press refers to as 'blind migration to the cities.' While the factors and forces which induce this migration are somewhat obscure, particularly since government policy frowns upon it, it is more than probable that the movement is primarily propelled by push rather than pull; that is, it may indicate a deterioration in rural economic conditions under the impact of government extractions to the point where at least some elements of the rural population seek escape in the cities. It may also be influenced by a general sense that the regime is concentrating its constructive efforts in the cities and that prospects there are more promising.

Urban unemployment and underemployment, however, may prove to be a transitory condition. Should industrialization proceed at the rates projected in our model,[10] the rising demand for labor could be met without reducing the size of the rural labor force. In fact, according to Table 9 the rural labor surplus would actually be augmented unless large tracts of new land are settled and brought under cultivation.

Unlike the problem of labor, the capacity of agriculture to expand output so as to meet a growing demand for its products is one of the most critical questions facing the regime. With this in mind, some of the salient factors affecting the demand for and supply of farm products will be explored below.

A. *Demand*

Proceeding from the assumptions underlying our model in Table 9 and assuming that the pattern of consumer expenditure will remain roughly constant during the coming decade—i.e., that the same proportion of the average household budget will be spent on food in 1962 as in 1952—just to meet domestic consumption requirements, food production in Communist China would have to increase by 10 per cent in 1957 and by 20 per cent in 1962.

Agriculture, however, will not only have to provide for domestic requirements but also for exports. Before the war about 70 to 80 per cent of mainland exports consisted of farm products of all kinds.[11] At the same time, the mainland was a net importer of rice and wheat, and a net exporter of coarse grains. This situation has changed since the Communist conquest; while agricultural exports have been maintained at roughly the prewar level, food imports have ceased, and a small net surplus has been generated. In 1952, for instance, possibly one million tons of grain, mostly coarse grain, were exported, which constituted less than 10 per cent of total exports, and only about 1 per cent of total mainland grain production.

From the model in Table 9 it is possible to calculate certain hypothetical levels of import requirements for the last year of the current Five Year Plan, 1957, and for 1962. These computations would tend to indicate that, to sustain the projected rate of industrial and aggregate growth, total imports would have to rise to about U. S. $1.6 billion in 1957 (1952 imports were roughly U. S. $1 billion); and to about U. S. $2.5 billion by 1962.

These estimates are based on the following assumptions:

1. That about 50 per cent of total gross investment will be in industry and transport. The 1953 budget actually allocated about 60 per cent of the investment funds to these purposes.

2. That 25 per cent of this industrial and transport investment will be in electric motors, generators, transformers, machine tools, and complex equipment of varying kinds which cannot be manufactured in China and must be imported. This percentage is based on Leontief coefficients with some qualitative adjustments for Chinese conditions.

3. That, *pari passu* with increases in industrial production, raw material import requirements will rise.

On the basis of these assumptions capital goods and raw material imports alone would have to be about U. S. $1.35 billion in 1957, and

$2.26 billion in 1962. To this total must be added imports of military equipment and some consumer goods. However, since there should be some raw material savings due to expanding domestic production, and since 25 per cent as the import component of capital formation may be too high, a total import estimate of U. S. $1.6 billion and $2.5 billion respectively may not be unreasonable.

Obviously a large share of these imports will have to be paid for with agricultural exports of all kinds. It is most unlikely that even the increased production of minerals such as coal, iron ore, tungsten, molybdenum, antimony, and others envisaged in Chinese Communist plans would be sufficient not only to maintain but raise the proportion of non-farm exports. Thus, assuming that the ratio of agricultural and non-agricultural exports remains constant, shipments of farm products of all kinds sent abroad would have to rise from about U. S. $700 million in 1952 to $1,120 million in 1957 and $1,750 million in 1962; that is, an increase of 60 per cent and 140 per cent, respectively, for the two years. Actually, this may be reduced somewhat by Soviet economic assistance; assuming such aid to be equivalent to about U. S. $100 million, farm exports may be projected, under these formal assumptions, as U. S. $1,050 million and $1,680 million, respectively.

The share of cereals in this agricultural export total will depend upon the success attained by the government in increasing the output and collection of grain and upon the availability of other farm products. On the basis of present indications, however, cereals are not likely to play a major role in the export trade. The burden will have to be borne by sectors of Chinese agriculture producing products other than the grains which constitute the bulk of the food supply at home.

In order to meet growing export requirements and to keep pace with rising consumer demand imposed by population growth and urbanization, according to the model in Table 9, the aggregate net product of agriculture would have to be raised from an estimated U. S. $12 billion in 1952 to about $13.5 billion in 1957 and $15.2 billion in 1962. This would mean an increase of approximately 13 per cent and 28 per cent, respectively.

B. *Supply Prospects*

The total cultivated area of mainland China may be estimated as 240–250 million acres,[12] which in 1952 yielded an estimated net product of about U. S. $12 billion or U. S. $48 per acre. This yield is attained with very small inputs of capital and a tremendous expenditure of labor. In this intensive, at times almost garden-type, agriculture the Chinese peasant has shown admirable ingenuity in maintaining the fertility of the soil, accomplishing this without a system of crop rotation and, in the south, on land which has produced two rice harvests for centuries.[13] Using these age-old practices, he obtains much higher rice and wheat yields than the Indian peasant and, to some extent, even the farmer of Meiji Japan. However, he has probably pushed these practices to the limit, so that further increases in yields will have to depend upon the introduction of modern farm technology.

In the following pages an attempt will be made to explore briefly the technical possibilities for increasing farm output, both through the extension of the cultivated area and through increases in per acre productivity, and some of the economic and institutional obstacles which may impede or limit the realization of these possibilities.

The most promising areas for new land settlement are found in Northern Manchuria, where, according to varying estimates, 20–30 million acres may be brought under cultivation. This is a dry-farming steppe-like region close to the northern limits of the wheat belt. Methods of cultivation would have to be extensive, and unit yields may be expected to be comparatively low; at the same time, owing to the rigors of climate, large annual fluctuations in output may be anticipated. The resource costs of reclaiming this land are probably fairly high, particularly if one considers that all external economies—roads, housing, schools, structures for the state apparatus and the party, electric power and other facilities—would need to be newly constructed. Therefore, it may be considered most unlikely that new land settlement on such a large scale is likely to be undertaken within the next five or ten years—although the Communist regime has already reclaimed some land in that area and probably will continue to do so on a modest scale. From the regime's point of view, this area provides an opportunity both for expanding agricultural output and for establishing state and collective farms in a setting where institutional resistances are minimal.[14]

There are also some opportunities for increasing the cultivated land area in a few of the old settled regions of China. For instance, it has been estimated that the wheat acreage in Northern and Central China can be increased by close to 10 million acres, while cotton acreage may be extended in the Yellow and Huai River valleys.[15] Provided that water conservancy projects currently in progress actually lead to improved flood control in the future, acreage extensions in such areas could probably be accomplished more easily and at much lower cost than those in Manchuria.

Buck's sample surveys show that almost 25 million acres of farm land are occupied by graves, ancestral shrines, etc., and that an unknown but considerable area is taken up by uncultivated strips separating the small land fragments belonging to different farmers. The institutional obstacles to bringing this land under cultivation are enormous. It is most doubtful that it could be accomplished without far-reaching collectivization. However, should the Chinese Communists seriously pursue their objective of 800,000 producers' cooperatives by 1957, they will have made considerable progress in consolidating farm holdings and eliminating the uncultivated strips.

On the basis of this brief survey, and assuming that the regime will undertake land development only where this can be accomplished with inputs of underemployed labor and relatively little capital, we may conclude that possibly about 15 million acres of currently uncultivated land may be brought under the plow within the next five to ten years. This would mean roughly a 6 per cent increase in the land cropped.

Judging by the Japanese experience, and taking account of the conditions just analyzed, one finds that if farm production is to be increased, major reliance will have to be placed upon raising unit yields. It may be interesting to note in this connection that in Japan average rice yields increased by about 20 per cent in the decade between 1880 and 1890. Similarly, the combined unit yield of six major crops rose by about 50 per cent between 1880 and 1920.[16] For the most part this was accomplished through increasing applications of commercial fertilizer. By 1936, 3.4 million tons of chemical fertilizer were applied in Japan on a crop area about one-sixteenth that of mainland China, as compared to only about 200,000 tons applied in the latter.[17]

Before the war the Chinese National Agricultural Research Bureau conducted experiments which indicated that, in order to raise unit crop yields by about 25 per cent, applications of 6,500,000 tons of ammonium sulphate, 3,800,000 tons of calcium superphosphate, and 300,000 tons of potassium sulphate per annum would be required. As of 1943–1944, the ammonium sulphate capacity of the mainland was about 320,000 tons, practically all of it concentrated in Manchuria. Most of this was exported to Japan before the war, but is now retained in China, so that, according to official Communist sources, about 350,000 tons were consumed in 1952. However, while this represents an increase over prewar consumption, it still represents very small applications indeed.

Since domestic capacity is so small, practically all of the required fertilizer would have to be imported, which means that, if the experimental increases in yield are to be attained, China would have to spend about U. S. $800 million on imports of ammonium sulphate alone (in 1952 prices); that is, about three-fourths of her total 1952 import value, an outlay obviously beyond the realm of reasonable expectations for a long time to come, and, more particularly, a line of policy at cross-purposes with the heavy industry emphasis of the Five Year Plan. Likewise, expansion of domestic productive facilities to anything approaching required levels seems most improbable within 5 to 10 years in view of high initial capital costs and high electric power requirements in current operations. Thus, raising chemical fertilizer applications to levels where they would significantly affect unit yields not only would be very expensive but also would force Chinese Communist policymakers to sacrifice many of their other current industrial objectives.

However, there are other possible ways of increasing unit yields in agriculture, even though they are likely to produce results more slowly, the most notable being improved water conservancy; that is, better flood control, extension of the irrigated area, and better use of water for irrigation. This is a field to which the Communists are devoting most attention, particularly since it can be largely effected through mass applications of labor underemployed in agriculture. Their efforts will undoubtedly have some effect on agricultural output within the next 5 or 10 years. In 1949, a particularly bad year, about 20 million acres were flooded; and in 1951, which can be considered a rather favorable harvest year, about 4 million acres were ravaged by floods.[18] As was indicated earlier, floods and droughts have been the major causes of famine throughout Chinese history.

Additional improvements could be expected from other comparatively capital-cheap measures such as better seed selection, introduction of new strains and varieties, plant and animal disease and pest control, grassland and forage crop improvements in the upland areas, and afforestation. Some of these measures are of a somewhat long-term character; and all require the organization of a capable and efficient network of farm extension. The Chinese Communists are attempting all of them to some extent—under the serious handicap of an acute shortage of technically qualified cadres.

Combining the possibilities of expanding acreage and raising yields within the technical and economic limitations discussed above, but excluding for a moment the possible effects of state grain collection and collectivization, it would seem most unlikely that farm output in

China could be raised by more than 10 per cent within five years and by a maximum of 20 per cent in a decade. This would mean that, in terms of purely technical considerations and within the context of current rates of agricultural investment, increases in output would fall somewhat short of the rising requirements posed by population growth, urbanization, and exports. However, there are other considerations than technical and economic factors to be reckoned with. Agricultural development will also revolve to a large extent upon government price, marketing, and land policies, and the Chinese peasant's reactions to these policies. Official Chinese Communist policy is openly and unequivocally based upon collectivization as a definite goal which is to be attained gradually and without either the loss of output which accompanied the Soviet experience or the stagnation which has accompanied the eastern European experience. To this end the regime has evolved a series of transitional forms of farm organization, each involving a more advanced form of 'cooperation.' A mutual-aid team, the most rudimentary type of agricultural cooperative, is essentially based on a more or less temporary pooling or exchange of labor with the individual farm operator retaining at least theoretical control over his production, consumption, and sales (after taxes). However, usually at least one member of the mutual-aid team is a Communist cadre whose function is to show the peasants the advantages of more advanced forms of cooperation. This 'education' is combined with economic incentives and pressures so as to induce the peasants to form producers' cooperatives, which are collectives in fact if not in name. The incentives seem to be both positive and negative: it is not only made attractive to come into, but also costly to stay out of, the cooperative.

The cooperatives involve the pooling of both labor and tools; and they call for joint cultivation and planning of production, with distribution of returns based on a complicated system of weights for labor and land input, with high premiums on the former and low premiums on the latter. Yet in the producers' cooperatives the peasant theoretically retains his individual right of ownership of land and his right to withdraw at any time. In the next stage, the collective, even these theoretical rights are abolished.[19]

In effect, the Chinese Communist strategy of collectivization bears a strong family resemblance to the methods tried and used in the east European satellites. The Chinese have, however, contributed to the 'storehouse of this strategy' by using as their point of departure the temporary or seasonal mutual-aid team, a form rooted in Chinese tradition but not generally applied in eastern Europe.

In appraising the possibilities for collectivization it should be noted that the Chinese system of farming *per se* does not present any insurmountable or inherent obstacles. Unquestionably rice culture presents very serious barriers to mechanization; but collectivization is perfectly feasible without mechanization. Under conditions where there are still large pools of unemployed and underemployed, as in China, the principal function of collectivization is to give the state more direct access to the farm produce. It was coupled with mechanization in the Soviet Union only because industrialization proceeded so rapidly that the demand for urban labor could not be met without introduction of labor-saving technology in agriculture. In China the barriers to collectivization are not primarily technical but, rather, cultural and institutional.

By 1953 close to half of the peasant households were organized in mutual-aid teams, and about 273,000 households had been organized into 14,000 producers' cooperatives. The regime plans to encompass 20 per cent of all farm households in such cooperatives by 1957.[20]

In the fall of 1953 the stepped-up drive towards collectivization was combined with a complete reorganization in the system of grain collections and the introduction of rationing.[21] The new system provides for compulsory deliveries, over and above the tax in kind, of grain to the state at fixed prices. Thus it is modeled after the east European system of collections, a system that has plagued the satellites since its inception. Generally, the growing similarities between Chinese and satellite economic policies are striking. It seems that in the early days of their rule, when their principal task consisted of organizing the state apparatus and the economy, the Chinese Communists drew on their own past experience, instituting policies essentially of their own making; and that, as they gradually entered into the development and industrialization phase of their program and faced problems which were unfamiliar, they turned to the Soviets for technical assistance in planning and administration.

The question is: What will be the impact of these collectivization and collection measures upon the structure of incentives in the countryside, both in and out of the collectives or producers' cooperatives? Will the satellite experience repeat itself, where such serious disincentives were set in motion that, despite considerable investments in agriculture, farm output still lags below prewar levels? [22]

One may also ask whether this problem has any relevance at all in the Chinese cultural setting. Judging by past experience, this last question can be answered in the affirmative: Chinese peasants seem definitely responsive to positive price and income inducements, as demonstrated, for instance, by the effectiveness of Chinese Communist policy measures like the raising of the cotton-grain ratio as a means of expanding cotton production. What about disincentives? In this respect the situation may be much more complex.

For agriculture in the process of gradual and 'peaceful' collectivization one might distinguish three effects, which may be termed the expectations effect, the tensions effect, and the disruption effect. The very fact of vigorous collectivization propaganda, pressure, and targets for organization of producer cooperatives is likely to set in motion a chain of expectations which will tend to discourage the peasant from making long-term improvements on his farm. Similarly, discriminatory measures directed against 'rich peasants' may actually induce the comparatively more capable and prosperous farming elements to curb their output and incomes so as to avoid being placed in this undesirable category. At the same time, the drive toward collectivization, compulsory grain deliveries, high tax rates, and a constant harassment of the 'rich peasants' is almost certainly bound to lead to a state of more or less permanent tension in the countryside. In turn, this state of tension may seriously inhibit that cooperation between farmers and technical cadres (government extension agents) which would be required to introduce better practices and modern technology. Finally, the very process of collectivization cannot help but entail at least some measure of disruption, the actual degree depending upon the manner and the speed of execution; if it is carried out quite slowly, the disruptive effects may be minimal and transitory.

Thus the cumulative impact of these three effects upon agricultural production may be considered as negative in the sense that they all would tend to discourage the farmer from adopting measures that might enable him to raise his output. The disruptive effect could easily lead to an actual decline in production.

On the other hand, high rates of net resource transfer out of agriculture may, under certain conditions, have just the opposite effect. A Chinese peasant who lives close to the margin of subsistence will tend to bend every effort to produce enough to meet his own needs and those of his family. In these terms, onerous extractions by the state may actually force him to increase output to the extent that it is possible for him to do so within the means at his disposal so as to satisfy his own demands as well as those of the state.

On balance, this analysis indicates that current and prospective agricultural policies in Communist China may tend to undercut the very measures which would make it possible to raise farm output. Therefore, unless these policies are reversed or relaxed, it is unlikely that agricultural production could be raised by the 10 to 20 per cent projected above on the basis of purely technical and economic considerations. If output lags, then the rising requirements imposed by growth of population, urbanization, and exports could not all be met simultaneously, in which case, given the over-all character and objectives of Chinese Communist policy, the regime may be expected to bend every effort to transfer the principal burden of this shortfall to the countryside.

The relationships emerging from this analysis are summarized in tabular form.

RELATION BETWEEN DEMAND FOR FARM PRODUCTS AND
AGRICULTURAL OUTPUT

(in millions of U. S. dollars at 1952 prices)

	1952	1957	1962
Demand for farm products:			
Domestic	11,300	12,430	13,560
Export	700	1,050	1,680
	12,000	13,480	15,240
Agricultural output:			
Case 1: Farm production attains levels postulated on the bases of technical possibilities and current rates of agricultural investment	12,000	13,200	14,400
Case 2: Farm production is stationary	12,000	12,000	12,000
Deficit:			
Case 1		280	40
Case 2		1,480	3,240

Under Soviet or Soviet-type institutional conditions, a lag in agricultural development need not present insurmountable barriers to industrialization and economic growth. For instance, at the height of the collectivization drive in 1930 and 1931, when farmers were slaughtering their cattle and agricultural production was seriously disrupted, the Soviet Union dumped about 5 million tons of grain on the world market. Thus, at a time when grain production was abnormally low, exports from the Soviet Union were higher than during any other interwar year. With a will and capacity to enforce a high rate of extraction upon the countryside, the Soviets utilized these grain exports to fulfill a very important function at a critical juncture in its industrialization program; they enabled the Soviet Union to increase its imports of capital goods for the First Five Year Plan. To be sure, this level of exports could not be maintained indefinitely in the face of stagnating or declining production without critically straining the political stability of the regime.

IV. The Five Year Plan

It is a curious fact that despite the official announcement of a Five Year Plan in 1953 the plan itself has not been published thus far. The launching of the plan was followed only by the publication of annual targets for the first year, i.e., 1953,[23] and by the definition of certain general goals in an article in *Pravda* published in Moscow on September 28, 1953.

Actually, it is rather doubtful that China's mainland economy is yet operating within the framework of a comprehensive and total economic plan of the Soviet type. It is more likely that annual targets are being fixed in terms of a broad set of five-year objectives, but without any attempt at detailed planning. Thus these plans may be viewed—to use Stalin's terminology—as "prognosis, guess-plans which bind nobody," [24] rather than plans based on a system of balanced estimates or definite interindustry relationships.

Within this context one must view planning in Communist China as evolving gradually from a series of loosely coordinated specific goals into a national plan, a process paralleled by a gradual shift from primary reliance upon indirect controls to increasingly direct controls. In China, with only a partially monetized rural sector, and with an underdeveloped bureaucratic and economic control apparatus, the task of planning resource use and resource allocation is difficult and complicated; and so, as the scope of Communist planning is widened and deepened, technical and administrative bottlenecks are becoming more serious—bottlenecks which Soviet advisers are called upon to resolve.

Viewed in these terms, 1953 may be considered an experimental and preparatory year. For instance, production targets were revised three times during the year; first, they were sharply curtailed, but toward the end of the year many of the cuts were partially restored.[25] One gets the general impression of a considerable measure of groping, uncertainty, and confusion during this first planning year, perhaps in part because of inadequate organization and lack of planning experience and skills, but most directly the result of a failure to come to an economic aid agreement with the Soviet Union until the middle of the year. Once the regime knew what it could expect from the Soviet Union, it apparently felt ready to embark upon a new phase of 'austerity' and 'bitter struggle'—marked by a general acceleration in the assumption of direct responsibility by the state and in collectivization within the framework of the new 'General Line of the state.' [26] In the course of the new drive the rate of resource mobilization is being stepped up, as illustrated by the new compulsory grain delivery scheme and the launching of another bond drive.[27]

TABLE 7. CHINESE COMMUNIST GOVERNMENT BUDGETS: 1953–1954 *

(in trillion JMP)

	1953 Budget	1953 Actual	1954 Budget
Expenditures:			
Military	52.3 ⎱		52.7
Government administration	23.8 ⎰ 95.9		46.9
Other	3.6 ⎰		
Economic construction:	103.5	86.0	113.2
Industrial enterprises under state budget:	47.6	42.9	54.1
Heavy industry			42.4
Light industry			11.7
Agriculture, forestry, and water conserv-			
ancy	11.8	11.3	11.9
Trade	4.4	9.9	12.8
Transport	14.8	12.4	17.6
Other	24.8	9.4	16.7
Cultural construction	34.8	32.0	36.7
Total	218.0	213.9	249.5
Revenues:			
Agricultural tax in kind	25.7 †	25.7 †	25.7 †
Taxes from industry and trade	87.5	92.5	104.4
Receipts from government enterprises	70.0	75.4	83.3
Other	11.9	6.4	4.6
Total	195.1	200.0	218.1
Deficit	22.9	13.8	31.4
Proceeds from special levies, bond issues, note issues, and other types of deficit financing	12.4	30.7	13.8
Carry-over	26.0	26.0	42.8
Cash balance	15.5	42.8	25.2

* Source: Teng Hsiao-ping, Minister of Finance, "Report on the 1954 State Budget at the Thirty-first Meeting of the Central People's Government Council," June 16, 17, 1954, *New China News Agency*, Supplement No. 204, London, June 24, 1954.

† Since the price of tax grain is not varied from year to year, the constancy of agricultural tax revenue indicates that the quantity levied remains unchanged. The differential between the price of tax grain and the market price is pocketed by the state trading companies and thus appears under 'receipts from government enterprises.'

Inadequate planning and failure to attain overambitious goals is also reflected in the government expenditure pattern as shown in Table 7. Thus, total 1953 outlay was somewhat lower than budgeted, and, although investment fell almost 20 per cent short of the goal, military expenditures substantially exceeded budgeted amounts.

After a series of protracted negotiations that lasted for about eight months, a Sino-Soviet economic aid agreement was finally announced in September 1953. The announcements refer only to 141 'enterprises,' 50 of which were already under way, that are to be rehabilitated or newly constructed with Soviet aid. The bulk of these 'enterprises' is in the fields of electric power generation, mining, chemicals, and producers' goods industries, particularly metals and engineering; however, they also include some fertilizer and textile plants.[28]

Information on the total value of Soviet aid is withheld, which is particularly strange in view of the fact that no secret was made of Soviet and Communist Chinese aid to North Korea or of the 1950 Sino-Soviet aid agreement, when the U. S. $300 million granted to China over a five-year period was hailed as an act of great generosity. These circumstances combined with the protracted nature of the negotiations would tend to suggest that the level of aid projected may not be very high.

There have been unconfirmed reports that the agreement provides for a 10-year aid program totaling U. S. $1 billion.[29] According to this version the agreement is retroactive to 1950 and thus includes the 300 million dollars originally granted. If this is correct, then the annual level of aid for the 1954–1959 period can be estimated as U. S. $117 million, i.e., an amount which, while representing close to a doubling of the 1950–1953 rate of aid, is still very modest measured by United States standards or by China's requirements.

According to the *Pravda* article referred to above, part of this Soviet aid will be used to achieve the production targets given in Table 8.

Should these targets be met, mainland China's crude steel capacity would exceed the current output of Canada, Belgium, and the other small countries of Europe but would still lag considerably behind the levels attained in Japan during the 1930's. At the same time, the projected levels of steel output would be roughly equivalent to those of the Soviet Union in 1928.[30]

On the basis of United States and Latin American investment costs, to expand mainland China's crude and finished steel output to the levels planned would call for an aggregate investment of about U. S. $600 to $900 million, depending upon the size of the newly built mills.[31] Actual costs in China would, of course, differ from these;

TABLE 8. SELECTED INDUSTRIAL PRODUCTION TARGETS FOR
COMMUNIST CHINA *

Product	Index 1952 = 100	Output		
		Units	1952	Target Date †
Crude steel	400	thousand MT	1,215	4,860
Rolled steel	250	thousand MT	740	1,850
Coal	160	thousand MT	53,000	84,800
Electric power	200	million kw	5,700	11,400
Mining equipment	200	n.a.	n.a.	n.a.
Metal-cutting machinery	350	n.a.	n.a.	n.a.

* Source: *Pravda*, September 28, 1953.
† No exact date is given, but it refers either to the last year of the Plan, 1957, or to when the current aid agreement expires, i.e., 1959.

construction labor costs would be lower in China than in the United States, but this may be counterbalanced to some extent by lower productivity.

A similar calculus for electric power plants would indicate that to expand generating capacity up to the planned levels would involve a total investment of about U. S. $340 million, basing our estimate on a United States investment cost per KW of installed thermal capacity of U. S. $120.[32] It should clearly be borne in mind that all of these estimates can represent no more than the crudest of approximations to the actual investment costs in China—even more true in the case of power than steel, since the former does not take account of the vastly different investment cost structure in hydroelectric power construction.

Thus the total capital cost of new steel mill and power plant production may be estimated as about one billion U. S. dollars. According to the stated plans, these projects are to be completed before 1959, in which case they would absorb about 10 per cent of the total industrial investment resources projected in Table 9 for 1953–1958. It may be assumed that about one-third of this total investment would have to be imported from the Soviet Union,[33] which would mean that about half of the estimated Soviet economic aid for this period would be channeled into expansion of power and steel production.

On the basis of these calculations and assumptions this rate of growth would not seem to lie beyond the resource capabilities of the Chinese Communist economy.

The only specific Five Year production target disclosed by official Chinese Communist sources is that which calls for a 30 per cent increase in annual grain output between 1953 and 1957. Unlike the industrial goals analyzed above, this target appears to be quite unrealistic, particularly if it is appraised against the background of agricultural investment, marketing, and land policies discussed in Section III above. A 30 per cent increase in crop production over a huge land area such as mainland China, where the opportunities for bringing new areas under cultivation are very narrowly circumscribed, and where the possibilities for raising fertilizer consumption are also quite limited, would be most extraordinary indeed. As was indicated in Section III, it is most unlikely that, given favorable farmer incentive conditions, crop production could be raised by more than 10 per cent within five years; and, in the face of current and prospective agricultural policies, the disincentives may become strong enough to block or seriously impede any increase in farm output.

V. Prospects for Economic Growth

Regardless of whether a detailed Five Year Plan is in operation or not, there is every indication of a determined, relentless, and massive effort to pursue a program of industrial expansion. The rapid rate of recovery, the restructuring of the institutional framework, possession of an industrial base in Manchuria, the termination of hostilities in Korea, and, above all, the application of political and social power to the mobilization of resources in the hands of the state have enabled the regime to raise the rate and level of investment considerably above that of the past. At the same time, the regime is mobilizing not only capital but technique and entrepreneurship as well. In essence, the Chinese economy, after being more or less stationary for centuries, with only erratic and partial spurts of growth in recent decades, seems to be entering, for better or for worse, a self-sustaining growth process.

Barring another world war or a major agricultural crisis in China, the long-run question before us is not whether the Chinese Communist economy will grow at all, but whether the rate of growth will be sufficiently rapid so that forces of the industrial revolution will be in a position to defeat the Malthusian counterrevolution. Given the previously discussed conditions and limitations, how rapidly may industrialization be expected to proceed? Obviously this question can be answered only conditionally and hypothetically. Before approaching this problem it may be well to take a schematic look at the size and structure of the mainland Chinese economy in 1952, which may be considered as the point of departure for the upward climb.

The accompanying data are based on tentative and crude calculations and are, therefore, intended merely as indications of approximate orders of magnitude rather than as actual estimates.

GROSS NATIONAL PRODUCT OF COMMUNIST CHINA IN 1952

By Economic Sector	Per cent	By Use	Per cent
Agriculture	40.0	Consumption in households	73.0
Small-scale and rural industry	15.0	Government administration	4.0
Trade and transport	24.0	Communal services	4.0
Factory industry and mining	7.0	Military expenditures	7.0
Dwelling services	4.0	Gross domestic investment	12.0
Government and other services	10.0		
Total (in billions of U. S. dollars)	$30.0	Total (in billions of U. S. dollars)	$30.0

In many respects the table shows a pattern that is fairly typical for underdeveloped areas. However, it exhibits several unique characteristics, the most outstanding of which is the large share mobilized by the government and appropriated for its own use—an indication of the degree to which the Chinese economy had been nationalized by 1952. This share is higher than that in any other country in Asia. Even more important in this context is the high rate of investment as compared to other underdeveloped countries. For example, the rate of investment in India was estimated as 8 per cent in 1949–1950.[34]

The investment share given above is based on government budget figures. Thus it leaves private investment out of account. By 1952 such investment was probably negligible in the urban sector; but in the rural sector there was undoubtedly some non-monetary investment.

According to the budget figures in Table 7, investment resources were allocated as shown in the accompanying table. Assuming that

ALLOCATION OF INVESTMENT RESOURCES

	1953 Budget, %	1953 Actual, %	1954 Budget, %
Industry	46.0	49.9	47.8
Agriculture, forestry, and water conservancy	11.4	13.2	10.5
Railways and communications	14.3	14.5	15.5
Trade and banking	4.3	11.5	11.3
Non-specified projects	24.0	10.9	14.9
Total	100.0	100.0	100.0

the Chinese follow Soviet budget practice, one may legitimately surmise that the non-specified projects may be partly military in character;
however, they may also include investments in government overhead
and a wide miscellany of small projects. In any case, about half of
the investment total seems to be channeled into factory industry, with
the bulk of this—close to 80 per cent—going into heavy industry.

Owing to the very character of government budgeting and accounting, a very broad concept of investment is used in Communist China.
The term officially applied is expenditures on 'economic construction';
these cover both outlays on fixed and on working capital, including,
for instance, raw material and fertilizer credits. For this reason it
may not be too far off the mark to conclude that in 1952–1953 about
40 per cent of total government disbursements on non-military construction was actually allocated to investment in fixed industrial capital. Given the general character of the Chinese Communist program,
with its great emphasis upon industrialization, one may assume that
over the Five Year Plan period and even the decade ahead industry's
share in the investment total will be at least maintained.

Heretofore our analysis of the dynamics of economic growth in Communist China has been confined to an examination of prospects in
terms of specific factors and sectors, such as resource endowments, agricultural policies, planning practices, and investment patterns. The
model in Table 9 attempts to combine these interrelated elements into
a projection of the potentialities for aggregate and industrial growth
in mainland China.

Using as a point of departure 1952 estimates of gross national product and its composition, and government budget data on patterns of
investment allocation, the model in Table 9 was constructed on the
basis of the following assumptions:

1. Population will grow at an aggregate rate of 1.2 per cent a year.
Owing to rural-urban migration under the dual impact of the industrial and other closely related demands for labor and rural poverty,
urban population will grow at a much more rapid rate than rural.
An examination of Japanese and Soviet rates of urbanization [35] showed
that in the first case roughly a trebling in industrial output was accompanied by a doubling in the urban population; in the second case
a doubling in urban population was paralleled by a quadrupling in industrial production. Given the respective characters of Japanese and
Soviet economic development, this is not at all surprising. The much
greater capital intensity of the Soviet process of economic growth, with
its emphasis upon expansion of producer goods industries, naturally
meant that the urban demand for labor per unit of incremental output

was lower than in Japan, where textiles and other light industries played a much greater role. On the basis of these considerations it is assumed that urbanization in China will proceed at a rate that would be closer to the Soviet than the Japanese tempo. This assumption is based on the fact that the Chinese Communist regime seems to place much greater emphasis upon development of heavy industry than the Japanese did in the first decades following the Meiji restoration. Recent evidence seems to indicate that Chinese Communist planners are allocating an even larger share of investment resources to the expansion of heavy industry than the Soviet Union did during the period of its first two Five Year Plans. Therefore, it was assumed for purposes of this model that a quadrupling in industrial output will require a doubling in urban population.

2. The level of aggregate consumption will be partly a function of this urbanization, since available evidence would tend to indicate that standards of consumption are higher in the cities than in the countryside. To this must be added the fact that the resource costs of maintaining a person in the cities would be higher in a largely pre-industrial society. Therefore, it was assumed that the resource cost of per capita consumption at the urban standard would be double that of the rural, i.e., about U. S. $60 as compared to U. S. $30. It was further assumed that the very process of industrialization and urbanization combined with the need to spur increases in industrial labor productivity will lead to some increases in per capita urban consumption despite probable efforts to keep consumption in check. Therefore, a 0.5 per cent annual rate of increase in urban per capita consumption was postulated.

3. Government consumption will increase at the same rate as gross national product. This highly arbitrary assumption is based on the hypothesis that maintenance and expansion of the state apparatus to assure the degree of control desired and required by the regime for resource mobilization and allocation and for non-economic ends will necessarily involve increasing unit costs. Moreover, with the high priorities assigned to modernizing and re-equipping the army, unit costs of maintaining a large standing army are also likely to rise.

4. The annual increases in gross national product and in industrial output were computed on the basis of aggregate and industrial incremental capital-output ratios. In this connection it was assumed that 40 per cent of total gross investment will be allocated to industry throughout the decade. In estimating output a one-year investment lag was used; that is, it was assumed that investment in one year will lead to increases in production the following year.

The choice of an incremental capital-output ratio is a most complex problem, particularly for a country like China where there is no sustained development experience to draw upon.[36] At best, the capital-output ratio is a rough-and-ready average which is the product of a host of counteracting tendencies and policies at work in the economy. For the model in Table 9, this choice was based on an analysis of the Soviet and Japanese growth experience on the one hand, and the current economic realities and policies in Communist China on the other. Moreover, our selection is based on the hypothesis that the capital-output ratio is ultimately determined by the resource-population balance, the pattern of investment, and the level of technology and entrepreneurship available in the economy. In other words, the more favorable the population-resource balance, the more advanced the technology and the entrepreneurial skills, and the lower the relative investment share of social overhead and other sectors in which the capital coefficient would be high, the lower will tend to be the aggregate incremental ratio.

On the basis of our current state of knowledge concerning national product and capital formation in the Soviet Union between 1928 and 1937, it would seem that the incremental capital-output ratio for that decade was no higher, and possibly lower, than 3.0.[37] Recent studies for Japan would tend to suggest that this ratio was at most around 4.0 for 1880–1900.[38]

In terms of the factors discussed heretofore, one could expect the incremental capital-output ratio in Communist China to be possibly lower than in Meiji Japan, but higher than in the Soviet Union. The resource-population balance was undoubtedly more favorable in the Soviet Union of 1928, but less propitious in Meiji Japan. The poor quality of Chinese coking coal and iron ore, coupled with the fact that frequently the distances between these two key raw material deposits are quite great, would tend to raise the capital-output ratio. As far as the level of technology and entrepreneurship is concerned, Communist China may again assume an intermediate position between the two countries; in this respect, China probably has a considerable advantage over Japan since it is starting with a relatively larger industrial base and at a more advanced stage of world technological development. On the other hand, the Russia of 1928 was technically and educationally much more advanced than the China of 1952. The rate of literacy, the number of technicians and skilled workers, and the general state of the arts were all higher.

A comparison of the pattern of investment in the three countries yields a less clear-cut conclusion as to the relative magnitudes of the capital-output ratios. China, with an even more underdeveloped transport system than the Soviet Union, is forced to allocate a significant share of its investment resources to this sector. Moreover, the bulk of this railroad development in China is concentrated in remote, sparsely populated areas where transport returns are bound to be low, and the sectoral capital-output ratio quite high. Owing to its geographic configuration, Japan was less dependent upon highly capital-intensive railroad development. On the other side of the balance-sheet, the Soviet Union had to pay relatively more attention than China to the expansion of its electric power facilities in view of its very small generating capacity in 1928. Housing, another sector with a high incremental capital-output ratio, was notoriously neglected in the Soviet Union, and China may be expected to follow suit. It must be noted, however, that the opportunities for economizing on housing space through overcrowding may be much more limited in China than they were in Russia. Moreover, while the initial cost of residential construction is undoubtedly lower in China, costs of replacement and maintenance are probably much higher.

However, differences in the patterns of investment allocation in the three countries are not confined to the social overhead sectors. Thus Meiji Japan concentrated its efforts upon the development of agriculture and of the textile industry, with the latter still based to a considerable extent upon small-scale, cottage type manufacture. In contrast, both the Soviet Union and Communist China seem to accord a considerably lower priority to agricultural development and a much higher priority to the expansion of producer goods industries. These factors, of course, would make for a comparatively lower capital-output ratio in Meiji Japan. The much more unfavorable terms of trade facing Communist China as compared to Meiji Japan would tend to work in the same general direction.

On the basis of all of these considerations combined, an aggregate and industrial ratio of 3.0 was selected as most reasonable for the purposes of the model in Table 9.

Calculating within this system of abstract assumptions, we may expect the Chinese Communist economy to grow quite rapidly, i.e., at an average rate of about 3 per cent a year over the decade, a rate lagging behind that of Meiji Japan and the Soviet tempo of 1928–1937.[39] The process of industrial expansion, however, would proceed much more speedily: industrial production would be more than trebled, and the share of mining and manufacturing in GNP would rise from 7 per cent to 17 per cent.

TABLE 9. MODEL OF ECONOMIC

(in billions of 1952

Year	Gross National Product		National In- come	Consumption			Aggregate Investment		Industrial Investment		Industrial Output	
	Dol- lars	Per Cent		Per- sonal	Govern- ment	Total	Gross	Net	Gross	Net	Dol- lars	Per Cent
1952	30.00	100.0	28.40	22.00	4.40	26.40	3.60	2.00	1.44	1.02	2.10	100.00
1953	30.61	102.0	29.11	22.45	4.49	26.94	3.67	2.13	1.47	1.08	2.44	116.19
1954	31.25	104.2	29.78	22.90	4.58	27.48	3.77	2.30	1.51	1.15	2.80	133.33
1955	31.96	106.5	30.55	23.35	4.68	28.03	3.93	2.52	1.57	1.23	3.18	151.43
1956	32.75	109.2	31.39	23.81	4.80	28.61	4.14	2.78	1.65	1.34	3.59	170.95
1957	33.62	112.1	32.32	24.27	4.93	29.20	4.42	3.12	1.77	1.48	4.04	192.38
1958	35.08	116.9	33.36	24.75	5.14	29.89	5.19	3.47	2.08	1.48	4.53	215.71
1959	36.26	120.9	34.51	25.19	5.31	30.50	5.76	4.01	2.30	1.66	5.02	239.04
1960	37.66	125.5	35.85	25.69	5.50	31.19	6.47	4.66	2.59	1.89	5.57	265.24
1961	39.28	130.9	37.40	26.21	5.73	31.94	7.34	5.46	2.94	2.18	6.20	295.24
1962	41.18	137.3	39.22	26.69	6.00	32.69	8.49	6.53	3.39	2.56	6.93	330.00

This rapid growth will have been made possible by rates of investment rising from about 12 per cent in 1952 to 20 per cent ten years later. The latter would correspond to the average rates in post-World War II Europe and would exceed the estimated Soviet rate of the 1930's.[40] It is most doubtful that this rate can actually be attained at such a low level of per capita product even within the context of a rigorous system of economic control. In reality this rising investment pattern is built into the model by virtue of the assumptions on which it is based, which means that the assumptions used become less and less applicable as they are projected further into the future. For the last few years of the projections, the investment assumptions would probably have to be modified with a downward adjustment in the speed of industrial and aggregate growth resulting therefrom.

One of the central elements in this process of growth is a rapidly rising productivity of labor under the impact of complex and interrelated forces. On the basis of all of the data available, it would seem that the more underdeveloped an economy the greater tend to be the differentials between the labor products of the economic sectors. Under such conditions the very shift of labor out of agriculture, a low productivity sector, into urban factory-industry, a high productivity sector, automatically results in rising per capita product in the economy. Under modern conditions of development this is reinforced by the advantages of delayed industrialization, inasmuch as the process

GROWTH IN COMMUNIST CHINA

U. S. dollars)

Population (in millions)			Personal Consumption		Total Capital Stock at Beginning of Year			Industrial Capital Stock at Beginning of Year		
					Old Capital Remaining	New Capital Remaining	Total	Old Capital Remaining	New Capital Remaining	Total
Total	Urban	Rural	Urban	Rural						
582	116	466	7.30	14.70	40.00	.....	40.00	6.00	.....	6.00
589	122	467	7.73	14.72	38.40	3.60	42.00	5.58	1.44	7.02
596	128	468	8.15	14.75	36.86	7.27	44.13	5.19	2.91	8.10
603	134	469	8.57	14.78	35.38	11.04	46.42	4.83	4.42	9.25
610	140	470	9.00	14.81	33.96	14.97	48.93	4.49	5.99	10.48
617	146	471	9.43	14.84	32.60	19.11	51.71	4.17	7.64	11.81
624	152	472	9.87	14.88	31.30	23.53	54.83	3.88	9.41	13.29
631	157	474	10.25	14.94	30.04	27.48	57.52	3.61	11.16	14.77
639	163	476	10.69	15.00	28.84	32.69	61.53	3.36	13.36	16.72
647	169	478	11.14	15.07	27.69	38.50	66.19	3.12	15.48	18.60
654	175	479	11.59	15.10	26.58	45.07	71.65	2.90	17.88	20.78

of industrial expansion in a country such as China is accompanied by discrete leaps in technology. Within this context, even the postwar dismantling of Manchurian plants by the Soviets may be considered as a blessing in disguise from the Chinese point of view. Japanese plant installations that were removed in 1945 have largely been replaced by now with more up-to-date Soviet equipment. The same applies to plants newly built; for instance, on the basis of eyewitness and other accounts, a flax mill located near Harbin and completed in 1952 seems to incorporate the advances of modern technology. Similarly, it may be assumed that the two new steel mills to be built in China by Soviet engineers with Soviet equipment will be based on modern Russian methods of steelmaking—methods which do not seem to lag far behind those applied in the United States.

The same may be put differently; i.e., high rates of investment in an economy in which the capital base is small will necessarily lead to rapid transformations in the age composition of capital. Thus, in our model, aggregate stock would be almost doubled while industrial capital would be trebled during the 10-year period. By 1962 practically all of the industrial capital will have been installed during the preceding decade, while for the economy as a whole only about one-third of the stock would still be old.

Of course this process of rejuvenation accelerates economic growth not only through its technological effects but also by virtue of the fact that as new capital displaces old the share of replacement allowances in the investment total declines. This tendency is reinforced in countries such as China which concentrate upon the development of producer goods industries with a longer life-span for equipment and, therefore, relatively lower rates of capital consumption.

While a number of factors seem to point to comparatively rapid rates of prospective growth in Communist China, even on the basis of the pace of expansion envisaged in our model, per capita gross product in 1962 would still be only around U. S. $65. In the context of Asia, growth at such speed would constitute a most impressive performance. Depending on the course of events elsewhere in Asia, a development of this kind in Communist China could significantly affect the regional political and power balance.

Notes for Chapter 14

1. Alexander Erlich, "Preobrazhenski and the Economics of Soviet Industrialization," *Quarterly Journal of Economics*, Vol. LXIV, No. 1, February 1950, pp. 57–88.

2. Bruce F. Johnston, "Agricultural Productivity and Economic Development in Japan," *Journal of Political Economy*, Vol. LIX, December 1951, pp. 498–513.

3. Shigeto Tsuru and Kazushi Ohkawa, "Long-Term Changes in the National Product of Japan Since 1878," *Income and Wealth*, Series III, Cambridge, England, pp. 19–44: Yuzo Yamada and Associates, *Notes on the Income Growth and the Rate of Saving in Japan*, Mimeo., Tokyo, 1953, 19 pp.

4. *China Yearbook, 1948* (in Chinese), China Yearbook Committee, China Nationalist Government, Nanking, September 1948; *World Iron Ore Resources and Their Utilization*, United Nations (New York), 1950; W. S. and E. S. Woytinsky, *op. cit.*

5. Edwin W. Pauley, *op. cit.*, p. 98.

6. The first portion of this railroad, running from Chungking to Chengtu is an exception inasmuch as it links the Szechwan rice basin to the rest of the country. Generally the motivation for concentrating on this western line is probably primarily strategic and political, designed to bring these remote areas under closer control by the center.

7. *Demographic Yearbook, 1952*, United Nations, pp. 224–231 and 264–269; also, W. S. and E. S. Woytinsky, *op. cit.*, Tables 63, 82, and 86.

8. *Demographic Yearbook, 1952*, United Nations; Kingsley Davis, *The Population of India and Pakistan*, Princeton, N. J., Princeton University Press, 1951, pp. 36–37.

9. There has been much evidence in the Chinese Communist press, in the spring and summer of 1954, that a sharp fall in the death rate has occurred. See, for example, New China News Agency, Peking, March 10, 1954, for a report on 60 per cent of the census results.

10. See Table 8.

11. Agricultural exports include not only modest quantities of grains, but a wide range of other farm products including: tung oil, soybeans, bean cake, rape seed, eggs and egg products, pork, hog bristles, and a range of vegetable oils.

12. T. H. Shen, *op. cit.*, Appendix Tables 3 and 5.

13. Pierre Gourou, "The Development of Upland Areas in China," *The Development of Upland Areas in the Far East,* New York, Institute of Pacific Relations, International Secretariat, 1949, p. 10.

14. As a matter of fact, the first collective farm in China, "The Spark," was established in this region.

15. T. H. Shen, *op. cit.,* p. 363.

16. B. F. Johnson, *op. cit.*

17. E. B. Schumpeter, ed., *The Industrialization of Japan and Manchukuo, 1930–1940,* New York, The Macmillan Co., 1940, p. 251, and T. H. Shen, *op. cit.,* p. 38.

18. It has been estimated that the average annual flooded area of major river basins in China was about 7 million acres; see "Economic Developments in Mainland China," *Economic Bulletin for Asia and the Far East.* The early indications are that 1954 will prove a year of serious flooding, despite recent water conservancy measures.

19. For a fuller discussion of these cooperatives see A. Doak Barnett, "China's Road to Collectivization," *Journal of Farm Economics,* May 1953, pp. 188–202.

20. "Decision on the Development of Agrarian Production Cooperatives," December 16, 1953, reported in *China News Analysis,* Hong Kong, February 12, 1953.

21. "Order of Government Administrative Council for Enforcement of Planned Purchase and Planned Supply of Grain," November 23, 1953, New China News Agency, Peking, February 28, 1954.

22. *Economic Survey of Europe Since the War,* United Nations, Economic Commission for Europe, Geneva, 1953, p. 166 and Chart 13, p. 177.

23. Po I-po, "Report on the 1953 State Budget," *op. cit.,* and Chou En-lai, "Report at the Fourth Session of the National Committee of the Chinese People's Consultative Council," *Ta Kung Pao* (Impartiality Daily), Hong Kong, February 5, 1953.

24. Speech at the Fifteenth Party Congress, verbatim report, p. 67.

25. Compare Po I-po, "Report on the 1953 State Budget," *op. cit.;* Chia To-fu, "Report to the Seventh Session of All-China Trade Union Congress," New China News Agency, September 25, 1953; and Wu Lun-hsi, "New China on the Road to Industrialization," *Ta Kung Pao* (Impartiality Daily), Hong Kong, October 1953.

26. This 'General Line' was first announced in an editorial in the *People's Daily,* Peking, October 1, 1953, under the title "Struggle for the Distant and Great Goal of Socialistic Industrialization." All of our references to collectivization include producers' cooperatives, on the assumption that the *de facto* distinction between the two is slight.

27. The new bond issue valued at 6 trillion JMP (about U. S. $240,000,000) was launched in December 1953. See *New York Times,* December 10, 1953; January 23, and February 9, 1954.

28. New China News Agency, Peking, September 15, 1953.

29. Harry Schwartz, "Soviet Aid to China," *New York Times,* October 5, 1953.

30. Table 6, and W. S. Woytinsky and E. S. Woytinsky, *op. cit.,* pp. 1118–1121.

31. *Study on Iron and Steel Industry,* Vol. II, E/CN. 12/293/Add. 2 & 3, Santiago, Chile, United Nations Economic Commission for Latin America.

This study gives the investment cost per ton of finished steel in a plant with a 250,000 ton capacity as U. S. $400. The investment cost per ton of crude steel is estimated as U. S. $170, all in terms of 1948 prices. In the 1 million ton plant at Sparrows Point, Maryland, unit investment cost is estimated as U. S. $283 per ton of finished and U. S. $126 per ton of crude steel.

32. *Steam-Electric Plant Construction Cost and Annual Production Expenses,* U. S. Federal Power Commission, Washington, D. C., 1950.

33. Input-output studies for the United States economy, conducted by the Harvard Economics Research Project, would tend to indicate that about one-third of the new investment required per unit of increased output in steel and power production would consist of complex types of equipment. It was assumed that this equipment could not be manufactured in China and would, therefore, have to be imported from the Soviet Union.

34. This relates the share of gross investment to gross national product. Derived from Mukharjee and Ghosh, "The Pattern of Income and Expenditure in the Indian Union, A Tentative Study," *Bulletin of the International Statistical Institute,* 1951.

35. This applies to Japan approximately between 1890 and 1915 and to the Soviet Union between 1928 and 1938.

36. The incremental capital-output ratio attempts to measure the amount of increase in output caused by an additional unit of investment. It is, therefore, a rough measure of how productive investment is likely to be. A low ratio indicates high capital productivity.

37. Tentatively estimated by the author on the basis of national income estimates by Bergson, Grossman, and Jasny, and investment estimates by Kaplan.

38. Shigeto Tsuru and Kazushi Ohkawa, *op. cit.;* and Yuzo Yamada and Associates, *op. cit.*

39. A. Bergson, ed., *Soviet Economic Growth,* Evanston, Ill., and White Plains, New York, Row Peterson and Company, 1953, p. 9.

40. *Ibid.,* Table 2–1, p. 41; and A. Bergson, *Soviet National Income and Product in 1937,* New York, Columbia University Press, 1953.

COMMUNIST POWER AND THE CHINESE

ECONOMY: CONCLUSIONS

Although the decision goes deep in basic Communist ideology, and was explicitly foreshadowed in 1952 if not earlier, it was toward the end of 1953 that the Communist regime firmly decided forthwith to press on with the building of a heavy industry base as a matter of overriding priority. This decision has had a number of ancillary consequences. It has meant that:

1. An increase in standards of welfare must, in general, be postponed; and the proportion of the budget to national income must be maintained (say, 30 per cent).

2. Given the complex nature of the industrial equipment required, a high and rising level of international trade must be sustained, and imports other than industrial raw materials, machinery, and military equipment must be minimized.

3. An increased volume of total agricultural output must be allocated to exports.

4. An increased volume of total agricultural output must be allocated to feeding expanding urban areas.

5. A very high proportion of industrial output must be reinvested in industry.

The decision on the priority of heavy industry has been taken in conjunction with a second decision: namely, that the size of the regime's armed forces be maintained and that its complement of modern equipment be steadily expanded. This latter decision is reflected in the official (and probably understated) scale of allocations to the Second Ministry of Machine Building (military production). It is altogether likely, although no evidence is available, that a high level of military equipment imports is maintained from the Soviet Union—financed by current Chinese exports.

The success of this program of combined heavy industry and military expansion hinges peculiarly on the government's ability to mobilize in its hands an increased absolute volume of agricultural output over a period where agricultural investment is likely to be exceedingly modest except for labor-intensive projects. The meaning of the regime's recent decision to proceed with an important degree of collectivization, and of its increasingly harsh and purposeful efforts at grain collection, is this: if there is to be a shortfall of food, it must be borne by the peasantry rather than the armed forces, cadres, industrial workers, or level of agricultural exports.

The regime must be aware that the prospects for a marked expansion in agricultural output are unlikely to be improved by its grain collection methods and by the announced collectivization program. Although never discussed in the Chinese Communist press, the course of events in Soviet and eastern European agriculture is undoubtedly known to the top leadership. But the regime has clearly been unwilling to accept a program of agricultural expansion based on market incentives to peasants and substantial industrial investment in fertilizers and agricultural equipment. These would not only require a diversion of resources to consumers' goods, as incentives, and to non-industrial investment; they would also commit the regime to accepting a private market economy over the face of agricultural China, with all the relaxation of political control and perpetuation of traditional Chinese peasant attitudes this would entail. The persistence of such attitudes down to 1954 is amply attested to in the Chinese Communist press. The regime has turned its face against a NEP for China. It is evidently prepared to accept the costs of a state-controlled grain market, of collectivization, and of the peasants' expectation of collectivization to ensure its hold over the disposition of agricultural output and to guarantee its political and social control of the peasant.

Within the tight limits of these overriding objectives, the regime will seek to do what it can to maintain, and if possible to expand, the total level of agricultural production and to gain the acquiescence if not the positive support of the peasantry. A considerable volume of labor-intensive investment will continue to go into irrigation and other water-control projects. Information on better seeds and methods will be spread through model farms and technically trained cadres. In the North the large-scale experimental state farms using modern equipment will be expanded. A vast propaganda effort to explain the new 'General Line' to the peasantry is under way. In theory the 800,000 producers' cooperatives are to be formed by persuading the peasantry that its material interest is to join; and there are certain to be disincentives set up for those who choose to remain outside. But the regime is evidently in a mood to face the worst.

Why has this policy of 'austerity' and 'bitter struggle' been adopted? At the most, if all goes well, it will yield in 1957 an industrial establishment based on, say, 3 to 5 million tons of crude steel, roughly equivalent to that of the Soviet Union in 1913, of Japan in 1930, and of contemporary Czechoslovakia or Poland. Communist China after a successful First Five Year Plan will remain an industrial country of the third rank, although second only to Japan in Asia. Its industrialization must be reckoned a process of decades, not years. Why, then, the great hurry? Why are grave risks of mass starvation being incurred, and the internal power machine strained to its limit? Why, at least, is not a phase of NEP sanctioned as it is in Communist theology for the first decade after successful revolution?

No dogmatic answer is possible. Like most major decisions of history, however, this has probably arisen out of different but converging elements.

1. As of 1953 the regime felt that its domestic power machine was fully consolidated—at least as well-consolidated as Stalin's in 1929; and, like Stalin in that period, the regime was not prepared to face the loosening consequences on political and social power of a peasant sector made up of small proprietors operating on private market incentives. A continuation of the 1953 relaxation would have carried this implication.

2. Unlike Lenin's Russia of 1921, Communist China is in the midst of a world arena of power engaged in a dour cold war. The leadership is certainly ambitious in Asia and must include in its calculations the possibility of engagement in major war with the United States even if it does not now intend to precipitate such war. It feels strongly the need for an independent industrial base capable of supplying a flow of modern military equipment and spare parts to its armed forces. It is not content to contemplate continued military dependence on the Soviet Union in the extreme degree to which such dependence now exists.

3. Even more specifically, there appears to be in Peking a powerful intent to increase at the maximum rate possible the degree of Chinese independence and authority within the continuing framework of the Sino-Soviet alliance. With respect to border issues, trade, the degree of dependence on Soviet military equipment, and the degree of Communist authority in Asia, Peking seeks greater freedom of action *vis-à-vis* Moscow. Mao and the Chinese Communists generally have never ceased to associate industrialization with military strength and mili-

tary strength with independence—a theme which, indeed, antedates Communism in the modern Chinese revolution.

Lacking information on Politburo and Central Committee discussion in Peking, we cannot weight these factors with precision. On the whole we would guess that the third may well have been decisive: that is, the Chinese Communists desire to increase as rapidly as possible the degree of their power, independence, and freedom for action within the Communist bloc.

Broadly speaking, in terms of aggregate resources, the goals of the First Five Year Plan appear to lie within Chinese Communist economic capabilities. The regime has demonstrated an ability to mobilize sufficient investment resources to expand industrial output at, roughly, the proposed rate and to maintain and modernize its armed forces.

Despite the aggregate feasibility of the scheme, there remains a series of important and difficult economic problems; and a massive political cloud hangs over the enterprise as a whole. These are the key problems:

1. *Foreign trade.* Given the primitive state of Chinese industrial technique and the low initial level of the Chinese industrial output, the regime will have to rely heavily on imports both for machinery and for military end-items. The Soviet Union does not appear willing to advance substantial credits; and there appear to be limits to the extent of the Communist bloc's willingness to trade such scarce items for Chinese foodstuff and raw material exports. Moreover, the terms of trade between China and the Communist bloc are not now so advantageous as they might be under more normal world trade circumstances. A strong impulse to enlarge trade with the Free World will probably exist. But it is by no means clear that it will prove easy for the Chinese Communists to sell available exports in exchange for the specific commodities they want, even if political barriers are lowered by an easing of international tension.

2. *Military versus industrial targets.* As nearly as we can make out, the regime intends simultaneously to expand its industrial base and to modernize its armed forces. In the short run these objectives conflict. Imports of military equipment from the Soviet Union are paid for with foodstuffs and raw materials which might buy machine tools either in the Communist bloc or outside. Equipment used by the Second Machine Tool Industry to equip the armed forces could be used substantially to produce industrial capital equipment. The military goals of the regime thus conflict with its industrial goals, and may pose awkward problems of priority and allocation despite the

fact that the industrial targets have been set in an initial relation to military targets.

3. *Industrial productivity*. China badly lacks skilled technicians and efficient managers. Its educational system has been turned with extremely sharp priority to producing engineers; and the criteria for promotion in the bureaucracy have been shifted so as to elevate rapidly those with managerial ability. Moreover, the resources of Soviet technical advice have been exploited on a large scale. Nevertheless, the First Five Year Plan undoubtedly will be hampered by a low average level of productivity in industry and by difficulties in turning out first-class precision equipment.

4. *Population*. It seems altogether likely that the natural death rate in China will fall and the birth rate remain high, creating increased population pressure. Quite persuasive evidence of this process has, indeed, begun to appear in the Communist press in the spring of 1954. The internal order of the country and substantial public health measures might be counted on to yield some decline in the very high death rates of the war and immediate postwar years. On the other hand, Marxist anti-Malthusianism merges with Chinese cultural values to maintain social pressure for large families. One cannot expect a drastic fall in the birth rate or purposeful state policies addressed to that end. There has been, of course, substantial loss of population due to certain of the regime's post-1949 policies: the Anti-Counter-revolutionary Campaign of 1951 resulted in millions of deaths; the Korean War, in extremely heavy casualties; the death rate under forced labor conditions must be high; the pressure for industrial output, which has clearly resulted in a sustained increase in accident rates, must also have affected the death rate as well. Nevertheless, looking ahead, we see that the economic problem of the regime, coming to rest as it does on food mobilization, may be complicated by a surge in the Chinese population. A 1 per cent per annum rise in population means more than an extra 6 million mouths to feed each year; and it is our guess that the current rate of natural increase is somewhat above 1 per cent.

In a situation where the margin of resources is being hard-pressed, a fall in the natural death rate could be an explosive factor, notably in the light of the regime's apparent decision to make the food supply in rural areas a low-priority residual affair; for this appears to be the fundamental policy which has been adopted, and it is likely to color the political mood of Communist China over the period of the First Five Year Plan.

The exact degree of pressure on the rural food supply, and the extent of actual starvation, cannot now be predicted. They will depend on many factors, notably the following:

1. The fall in the death rate due to other causes.

2. The peasants' reaction, in terms of effort and output, to collectivization efforts and to the prospect of collectivization.

3. The weather and its impact on the harvests.

4. The extent to which the regime's investment in water control and the spreading of new farming techniques yield positive results.

5. The average level of skill of the cadres at the village level in mitigating the effects on output of the collectivization program.

The willingness and ability of the regime to corral the grain it requires and to distribute it with considerable efficiency can hardly be questioned on the basis of its performance since 1949.

On the whole it is proper to assume that there will be substantial hunger and even a measure of starvation in China over the period of the First Five Year Plan; and that, by and large, the peasant will not be content. This certainly appears to be the current (August 1954) appreciation of the regime. What importance is to be attached to this probability?

It is evidently the regime's view that its instruments of control can successfully contain whatever situation may develop. And, in general, there is little reason to challenge this apparent judgment. The cadres are tightly bound to the regime and seek to carry out its instructions. The armed forces are under effective centralized discipline, and the military leaders are closely bound to Mao. The militia and the secret police are capable of applying overwhelming force at any given point of revolt. So long as the instruments of control remain unified at the apex of the system, and so long as the cadres, militia, and secret police remain under effective discipline, the regime need not fear that its policies or its rule will be effectively challenged by a hungry, dissident peasantry unless starvation reaches mammoth proportions. A danger to the regime would arise only if men high in its councils, with authority or influence over major instruments of power, should differ on the wisdom of the policies being pursued or should use differences over policy as an occasion to seek enlarged power for themselves and the bureaucratic agencies they represent. Undoubtedly, if things go badly in the countryside, personnel within the cadres and militia will be somewhat infected with peasant discontent; but without a split at the top this factor is unlikely to be important. The bureaucratic agents of the regime have nowhere to go outside the protecting and threatening confines of the regime's structure of organization. Their status, their food, and their lives are at the regime's disposition.

What, then, are the prospects for a high-level split over the issue of economic policy? There is some evidence that the austerity and 'bitter struggle' decisions of late 1953 were not taken without conflict at reasonably high levels in Peking. The intense and pointed character of Liu Shao-ch'i's warning against party factionalism, early in February 1954, is noteworthy. It does not have the character of a routine pronouncement on the perennial theme of party unity, but appears to reflect the will to impose effectively a command decision on actual or believed dissidents.

We do not know either the terms in which the policy decision was argued out or the alternative course which may have been put forward. We do not know the extent and character of whatever opposition there may have been. The most likely conclusion is that so long as Mao is alive and effective the regime's leadership will remain unified and that its policy line will be maintained—with some tactical variation and adjustment over the next several years.

But what if Mao should die in the near future? Would the struggle for power, if any, interweave with differences over economic policy? Here again, any judgment must be extremely tentative. There is, however, one possible chain of connection that should be noted: if the decisive consideration in Peking was the desire to diminish its military dependence on Moscow, within the orbit of the alliance, then the economic plan must have the backing of key military figures; and, if our argument on the succession problem is correct, these men will hold the key to the regime's stability after Mao's death. Our tentative and precarious line of argument leads, then, to the conclusion that, barring a gross failure in the agricultural sector, the decisions surrounding the Five Year Plan are likely to persist after Mao's death, should he die in the near future, unless his military and civil successors fall out.

PART

6

THE PROSPECTS FOR COMMUNIST CHINA

THE PROSPECTS FOR COMMUNIST CHINA

I. The Vision of the Top Leadership: China and the Soviet Model

The vision of the next decade which controls the policy of Peking is clear enough. The top leadership seeks to repeat on the Chinese scene the pattern of domestic transformations carried out by Stalin in the early 1930's, with a specially urgent emphasis on the creation of a Chinese industrial base for the maintenance of its modernized armed forces. It seeks simultaneously a related goal: to increase the independent authority of Peking in Asia within the limits permitted by the need to maintain the Sino-Soviet alliance, and by the resource requirements of the industrialization program. For the moment, where internal and external ambitions conflict (or are made to conflict by an effective Free World policy), the present leadership in Peking is likely to accord priority to expansion of its domestic power base.

In terms of political, social, and cultural policy, as well as in economic objectives and technique, the actions of the Chinese Communist regime as of 1954 strongly recall those of Stalin in 1930, the most notable exceptions being the priority accorded by Peking to current military strength and the pace of planned collectivization, in which Mao is proceeding more in the manner of the post-1945 European satellites than with the ruthless urgency of Stalin in the Soviet First Five Year Plan. By and large the regime's order to the cadres—to take their guidance from Chapters 9–12 of Stalin's *Short Course*—reflects a deep reality: the regime intends, essentially by Stalin's methods, to duplicate in China the results achieved by Stalin in the 1930's.

It is, therefore, worth examining the relevance of this analogy which operates so powerfully on the minds of Peking's rulers.

The tables in Appendix 2, at the end of this chapter, set out estimates for the Chinese and Soviet positions for the historically comparable years 1952 and 1928. In China 1952 marked the virtual completion of the postwar rehabilitation process and, roughly, the attainment of pretakeover peak levels of output (1943 for Manchuria; 1936 for the rest of China). In the Soviet Union 1928 marked the reattainment of, roughly, 1913 output levels. In 1929 and 1953, respectively, the Soviet and Chinese Communist First Five Year Plans were launched. The following key features emerge from the tables of Appendix 2:

1. By the end of the 1920's the Soviet Union had already passed through the massive decline in the death rate that results from the application of basic modern public health measures. Communist China is probably now in the midst of this process and will confront a great population bulge in the course of its First Five Year Plan.

2. The Soviet Union enjoyed an enormous superiority in agricultural population per acre of cultivated land (0.2 to 1.7).

3. In imposing austerity measures on the Russian peoples, the Soviet regime had the advantage of a substantial margin above subsistence into which to cut: 1928 real income per capita was about four times as high in the Soviet Union as in 1952 Communist China.

4. On the eve of the First Five Year Plan the Soviet Union was able to mobilize for investment a substantially higher proportion of the national income than Communist China can, not because of the Soviet Union's greater wealth or the superior tax collection abilities of its regime, but because of Peking's higher military outlays.

5. The absolute level and scale of current allocations to the armed forces in 1952 Communist China were about four times those of the Soviet Union in 1928.

6. The industrial base of Communist China in 1952 was roughly that of Russia in the 1890's, as measured by pig iron and steel output; and the First Five Year Plan in Communist China, if successful, will expand the industrial base roughly to the 1913–1928 Soviet level.

7. Largely because of the initial inadequacy of its industrial base, Peking must count on an enlarged level of foreign trade in its First Five Year Plan, while the Soviet Union could achieve its goals despite a sharp decline in external trade.

Broadly speaking, then, Communist China in 1952 was industrially nearer the position of Russia in the 1890's than of the Soviet Union of 1928; Communist China's First Five Year Plan is more heavily dependent on a maintained or expanded level of foreign trade; its ambitions demand an important allocation to military purposes which

Stalin avoided in 1929; China faces a population growth and urbanization problem of unknown but potentially serious dimensions which
may well conflict with the maintenance of minimum welfare standards. All of these special pressures come to rest on a level of agricultural output which, unlike that of the Soviet Union, was not geared
in the pretakeover period to a large export surplus. Moreover, China
lacks the timber and gold which the Soviet Union could throw in as
its grain export capabilities declined under the impact of collectivization and population increase.

In the attempt to realize the Chinese Communist leaders' vision,
therefore, much hinges on the course of agricultural output and, especially, on the peasants' productivity response to the regime's grain
control and collectivization measures. The Chinese Communist
regime's problem is thus essentially more difficult than Stalin's, and
success is not assured. A repetition in China of the 20 per cent fall
in agricultural output which marked the First Soviet Five Year Plan
would constitute a disaster not to the Chinese people alone, but to
the regime's ideological pretensions, and, probably, to its control machinery and unity as well.

II. The Regime's Tactical Goals

It is evident that, although the Chinese Communists had long
pointed to the major goals of industrialization and modernized armed
forces, they were unable in the period 1949–1953 to decide on the
pace, sequence, and tactics of the Chinese 'transition to socialism.'
Now, as of August 1954, key decisions have been made or have emerged
from an accumulation of *ad hoc* policies.

Within the broad strategy of the over-all vision, the internal tactical
goals appear to be these:

1. An industrial complex in 1957–1959 roughly on the scale of
Russia in 1928.

2. Armed forces substantially modernized in equipment, staff work,
and organization, and supplied increasingly from Chinese resources.

3. Consolidation of state control over agricultural output and its
distribution, including the movement of at least 20 per cent of the
peasantry into producers' cooperatives by 1957.

4. A maximum effort to increase agricultural output compatible
with the overriding decision on collectivization and the higher priority
assigned to investment allocations for the armed forces and heavy
industry.

5. The training of a generation of technicians capable of operating China's industry and administering its massive state apparatus.

6. Further bureaucratization of techniques for maintaining absolute central control over the armed forces, the Communist Party membership, the non-Communist Party cadres, and the Chinese people down to the level of villages and city blocks.

7. The spread of literacy by means most conducive to indoctrination in Chinese Communist dogma.

External goals would appear to be:

1. Maximum expansion of Peking's authority in Asia compatible with the avoidance of major diversion of resources from domestic tasks; at the minimum, the maintenance of a political and ideological base for later assertion of leadership, if not hegemony, in Asia.

2. Maintenance and development of the maximum degree of freedom of action *vis-à-vis* Moscow compatible with maintaining the security and economic advantages of the Sino-Soviet alliance.

That the Communist leaders have recognized the possibility of serious problems arising as they attempt to reach their immediate goals is already evident from the regime's recent moves. Briefly:

1. Mao may die in the course of the next several critical years, removing the most powerful, most unifying personal force. The regime has begun to lay the foundations for collective leadership in public doctrine and, quite possibly, in administrative practice.

2. The limits in Sino-Soviet trade and credit set by Moscow may prove incompatible with the machinery import requirement of the industrialization plan. There are signs that the regime looks to the development of an increased margin of East-West trade over the course of the First Five Year Plan.

3. The peasants' reaction to agricultural policy and the course of the harvests may produce widespread hunger and discontent. The regime is evidently gearing its instruments of control to new levels of discipline and efficiency to cope with this possibility.

4. The new technical and bureaucratic standards of value imposed on the literate will require the replacement of many of the older cadres. The leadership has indicated that it is prepared to cope with the resultant dissidence by measures of purge if necessary.

5. The evident waning of popular enthusiasm for the regime has led to an increased relative reliance on appeals to fear and to sentiment rooted in nationalism as opposed to promises of welfare and reform.

The situation, then, is one in which the regime has set maximum current goals which are very modest. They involve no rise in standards of welfare per capita; and they look to the creation of an industrial base founded merely on some 4 million tons of unprocessed steel at the end of the Five Year Plan. To achieve this result the regime, fully aware of possible obstacles, counts on the maintenance of a ruthless and unpopular system of controls over peasant and worker, the denial of all meaningful freedom to the literate Chinese. It is prepared to 'struggle bitterly' for its limited ends.

III. The Nature of Possible Internal Crisis

Although it is plain that there will be continuing and probably increasing strain between the regime's doctrines and ambitions on the one hand and its human and material resources on the other, it would be foolhardy to predict a major crisis. All that we can see now is that, given a convergence of certain conditions, such a crisis is possible; and it may be useful, therefore, to outline very briefly an extreme case.

The regime is committed to a policy of agricultural output mobilization sufficient to cover a set of key requirements: minimum peasant consumption, urban needs, labor-intensive project needs, military and all official needs, and export. It is prepared, up to a point, to regard the food supply left to the peasant as residual; that is, it is prepared to balance its books, as in 1953–1954, with starvation on a considerable scale—but well short of major crisis.

Nevertheless, a rising population in the face of an agricultural output either static or decreased by unfavorable peasant response or natural disaster would immediately raise serious questions. To what extent should rural starvation be accepted in lieu of reduced allocations to other categories? It is evident that the control system in Communist China can maintain order in the face of substantial starvation; but how much starvation over what period would crack the morale of the cadres and the peasant-born army? At what stage would some in the top leadership question the relevance of the Soviet model for China? How would the prestige effects on Asia of massive Chinese starvation be weighted by Peking's leaders? At what stage would a cut-back in foreign trade and investment be accepted in place of starvation? And, in the extreme, what would happen if a population increase and accelerated urbanization should so silt up the Chinese economy that the regime would be confronted with the choice of unacceptable levels of starvation or a virtual abandonment of its further development plans?

These are questions of quantity and degree; and it should be strongly emphasized that an extreme crisis which would pose them all cannot be predicted on present evidence. Moreover, should such a situation arise, the regime, aside from cutting back its level of foreign trade and investment, might lay an effective claim in Moscow for food imports on credit. Finally, such a definitive crisis could come about only as the result of a process lasting for several years—not as the consequence of a single bad harvest season.

With this in mind, it is still worthwhile to underline the five convergent factors which, if they persisted, might yield major crises, for all are to some extent present or possible in the Chinese scene:

1. A sharp fall in the natural death rate.

2. A disproportionate rise in the urban population.

3. An adverse productivity reaction of the peasantry to the regime's agricultural policy, yielding static or declining output.

4. A relative neglect of agricultural in favor of industrial investment.

5. A succession of bad harvest years.

An extremely crude set of calculations in Appendix 3 at the end of this chapter attempts to set out the alternatives. Roughly speaking, we would hold that the fulfillment of Peking's current objectives requires something like a 10 per cent increase in agricultural output over the 1952 level by, say, 1957–1959; and that a 10 per cent fall in output from the 1952 level, if it persisted for several years, could generate a decisive crisis. Moreover, such a crisis would be unlikely to be only a domestic affair. Its existence would constitute a demonstration that the Soviet model is inappropriate to the Chinese scene; and that the network of ties to the Soviet Union failed to carry China over the hump into sustained industrial growth. And in such an extreme setting the leadership might well split and Peking's international orientation as well as its domestic policy come under re-examination in the course of subsequent conflict.

Thus, while emphasizing the fact that a decisive crisis on the mainland cannot be firmly predicted, we can say with confidence that one critical test of the regime over the next several years will lie in its ability to move toward its announced goals in the face of China's fundamental problems of overpopulation and low agricultural productivity by techniques which violate the peasant's incentive to produce.

IV. THE PATTERNS OF INTERNAL EVOLUTION—WITHOUT
MAJOR CRISIS OR WAR

Assuming that Communist China avoids a major internal crisis and remains at peace, we can make certain observations on the implications for the future of the forces which are now in motion within Chinese Communist society.

Top Leadership

At the moment the top leadership of the regime represents a continuity stretching back to the earliest days of Chinese Communism. This homogeneous group of individuals, now mainly in their fifties, will continue to control the Chinese Communist regime over, say, the next decade whether or not Mao survives, and to remain unified and fairly impervious to change until the 1960's. But it is worth noting, as we look ahead, that the inevitable process of wholesale replacement, whether gradually prepared for or occurring over a relatively short period, could have significant meaning. The older leaders like Chu Teh, Lin Tsu-han, and Tung Pi-wu, who now lend great prestige to the regime and still exert influence on policy, will presumably be dead or without real power. The same holds true for the famous military veterans, the very core of Mao's strength and of the unique Chinese Communist administrative system, all but, possibly, Lin Piao, who is only forty-six—and Lin is thought by some to be already disabled by serious illness. And two other groups, the Communist Party veterans who were subject to western education and many of those who studied in the Soviet Union, will be reaching the end of their active years. By 1965 the elders may well be Chou En-lai, Liu Shao-ch'i, P'eng Chen, Ch'en Yun, P'eng Te-huai, and Li Fu-ch'un. There is only one full-scale military man here—P'eng Te-huai.

There is a sizable group of Communist Party veterans in their forties; [1] and there have appeared in recent years important new leaders, like An Tzu-wen, Lai Jo-yu, and Hu Yao-pang, who seem to be without any known history of distinction in the Chinese Communist movement and to have moved suddenly from the regional periphery to the power center. Here is the material of future leadership— a mixture of what we might call second-generation veterans whom we recognize at least in part and of newcomers just beginning to show.

There is little to be said about the newcomers except that they are likely to be different in experience and outlook from their predecessors in Communist command. The rising military men will have had their training in conventional military units, rather than guerrilla operations; they will be more expert in staffwork, logistics, and the handling of modern equipment than Chu Teh and his colleagues who now run the Chinese Communist armed forces. The politicians will be experts at the bureaucratic manipulation of organized instruments of power, administrators rather than experts in the politics of insurrection. If present modes of education and criteria for promotion persist, the new generation will be heavily laced with engineers, industrial managers, and planners. In short, we can expect, slowly or suddenly, a transition in Communist China similar to that engineered by Stalin in the Soviet Union in the 1930's. It is still a decade, however, before this new generation emerges and bids for (or inherits peacefully) the posts of command.

The Bureaucrats

The process of converting the humanistic tradition of China to the technocratic standards of entrenched Communism is well under way. Here, too, if the Chinese Communists remain in power, a version of the transition in style, manners, and values familiar in the Soviet Union during the 1930's can be anticipated. By 1953 about half of all students getting a higher education were being trained as engineers. If the regime succeeds it will breed up a new hard-faced generation paralleling that known to the West in the persons of Gromyko and others of the younger Soviet diplomats: technically trained bureaucrats, men who have known only the Communist system, and who owe everything to that system. Neither in Moscow nor in Peking can we yet predict how such men will manage the power system they inherit from figures like Stalin and Mao.

Among the arms of the bureaucracy the central long-term issue is likely to be whether and to what extent the civil powers now held by the armed forces are allocated to the civil government chain of command, to the secret police, and to the Communist Party. Thus far pressures toward such a transfer have been evident, notably a relative expansion in the instruments of central government; but the army still retains powerful positions of administration, and a heavy claim both to the allocation of resources and in the making of high policy decisions, which stem directly from Mao's mixed military-political experience and outlook. They are reflected in that unique and powerful instrument, the National Defense Council. Whether and at what stage a cleavage develops in this matter of military authority depends on many factors which cannot now be predicted. If, as is altogether possible, the ambitions of Peking and the international context in which Peking seeks to achieve them remain highly military, the Chinese Communist military leaders may well maintain their present exalted role in civil policy and administration. If a protracted period of military quiescence should emerge from the present chronic crisis in Asia, forces might develop, notably after Mao's death, which would successfully reduce the civil role of the military.

The part of the non-Communist collaborators in the government bureaucracy and the fact that their parties have no real power have already been made amply clear by the regime. The nominal survival of these men and their parties would seem to depend on two factors: the need for their skills, and the degree to which the regime still feels compelled to appeal to incentives provided by the semblance of united-front government. Not only will both of these be diminished as rapidly as the regime finds it possible, but also there will be fewer and fewer centers of non-Communist collaboration as the foci, the non-Communist prestige figures like Chang Lan, Chang Po-chün, Chen Ming-shu, Ch'en Shu-t'ing, Ch'eng Ch'ien, Huang Yen-pei, Li Chi-shen, and Shen Chün-ju, all elders now, disappear from the scene. With their going we would expect also the virtual abandonment of the united-front fiction, now considerably diluted in the 1954 Draft Constitution.

It should be noted that the Chinese Communist Party as such—that is, as a bureaucratic and policymaking structure—is unlikely to go through a passage of primacy like that of the Soviet Union in the 1920's and early 1930's. In insurrection the Chinese Communist Party was largely an adjunct of the armed forces, carrying out those political operations judged likely to make military victory most possible. In 1949, with military administration the core of its structural framework, there was in Mao's Communism none of Lenin's initial inhibitions about the use of bureaucratic administration—only a will to seize, build, and consolidate the arms of administration. In part this skipping of a stage in Soviet evolution, the stage of party dominance, stems not merely from a difference in ideological background but also from a difference in history. The rudiments of governmental operation were too familiar to the Chinese Communists for them to revert to the more primitive techniques of party-government employed by Lenin and by Stalin in his early days. As in the Soviet Union, the Communist Party is likely to remain the binding political link among the society's elite and an important arm of administration; but the operational functions of the party apparatus are likely to narrow toward propaganda, surveillance of policy execution, reporting upward, and to some extent local and regional coordination of other arms of the bureaucracy.

The People

Assuming that the Communist regime remains in power, there are implicit in the present situation several characteristics of the position and outlook of the Chinese population at large which are likely to develop along the following lines:

1. Literacy will certainly increase, and with it an increased awareness of national and international life as set forth in the regime's propaganda and indoctrination. The scope of popular rumor and of reading between the lines of official pronouncements can be expected to grow.

2. An increased proportion of the population will be urbanized.

3. The family, although reduced somewhat in function, is likely to retain its essential core of social importance as the last area of retreat from the pressures of the regime. It is not at all unlikely that when the regime completes its structural changes, notably agricultural collectivization, it will officially reaffirm the sanctity of the family, as the Soviet Union did in the mid-1930's, as a device of civil order and a concession to intractable cultural pressures.

4. Popular pressure for increased allocations for welfare purposes will increase as the regime continues to minimize the level of current consumption in favor of military and industrialization outlays.

5. The people will become increasingly aware of the real privileges and status for those who rise within the regime; they will increasingly accept the image of the regime as a powerful 'they' to be dealt with as an inescapable and totally effective authority. The regime will seek to counter the diminished popular sense of identification by increased reliance on appeals to nationalism—which already figure strongly in Peking's massive propaganda and indoctrination efforts.

Such appear to be the general, one could almost say the abstract, lines of development of the Chinese people's position and attitudes in a future the first period of which the regime has already characterized as animated by the spirit of 'bitter struggle': a period in which the regime obviously intends to mold Chinese society, by force and starvation if necessary, to Communist-dictated ends. The mood of the people as a whole and as individuals can be predicted—in considerable detail if necessary. It is sufficient for our purpose here to note that there are three already existing broad human bases of popular discontent in Chinese society: the peasant's dislike of state grain collection and collectivization; the urban worker's dislike of both his low standard of welfare and the intensity of effort which the regime seeks to evoke from him; and a general popular dislike of the cumulative inescapable pressures and threats with which the regime surrounds the life of the individual, clashing as they do with deep forces in the Chinese culture. These pressures are likely to be steadily increased over the foreseeable future. There is also the very strong likelihood of increasing suspicion and disapproval of the Sino-Soviet tie.

With the exception of the last, these parts of the picture of the Chinese people in the next years under Communism offer nothing new to the observer of either Soviet Russian or European satellite history. The principal outlines of the pattern of impact of Communist totalitarianism on human society are widely known to be about the same everywhere; and the Chinese Communists run generally true to form. And so, also, unless the established pattern of modern totalitarian history is violated, no popular outbreak against the Chinese Communist regime can be anticipated unless there is a split among the leadership and a consequent loss of unity among the instruments of control. At a time of crisis, when new political paths for China again would become a realistic possibility, popular pressures would probably be reflected in public policy.

V. Free Asia and the Future of Chinese Communism

The regime is not merely engaged in a struggle against China's basic problems, its people, and its culture; it is in a competitive race with Free Asia. Despite the political isolation of Communist China from the external world, and the effective control system which makes this isolation possible, the great test of Communism in Asia is not being carried out in a vacuum. The evolution of Communist society in China will be profoundly affected by the course of events in Free Asia; and the full success of the Chinese Communist regime—both in Asia and, ultimately, in mainland China—depends in part on what happens over the next decisive years in Free Asia. The Chinese Communists came to power essentially because the only alternative available was weak in the field, ineffective in administration, and, to many, unattractive. In a larger sense the meaning of what Communist China accomplishes or fails to accomplish will be measured against the strength and attractiveness of Free Asia's performance.

There is an important military component to this issue, as indeed there was in the Communist takeover of 1947–1949. Military success can be an effective political substitute, in the short run, for domestic performance. Regimes which are achieving international success seldom break up in their period of expansion. Free World military weakness in Asia could thus strengthen the prestige and power of the Peking regime within China, and cushion the consequences of a mediocre domestic performance.

Although Chinese Communist direct military aggression is not to be ruled out, it is evident that the regime wishes to avoid a major war, and that it intends to pursue its ambitions for expansion in Asia by a mixture of political aggression with those limited forms of military action which minimize the risks of major war, and which cost little in resources. We can count on a determined effort to complete the conquest of Indo-China; and incipient operations in this style may be in the making, directed against Thailand, certain northern provinces of India, Burma, and, perhaps, Indonesia. The Chinese Communists hope to link such direct pressures on the Asian states to more conventional political efforts to pose as the leading power of Asia and as the repository of the correct line of approach to Asia's great problems of overpopulation and agrarian poverty.

The effectiveness of this program of quasi-military erosion and political posturing obviously hinges on the military and political performance of Free Asia. If Japan is left to wallow along from year to year in the trough of a chronic balance-of-payments crisis; if the Philippines fail to make good in concrete results the social and economic promise of Magsaysay's political success; if Indonesia remains indolent and distracted in the face of its growing population problem; if India fails to produce major results from its effort at a democratically engineered rural revolution; if Formosa fails to develop both as a creative element in Free Asia and a political rallying point for a new China—if, in short, Free Asia does not substantially improve its performance, an indifferent outcome on mainland China could still represent an important relative achievement both to the Chinese and to Asians generally.

On the other hand, the evolution of solid military, political, and economic policies in Free Asia could deny Peking its claim to military and ideological primacy in Asia, and help force, over a period of time, a fundamental re-evaluation of the Chinese Communist regime's domestic and foreign policies.

There thus appears to be a distinct, if somewhat subtle, difference between the present position of Communist China and that of the Soviet Union during the interwar period. The Soviet Union never abandoned its pretensions to international leadership and never dismantled its apparatus of connection and control over the Communist parties throughout the world. Nevertheless, Russia was a unique continental society capable of evolving on a national basis. It restrained its international ambitions in favor of domestic tasks until the course of World War II gave it important opportunities for directly extending its national authority. Until the rise of Hitler made the Soviet Union an important and even decisive element in the world's balance of power, wooed by both sides as the showdown approached in 1939, Moscow was a negligible element on the world power scene in its decisive period of domestic transformation.

Mainland China, too, represents an old and unique civilization. But it is caught up in Asia more intimately than postrevolutionary Russia was ever caught up in Europe; and Asia is an active major theater in the intensive worldwide power struggle. Peking's ambitions in Asia are being pursued with urgency and vigor. And the playback on China of events in Asia is likely to be more powerful over the coming years than the impact of the outside world on the Soviet Union from, say, 1920 to 1935.

This point must not be pushed too far. It is possible to envisage a Communist China blocked politically and militarily by a successful Free Asia but persisting for many years along its present course. If even modest success can be achieved in increasing agricultural output, the unity and power of the control system are likely to translate the surplus into increased industrial and military strength, while a growing population, apathetic and helpless, continues to live at present minimal welfare standards. In the short run the regime could survive and persist even if Free Asia offered a more successful and attractive alternative. In the long run, however, the fate of Communist China will be powerfully affected by Free Asia's strength or weakness, and by its success or failure in coping with Asia's great problems of transition.

VI. CONCLUSIONS

The procedure throughout our examination of Communist China has been to attempt a kind of trial balance as of mid-1954. This exercise leads to the judgment that, despite widespread politically unfocused popular discontent, the present position of the Chinese Communist regime on mainland China is internally secure—because of its unity and its instruments of control.

Looking ahead, we believe that the regime's continued stability depends principally on the following four interconnected factors:

1. *The policy and performance of Soviet Russia.* Moscow must continue to deny itself direct intervention in Peking's internal control system; and Moscow must avoid an internal Soviet crisis that would

gravely weaken Soviet strength on the world scene. A weak Soviet Union would force a reappraisal of the lean-to-one-side policy, as would an attempt to extend Soviet strength into Peking's domestic power machinery.

2. *Competition with Free Asia.* Peking must persuasively maintain its posture as Asia's wave of the future, both in terms of military strength and, especially, as possessor of the 'correct' formula for the solution of Asia's problems; and Peking's ability to do this lies largely in the hands of the Free World: in Free World actions and policies, and in the image the Free World impresses on the minds of Asia's citizens.

3. *The economic problem.* Peking must achieve industrialization, without excessive starvation, in the face of China's underlying problems of overpopulation and low agricultural productivity. This outcome hinges on the balance between measures to increase agricultural output and the human response of the peasantry to collectivization—with the luck of the harvests an important random variable.

4. *Top leadership unity.* Unity and continuity must be maintained in the top leadership of the regime, a problem which is likely to hinge in the foreseeable future more on the success of Peking's substantive internal and external policies, and the leadership's continued agreement on them, than on personal or bureaucratic struggles for power within Peking's control structure.

All this is said on the assumption that major war will not come. The question arises: Is Peking likely to launch a major war—for example, by pouring its ground forces south into Burma, Thailand, Malaya, and Indonesia, taking the risks that would be involved, as the Japanese did in 1941?

For the moment such premeditated military aggression seems unlikely. Peking's leaders have a strong sense of history. They see China in a tactically strong position but without the strategic underpinnings for independent major-power status. For the moment their main purpose is to concentrate on the creation of the industrial and military foundations for major-power status; and they are not in a mood for reckless military adventure which would risk their hard-won base of power in China. But it cannot be too strongly emphasized that the determination of the cost of military adventure to Peking is a matter of the Free World's strength, unity, and will. Communism is never a self-containing phenomenon.

If their present industrialization plan should clearly fail—in the specific sense that agricultural output does not expand enough to feed the rising population and supply the further margins necessary for industrial growth, then the leadership will face a critical choice: whether to change the whole cast of their policy, or to strike out into Asian food-surplus areas of Indo-China, Thailand, Burma, and Indonesia. Here the leadership might split. In any case, the situation as a whole would present grave dangers but also enormous opportunities to the Free World.

Major war could arise from less purposeful movements than a pouring of Chinese troops across frontiers. War might arise, for example, between the Soviet Union and the West, drawing Communist China in its wake. Initially Peking, in its present mood, would almost certainly meet its obligations to Moscow under the 1950 pact, exploiting the possibilities of open conflict to expand its holdings in Asia. However, Peking's behavior in the course of the war would depend significantly on the prospects of Soviet victory and on the terms of withdrawal available to Peking from the West should Soviet defeat appear likely. The overriding priority of the Chinese Communists is to maintain their base of power in China. Should the West offer terms which appeared to permit the maintenance of China's national integrity— that is, terms well short of unconditional surrender, important groups in Peking would probably seek those terms rather than fight to the limit once Soviet defeat appeared likely.

What are likely to be Peking's intentions in the face of limited unstable conflicts? Peking is likely to press its interests coolly and ruthlessly by political schisms and weaknesses. It will abandon no positions cheaply, but will assay the real power position it confronts in the mixed political-military terms that have marked Chinese Communist thought since Mao's ascendancy. We believe that, if the regime is confronted with the choice of postponing the achievement of its external ambitions or facing either major war or operations costly to industrialization, it is prepared to postpone its expansion in Asia. If confronted with a situation which would seriously endanger the regime's hold on its domestic base (and in the context of Sino-Soviet relations the UN advance to the Yalu and Manchuria was so judged in 1950), Peking is likely to fight to the limit.

This, then, is the phenomenon we confront. A unified, confident, ambitious group of men deeply committed to the use of totalitarian techniques have mastered mainland China. They are driven on by their internal and external ambitions to industrialize rapidly and expand the modern units of their armed forces. They are driven on by the requirements of these tasks combined with their ideological commitment to total political control to employ techniques which may or may not be consistent with their aims. They face in the coming years a decisive passage of modern history at a time of intense power struggle in which they are caught up two ways: in the Sino-Soviet Alliance, and in the interaction of China and the rest of Asia. Thus, despite the unique powers the Communist regime exercises on the mainland, its fate rests substantially with the peoples of the Free World and their governments.

NOTE FOR CHAPTER 16

1. Among them: Liao Ch'eng-chih, Liu Ning-i, General Su Yu, Sung Shao-wen, Li K'e-nung, General Li Hsien-nien, Chang Han-fu, Hsiao Hua, Wan I, Wang Cheng, Wang Chia-hsiang, Wang Shou-tao, Wu Hsiu-ch'uan, Wu Liang-p'ing.

APPENDICES

APPENDIX
———— 1 ————

INDICES OF INDUSTRIAL PRODUCTION
IN COMMUNIST CHINA, 1949–1952

The purpose of this appendix is to compile systematically the different indices of industrial production published in Communist China, to cross check them for internal consistency, and thus provide the basis for computing an adjusted and revised series.

TABLE I

	Official Chinese Communist Indices							
Product	1949 = 100						1951 = 100	
	1950		1951		1952		1952	
	(a)	(b)	(a)	(c)	(a)	(d)	(e)	(f)
Pig iron	394	390	597		764	750	131	128
Steel ingots	383		566		846	940	141	150
Rolled steel	288		496		848	820		
Electric power	106	113	134		164	180	129	122
Coal	132	125	164		202	200	118	123
Crude oil	166	158	248		358	310	125	144
Cement	213	210	376		433	350	111	115
Metal cutting machine tools	200		362		650			
Cotton yarn	134	118	149	124	201	200	130	134
Cotton cloth	154	108	197		287	230	136	146
Paper	130		223		332		151	149
Flour	93		143		220			
Sugar	121		151		199		128	132
Matches	87		107		129			
Cigarettes	116		116		151			

Sources: (a) *Communiqué on Rehabilitation and Development of National Economy, Culture and Education during 1952*, Peking, State Statistical Bureau, September 29, 1953.

(b) Chen Chien-ke, "China's Outstanding Financial and Economic Achievements," *People's China*, October 16, 1951.

(c) Chen Yun, "Address to the Preparatory Conference of the All-China Federation of Industrial and Commercial Circles," on June 24, 1952, *New China's Economic Achievements*, Peking, 1952, p. 141.

(d) Chia To-fu, "The Advance of China's Industry," *People's China*, June 1, 1953, p. 10.

(e) Po I-po, "The 1953 State Budget of the People's Republic of China," Supplement to *People's China*, March 16, 1953.

(f) Calculated from source (a).

TABLE II

Product	Official Chinese Communist Indices Past Peak = 100							
	1949	1950		1951		1952		
						Plan	Actual	
	(a)	(d)		(d)		(a)	(g)	(h)
	(1)	(2)	(3)	(4)	(5)	(6)	(7)	(8)
Pig iron	11	48 ⎫ (c)		64 ⎫ (c)		104	115	84
Steel ingots	16	68 ⎬		97 ⎬		155	183	135
Rolled steel	18	67 ⎭		120 ⎭		167	237	153
Electric power	72	77 ⎫ (d)		95 ⎫ (d)		115	114	118
Coal	45	59 ⎭		69 ⎭		90	92	91
Crude oil	38					136	150	136
Cement	31	66(c)		107(c)		148	146	134
Metal cutting machine tools								
Cotton yarn	72	100 ⎫ (c)		106 ⎫ (c)		144	155	145
Cotton cloth	73	109 ⎭		113 ⎭		161	176	209
Paper	90	85 ⎫	114	146 ⎫	155	234	241	299
Flour	78	49 ⎪		82 ⎪		106(b)		172
Sugar	40(b)	73 ⎬ (e)		73 ⎬ (e)		100(f)		80
Matches	85	85 ⎪		85 ⎪		111		110
Cigarettes	83	110 ⎭		110 ⎭		145	178	125

Sources: (a) Li Fu-chun, "The Restoration and Development of Our Industries in the Past Three Years," *New China's Economic Achievements*, October 2, 1952, p. 180.

(b) Li Fu-chun, "The Present Situation of China's Industries and the Direction of Our Future Work," *New China's Economic Achievements*, October 31, 1951, p. 124.

(c) Ke Chia-lung, "China Builds a New Democracy," *People's China*, December 16, 1951.

(d) Wu K'ang, "Consolidate the Victory, Continue to Advance," *The Economic Weekly*, Shanghai, January 3, 1952, in K. C. Chao, *Source Materials from Communist China*, Vol. 2, p. 14.

(e) Huang Yen-pei, "Progress in China's Light Industry," *People's China*, December 16, 1952.

(f) Po I-po, "Three Years of Achievement of the People's Republic of China," in *New China's Economic Achievements*, p. 157.

(g) Calculated on basis of Plan Fulfillment indices given in source (a).

(h) Calculated by applying 1952 index (1949 = 100) as given in source (a) to 1949 index (past peak = 100) as given in sources (g) and (h).

Table III. Corrected Indices of Industrial Production in Communist China

Product	1949 = 100			Past Peak = 100	
	1950(a)	1951(a)	1952(a)	1949	1952(b)
	(1)	(2)	(3)	(4)	(5)
Pig iron	394	597	750	11	83
Crude steel	383	566	846	16	135
Rolled steel	288	496	820	18	148
Electric power	106	134	158	72	114
Coal	132	164	202	45	91
Crude oil	166	248	310	38	118
Cement	213	319	350	31	108
Cotton yarn	118	124	161	72	116
Cloth	108	138	189	73	138
Paper	94	162	245	90	220
Flour	63	105	162	78	126
Sugar	121	151	199	40	80
Matches	87	100	120	85	102
Cigarettes	116	132	151	83	125

(a) Correction based on elimination of internal inconsistencies in the indices in Tables I and II. As a rule, the lower figure was adopted, except that whenever the differences were minor the latest data were used.

(b) Calculated by applying revised 1952 index with 1949 as a base, column (3) of this table, to 1949 index with 'past peak' as a base, column (4) of this table.

TABLE IV

Product	Indices of 1952 Plan Fulfillment		
	Official		Revised
	(*a*)	(*b*)	(*c*)
Pig iron	111	81	80
Steel ingots	118	87	87
Rolled steel	142	92	89
Electric power	99	103	99
Coal	106	101	101
Crude oil	110	100	87
Cement	99	90	73
Cotton yarn	106	100	80
Cotton cloth	109	130	86
Paper	103	128	94
Flour		162	119
Sugar	156	80	80
Matches		100	92
Cigarettes	123	83	86

Sources: (*a*) Same as source (*a*) in Table I.

(*b*) Calculated by applying column (8) of Table II to column (6) of the same table.

(*c*) Calculated by applying indices in column (5) of Table III to indices in column (6) of Table II.

THE SOVIET UNION, 1928; COMMUNIST CHINA, 1952

	Units	U.S.S.R.		China	
Population	Millions	147.0	1926	About 600	
Crude birth rate	Per 1,000	43.5(a)	1926	40.0 }	1930–35
Crude death rate	Per 1,000	19.9(a)	1926	34.0 }	
Rate of increase per year	Per cent	2.4%	1926	0.6(?)	
Population increase during First Five Year Plan period	Per cent	n.a.(b)			
Proportion rural	Per cent	82.1%	1926	80–85%	1926
Proportion urban	Per cent	17.9%	1926	15–20%	1926
Total labor force	Millions	86.2(c)	1926	250(?)	1926
Working force in non-agricultural employment	Millions	15.7	1926	50–55	1926
Working force in modern industry	Millions	3.35(d)	1928	1.9	1928
Agricultural population per acre cultivated land	Units	0.2	1926–8	3 (including mining & transport)	
Gross National Product	Billions 1952 U. S. dollars	$35	1928	$30	1952
GNP per capita	1952 U. S. dollars	$240	1928	$50	1952
Per cent GNP invested	Per cent	20%	1928	12%	1952
Output per worker in modern industry	1952 U. S. dollars	About $900–1,100(f)		$700(?)	1952
Output per person engaged in agriculture	1952 U. S. dollars	About $230–270(f)		$45(?)	1952
Output per person dependent on agriculture	1952 U. S. dollars	About $140–170(f)		$25(?)	1952
Size of military establishment	Billions 1952 U. S. dollars	About 0.8	1928	2.0	1952
Percentage of GNP put into military budget	Per cent	2%	1928	7%	1952
Percentage of GNP included in the government budget	Per cent	25%	1928	27%	1952
Production					
Coal Total	Million metric tons	40.1	1929	48.2	1952
Per capita	Kilograms	273	1929	96	1952
First Five Year Plan goal	Million metric tons	75	1932/3	77.2	1957–59
Crude steel Total	Million metric tons	4.3	1927–8	1.2	1952
Per capita	Kilograms	29	1927–8	2	1952
First Five Year Plan goal	Million metric tons	10.4	1932/3	4.8	1957–59
Finished steel Total	Million metric tons			0.7	1952
Per capita	Kilograms			1	1952

	Unit					
First Five Year Plan goal	Million metric tons		3.3	1927-8	1.85	1957-59
Pig iron	Million metric tons		22	1927-8	1.6	1952
	Kilograms		10	1932/3	3	1952
First Five Year Plan goal	Million metric tons				n.a.	
Electric power generating capacity	Thousand kilowatts	Total	1,900	1928	2,850	1952
	Kilowatts	Per capita	0.013	1928	0.006	1952
First Five Year Plan goal			About 3½ times the 1928 level	1932/3	11,400	1957-59
Cotton spindleage in industry	Thousands	Total	7,465	1929	5,000	1952
	Units	Per capita	0.051	1929	0.010	1952
Cement	Million metric tons	Total	1.90	1928	2.3	1952
	Kilograms	Per capita	0.013	1928	5	1952

Soviet Union

	Grain Exports (1,000 tons)	Percentage Share in Total Exports of Grain Exports
1909–13	10,533	40.1
1913	9,185	33.7
1923–24	2,596	37.7
1924–25	569	8.5
1925–26	2,017	22.6
1926–27	2,099	24.6
1927–28	289	3.3
1929	178	1.1
1930	4,765	19.4
1931	5,057	18.5
1932	1,728	9.6
1933	1,686	8.2
1934	771	4.5
1935	1,519	10.1
1936	322	2.6

Principal source: Alexander Baykov, *Soviet Foreign Trade*, Princeton, Princeton University Press, 1946.

(a) European Russia.
(b) The average annual rate of increase of population between the 1926 and 1939 censuses was 1.3% per year (1.4% for those over 15 years of age).
(c) Both sexes, all ages.
(d) Large-scale industry.
(e) The component parts of national product were measured at 1926/7 prices and percentages computed.
(f) Estimates.

APPENDIX
3

AGRICULTURAL OUTPUT AND THE CHINESE
COMMUNIST FIRST FIVE YEAR PLAN

·The following crude arithmetic calculations are designed for a limited purpose only: to illustrate roughly the relation between the course of agricultural output in Communist China in the period 1954–1957 and the goals of the First Five Year Plan.

The calculation is set out in terms of current U. S. dollars. The following assumptions and calculations have been made, which are broadly consistent with those made in Chapter 14.

1. It is assumed that population is rising at 1.2 per cent per annum, and it is arbitrarily assumed here that virtually the whole of the increase will be in the urban sector.

2. It is roughly estimated that more than one-half of Chinese consumption expenditures are on food for normally poor rural families, somewhat less than one-half in cities; but that special allowance must be made for the armed forces and the civil employees of the state, including those in forced labor. Taking the Chinese population at 582 million for 1952 and making allowances for differences in the value of rural and urban food consumption, total initial food outlays (excepting special categories) come to $10.3 billion. An extra $1.0 billion is allowed for those fed directly by the state. The agricultural component in 1952 foreign trade is taken as about $0.7 billion.

3. The implication of these figures is that in 1952 something like $4 billion in foodstuffs was mobilized from the countryside, or about one-third of total output. From independent estimates based on Communist sources this is not far off the mark.

4. It is assumed that the First Five Year Plan must make allowance for feeding an increased population, requiring an additional $1.0 billion; and that the regime aims to expand its agricultural exports by, say, an extra $.4 billion.

5. If there is any validity in these calculations the regime must seek an increase of about one-third in the foodstuffs mobilized in its hands in the course of the First Five Year Plan.

Again it should be emphasized that the absolute figures used in this exercise are highly arbitrary and the orders of magnitude exceedingly rough. This is merely a quantitative version of the qualitative argument presented in Chapters 14 and 16.

CASE 1. APPROXIMATE CONDITIONS FOR SUCCESS OF THE FIRST CHINESE COMMUNIST FIVE YEAR PLAN

(in billion $U. S.)

	1952	1957–1959 Requirements
Rural food requirements	7.5	7.5
Urban food requirements	2.8	3.8
Military and civil state employees (extra rations)	1.0	1.0
Agricultural exports	0.7	1.1
Total	12.0	13.4
	Output	13.4
Government collection	4.5	5.9

An increase in agricultural output, in 5 years, of something just over 10 per cent is likely to be required to fulfill the objectives of the plan, with the increase effectively mobilized by the state to meet expanded urban and export requirements.

CASE 2. STAGNATION

(in billion $U. S.)

	1952	1957–1959 Requirements
Rural food requirements	7.5	7.5
Urban food requirements	2.8	3.8
Military and civil state employees (extra rations)	1.0	1.0
Agricultural exports	.7	1.1
Total	12.0	13.4
Assumed output		12.0
Deficit		1.4

In Case 2 the rise of urban food requirements can be met only by some combination of a decline in other categories: that is, either a decline in peasant food consumption, urban food consumption, the food consumption of government-fed groups, or in agricultural exports. Stagnation is likely to be reflected in all categories to some degree. The regime would accord a likely priority, however, to the maintenance of exports. Second priority might well be the maintenance of privilege in the armed services and among the civil cadres. Third priority would go to feeding the cities. The bulk of the gap would be filled by peasant starvation and malnutrition.

CASE 3. A CRISIS SITUATION: A 10% DECLINE

(in billion $U. S.)

	1952	1957–1959 Requirements
Rural food requirements	7.5	7.5
Urban food requirements	2.8	3.8
Military and civil state employees (extra rations)	1.0	1.0
Agricultural exports	.7	1.1
Total	12.0	13.4
Assumed output		10.8
Deficit		2.6

In Case 3 the scale of the shortage, if totally allocated to the peasantry (with other categories fully maintained), would produce a food deficit of one-third in the countryside. This we would take to be beyond tolerable limits, even with the regime's massive control capabilities. Evidently, sacrifices in other categories would have to be made which would strike at the success of the industrialization plan, at morale in the military and bureaucratic ranks, and at the urban standard of welfare. It is to be noted that minimum rural and urban food requirements (11.3) would exceed assumed output (10.8), even if extra rations and agricultural exports were abandoned. Should such a situation persist for several harvest seasons, we believe it likely to produce a general political crisis on the mainland and in Sino-Soviet relations.

A SELECTED BIBLIOGRAPHY IN WESTERN
LANGUAGES

This Bibliography was compiled by Martha T. Henderson under the over-all editorship of W. W. Rostow and with the assistance of the members of the staff of the Center for International Studies and certain of the faculty and graduate students of Harvard University. Indebtedness is acknowledged especially to the authors of the other bibliographies listed in Section I.

The analysis of Communist China from the outside requires certain special techniques somewhat similar to those required for study of the Soviet Union. Since few relatively objective observers are allowed extensive access to Communist China, the bulk of the data must be that released from official Communist sources, especially the Communist Chinese press. Although the use of this material poses many difficulties, it appears to be the case that a major modern society—even a totalitarian society—cannot be maintained without revealing the main lines of its evolution in some open sources. This statement holds particularly true of the important events and trends in economic and political affairs. It is more difficult to ascertain the mood of the Chinese people because of the size and variety of the country as well as the censorship. But it is possible to discern certain attitudes from the reports of a few observers, and by reading the official directives to the cadres with respect to their own behavior, their treatment of the peasantry, industrial workers, and other groups.

Fortunately good translations of the Communist press are issued regularly (see Section II), so that a good part of this primary material is easily available to a western reader.

A. Sources.
    I. Other bibliographies.
    II. Press, radio, and other translations and commentaries (from many coun·
        tries).
    III. Newspapers.
    IV. Periodicals:
        A. American.
        B. Australian.

    C. British.

    D. *a.* Non-Communist Chinese (in English).

       b. Communist Chinese (in English).

    E. French.

    F. Japanese (in English).

    G. Indian (in English).

    H. Indonesian (in English).

    I. Korean (in English).

    J. Filipino (in English).

    K. United Nations (in English).

B. Subjects.

    V. History, 1848–1949 (selected list).

    VI. Communist period, 1949–1954 (and including certain background sources; emphasis on the period 1951–1954 throughout).

      A. General.

      B. Ideology.

      C. Top leadership and Communist Party.

      D. Army and Korean War.

      E. Foreign relations; trade (excluding Sino-Soviet relations).

    VII. Sino-Soviet relations.

    VIII. Chinese society.

    IX. Chinese economy.

C. Appendices.

    1. Papers of the China Project, Center for International Studies, Massachusetts Institute of Technology, Cambridge, Mass., 1952–1954.

    2. *Papers on China,* Regional Studies Program on East Asia, Harvard University, Cambridge, Mass., 1949–1954 (selected list of those pertaining to Communist China).

    3. *Studies on Communist China,* papers under the direction of Theodore H. E. Chen, University of California, Los Angeles, 1952–1953.

I. OTHER BIBLIOGRAPHIES

1. *Annals of the Academy of Political and Social Science,* Vol. 277, "Report on China," Philadelphia, Pa., September 1951. Note especially Mary C. Wright, "How We Learn about Communist China," pp. 224–228, which reviews bibliography on Communist China up to 1951.

2. Chao Kuo-chün, comp., *Selected Works in English for a Topical Study of Modern China, 1840–1952* (mimeo.), Cambridge, Mass., Regional Studies Program on East Asia, Harvard University, November 1952.

Includes references to other bibliographies and reference works, and gives a detailed list of books and articles according to political, economic, and social topics, certain political movements, leading personalities, etc.

3. External Research Report, *Unpublished Research on China, in Progress and Recently Completed.* Most recent compilation dated April, 1954, ERS List #2.2, 11 pp.; see also reports of April 1953, ERS List #2.1; August 15, 1952, ERS List #22; January 16, 1952, and one previous. Note also *Unpublished Research on Far East and Asia, General and Regional, Completed and in Progress.* All are compiled

and distributed by the External Research Staff, Office of Intelligence Research, Department of State, Washington 25, D. C.

Useful lists of social science research contributed by faculty and graduate students throughout the United States. It includes books and articles in progress, graduate theses, projects, etc.

4. Fairbank, J. K., ed., *Bibliographical Guide to Modern China, Works in Western Languages,* 1948, 80 pp.; Fairbank, J. K., comp., *Bibliographical Guide to Modern China, Works in Western Languages* (revised), Section 5: *Economics,* with Douglas S. Paauw, 1951, 49 pp. Both for the Regional Studies Program on China, mimeographed for private distribution by the Committee on International and Regional Studies, Harvard University, Cambridge, Mass.

Invaluable annotated guides to modern China which list materials through the period just preceding, or, in the revised section, just after, the Communist takeover. Other bibliographies and reference works are noted.

5. *Far East Digest,* Summaries of current articles on the Far East and the Pacific Area, 12 numbers per year (usually issued bimonthly); published by the Institute of Pacific Relations, New York, N. Y.

Contains summaries of articles from both American and foreign periodicals, including key articles from Communist Chinese publications. Excellent source for up-to-date references.

6. *Far Eastern Quarterly,* published for the Far Eastern Association, Inc., by the Science Press, Lancaster, Pa. The August issues have a bibliography of books and periodicals listed by country, which has been compiled in recent years by Miss Gussie Gaskill. These lists are an invaluable source for materials of the calendar year previous to date of issue.

7. Thomas, S. B., and Knight Biggerstaff, *Recent Books on China, 1945–1951* (1945–47 compiled by Biggerstaff; 1948–51 by Thomas), New York, American Institute of Pacific Relations, 1951, 16 pp. Contains list of titles plus reviews of certain recent books.

II. Press, Radio, and Other Translations and Commentaries: Communist China

The major items constitute the most important primary sources and/or reports available.

1. American Consulate General, Hong Kong. Three invaluable sources providing news from the mainland:

a. Current Background, founded June 1950. Mimeographed. Occasionally. Topical analyses which give translations of pertinent data, ranging over economic, political, social, and cultural affairs. Material is usually from the Communist New China News Agency (NCNA). The first 200 issues are indexed.

b. Survey of the China Mainland Press, founded November 1, 1950. A mimeographed, translated survey, issued almost daily, of the Chinese mainland newspapers. It usually carries important editorials from the Peking *People's Daily,* plus other major policy statements and many smaller items. Most material is from NCNA. Issues run from about 20–60 pp. and are carefully indexed under headings such as Korean News, International Affairs, National and Regional Affairs. Also periodic indices of other untranslated articles in the press.

c. Review of the Hongkong China Press, issued since 1946. An almost daily mimeographed translated review of the Chinese newspapers appearing in Hong Kong. The political bias of the newspapers is noted. Later issues have been carefully indexed. While less informative on the internal situation on the mainland than items *a* and *b* above, this source contains data on the migration of overseas Chinese students, local affairs of Hong Kong or Formosa, and does include some notes and occasional articles on mainland affairs, especially in the Kwangtung area.

2. American Universities Field Staff, 522 Fifth Ave., New York 36, N. Y., Phillips Talbot, Exec. Dir. This organization issues mimeographed newsletters which may not be used for other publication, but may be used as sources for research papers. The letters of A. Doak Barnett from Hong Kong and Albert Ravenholt from Formosa should be noted, since they contain information from interviews and from the press, with interesting interpretations. Earlier letters by the same authors and others from Hong Kong, Formosa, and the China mainland were sent out in the same manner by the Institute for Current World Affairs at the above address. These date back to postwar times. A valuable source.

3. *Antara Daily News Bulletin,* the semi-official news service of Indonesia; mimeographed from Amsterdam in English, but strictly Indonesian in approach. Each weekly edition contains articles with reference to China, especially respecting international relations or the impressions of Indonesian overseas Chinese students returning from the mainland.

4. *China News Analysis,* a weekly printed newssheet published in Hong Kong. The first issue was on August 25, 1953, and it has been appearing regularly ever since. The editor is a multilingual Hungarian Jesuit priest named Ladany. This is a good summary of events handled topically and is carefully footnoted and indexed. It is based on the Communist press and is commonly about 7 pp. A very useful source.

5. *China Bulletin* of the Far Eastern Joint Office, Division of Foreign Missions, NCCC/U.S.A., 156 Fifth Ave., New York 10, N. Y. Founded 1951, a monthly; usually 4 pp., printed. Francis P. Jones, editor. A Protestant bulletin which briefly reports on the church in China and also on mainland news, including educational and general affairs.

6. *Chinese News Service,* Nationalist government agency. A mimeographed weekly newssheet published in New York. See also their *News Bulletin of the China News Service.* Mainly dedicated to international affairs, there is little on internal mainland matters. Not very informative.

7. *Chinese Communism in Action,* H. Arthur Steiner, compiler. Three mimeographed volumes of translated source materials on political developments in mainland China. Materials are often taken from the Communist press. Published by the University of California Press, Los Angeles, November 1953, 313 pp. A valuable compilation, indexed.

8. *Communist China Problem Research Series,* founded November 1953. A mimeographed topical series put out by The Union Research Institute, P. O. Private Bag K-1, Kowloon, Hong Kong. Carefully documented interpretations by a non-Communist group, based largely on the Communist press. The first issue of November, 1953, was on "Campaign of Party Expansion of the Chinese Communist Party in 1952," by Fang Shu. The second, December, 1953, dealt with "Higher Education in Communist China," by Chung Shih. Subsequent items listed in appropriate sections.

9. *The Current Digest of the Soviet Press,* published weekly since 1949 by the Joint Committee on Slavic Studies, appointed by the American Council of Learned Societies and the Social Science Research Council. Contains indexed translations frequently condensed from various press items in *Pravda,* etc., of about one month

previous to the *Digest's* publication. There are frequent references to China, especially regarding international relations.

10. *Daily News Release* of the Hsinhua (New China) News Agency, published monthly in Communist China by the People's Government. A printed, paper-bound, indexed volume consisting mainly of short news items. Not very useful.

11. *Daily Report Foreign Radio Broadcasts*, Section on Far East. Monitoring of Peking, etc., newscasts. It is often repetitions of newspaper NCNA accounts, but valuable for the Communist line to the outside world. An open U. S. government series which may not be cited as a source.

12. *Developments in China*, British press summary and analysis issued in Hong Kong, and giving daily coverage. Useful, but not easily available in the United States.

13. *Freedom Front*. A fortnightly report of Chinese news and views, published in Hong Kong beginning July 29, 1950. Also published in Chinese. Editor: Hsieh Chen·ping. A mimeographed English report which is based on the Communist press and apparently also on interviews with refugees. Politically it is both anti-sheet has some useful data, especially on what is wrong in China.

14. *For Lasting Peace, for a People's Democracy*, the Cominform Bulletin, published weekly in Bucharest. Useful for indication of policy lines of international Communism.

15. *Indian Press Digest*, published periodically since March 1952, by the Bureau of International Relations of the Department of Political Science, University of California, Berkeley. Based on 23 daily and weekly periodicals. March 1954 issue covers through December 1952 period. Largely useful for international relations with China.

16. *Inside China*. A British government commentary on events, issued in Singapore. Difficult to obtain in the United States.

17. *Japanese Press Summary*, issued nearly daily by the American Embassy, Tokyo, Political Division, Language Services Branch. Mimeographed and translated summary which gives occasional news of Sino-Japanese trade, or comments by repatriates. Peripheral source. There are similar press translations emanating from American Embassies in all Southeast Asian countries.

18. *Library Notes*, published weekly by Committee for Free Asia, Inc., San Francisco, California. (See also their *Asian Student*.) A review of materials received for staff use by the library, starting in 1952. Quotes from periodicals, some infrequently seen, and has rare items on Communist China. It also contains notice of new books and pamphlets. Peripheral source.

19. *New China News Agency*. Official English translations of the Chinese Communist press published daily since 1950 in London. Mainly oriented toward international affairs, it carries less frequent coverage of internal matters. Any important items quoted in this source are almost always to be found in the more comprehensive *Survey of the China Mainland Press*.

20. *Pacific News Digest, China Section*, published intermittently in Tokyo. #1, April 1, 1953; #2, April 6, 1953; #3–4, May 20, 1953; #5, end of 1953. Printed sheets, anti-Communist. Aims to provide intelligence ·on politics, finance, and culture in China, based on the press. It also reports interviews. Quite useful when available.

21. *Radio Free Asia monitoring of Hsinhua (New China) News Agency Morsecast*, printed sheets which ceased publication in April 1953. Sponsored by a private, non-Communist group in the United States.

22. *Soviet Press Translations*, published twice monthly by the Far Eastern and Russian Institute, University of Washington, Seattle, from 1946 to March 15, 1953. It contained frequent references to China translated both from Russian sources such as *Pravda* or *Voprosy ekonomiki*, and Chinese sources such as *Hsüeh hsi*, which ranged over Chinese ideological, political, economic, and cultural affairs. It was a very useful source for official Russian or Chinese viewpoints on important issues, plus general information.

23. United States Information Service (Hong Kong), *Chinese Communist Propaganda Review*, October 1951–August 1, 1953. Mimeographed translations issued bimonthly which included sections on: Propaganda Review, Methods and Techniques, and Theme and Content. Sources were periodicals such as *Hsüeh hsi* and the press.

III. Newspapers (see also Section II, for press digests and reviews)

American (U.S.A.)

Christian Science Monitor, published daily, Boston, Mass. Excellent reports, such as 12 articles on China by correspondent Frank Robertson, March 10–April 14, 1952; and the series of 10 articles, "Peace for Asia," by Gordon Walker, April 12–May 3, 1954, first article specifically on Communist China.

New York Times, especially for articles by foreign correspondents, such as those of Henry Lieberman from Hong Kong.

British

The Times, published daily, London, especially for about three brief articles monthly on the internal situation in China, usually by the China correspondent, Richard Harris. See also the *London Times Review of Industry* article by Harris on "China's Industrialization," January 16, 1954.

Manchester Guardian, published daily, Manchester. Periodic reports on China. See also *The Manchester Guardian Weekly:* Vol. 63, No. 15, through Vol. 64, No. 5 (1950–1951), series of good articles on "Communist China" by Leonard Consandine. See also "The New China: Whirlpool of Revolution" and "The New China: Terrorism and Resistance," by Robert Guillain, May 24 and May 31, 1951. "Becoming a Military Power," December 20, 1951, R. Guillain. "Revolution in China: A War of Long Duration," R. Guillain, December 28, 1951. December 17, 1953: editorial on China, p. 8. Series, December 24, 1953–January 7, 1954, 3 articles on "Industrializing China" by special correspondent. Last one had subheading, "Education's Hurried Task." "Labour's Delegation to China," from "our own correspondent," June 3, 1954. "China's Interest in Trade with the West," by Rt. Hon. Harold Wilson, M.P., June 10, 1954, p. 3. Editorial, same issue, "Trade with China," p. 9. "Chou En-lai and Britain," by Rt. Hon. Harold Wilson, M.P., June 17, 1954, p. 5. "United States and China," from "our own correspondent," July 8, 1954, pp. 1–2. "Limitations of British Trade with China," from our financial staff, July 15, 1954, p. 2. "Britain, America, and the Chinese Fighters," from "our own correspondent," Max Freedman, additional notes by the diplomatic correspondent, July 29, 1954, p. 3.

Switzerland

Neue Zürcher Zeitung, published daily in Zurich, carries learned articles on international current affairs. The *"Christian Science Monitor"* of Europe.

IV. PERIODICALS

A. American.
B. Australian.
C. British.
D. *a.* Non-Communist Chinese (in English).
   b. Communist Chinese (in English).
E. French.
F. Japanese (in English).
G. Indian (in English).
H. Indonesian (in English).
I. Korean (in English).
J. Filipino (in English).
K. United Nations (in English).

A number of periodicals which are likely to carry articles or commentary upon Communist China are listed below, with annotations. The best up-to-date guide to specific articles will be found in the *Far East Digest,* see Section I, and in the yearly bibliographies given in the August issue, *Far Eastern Quarterly,* Section I.

A. American

1. *Annals of the American Academy of Political and Social Science,* published bimonthly, Philadelphia, Pa. Note issue of September 1951, #277, "Report on China," edited by H. Arthur Steiner. A learned journal devoted to current issues, with scholarly and informative articles assembled topically.

2. *American Political Science Review,* published quarterly by the American Political Science Association, Washington, D. C. Official organ of the Association. Publishes fairly frequent scholarly or informative articles on current issues in China.

3. *Current History,* the Monthly Magazine of World Affairs, published by Events Publishing Co., Philadelphia, Pa. A reputable learned journal, useful source of factual and analytical data, handled topically. Contains fairly frequent articles on Communist China.

4. *The Department of State Bulletin,* published weekly by Department of State, U. S. Government Printing Office, Washington, D. C. Contains frequent, usually brief, statements and speeches on China policy by State Department officials. Indispensable for official United States viewpoint.

5. External Research Staff, Office of Intelligence Research, Department of State, Washington, D. C. Periodic footnoted articles on specific aspects of the China situation.

6. *Far East Digest* (see Section I).

7. *Far East Trader,* published weekly in New York by American International Publications, 1951–present. Mimeographed sheets (usually about 8 pp. per issue), containing very short summaries of NCNA reports mainly on trade, some trade statistics from Hong Kong, Shanghai, etc., and infrequent articles.

8. *Far Eastern Quarterly* (see also Section I), published for the Far Eastern Association, Inc., by the Science Press, Lancaster, Pa. Official organ of scholars interested in the Far East. A basic source, although articles on current affairs in China are infrequent. Indexed yearly. August issue contains an excellent bibliography for the previous calendar year.

9. *Far Eastern Survey,* published monthly by the American Institute of Pacific Relations, New York, N. Y. A standard source for Far Eastern affairs with contributions by scholars and men of affairs. Indexed yearly. Subjects range over political, economic, and social affairs and Sino-Soviet and international relations. Relatively frequent articles on Communist China.

10. *Foreign Affairs,* an American Quarterly Review, published by the Council on Foreign Relations, Inc., New York, N. Y. Authoritative scholarly source. Infrequent articles on China.

11. *Foreign Policy Bulletin,* an analysis of current international events, published twice monthly by the Foreign Policy Association, Inc., N. Y. Occasional news notes or brief articles on China, especially U. S.-China policy. Too brief to be very informative.

12. *Monthly Labor Review,* published by Department of Labor, U. S. Government Printing Office, Washington, D. C. Has treated Chinese labor problems.

13. *Pacific Affairs,* published quarterly by the Institute of Pacific Relations at Richmond, Va. A fundamental source on Far Eastern affairs with contributions by well-known scholars and men of affairs. Carries frequent informative, critical articles on China which are usually well documented.

14. *Problems of Communism,* periodic (usually bimonthly) publication for reference use and limited circulation. Published by Documentary Studies Section, International Information Administration, U. S. Government, Washington, D. C., since 1951. Deals mainly with the Soviet Union, but has an occasional section on China with documented, useful articles by scholars or officials.

15. *World Politics.* A Quarterly Journal of International Relations, published at Princeton, N. J., under the editorial sponsorship of the Center of International Studies, Princeton University. Sound source which carries scholarly and essay-type articles of special interest to experts in international affairs. Occasional articles are on China.

See also: Section II on Press translations, etc. *Reader's Guide to Periodical Literature* for notice of articles or editorials in magazines such as *Time, Newsweek, The Nation, The Atlantic, Harper's,* etc., or certain religious periodicals. Other learned journals or reviews such as the *American Journal of Sociology, Geographic Review, The Review of Politics, Proceedings of the American Philosophical Society, Psychiatry, Yale Review,* etc., all of which have carried specialized articles on China.

B. Australian

1. *Australian Outlook,* The Journal of the Australian Institute of International Affairs, affiliated to the Royal Institute of International Affairs, and constituting the Australian National Council of the Institute of Pacific Relations, published quarterly, Melbourne. Founded 1947. It incorporates the *Austral-Asiatic Bulletin.* Has fairly frequent informative, analytical articles on different aspects of China.

2. *Australian Quarterly,* published in Sydney for the Australian Institute of Political Science. A semi-scholarly review, more oriented towards literature and the humanities than the sciences, which carries infrequent articles on China.

C. British

1. *Asian Review,* incorporating *The Asiatic Review* and *The Journal of the East India Association,* founded in the 1880's; published quarterly in London by the

East India Association, a group with both English and Indian membership. Predominantly oriented toward India, it runs occasional articles on China by international contributors. A secondary source with brief anti-Communist commentaries.

2. *Eastern World,* published monthly, London. Indexed yearly by country. It attempts to have non-partisan contributions. It carries frequent articles on China, especially relating to culture, industry, and agriculture, which are usually brief, editorial-type statements of a relatively conservative slant. It is an informative secondary source.

3. *The Economist,* published weekly, London. Contains fairly frequent references to China trade and foreign policy, occasional articles on China's internal economic and political situation.

4. *Far Eastern Economic Review,* published weekly, Hong Kong. Contains editorials and notes on mainland China in nearly every issue, plus occasional signed articles, and trade statistics. Topics range from discussions of economics and political affairs to their effect on cultural and social matters. About 60 per cent of the editorials, which are unsigned, are by the editor, Eric Halpern, a former finance and commerce man in Shanghai, while most of the remainder are by local British correspondents, notably Richard Harris of the *Times;* a few are by E. Stuart Kirby, Professor of Economics, University of Hong Kong. These editorials and the notes are based on the China press, other Far Eastern journals, interviews, etc. Footnoting and documentation is a little haphazard, but this magazine can be counted a very useful primary source, containing many valuable quotations from mainland publications and good "feel" for the mainland situation. It is indexed every six months.

5. *Great Britain and the East,* published monthly, London. Established in 1911 and incorporating *The Near East* and *The Near East and India.* It covers industry, economics, and current affairs and has some articles on China which are fairly brief but informative. Trade commentaries and some statistics are also included.

6. *Hongkong Annual Reports,* published by Great Britain Colonial Office, London, H. M. Stationery Office. Mainly about the colony, it carries some data on mainland refugees, population notes, references to Hong Kong's relations with mainland China, etc.

7. *Hongkong Government Gazette,* the official publications of the Hong Kong government, more or less equivalent to the Federal Register.

8. *International Affairs,* published quarterly by the Royal Institute of International Affairs, London. Authoritative journal of international affairs; excellent bibliography. Carries various analytical articles on China.

9. *Journal of the Royal Central Asian Society,* published monthly, London. Scholarly emphasis, but some informative general articles on Tibet, and occasionally on China proper, China trade, etc.

10. *Keesing's Contemporary Archives,* Keesing's Publications, Ltd., London. A weekly diary of world events with index kept constantly up-to-date.

11. *World Today,* Chatham House Review, published monthly by the Royal Institute of International Affairs, London. Carries up-to-date informative articles and editorial comment, occasionally on China. Supplement: *Chronology of international events and documents.*

See also popular magazines and learned journals and reviews.

D. a. Non-Communist Chinese (in English)

1. *Chinese Association for the UN,* newsletter monthly, Taipei, Taiwan (Formosa). Pro-Nationalist sheet mainly on international affairs.

2. *Free China Review,* a monthly founded in 1951 and published in Taiwan by the Nationalists. Strongly anti-Communist. Runs occasional articles on mainland China and regularly carries a section on "News from the Mainland," which contains quotations from the press with comments.

3. *Newsdom,* the biweekly magazine of the Far East. Published Hong Kong, 1950–1951.

4. *Modern China,* monthly or bimonthly, Taiwan, Taipei. A *"Reader's Digest"*-type magazine with occasional anti-Communist articles about the mainland. Issued October 1950–1951.

b. Communist Chinese (in English)

5. *China Monthly Review,* ceased publication summer 1953, formerly published in Shanghai. Editor: John Powell, a left-wing American. Used to carry various editorials and descriptive articles about China which favored the regime. Covered economic, political, and social matters. Biased, but useful for description of life according to the Communists.

6. *China Pictorial,* published in Peking, founded 1952. The Communist China propaganda version of *"Life,"* containing happy, descriptive articles and some striking photographs.

7. *China Reconstructs,* a bimonthly published in Peking beginning in January 1952. Although a propaganda magazine, it contains articles by some of China's leading pre-takeover non-Communist intellectuals on university life, industry, natural resources, women, etc. Properly viewed, it can be a useful source. It is a Communist Chinese propaganda version of the *"Nation"* or the *"Atlantic"* with an admixture of illustrations, some lighter reporting, and straight propaganda articles.

8. *People's China,* published semimonthly in Peking. Formerly the *China Digest,* it began in its present form in January 1950. It is the official propaganda organ of the Peking government for foreign consumption. It is useful since it contains many official speeches and policy statements, plus glowing, but occasionally illuminating, articles about such matters as life on a collective farm or as an industrial worker in a factory.

E. French

1. *Asia,* Asian Quarterly of Culture and Synthesis, published in Saigon, French Indochina, with a French editor. Contains a section entitled News from Far East, which is largely repetitive of news more easily acquired through press translations. It also has occasional articles on China, usually on cultural affairs.

2. *B.E.I.P.I., Bulletin de L'Association d'Études et d'Informations Politiques Internationale,* published bimonthly, Paris. A commentary, mainly about the Soviet orbit, which contains well-documented, anti-Communist critiques, some of them dealing with China.

3. *La Documentation Française, Articles et Documents, Bulletin d'informations et de Presse Étrangère,* published three times a week by the Présidence du Conseil, Sécrétariat Général du Gouvernement, Direction de la Documentation, Paris. Contains three sections: *Problemes d'Actualité, Testes du Jour, Faits et Opinions.* In-

cludes some French translations of NCNA plus French summaries of press and periodical articles, some of which are about China. Most of the relevant materials can be found in English sources, but occasionally there are quotations from French, German, Swiss, or other publications rarely seen here.

4. *France-Indochine,* published monthly, Paris. A news magazine with occasional informative articles on China, economics, society, etc. It is mainly concerned, as the title suggests, with Indochina.

5. *France-Asie,* the French version of *Asia,* (*op. cit.*).

6. *Politique Étrangère,* published bimonthly, Paris, by the Centre d'Études de Politiques in cooperation with the Centre National de la Recherche Scientifique. The French equivalent of *International Affairs.* Contains useful lengthy analytical articles or reports, occasionally about China. (The *Far East Digest* usually carries translated summaries of articles on China.)

F. *Japanese* (*in English*)

1. *Contemporary Japan.* A Review of Far Eastern Affairs, founded in 1931, published quarterly by the Foreign Affairs Association of Japan, Tokyo. Carries occasional articles of reporting and analysis on China. Conservative, popular, of no great research value.

2. *The Oriental Economist,* published monthly, Mihombashi, Tokyo, Tanzan Ishibashi, President and Editor. Largely devoted to business interests; a popular, fairly conservative journal with some informative economic articles. Contains occasional commentaries on China trade, industrialization, etc.

3. *Translation of Special Magazine Articles,* American Embassy, Tokyo, Political Division, Language Services Branch. A mimeographed weekly which gives translations of articles, usually in summarized form, from such Japanese magazines as *Bungei Shunju, Kaizo, Shukan Sankei, Toyo Keizai Shimpo, Nippon Shuho, Sekai, Economist, Secho, Shukan, Yomiuri, Zenei, Diamond, Atarashii Sekai, Nippon Oyobi Nipponjin, Akahata.* Many of these magazines have a leftist slant. A few articles which relate to Communist China are especially useful for the Japanese point of view.

See also daily *Japanese Press Summary,* Section II.

G. *Indian* (*in English*)

1. *Cross Roads,* English-language weekly newspaper of the Indian Communist Party. Ceased publication September 1953. Succeeded by *New Age* (weekly). Both carry a great deal of Communist-line material on China.

2. *The Eastern Economist,* printed and published weekly by Devi Prasad Sharma at the Hindustan Times Press for the Eastern Economist, Ltd., New Delhi. Journal of leading Marwari businessmen. It contains occasional (not always accurate) articles and editorials on China.

3. *Economic Weekly,* Bombay. A genuinely liberal, independent journal focusing on current events. Rather like the *Nation,* but weightier. Occasional articles on China indicate Indian slant.

4. *Foreign Affairs Report,* published bimonthly by the Indian Council of World Affairs, New Delhi. Modeled on the *Foreign Policy Bulletin,* it contains brief news notes and short articles on current affairs occasionally relating to China.

5. *India Quarterly,* A Journal of International Affairs, published by the Oxford University Press, Calcutta, Bombay, Madras, by the Indian Council of World Affairs, an unofficial non-political group, founded in 1943 to study Indian and international problems. Views are those of authors. Magazine with great prestige; considered, detached, and scholarly. Carries fairly frequent articles about China.

6. *The Indian Economic Review,* published twice yearly by the Publications Department of the Delhi School of Economics. Contains very little on China, but is considered a sound academic journal. Official organ of the Indian Economics Association. International contributors.

7. *The Modern Review,* published monthly in Calcutta. The oldest and best established scholarly review containing discussions of broad social subjects, some of which relate to China. It is like a scholarly *Atlantic* or *Harper's.*

8. *New Age,* monthly, succeeded *Communist* in January 1952. The earlier publication contained little on China, but the *New Age* has considerable Communist material on China.

See also *The Indian Press Digest,* Section II.

H. Indonesian (in English)

1. *Ekonomi Dan Keuangan Indonesia* (Economics and Finance in Indonesia), published monthly, Jakarta. A multilingual learned journal of economics, comparable to the *American Economic Review.* Considered a reputable source, though fewer research facilities are available than in more urbanized areas. Runs occasional articles on Chinese economic matters.

2. *Indonesian Review,* published quarterly, Jakarta. A semi-learned journal, rather like the *Atlantic* or *Harper's,* which runs occasional articles usually oriented to overseas Chinese but bearing on mainland Chinese problems.

See also *Antara Daily News Bulletin,* Section II.

I. Korean (in English)

Korean Survey, published by the Washington, D. C., Bureau of the Korean Pacific Press, foreign agency of the *Korean Pacific Press,* an association of Korean newspapers. Little on China, but section entitled "In Print" reviews notices in press and popular publications which occasionally note Chinese activity in North Korea.

J. Filipino (in English)

The University of Manila Quarterly, Manila. A reputable scholarly source. Occasional articles on China, often historical.

K. United Nations

1. *Economic Bulletin for Asia and the Far East,* published quarterly, Bangkok, by the Economic Commission for Asia and the Far East, United Nations, Economic and Social Council.

2. *Economic Developments in Asia and the Far East,* yearly, ECAFE, etc. (see above).

3. *United Nations,* ECAFE, Asian Bibliography, for periods since 1951. Earlier period, see "Consolidated list of publications from the ECAFE library," supplement No. 108, 31 March, 1950–1951. December 1951, Bangkok.

V. History, 1848–1949

The following list is highly incomplete. It is designed to include only selected standard works. Note that certain books are repeated later for convenience and that further background sources are listed separately under sections:

VI. Communist period, 1949–1954, including background sources on Communism.

VII. Sino-Soviet relations.

VIII. Chinese society, including village studies of pretakeover origin.

IX. Chinese economy.

1. Brandt, C., B. I. Schwartz, and J. K. Fairbank, *A Documentary History of Chinese Communism*, Cambridge, Harvard University Press, 1952, 552 pp. (Russian Research Center Studies, 6). A fundamental research source containing the policy statements and speeches which form the basis for the Chinese Communist movement.

2. Buck, J. L., *Land Utilization in China*, 3 vols., Chicago, University of Chicago Press, 1937. Based on careful field work, this remains the standard source of factual data on China's agrarian economy.

3. Chang Kia-ngau (Chang Chia-ao), *China's Struggle for Railway Development*, New York, John Day, 1943, 325 pp. The major survey available of railway transport development in China and Manchuria. It covers to the end of 1942, with some comments on the future. Author was a banker, Minister of Railways, and Minister of Communications.

4. Chiang Kai-shek, *China's Destiny*, authorized translation by Wang Chung-hui, introduction by Lin Yu-tang. New York, The Macmillan Co., 1947, xi, 260 pp. Chiang's basic statement of policy and aspiration.

5. Ch'ien Tuan-sheng, *The Government and Politics of China*, Cambridge, Harvard University Press, 1950, 526 pp. A thorough study by an American-educated Chinese scholar. It emphasizes twentieth-century developments.

6. Clyde, Paul H., *The Far East, A History of the Impact of the West on Eastern Asia*, New York, Prentice-Hall, 1948, 862 pp. A broad survey, emphasizing political development during the twentieth century, especially since World War I. It is accurate and has an excellent bibliography.

7. Cressey, George B., *China's Geographic Foundations, A Survey of the Land and Its People*, New York, McGraw-Hill, 1934, 436 pp. The best introduction to the human geography of China, not superseded by the author's later book.

8. Cressey, George B., *Asia's Lands and Peoples, a geography of one-third the earth and two-thirds its people*, 2nd ed., New York, McGraw-Hill, 1951, 597 pp., of which 130 are on China.

9. Fairbank, John King, *Trade and Diplomacy on the China Coast; the Opening of the Treaty Ports, 1842–1854*, Cambridge, Harvard University Press, 1953,* 2 vols. Vol. I, 468 pp. and index, pp. 469–489; Vol. II, Notes, 65 pp., bibliography, pp. 66–88. Includes appendices and a glossary of Chinese names and terms. Published under the direction of the Department of History. A comprehensive basic work on the treaty ports during a crucial period of China's relations with the West, by an authority on this field.

* From the income of the Henry Warren Torrey Fund, Vol. LXII.

10. Fairbank, John King, *United States and China*, Cambridge, Harvard University Press, 1948, 384 pp. An excellent short survey of pre-1948 modern Chinese history.

11. Fei Hsiao-tung, *Peasant Life in China, A Field Study of Country Life in the Yangtze Valley*, London, George Routledge, 1939, 300 pp. A brilliant anthropological study of one village, covering family life, rice culture, and village organization. A pioneering study of this type.

12. Feng Yu-lan, *A History of Chinese Philosophy*, translated by Derk Bodde, Princeton, Princeton University Press, 1952 and 1953, 2 vols., 1200 pp. A good translation of one of the only compilations of Chinese philosophy.

13. Feis, Herbert, *The China Tangle; the American Effort in China from Pearl Harbor to the Marshall Mission*, Princeton, Princeton University Press, 1953, 445 pp. A balanced study of a decisive phase in Sino-American relations, with extensive documentation.

14. Fitzgerald, Charles P., *China, A Short Cultural History*, New York, Frederick A. Praeger, 1950, 619 pp. A biased but stimulating cultural history, neither comprehensive nor entirely reliable, but propounding many interesting ideas.

15. Hummel, Arthur W., ed., *Eminent Chinese of the Ch'ing Period*, Washington, Government Printing Office, Vol. 1, 1943, 604 pp.; Vol. 2, 1944, 498 pp. A dictionary of 800-odd biographies, based on exhaustive, long-term scholarship by Chinese, Japanese, and American scholars. Excludes men who died after 1911. An outstanding contribution with excellent bibliography.

16. Isaacs, Harold R., *The Tragedy of the Chinese Revolution* (revised ed.), Stanford, Stanford University Press, 1951 (original ed., 1938), 382 pp. Careful historical study, based on Chinese sources, of the crucial period 1923–1927. A critique of Stalin's early policy toward China.

17. Latourette, Kenneth Scott, *The Chinese, Their History and Culture*, New York, The Macmillan Co., 3rd ed., rev., 1946 (original, 1934), 847 pp. The most reliable historical text, comprehensive and carefully organized. Part I discusses historical periods; Part II has sections on religion, economics, etc.

18. Lattimore, Owen, *Inner Asian Frontiers of China*, American Geographical Society, Research series No. 21, London and New York, 1940, xxii, 585 pp. 2nd ed., Irvington-on-Hudson, N. Y., Capitol Publishing Co., 1951, lxi, 585 pp., maps. Basic data for China's relations with the frontier, including an excellent long bibliography.

19. Linebarger, Paul M. A., *The China of Chiang K'ai-shek*, Boston, World Peace Foundation, 1941, 449 pp. A comprehensive factual analysis of the Chinese National Government in early 1941, which also covers the Chinese Communists, the Japanese, etc. Appendix has 150 pp. of documents.

20. Mao Tse-tung, *China's New Democracy*, New York, New Century Publishers, 1945, 72 pp. Originally appeared in 1941. Introduction by Earl Browder. An influential statement by the Chinese Communist leader which was a major propaganda item during the United Front period.

21. MacNair, H. F., ed., *China*, Berkeley, University of California Press, 1946, xxix, 573 pp. A collection of 34 chapters by many authors on the history of Chinese politics and culture. Uneven, but useful brief commentary on Chinese civilization.

22. Mitchell, Kate L., *Industrialization of the Western Pacific*, New York, Institute of Pacific Relations, 1942, xv, 317 pp., Part III of *An Economic Survey of the Pa-*

cific Area. The most valuable single survey of countries bordering on the Western Pacific. Many statistics, which are not always accurate.

23. North, Robert C., *Moscow and the Chinese Communists,* Stanford, Stanford University Press, 1953, 286 pp. A history of the Chinese Communists and discussion of the modern period, based on Chinese sources. A basic source.

24. Morse, H. B., *The International Relations of the Chinese Empire,* Shanghai, 3 vols., 1910–1918. Vol. I, *The Period of Conflict,* 1834–1860, the best treatment of that period. Vol. II, 1861–1893; Vol. III, 1894–1911. Classic work by a Chinese Customs Service official and scholar who has written other important works on related topics.

25. Rowe, David B., *China among The Powers,* New York, Harcourt, Brace and Co., 1945, 205 pp. An original, important analysis of China's great power potentialities, economic, social, and political, with pessimistic conclusions.

26. Schwartz, Benjamin I., *Chinese Communism and the Rise of Mao,* Cambridge, Harvard University Press, 1951, 258 pp. (Russian Research Center Studies 4). A fundamental text on Chinese Communism which uses both Chinese and Russian sources.

27. Shen, T. H., *Agricultural Resources of China,* Ithaca, Cornell University Press, 1951, 407 pp. This book up dates Buck (*op. cit.*) and other works and analyzes different crops and resources. Many statistics and tables are given.

28. Sun Yat-sen, *San Min Chu I: The Three Principles of the People,* translated by Frank W. Price, edited by L. T. Chen, under the auspices of China Committee, Institute of Pacific Relations, International Understanding Series, Chungking, Ministry of Information of the Republic of China, 1943, vii, 514 pp. First published in 1927, the standard translation. Extremely influential work by the "founder of the Chinese Republic."

29. Tamagna, Frank M., *Banking and Finance in China,* New York, Institute of Pacific Relations Inquiry Series, 1942, 400 pp., selected bibliography, pp. 367–375. A comprehensive study by a Federal Reserve Board expert which covers pre-1927 historical development, native, foreign, and modern, and analyzes the money market of 1927–1937 and 1937–1942. An extremely useful bibliography, statistics, and tables are included.

30. Tawney, R. H., *Land and Labor in China,* New York, Harcourt, Brace and Co., 1932, 207 pp. This text remains a classic on China's modern problems.

31. Teng Ssu-yu and John King Fairbank, *China's Response to the West, A Documentary Survey, 1839–1923;* Cambridge, Harvard University Press, 1954, 276 pp., notes, pp. 276–296. With E-tu Zen Sun, Chaoying Fang, and others. A documentary history of the response of China's leaders to the invasion of western materiel, men, and ideas. A basic source.

32. U. S. Department of State, *United States Relations with China, with Special Reference to the Period 1944–1949,* Washington, D. C., Department of State Publication 3573, August 1949, 1054 pp. The famous "White Paper."

33. Weber, Max, *The Religion of China,* Glencoe, Ill., The Free Press, 1951, 308 pp. Translated and edited by Hans H. Gerth. An analysis of Chinese religion, including its sociological implications, by a famous German sociologist.

34. White, Theodore H., and Annalee Jacoby, *Thunder Out of China,* New York, William Sloane Associates, 1946, 331 pp. A best-seller on the war years in China, including background conditions, by correspondents familiar with the leading

figures and events. It has an anti-Nationalist, pro-Stilwell slant, but gives a vivid picture of the period.

35. Wright, Stanley F., *China's Struggle for Tariff Autonomy: 1843–1938,* Shanghai, 1938. The fundamental work on an important subject by a former Commissioner of Customs.

36. Wright, Arthur F., ed., *Studies in Chinese Thought,* vol. in series on *Comparative Studies in Cultures and Civilizations,* edited by Robert Redfield and Milton Singer, Chicago, University of Chicago Press, 1953, 317 pp. Also published as *Memoir No. 75* of the American Anthropological Association. A collection of papers by various Far Eastern and other authorities dealing with Chinese history, religion, Western impact, language, etc., which attempt to present the Chinese approach to different issues in their historical context.

VI. COMMUNIST PERIOD, 1949–1954

Note that certain background materials are included; see also later sections which give further specialized references.

VI. Communist period, 1949–1954.
    A. General.
    B. Ideology.
    C. Top leadership and Chinese Communist Party.
    D. Army and Korean War.
    E. Foreign relations; trade (excluding Sino-Soviet relations; Section VII).

A. General

1. "Atlantic Report on the World Today: China," *Atlantic Monthly,* Boston, March 1954. Editorial comment on China's present situation.

2. Balazs, Etienne, "Tradition et révolution en Chine," *Politique Étrangère,* Juin–Juillet 1954, pp. 291–308. Author is chief of research, C. N. R. S.

3. Ball, W. MacMahon, *Nationalism and Communism in East Asia,* Melbourne, Melbourne University Press; New York, Cambridge University Press, 1953, 210 pp. A chapter is devoted to China. The author is an Australian specialist in Far Eastern affairs.

4. Barnett, A. Doak, *Profile of Red China,* Foreign Policy Report, New York, Foreign Policy Association, February 15, 1950, 15 pp. An analysis of the takeover and the structural program of the Chinese Communist Party and of the problems it faces.

5. Brieux, Jean Jacques, *La Chine du nationalisme au communisme,* Paris, Editions du Seuil, 1950, 445 pp., maps.

6. Chang, Carsun, *The Third Force In China,* New York, Bookman Associates, 1952, 345 pp. Despite its title, essentially a history of modern China. The author is head of the Social Democratic party of China.

7. Chao Kuo-chün, *The Communist Movement in China: A Chronology of Major Developments, 1918–1950,* Russian Research Center, Harvard University, 1950, 31 pp. A useful guide.

8. *China Handbook, 1950,* compiled by Hollington K. Tong (former Director of China Government Information office), New York, Rockport Press, Inc., 1950, 799 pp.

9. *The Chinese Yearbook,* Council of International Affairs, Shanghai, The Commercial Press, 1935–1936, 1936–1937, 1937, 1938–1939, 1940–1941, 1943, and 1944–1945.

10. *The Common Program and Other Documents of the First Plenary Session of the Chinese People's Political Consultative Conference,* Peking, Foreign Languages Press, 1950.* Basic policies of Communist China.

11. Constantine, Leonard, "Inside Communist China," *New Republic,* New York, Part I: January 8, 1951, pp. 10–14. Part II: January 18, 1951, pp. 25–27. Report by a correspondent who has also written articles for the *Manchester Guardian Weekly.*

12. Durdin, Tillman, and Robert Aura Smith, *China and the World* ('Headline Series,' No. 99), New York, Foreign Policy Association, 1953, 63 pp. Part I by Durdin is on China in 1949; Part II by Smith is on *The Rebirth of Formosa.* The authors are well-known correspondents.

13. "European Refugees in China," *Eastern World,* July 1954, pp. 20–21. Discussion of situation of about 15,000 European refugees in China.

14. Fitzgerald, C. P., *Revolution in China,* London, Cresset Press, 1952, 289 pp., New York, Frederick A. Praeger. A controversial discussion of Communist China in the light of Chinese history; weak on totalitarian practice, but a stimulating commentary of a scope rarely essayed.

15. Ginsburg, Norton S., "China's Changing Political Geography," *Geographical Review,* 42, January 1952, pp. 102–117.

16. Green, O. M., "China's Testing Year," *Fortnightly,* April 1954, pp. 231–235. Comments upon the new "General Line" as it affects the party, private business, and the peasantry.

17. Grosbois, Charles, "La Chine et Nouvelle Democratie," *Politique Étrangère,* Part I: May 1952, pp. 29–48. Part II: July 1952, pp. 155–186. Part I analyzes the practical functioning of the Chinese Communist government in its organization of power, the military system, and economic policy. Part II studies the economy, social problems, and foreign affairs. Summarized in English in the *Far East Digest,* No. 63, July 1952.

18. *A Guide to New China* (2nd ed., revised), Peking, Foreign Languages Press, 1952, iv, 117 pp. Contains official brief descriptions of government organs, political parties, popular organizations, etc.

19. Holland, William L., editor, *Asian Nationalism and the West,* New York, The Macmillan Co., 1953, 449 pp. Includes a brief section on China, but is mainly about Southeast Asia. A useful survey.

20. Hucker, Charles O., "The traditional Chinese censorate and the new Peking regime," *American Political Science Review,* 45, December 1951, pp. 1041–1057.

21. Hummel, Arthur W., "Some basic principles in Chinese culture," *Proceedings of the American Philosophical Society,* 95, 1951, pp. 453–456.

22. Hutheesing, Raja, *The Great Peace,* New York, Harper & Bros., 1953, 240 pp. One of the best reports of a visit to Communist China. The author is an Indian businessman, brother-in-law of Nehru, who was in China on two conducted tours in the autumn of 1951 and in May–June 1952.

* All post-1949 Peking publications are subject to censorship by the Chinese Communist government and therefore may be taken as official sources. The New China News Agency, to be referred to as NCNA throughout, is the Peking official news agency, even when published in translation in London.

23. Isaacs, Harold R., "The Blind Alley of Totalitarianism," *Annals of the Academy of Political and Social Science,* 276, July 1951, pp. 81–90. A survey and analysis of the history of the Chinese Communist Party's rise to power and its direction after the takeover.

24. Levenson, Joseph R., "Western Powers and Chinese Revolutions: The Pattern of Intervention," *Pacific Affairs,* 26, September 1953, pp. 230–236. Discussion by a scholar in the field of modern Chinese intellectual history.

25. Ling Nai-jui, "Three Years of Communist Rule in China," *The Review of Politics,* January 1953, pp. 3–33. Analysis of the Chinese Communist Party's rise to power, steps to consolidate their rule, and differences with Russia. The author regards Formosa as an important rallying point for the free Chinese.

26. Littlejohn, Justin, "China and Communism," *International Affairs,* 27, April 1951, pp. 137–150. A generally balanced report by a British businessman with long experience in China. He examines the regime with respect to the peasantry, workers, private-state enterprise, and Sino-Soviet relations, and draws up a balance sheet. In general he admires the centralized order, especially financial, but deplores the use of controls to inhibit freedom of thought or action.

27. Mao Tse-tung, *China's New Democracy,* 1941, New York, New Century Publishers, 1945, 72 pp. Influential propaganda during the United Front period, stressing Sun Yat-sen's three principles and underemphasizing, though not excluding, the Communist Party line.

28. Magnenoz, Robert, "De Confucius à Lénine," *France-Asie,* 6, February 1951, pp. 839–847. A brief analysis of the historical reasons for the appeal of Communism to China and tentative comments on its feasibility as a method of solving modern Chinese problems.

29. *Manchester Guardian* and the *Manchester Guardian Weekly*—see Section III for special articles and editorials.

30. Moraes, Frank, *Report on Mao's China,* New York, The Macmillan Co., 1953, 212 pp. Probably the best single visitor's report on the recent Chinese scene. The author is an Indian newspaperman who was in China in the spring of 1952. He both reports on and analyzes political, social, economic, and diplomatic affairs.

31. Possony, Stefan T., *A Century of Conflict,* Chicago, Henry Regnery, 1953, 439 pp. A history of Communism which contains an excellent well-documented account of the 1945–1949 period in China.

32. Seton-Watson, Hugh, *From Lenin to Malenkov,* New York, Frederick A. Praeger, 1954 (originally published in London). One of the few comprehensive discussions of Communism as a worldwide movement which includes China. It is a good balance for Fitzpatrick (*op. cit.*) and discusses at length the social factors favoring or hindering the spread of Communism.

33. Stein, Gunther, *The Challenge of Red China,* New York, London, McGraw-Hill, 1945, 490 pp. The Yunnan regime of the Communists as viewed by the first group of correspondents to visit there in 1944. The author is a former correspondent whose writing is occasionally overfacile, but who had long experience in China and gives many facts.

34. Steiner, H. Arthur, editor, "Report on China," *Annals of the American Academy of Political and Social Science,* 277, September 1951, 291 pp. One of the most valuable sources on Communist China, consisting of articles by various authorities. Almost all the chapters are referred to separately throughout this bibliography.

35. Taylor, George E., "The Hegemony of the Chinese Communists, 1945–1950," *Annals of the American Academy of Political and Social Science*, 277, September 1951, 291 pp., pp. 13–21. Account by an historian of China of the rise to power and the consolidation of conquest.

36. Taylor, George E., "The Intellectual Climate of Asia," *Yale Review*, XLII, No. 2, December 1952.

37. Thomas, S. B., *Government and Administration in Communist China*, New York, Institute of Pacific Relations, November 1953, 150 pp. A good, fairly technical survey of recent political events.

38. *Recent Political and Economic Development in China*, New York, 1950, 130 pp. (Institute of Pacific Relations, 11th Conference, 1950, Secretariat paper.) A useful early survey.

39. War Department, Military Intelligence Division, *The Chinese Communist Movement*, Washington, D. C., 1945 (July).

40. Wright, Arthur F., "Struggle versus Harmony, Symbols of Competing Values in China," *World Politics*, October 1953, pp. 31–44. An historian's discussion of the basic philosophical differences between traditional and Communist views.

B. Ideology

1. Bodde, Derk, "The New Ideology in the Old China," based on an address delivered to the Episcopal League for Social Action, St. John's Cathedral, Wilmington, Del., February 22, 1951; New York, Institute of Pacific Relations, 1951, 12 pp.

2. Brandt, Conrad, Benjamin Schwartz, and John K. Fairbank, *A Documentary History of Chinese Communism*, Cambridge, Harvard University Press, 1952, 552 pp. (Russian Research Center studies 6). Published in London by Allen & Unwin. A fundamental research source containing the policy statements and speeches which form the basis for the Communist movement.

3. *Chung-kuo-jên-min-chêng-chih-hsieh-shang-hui-i* (The Common Program and Other Documents of the First Plenary Session of the Chinese People's Political Consultative Conference), Peking, Foreign Languages Press, 1950, 44 pp. Contents: The Common Program of the Chinese People's Political Consultative Conference. The Organic Law of the Central People's Government of the People's Republic of China. The Declaration of the First Plenary Session of the Chinese People's Political Consultative Conference. These constitute the initial basic policy statements of Communist China.

4. Compton, Boyd, translation and introduction, *Mao's China; Party Reform Documents, 1942–44*, Seattle, University of Washington Press, 1952, lii, 278 pp. (University of Washington Publications on Asia). Reports, etc., by Mao, Ch'en Yün, Liu Shao-ch'i, and Stalin on party reform.

5. Liu Shao-ch'i, *How to Be a Good Communist*, Peking, Foreign Languages Press, 1951, 122 pp. A basic directive especially for cadres and study groups by the second ranking leader, who is known as the party theoretician.

6. Liu Shao-ch'i, *Internationalism and Nationalism*, Peking, Foreign Languages Press, 1951 (?), 54 pp. A rebuttal to Titoism.

7. Liu Shao-ch'i, *On Inner-Party Struggle*. (A lecture delivered on July 2, 1951, at the party school for Central China.) Peking, Foreign Languages Press, 1951 (?), 92 pp. Directives on party discipline, including an attack on "bourgeois concepts" such as liberalism.

8. Liu Shao-ch'i, *On the Party* (2nd edition), Peking, Foreign Languages Press, 1950, 206 pp. "The Constitution of the Communist Party of China," pp. 155–204. A collection of various articles on party theories and general discipline.

9. Magnien, Marius, "La victoire de la politique Stalinienne en Chine," *Cahiers du Communisme*, 27, Mars 1950, pp. 48–59.

10. Mao Tse-tung, *Collected Works*, New York, International Publishers. The four volumes are being gradually translated; only Vol. I is completed to date.

11. Mao Tse-tung, "Concerning Practice; On the Relation between Cognition and Practice—between Knowledge and Action," *Soviet Press Translations*, 6, February 15, 1951, pp. 74–82. Translated from *Bolshevik*, No. 23, 1950. A discussion of Marxist theory as it touches on the need for practical experience during the revolutionary struggle.

12. Mao Tse-tung, *On Practice, On the Relation between Knowledge and Practice, between Knowing and Doing*, Peking, 1951, 23 pp. (Different edition of "Concerning Practice," *op. cit.*)

13. Mao Tse-tung, *The Dictatorship of the People's Democracy*, edited by Tien-yi Li, New Haven, Institute of Far Eastern Languages, Yale University, 1951, 13 pp., 21 pp. (Mirror series C, No. 5). Chinese text with Chinese-English vocabulary. (See translation following.) A basic document.

14. Mao Tse-tung, *On People's Democratic Dictatorship*, together with his two speeches delivered at the preparatory committee meeting and the first plenary session of the Chinese People's Political Consultative Conference (3rd ed.), Peking, Foreign Languages Press, 1950, 45 pp. (See other version, *op. cit.*)

15. Mao Tse-tung, "On Contradiction," *Soviet Press Translations*, 7, November 15, 1952, pp. 403–416. Translated from *Hsüeh hsi*, April 1952. Text for study by cadres and others. A discussion of Marxist theory.

16. Schwartz, Benjamin, "A Marxist Controversy on China," *Far Eastern Quarterly*, 13, February 1954, pp. 143–153. A discussion of the use of Marxism as an explanation of China's history and modern pre-Communist conditions, including a description of the fierce controversy this topic aroused among intellectuals, especially during the period 1928–1937.

17. Stalin, J., *Stalin on China; A Collection of Five Writings of Comrade Stalin on the Chinese Question*, Bombay, People's Publishing House, 1951, 106 pp.

18. Sung Ch'ing-ling (Mme. Sun Yat-sen), *The Struggle for New China*, Peking, Foreign Languages Press, 1952, xiv, 4, iv, 398 pp. A collection of the articles, speeches and statements made between July 1927 and July 1952 by a Chinese woman leader who is nominally a non-Communist vice-chairman of the Peking government.

19. Szczepanik, F. F., "On Economic Theory of Maoism," *Ekonomi Dan Keuangan Indonesia* (Economics and Finance in Indonesia), January 1954, pp. 4–16. Discussion by a lecturer at the University of Hong Kong.

20. Steiner, H. Arthur, *Maoism, A Sourcebook; Selections From the Writings of Mao Tse-tung*, introduced and edited by Steiner, Los Angeles, University of California, 1952, 142 pp.

21. "Thoughts on Reading Mao Tse-tung's 'Anti-Liberalism,'" *Soviet Press Translations*, 9, January 15, 1953, pp. 19–20, translated from *Hsin Chien She*, November 1952.

22. Thomas, S. B., "Structure and Constitutional Basis of the Chinese People's Republic," *Annals of the American Academy of Political and Social Science*, 277, September 1951, pp. 46–55. A discussion of both ideology and the structure of the government by a student of the Chinese Communist government.

23. Wittfogel, Karl A., "The Influence of Leninism-Stalinism on China," *Annals of the American Academy of Political and Social Science,* 277, September 1951, pp. 22–34. A discourse by a well-known Sinologist, an ex-Communist, who has much interest in ideological problems and their sociological significance.

C. Top Leadership and Chinese Communist Party

See also Sections *A, B, D,* and *E.*

1. Borkenau, Franz, "The Chances of a Mao-Stalin Rift," *Commentary,* 14, August 1952, pp. 117–123. An article by a German refugee expert on international Communism. He discusses Sino-Soviet relations in the light of the Indian Communist Party shifts.

2. Band, C. and W., *Two Years with the Chinese Communists,* New Haven, Yale University Press, 1948, 347 pp. Supplementary facts and views on the Yunnan period by an English physicist and his wife who were there from December 1941 to early 1944.

3. Chang Kuo-tao, "Mao—A New Portrait by an Old Colleague," *New York Times,* Magazine section, August 2, 1953.

4. Chassin, General L.-M., "Mao Tse-tung, Stratège et poète (I)," *France-Asie,* 956, Avril–Mai 1954, pp. 553–65. A rather hero-worshiping appraisal of Mao.

5. Elegant, Robert S., *China's Red Masters; Political Biographies of the Chinese Communist Leaders,* New York, Twayne Publishers, 1951, 264 pp. Reports by a newspaperman on the political and military leaders.

6. Green, O. M., "The Deification of Mao Tse-tung," *Fortnightly,* 178, October 1952, pp. 228–231.

7. Hu Ch'iao-mu, *Thirty Years of the Communist Party of China,* Peking, Foreign Languages Press, 1951, 94 pp. The official chronology of the Chinese Communist Party.

8. Hu Shih, "My Former Student, Mao Tse-tung," *Freeman,* July 2, 1951, pp. 636–639. Brief comments by one of China's leading refugee intellectuals.

9. Keesing, Donald B., "Use of Top-Level Personnel by the Chinese Communist government, 1949–53," submitted as a history honors thesis for the A.B. degree at Harvard University, April 2, 1954, 60 pp. and notes. (To be revised in the future.)

10. "Leadership in New China," *Economist:* series 1, "The Men at the Top," June 19, 1954, pp. 978–980; series 2, "Soldiers around Mao," June 26, 1954, pp. 1064–1065; series 3, "The Economic Planners," July 3, 1954, pp. 40–41; to be continued.

11. North, Robert C., "The Chinese Communist Elite," *Annals of the American Academy of Political and Social Science,* 277, September 1951, pp. 67–75. Description of the top leadership of the Chinese Communist Party by a specialist on China.

12. North, Robert C., *Kuomintang and Chinese Communist Elites,* with the collaboration of Ithiel deSola Pool. Introduction by John K. Fairbank. Stanford, Stanford University Press, 1952, vii, 130 pp. (Hoover Institute Studies, Series B: Elite studies, No. 8). A study of the top leadership of the KMT and CCP, including background data on personnel.

13. North, Robert C., "The Rise of Mao Tse-tung," *Far Eastern Quarterly,* 11, February 1952, pp. 137–145.

14. Palmer, Norman D., and Shao Chuan Leng, "Organization of the Chinese Communist Party," *Current History,* 23, July 1952, pp. 13–19.

15. Payne, Robert, *Mao Tse-tung, Ruler of Red China,* New York, Henry Schuman, 1950, 303 pp. The first full-length English biography. The author tends to view Mao as Chinese first and Communist second, and makes some unsubstantiated comments, but the book remains an interesting and well-written biography.

16. Snow, Edgar, "Mao Tse-tung as I Knew Him," *The Reporter,* January 3, 1950.

17. Snow, Edgar, "Red China's Gentleman Hatchetman," *Saturday Evening Post,* March 27, 1954. Article on Chou En-lai.

18. Snow, Edgar, *Red Star over China,* The Modern Library, Random House, New York, 1944 (original, 1938), 529 pp. This famous book gives an account of Mao, the Long March, and the Communist Reform Program. It has some unique first-hand data.

19. Steiner, H. Arthur, "Recent Literature on Chinese Communist Party History," *American Political Science Review,* 46, June 1952, pp. 542–549.

20. Strong, Anna Louise, "The Thought of Mao Tse-tung," *Amerasia,* XI, June 1947, pp. 161–174.

21. "Thoughts on Reading Mao Tse-tung's 'The Chinese Revolution and the Chinese Communist Party,'" *Soviet Press Translations,* 8, March 1, 1953, pp. 67–78. Translated from *Hsin Chien She,* December 1952.

22. Wales, Nym (pseudonym), *Red Dust, Autobiographies of Chinese Communists as told to Nym Wales* (Helen Foster Snow). With an introduction by Robert Carver North, Stanford, Stanford University Press, 1952, 238 pp. First-hand accounts by the wife of Edgar Snow.

23. *Who's Who in Modern China* (from the beginning of the Chinese Republic to the end of 1953). Over 2,000 brief but detailed biographies, including detailed histories of political parties, government organizations, and a glossary of contemporary Chinese terms, indexed in Chinese and English. Compiled by Max Perleberg, Hong Kong, Ye Olde Printerie, Ltd., 1954, 429 pp. and glossary. Mainly presents Nationalist leaders, but some Communists are included, plus various men who went over to the Communists.

24. Yu, Frederick T. C., *Key Leaders in Communist China,* Los Angeles, University of Southern California, 1953, 152 pp. (Unpublished series of *Studies in Chinese Communism,* see Appendix 3.)

D. Army and Korean War

1. Baldwin, Hanson W., "China as a Military Power," *Foreign Affairs,* 30, October 1951. An analysis by the *New York Times'* military expert.

2. *China Fights for Peace,* Peking, Foreign Languages Press, 1950, iv, 64 pp. Texts from Soong Ching-ling, Kuo Mo-jo, Emi Siao, Liu Ning-yi, and appendixes.

3. *The Chinese People's Liberation Army,* Peking, Foreign Languages Press, 1950, 62 pp.

4. Chou Keng-sheng, "The Legal Responsibility of the American Aggressor in Waging Germ Warfare and Violating Our Air Borders," *Soviet Press Translations,* 7, October 15, 1952, pp. 376–379. Translated from *Hsin Chien She,* April 1952.

5. Chu Teh, *On the Battlefronts of the Liberated Areas,* Peking, Foreign Languages Press, 1952, 91 pp. Comments by the Communists' top military man.

6. Hanrahan, Gene Z., "The People's Revolutionary Military Council in Communist China," *Far Eastern Survey,* 23, May 1954, pp. 77–78.

7. Hanrahan, Gene Z., "Report on Red China's New Navy," *United States Naval Institute Proceedings* (published monthly, Menasha, Wisc.), August 1953, pp. 847–854. Reported in *Far East Digest*, January 1954, p. 15.

8. Hanrahan, Gene Z., "Red China's Three Top Field Commanders," *Marine Corps Gazette*, 36, February 1952, pp. 54–61.

9. "How Strong Is Red China" *U. S. Army Combat Forces Journal*, II, January 1952, pp. 34–38.

10. Mao Tse-tung, *Strategic Problems of China's Revolutionary War*, Bombay, People's Publishing House, 1951, 82 pp.

11. Marshall, S. L. A., *The River and the Gauntlet*, New York, Morrow, 1953, 385 pp. The defeat of the Eighth Army by the Chinese Communist Forces, November 1950, in the Battle of Chongchun River, Korea. Written by an infantry analyst and army historian, this book is mainly a description of U. S. Army operations, but some account of Chinese Communist forces is included.

12. Rigg, Lt. Col. Robert B., *Red China's Fighting Hordes*, a realistic account of the Chinese Communist Army by a U. S. Army officer who fought in the Korean War. Harrisburg, Pa., Military Service Publishing Co., 1951, xiv, 378 pp. The only full-length treatment of this subject. It is fairly technical.

13. Ryder, Wilfred, "China—A New Military Power," *Eastern World*, April 1952, pp. 15–16. Brief general comments.

14. Shuang Yun, "The Marxist Military Line," *People's China*, September 1, 1950, pp. 6–7.

15. Wu Hsiu ch'üan, *China Accuses!* Speeches of the Special Representative of the Central People's Government of the People's Republic of China at the United Nations, Peking, Foreign Languages Press, 1951, 107 pp.

16. United Nations, General Assembly. Delegation from China. *China Fights for Peace and Freedom*, New York, 1951, 99 pp.

E. Foreign Relations

(Note especially the separate Section VII, Sino-Soviet Relations.)

1. Acheson, Dean, "Our Far Eastern Policy; Debate, Decision and Action," an address delivered before the Women's National Press Club, Washington, D. C., April 18, 1951. Washington, D. C., Department of State (Division of Publications, Office of Public Affairs, 1951), 11 pp. (Department of State Publication 4201, Far Eastern Series, 41.)

2. Angus, H. F., *Canada and the Far East, 1940–1953*, Toronto, University of Toronto Press, for the Canadian Institute of International Affairs and Institute of Pacific Relations, 1954, 130 pp. A summary by a Canadian economist with government experience.

3. Bagchi, P. C., *India and China, A Thousand Years of Cultural Relations*, Bombay, Hinds Kitab, Ltd., 1950.

4. Berger, Ronald, "Opening a Path of Trade," *Great Britain and the East*, October 1953, pp. 9–11, and 33. Comments on China's industrialization plans and their effect on Britain's (and other nations') trade. The issue contains other articles on British-Chinese trade by businessmen members of the British Trade Delegation to Peking, representing some 200 firms.

5. Chen, Theodore H. E., "Relations between Britain and Communist China," *Current History*, 23, November 1952, pp. 295–303.

6. Clubb, O. Edmund, "Chinese Communist Strategy in Foreign Relations," *Annals of the American Academy of Political and Social Science*, 277, September 1951, pp. 156–166. Comments by a former member of the U. S. Foreign Service with many years experience in China.

7. Collar, H. J., "Recent Developments of British Commercial Relations with China," *Royal Central Asian Society Journal*, January 1954, pp. 26–37. A description of the Communist regime's pressure on British firms in China.

8. Collar, H. J., "British Commercial Relations with China," *International Affairs*, October 1953, pp. 418–428. The author is a man with long business experience in China and Hong Kong, who gives a review of commercial relations with China and hopes for light industry priorities there.

9. Collar, H. J., "China and Hongkong," *Asian Review*, April 1954, pp. 64–65. Very brief general comments.

10. *Department of State Bulletin.* Frequent brief speeches by various State Department officials on United States-China policy. (See Section IV*A*.)

11. *The Economist*, weekly, London. Frequent trade statistics and commentary on economics and foreign affairs. (See Section IV*C*.)

12. *Far Eastern Economic Review*, weekly, Hong Kong. Frequent trade statistics, plus notes and articles on trade, Sino-Soviet relations, industrialization, and so on. (See Section IV*C*.)

13. *Far East Trader*, weekly, New York. Frequent trade statistics and commentary. (See Section IV*A*.)

14. Feer, Mark, "Tibet in Sino-Indian Relations," *India Quarterly*, October–December 1953, pp. 367–381. An analysis by an American graduate student studying in India.

15. Fitzgerald, C. P., "The Chinese Revolution and the West," *Pacific Affairs*, 24, March 1951, pp. 3–17. Comments on differing reactions to China by the United States, Britain, and the rest of Asia.

16. Fitzgerald, C. P., "Peace or War with China?" *Pacific Affairs*, 24, December 1951, pp. 339–351. Further comments on policy toward China.

17. *Foreign Policy Bulletin*, twice-monthly, New York. Fairly frequent notes on United States-China policy.

18. "Foreign Trade Policy: China," *Far East Trader*, January 13, 1954, pp. 315–316. An editorial.

19. Forster, Lancelot, "China and the United States," *Contemporary Review*, 181, May 1952, pp. 274–278.

20. Holland, William L., editor, *Asian Nationalism and the West*, New York, The Macmillan Co., 1953, 449 pp. A very short treatment of China.

21. Hu Shih, "How to Understand a Decade of Rapidly Deteriorated Sino-American Relations," *Proceedings of the American Philosophical Society*, 95, 1951, pp. 457–459.

22. Huan Hsin-yi, "The Foreign Policy of the People's Republic of China during the Last Two Years," *Soviet Press Translations*, 6, December 15, 1951, pp. 667–677. Translated from *Hsin Chien Sheh*, Vol. 5, No. 1.

23. Kirby, E. Stuart, "The British and the Chinese," *Far Eastern Survey*, 20, April 18, 1951, pp. 74–76. Comments by an English economist from the University of Hong Kong with long Far Eastern experience.

24. Kirby, E. Stuart, "Hongkong and the British Position in China," *Annals of the American Academy of Political and Social Science*, 277, September 1951, pp. 193–202.

25. Leng, Shao-chuan, "India and China," *Far Eastern Survey*, May 21, 1952, pp. 73–78.

26. Levi, Werner, *Modern China's Foreign Policy*, Minneapolis, Univ. of Minnesota Press, 1954, 399 pp. A presentation of recent materials on the subject which gives a fairly useful summary of events and has a good bibliography.

27. Li Chang, "Ceylon's Trade with Communist China," *Far Eastern Survey*, 22, May 1953, pp. 70–72.

28. Linebarger, Paul M. A., "Outside Pressures on China, 1945–1950," *Annals of the American Academy of Political and Social Science*, 277, September 1951, pp. 177–181. Comments by a Far East expert on the United States and Soviet pressures on China just before the takeover.

29. Lu Hsu-chang, "China's Foreign Trade Expands," *Eastern World*, July 1954, pp. 40–42. Author is the managing director of the China Import and Export Corporation, Peking. He comments on China's capacity to import and to trade with the West.

30. North, Robert C., "The Chinese Revolution and Asia," *International Journal*, 6, winter of 1950–1951, pp. 20–28.

31. Palmer, Norman D., "Factors Shaping U. S. Policy towards China," *India Quarterly*, July–September 1953, pp. 227–248.

32. Panikkar, Sardar K. M., "India and China through the Ages," *Asiatic Review*, 48, April 1952, pp. 86–95. Report by the currently fellow-traveling former Indian ambassador to Peking, whose opinions vary with the climate, but who has some claims to scholarship and has had wide experience.

33. Spender, P. C., "Partnership with Asia," *Foreign Affairs*, January 1951, pp. 205–218.

34. Steiner, H. Arthur, "The United States and the Two Chinas," *Far Eastern Survey*, 22, May 1953, pp. 57–61.

35. "United Kingdom Trade with China," by a correspondent, *Great Britain and the East*, September 1953, p. 37.

36. *U. S. Department of State*, transcript of a round-table discussion on American policy toward China, held in the Department of State, October 6, 7, and 8, 1949. (Reported by E. Moyer and E. Voce.) Washington, 1949, 1 vol.

37. Walker, Richard L., "Communist China Looks at the United States," *Yale Review*, 41, Autumn 1951, pp. 25–43.

38. Wint, Guy, *The British in Asia*, London, Faber and Faber, Ltd., 1954.

39. Zinkin, Maurice, *Asia and the West*, revised edition, New York, Institute of Pacific Relations, 1953, 304 pp. Mainly on Southeast Asia.

VII. SINO-SOVIET RELATIONS: COMMUNIST CHINA

Reference should also be made to:

1. Books and articles listed under Section VI, the Communist Period.

2. Certain books under Section VIII, Chinese Society. Many accounts of trips, such as Frank Moraes' *Report on Mao's China*, discuss the presence of Russians in China and their possible influence.

3. Press translations and so forth listed under Section II which have almost continuous references to this subject and are the best primary source.

4. Periodicals not listed here by article owing to the frequency of occurrence: (*a*) Chinese periodicals listed under Section IV, Part *D*; especially *Free China Review*, *China Reconstructs*, and *People's China*. (*b*) *Far Eastern Economic Review*— Section IV, Part *C*.

Sino-Soviet Relations

1. Ballis, William B., "The Pattern of Sino-Soviet Treaties, 1945–1950," *Annals of the American Academy of Political and Social Science*, 277, September 1951, pp. 167–176. A discussion by an expert on Russia concerning the treaties and their significance in Sino-Soviet relations.

2. Ballis, William B. and Emily Timmins, "Recent Soviet Writings on the Far East," *Pacific Affairs*, 25, March 1952, pp. 59–75. A review of some recent Russian language articles; mainly historical.

3. Beloff, Max, "Soviet Policy in China," *International Affairs*, 27, July 1951, pp. 285–296. A description and analysis by an authority in the field.

4. Beloff, Max, *Soviet Policy in the Far East, 1944–1951*, London, New York, Toronto, Oxford University Press, 1953; issued under the auspices of the Royal Institute of International Affairs, 259 pp. One of the better-documented histories.

5. Boorman, Howard L., "Chronology of Sino-Soviet Relations," *Problems of Communism: China*, III, 3, May–June 1954, pp. 14–21. (Accompanies the article by R. L. Walker; see below.)

6. Chang Li (pseudonym), "The Soviet Grip on Sinkiang," *Foreign Affairs*, April 1954, pp. 491–503. A history of the border province since 1928 by a Chinese scholar.

7. Crocker, H. E., "Russian Communism in Asia," *Contemporary Review*, 182, September 1952, pp. 134–138.

8. Dallin, David J., *The Rise of Russia in Asia*, New Haven, Yale University Press, 1949, 292 pp. Covers the period from the mid-nineteenth century to the Manchurian incident of 1931. While good on Soviet thought, it is less helpful on specifically Chinese attitudes and is not thoroughly documented. It does, however, contain much useful background material.

9. Debau, E. J., "La Chine et Moscou," *Revue des deux mondes*, 15, September 1951, pp. 296–303.

10. Donnelly, Desmond, "Red China Diary, I, Prague to Peking," *The Nation*, March 28, 1953, pp. 262–264. Mainly a description of China by an English Member of Parliament on tour.

11. Fitzgerald, C. P., "Does China's Foreign Policy Fit into the Kremlin's Pattern?" *Voice* (published monthly, Sydney, Australia), July 1952, pp. 18–19. Reviewed in *Far East Digest*, No. 66, October 1952.

12. Freadman, Paul, "Sino-Soviet Relations," *Australian Outlook*, 6, March 1952, pp. 27–39.

13. Green, O. M., "Russia in China," *Eastern World*, April 1953, pp. 19–20. A brief historical review.

14. Hao To-fu, "Soviet Assistance and the Development of Chinese Economic Reconstruction in the Past Two Years," *Soviet Press Translations*, 7, May 1, 1952, pp. 237–240. Translated from *Chung su yu hao*, No. 5, 1952.

15. Hu Shih, "China in Stalin's Grand Strategy," *Foreign Affairs*, 29, October 1950, pp. 11–40. A discussion by a leading Chinese intellectual liberal who fled the Communists.

16. Krakowsky, Édouard, "Le Mystère russe et le secret Chinois," *Politique Étrangère*, Juin–Juillet 1954, pp. 309–316. An historical survey of the current situation.

17. Lattimore, Owen, and associates, *Pivot of Asia*, Boston, Little, Brown and Co., 1950, 288 pp. Largely about the border province of Sinkiang, it is particularly

useful because of the extreme dearth of information elsewhere on this important subject.

18. "Le rôle de Moscou et de Mao Tse-Tung dans la révolution Chinoise," *B.E.I.P.I.*, 16/31 March 1954, pp. 12–18. Careful article by a group from "le collège d'Europe," Bruges.

19. Lieberman, Henry R., "How Firm is the Moscow-Peiping Axis?" *New York Times,* Magazine section, March 3, 1953.

20. Linebarger, Paul M. A., "Outside Pressures on China, 1945–1950," *Annals of the American Academy of Political and Social Science,* 277, September 1951, pp. 177–188. Mainly a discussion of United States-China relations, but also gives some comments on the Sino-Soviet picture.

21. Lobonov-Rostovsky, Prince Andrei, *Russia and Asia,* Ann Arbor, Mich., G. Wahr Publishing Co., 1951, 342 pp., illustrated. Originally published edition, New York, The Macmillan Co., 1933.

22. "Malenkov and Mao Tse-tung," by a special correspondent, *Eastern World,* December 1953, pp. 14–15.

23. Mosely, Philip E., "Soviet Policy and the Revolutions in Asia," *Annals of the American Academy of Political and Social Science,* 276, July 1951, pp. 91–98.

24. Mousset, Albert, "Ties between Peking and Moscow" (in French), *France-Indochine,* June 1953, p. 162.

25. North, Robert C., *Moscow and the Chinese Communists,* Stanford, Stanford University Press, 1953, 286 pp. Includes both past history and the modern period, based on Chinese sources. The discussion tends to be on an abstract level with considerable emphasis on American relations to the problem. A highly informative, accurate, and well-organized book basic to the study of the field.

26. North, Robert C., "The NEP and the New Democracy," *Pacific Affairs,* 1, March 1951, pp. 52–60.

27. North, Robert C., "Sino-Soviet Partnership," *Foreign Policy Bulletin,* February 15, 1952, pp. 1–2.

28. Pavlovsky, Michel N., *Chinese-Russian Relations,* New York, Philosophical Library, 1949. Principally on the seventeenth and eighteenth centuries.

29. Plunkett, Richard L., "China Views Her Russian Tutor," *Far Eastern Survey,* 22, July 1953, pp. 95–101.

30. Priestley, K. E., "The Sino-Soviet Friendship Association," *Pacific Affairs,* 25, September 1952, pp. 287–292.

31. O. E. C., " 'Titoism' and the Chinese Communist Regime: An American View," *The World Today,* December 1952, pp. 521–532. Author thinks there will be no Titoism until China no longer needs Russian aid, which he thinks might come about in time.

32. Sachs, Milton, "The Strategy of Communism in Southeast Asia," *Pacific Affairs,* 23, September 1950, pp. 227–247. By an expert on Indochina. The first half deals with the 1949 W.F.T.U. Conference in Peking and its influence in Southeast Asia. The second half is on Indochina.

33. Schwartz, Benjamin, *Chinese Communism and the Rise of Mao,* Cambridge, Harvard University Press, 1951, 258 pp. (Russian Research Center Studies 4). A fundamental text on Chinese Communism which uses both Chinese and Russian sources.

34. *700 Millions for Peace and Democracy,* Peking, Foreign Languages Press, 1950, ii, 82 pp. Concerns Sino-Soviet relations and includes speeches by Mao, Chu-teh,

Liu Shao ch'i, Soong Ching-ling, Kuo Mo-jo, and Chen Po-ta, plus an N.C.N.A. editorial.

35. Stalin, J., *Stalin on China; a Collection of Five Writings of Comrade Stalin on the Chinese Question*, Bombay, People's Publishing House, 1951, 106 pp.

36. Steiner, H. Arthur, "Maoism or Stalinism for Asia?," *Far Eastern Survey*, 22, January 14, 1953, pp. 1–5.

37. Swank, Emory C., *The Moscow-Peking Axis; An Interpretation Based Primarily on Communist Source Materials*, 1949, February 1953. External Research Staff, OIR, Department of State, 1953, 39 pp. and a bibliography.

38. Thompson, Pauline, *American-Russian Relations in the Far East*, New York, The Macmillan Co., 1949, 426 pp. Covers the period from the end of the nineteenth century to 1948. Largely relates to the diplomatic level, is occasionally unbalanced in treatment of economic and social problems, and is unevenly documented.

39. Walker, Richard L., "Pattern of Sino-Soviet Relations," *Problems of Communism: China*, III, 3, May–June 1954, pp. 5–13. (Accompanies article by H. L. Boorman, *op. cit.*)

40. Werth, Alexander, "Moscow-Peking Axis," *The Nation*, April 11, 1953, pp. 308–309. Author comments on the strength of the bond between Peking and Moscow, and on Russia's stake in keeping China.

41. Woodman, Dorothy, "As China Sees It," *New Statesman and Nation*, London, April 15, 1950, pp. 420–421. A review of postwar relations between China, Russia, and the United States.

42. Wu, Aitchen K., *China and the Soviet Union*, New York, John Day, 1950, xvi, 434 pp. Summary of relations from 1618 to 1950 which reveals careful scholarship if little new data, and suffers from poor editing. The author was a Nationalist diplomat who served in Russia. Useful despite interjection of somewhat odd political judgments.

43. Yefimov, G., "The Soviet Union—the Great Friend of the Chinese People," *Soviet Press Translations*, 6, June 15, 1951, pp. 323–337. Translated from *Voprosy ekonomiki*, No. 3, 1951.

VIII. CHINESE SOCIETY

Material on social forces and patterns in Chinese life is poor both for current and for background data. Since material on the question of present attitudes toward the regime is particularly sparse, it is necessary to study such relevant background data as exist as a basis for even surmising how Communist plans and actions are actually striking the population.

Particular reference should be made to Section II, Press, Radio, etc., which forms the major source material for this section. There is also considerable overlapping with Section IX, Chinese Economy.

The following are surveys which serve to point up vast fields. See other bibiographies for further reference.

Philosophy

1. Creel, Herrlee G., *Chinese Thought from Confucius to Mao Tse-tung*, Chicago, University of Chicago Press, 1953, 292 pp. A brief review by a Sinological philosopher.

2. Feng Yu-lan, *A History of Chinese Philosophy,* translated by Derk Bodde, Princeton, Princeton University Press, 1952 and 1953, 2 vols., 1200 pp. An excellent survey, well-translated, of the major trends of Chinese philosophy.

3. Russell, Bertrand, *The Problem of China,* New York, Century Co., 1922, 276 pp. Stimulating comments on China, based on a trip and on extensive reading, by a famous British philosopher and mathematician.

4. Waley, Arthur, translator, *Three Ways of Thought in Ancient China,* London, G. Allen & Unwin, Ltd., 1939, 275 pp. An introduction to Confucianists, Legalists, and Taoists by a brilliant writer.

5. Wright, Arthur F., editor, *Studies in Chinese Thought,* volume in series on *Comparative Studies in Cultures and Civilizations,* edited by Robert Redfield and Milton Singer, Chicago, the University of Chicago Press, 1953, 317 pp. A compilation of chapters on various aspects of Chinese thought, religion, language, literature, etc., by a group of qualified scholars which provides useful background on various thought patterns in China.

Fiction

Noted for their vivid pictures, albeit imaginative, of certain aspects of Chinese life. Many others could be cited, especially in the modern period.

6. *All Men Are Brothers* (Shui Hu Chuan), translated by Pearl Buck, New York, John Day Co., 1933 and 1937, 1279 pp. One of China's most famous novels, set in the fourteenth century during the decay of the Sung dynasty when semi-bandit, fraternal groups grew up among those forced to flee an oppressive government, from which these groups supposedly protected the poor.

7. *Chin P'ing Mei,* The Adventurous History of Hsi Men and His Six Wives, introduction by Arthur Waley, New York, G. P. Putnam's Sons, 1940, 2 vols., 863 pp. A history of the decline of a family which gives vivid descriptions of the lower social classes in China during the late Ming Dynasty. This book was allegedly written to avenge the author's father, who was wronged by the subject of this "history."

8. *The Dream of the Red Chamber,* by Ts'ao Hsueh-chin and Kao Ngoh. Translated and adapted from the Chinese by Chi-chen Wang, with a prologue by Arthur Waley, London, G. Routledge & Sons, Ltd., 1929. An often-quoted novel of gentry family life during the early Ch'ing period.

9. *Book of Lord Shang,* by Kung-sun Yang (d., B.C. 338), translated by J. J. L. Duyvendack, London, A. Probstain, 1928, 346 pp. A good translation of a classic of the Chinese Legalist School.

10. Lusin, *Ah Q and Others: Selected stories of Lusin,* translated by Wang Chi-chen, New York, Columbia University Press, 1940, 219 pp. A translation of some of the best stories of the most famous modern short-story writer.

11. *Rickshaw Boy,* by Lau Shau (Lao She), translated by Evan King, New York, Reynal and Hitchcock, 1945, 315 pp. An excellent translation of the famous modern novel which includes penetrating descriptions of the life of Peking in the 'twenties.

Social Biography

12. Chao, Buwei Yang, *Autobiography of a Chinese Woman,* put into English by her husband, Yuenren Chao, New York, John Day (Asia Press Book), 1947, xi, 327 pp. A sprightly autobiography by a woman physician, wife of a well-known Sinologist now at the University of California, Berkeley.

13. Chiang Monlin, *Tides from the West, A Chinese Autobiography,* New Haven, Conn., Yale University Press, 1948, 282 pp. Recollections of a well-known educator, which are very good on his early family life and his start in an official career in revolutionary times.

14. Pruitt, Ida, *A Daughter of the Han, The Autobiography of a Chinese Working Woman, as told by Ning Lao T'ai,* New Haven, Conn., Yale University Press, 1945, 249 pp. The story of an old village woman and her family; a vivid picture of the life of a poor but spirited Chinese.

15. Tretiakov, Serge, *A Chinese Testament: The Autobiography of Tan Shih-hua as Told to S. Tretiakov,* New York, Simon and Schuster, 1934, 316 pp. The story of a student, son of an early Kuomintang revolutionist, who joined the student movement at Peking National University. A vivid picture of revolutionary ferment and traditional life up to 1926.

Anthropology-Sociology

16. Belden, Jack, *China Shakes the World,* New York, Harper & Bros., 1949, 524 pp. First-hand vivid reporting and biographies from both Communist and KMT areas, 1946–1949. It emphasizes the peasantry and has many comments on the status of women. Emotional and biased, but useful for primary source material.

17. Bunzel, Ruth, *Explorations in Chinese Culture, Research in Contemporary Cultures,* New York, Columbia University, 1950, 231 pp., bibliography and appendices. I, Introduction; II, The Structure of Chinese Society; III, Aspects of the Development of the Chinese Child; IV, Men and Women; V, Some Characteristics of Chinese Thinking; VI, Configurations in Chinese Culture. Preliminary dittoed copy presenting various interesting, occasionally controversial, ideas. It is one of few such treatments.

18. Crow, Carl, *Four Hundred Million Customers,* New York, Harper & Bros., 1937, 316 pp. Reminiscences of an advertising man which give a good picture of reactions to Western commerce.

19. Eberhard, W., *Conquerors and Rulers: Social Forces in Medieval China,* Leiden, Brill, 1952, xi, 129 pp.

20. Epstein, Israel, *Notes on Labor Problems in Nationalist China,* New York, Institute of Pacific Relations, January 1949, 159 pp. A description of the effects of the Japanese War on labor and of conditions, policy, and organization under the KMT, written from a Communist point of view.

21. Fei Hs'ao-t'ung, *China's Gentry; Essays in Rural-Urban Relations,* revised and edited by Margaret Park Redfield, with *Six Life-Histories of Chinese Gentry Families* collected by Yung-teh Chow and an Introduction by Robert Redfield, Chicago, University of Chicago Press, 1953, issued in cooperation with the International Secretariat, Institute of Pacific Relations, 287 pp. A valuable study, by a Chinese social anthropologist of international reputation, discussing the gentry during the period up to 1948. The six life histories are rare and interesting sources.

22. Fei Hs'ao-t'ung and Chang Chih-i, *Earthbound China,* Chicago, University of Chicago Press, 1945, 319 pp. A study of three villages in Yunnan Province at varying stages of agricultural self-sufficiency and commercial development, based on 1939–1943 field work.

23. Fei Hs'ao-t'ung, *Peasant Life in China,* London, George Routledge & Sons, 1939, 300 pp. A pioneering classic study of the Chinese peasantry and their place in society, based on a village study.

24. Fei Hs'ao-t'ung, "Peasantry and Gentry, An Interpretation of Chinese Social Structure and Its Changes," *American Journal of Sociology*, 52.1, July 1946, 17 pp. A brief but brilliant statement about the structure of society and its signs of strain. *China's Gentry* (see above) is in part an expansion of this article, which remains an excellent short statement.

25. Fried, Morton H., *Fabric of Chinese Society: A Study of the Social Life of A Chinese County Seat*, New York, Frederick A. Praeger, 1953, xi, 243 pp. An anthropological study of the town of Ch'u hsien, just north of Nanking. The field work was done in 1947–1948 when the author lived in the town. It gives a description and analysis of the community with special attention to non-kin relationships, including an analysis of *Kan-ch'ing* (roughly, the warmth and intensity of relationships).

26. Gamble, Sidney D., *Ting Hsien, A North Chinese Rural Community*, Introduction by Y. C. James Yen, New York, Institute of Pacific Relations, 1954, 500 pp. Survey of a Chinese agricultural community based on work done in 1926–1933 in cooperation with the Chinese Mass Education Movement. The emphasis is on demography and economy.

27. Hsiao Kung-ch'uan, "Rural Control in Nineteenth Century China," a paper presented at the Far Eastern Association Meeting, Boston, 1952.

28. Hsü, Francis L. K., *Americans and Chinese: Two Ways of Life*, New York, Henry Schuman, 1953, 457 pp. A comparative study, by an anthropologist, of Chinese and American attitudes to personal, communal, and certain national problems.

29. Hsü, Francis L. K., *Under the Ancestor's Shadow*, New York, Columbia University Press, 1948, 317 pp. A study of kinship patterns which is particularly useful for providing a rarely found analysis of ancestor worship and its place in the social structure. The book is based on field investigation of a semi-rural Yunnan community.

30. Kiang Wen-han, *The Chinese Student Movement*, New York, King's Crown Press, 1948. A good description of intellectual developments which were influential not only in academic circles but also in political affairs. A discussion of a rarely considered and important topic.

31. Kracke, E. A., Jr., "Sung Society: Change within Tradition," paper presented before the Far Eastern Association, New York, April 14, 1954.

32. Kracke, E. A., Jr., *Civil Service in Early Sung China, 960–1067*, with particular emphasis on the development of controlled sponsorship to foster administrative responsibility, Cambridge, Mass., Harvard University Press, 1953, 262 pp.

33. Lang, Olga, *Chinese Family and Society*, New Haven, Conn., Yale University Press, 1948, 317 pp. A thorough study of the family and its changing role in society.

34. Levy, Marion J., Jr., *The Family Revolution in Modern China*, Cambridge, Mass., Harvard University Press, 1949, 390 pp. A sociological and historical analysis of the family with special attention to points of strength and strain in a time of drastic changes.

35. Levy, Marion J., Jr., and Shih Kuo-hung, *The Rise of the Modern Chinese Business Class*, New York, Institute of Pacific Relations, 1949, 64 pp. A good, if tentative, study of a topic rarely covered. Levy's section is a sociological analysis of the background of the business class; Shih gives an historical study showing early problems of development.

36. Lin Yueh-hua, *The Golden Wing, A Sociological Study of Chinese Familism,* London, Institute of Pacific Relations, 1948, 234 pp. A semi-analytical, somewhat fictionalized, description of a Fukien family which started on the land and branched out into commerce, in which one line of the family did very well, while another slipped into oblivion. It mainly covers the first four decades of this century, with brief comments on the 1940's as well. It is a vivid description of social change in disrupted times.

37. Mitrany, David, *Marx against the Peasant, A Study in Social Dogmatism,* Chapel Hill, University of North Carolina Press, 1951, 301 pp. A good analysis of the peasant problem under Communism which is valuable to Far Eastern study although based on European situations.

38. Sanders, Irwin T., editor, *The Chinese Peasant: Habitat and Social Structure,* Lexington, Ky., 1952, 267 pp. (Societies around the World), compilations of excerpts from leading experts such as Fei Hs'ao-t'ung, J. L. Buck, etc., which form a useful summary.

39. Shih, Kuo-heng, *China Enters the Machine Age,* Cambridge, Mass., Harvard University Press, 1944, 206 pp. A description of a wartime factory in Yunnan and the problems of achieving labor efficiency with a mixed group of east-coast industrial worker refugees and of untrained local peasants. While some of its generalizations may be questioned, it remains a stimulating discussion of a rarely treated topic.

40. Tawney, Richard H., *Land and Labor in China,* New York, Harcourt, Brace & Co., 1932, 207 pp. The first section on agriculture remains of fundamental importance for the understanding of the position of the peasantry, while the second section on industry is somewhat outdated. The book as a whole remains valuable as a basic economic and social text. Other works listed under the chapter on economics should also be noted for background.

41. Yang, Martin C., *A Chinese Village: Taitou, Shantung Province,* New York, Columbia University Press, 1946, 275 pp. A sociological study with special emphasis on family relationships. Field work was done in the early 1940's.

Communist Period

42. *The Agrarian Reform Law of the People's Republic of China,* Peking, Foreign Languages Press, 1950, 104 pp.

43. Allen, Stewart, "China under Communist Control," *Behind the Headlines* pamphlet series, issued seven times a year, Canadian Institute of International Affairs, Toronto, February 1954, 18 pp. A résumé of Communist achievements and faults by a Canadian medical missionary deported in 1951.

44. Alley, Rewi, *Yo Banfa!* (We Have a Way), edited by Shirley Barton, foreword by Joseph Needham, Shanghai, China Monthly Review, 1952, 193 pp. A pro-Communist account by a New Zealander with long experience in China.

45. Ayers, William, "Labor Policy and Factory Management in Communist China," *Annals of the American Academy of Political and Social Science,* 277, September 1951, pp. 124–134. A useful study covering the early years of Communist rule.

46. Barnett, A. Doak, "Social Controls in Communist China," *Far Eastern Survey,* April 22, 1953, 22, pp. 45–48. A description by a trained observer with long experience in China.

47. Barnett, A. Doak, "Mass Political Organizations in Communist China," *Annals of the American Academy of Political and Social Science,* 277, September 1951, pp.

76–88. A discussion of one of the important means of propaganda and control in Communist China.

48. Bodde, Derk, *Peking Diary, A Year of Revolution,* New York, Henry Schuman, 1950, 292 pp. A report by an American Sinologist of the takeover of Peking. The author was impressed by the great orderliness of the Communists after KMT chaos, but noted unfavorably the early manifestations of restrictions on freedom.

49. Borowitz, Albert, *Fiction in Communist China,* Cambridge, Center for International Studies, Massachusetts Institute of Technology, April 1954, 124 pp. A study based on wide reading of Communist literature. The life of writers under Communist rule is also discussed.

50. Brenier, Henri, "Les Femmes et la Famille en Chine Communisme," *France-Indochine,* Fevrier 1954, pp. 31–35. An analysis of the Marriage Law and of the place of women in Chinese Communist society.

51. Bunzel, Ruth, and Weakland, John Hast, *An Anthropological Approach to Chinese Communism.* A report done under Task Order III, Contract N 6 ONR-271, Amendment 9; Research on Contemporary Cultures, April 1952, 227 pp., appendixes and bibliography, dittoed.

52. Burchett, Wilfred, *China's Feet Unbound,* London, Laurence and Wishart, 1952, 190 pp. Published in Melbourne by World Unity Publications. A party-line account by an Australian newspaper correspondent.

53. Chang, C. M., "Mao's Strategem of Land Reform," *Foreign Affairs,* July 1951, pp. 550–563.

54. Chao, K. C., *Mass Organizations in Communist China,* Cambridge, Center for International Studies, Massachusetts Institute of Technology, November 1953, 157 pp. Description and analysis of the major instruments whereby the Communist government attempts to reach the masses via propaganda and organization in the use of Communist ideas and methods of operation. It has detailed descriptions of the labor, women's, and youth organizations.

55. Chen, Theodore Hsi-en, "China: Communist Reform," *Current History,* November 1953, pp. 261–268. One of a series of articles on land policies in Asia.

56. Chen, Theodore Hsi-en, "Education and Propaganda in Communist China," *Annals of the American Academy of Political and Social Science,* 277, September 1951, pp. 135–145.

57. Chen, Theodore Hsi-en, "New Schools for China," *Current History,* June 1952, pp. 328–333.

58. Chen, Theodore Hsi-en, "Observable Weaknesses of the Chinese Communist Regime," *World Affairs Interpreter* (published quarterly, Los Angeles), Summer 1953, pp. 200–208. A discussion of problems of party organization, discipline, and membership, and of economic, financial, and Sino-Soviet difficulties.

59. Chen, Theodore Hsi-en, and Chen Wen-hui, "The 'Three-Anti' and 'Five-Anti' Movements in Communist China," *Pacific Affairs,* March 1953, pp. 3–23. A brief summary of the clean-up movements of 1951–1952 directed against first the Communist Party and subsequently the business classes.

60. Chen, Theodore Hsi-en, *Studies on Chinese Communism,* papers under the direction of Theodore H. E. Chen, Department of Asiatic Studies, University of Southern California. See Appendix 3 for titles. The material gathered is very useful although analyses are preliminary.

61. *China Monthly Review* (see Section IV, Part C), includes descriptions of life in China up to the summer of 1953.

62. *China Reconstructs,* Peking, bimonthly, many articles and stories on intellectuals, industry, etc., which are pro-regime, but some famous scholars contribute comments.

63. "The Chinese Labor Movement on the Eve of the Formation of the National, Anti-Imperialist United Front," *Soviet Press Translations,* 8, February 15, 1953, pp. 51–56, and *Soviet Press Translations,* 8, March 1, 1953, pp. 70–79, translated from *Voprosy Istorii,* No. 10/52.

64. Chun Chee Kwon, "Agrarian Unrest and the Civil War in China," *Land Economics,* 26, February 1950.

65. Clubb, O. Edmund, "Plus ça Change . . . in China," *Far Eastern Survey,* January 28, 1953, Vol. XXII, 2, pp. 18–19. A review of Fitzgerald's *Revolution in China (op. cit.).*

66. *Culture and Education in New China,* Peking, Foreign Languages Press, 1950. 82 pp. Includes a talk by Kuo Mo-jo, an education policy statement, and comments on the radio, films, and other media.

67. Davidson, Basil, *Daybreak in China,* London, Jonathan Cape, 1953, 191 pp. A report on a 1953 visit to China at the invitation of the Chinese People's Institute of Foreign Affairs. A rather naive account by an Englishman who appears to be very favorable to the regime.

68. "Decision of the Central People's Government on the Problem of Unemployment," *Soviet Press Translations,* 7, December 15, 1952, pp. 435–438. Translated from *Hsüeh hsi* for September 1, 1952. Official CCP version, designed for study groups.

69. De Francis, John, "National and Minority Policies," *Annals of the American Academy of Political and Social Science,* 277, September 1951, pp. 146–155.

70. *Eastern World,* published monthly, London (see Section IV, Part C). Includes many short articles which form a useful secondary source.

71. Endicott, Mary Austin, *Five Stars over China,* Toronto, published by the author, 1953, 464 pp. An account of a trip by the wife of Dr. James Endicott, winner of a Stalin Peace Prize and former China missionary. It is blatant propaganda.

72. *Far Eastern Economic Review,* weekly, Hong Kong (see Section IV, Part C). Contains frequent useful material on economic matters with an analysis of their effect on social and political affairs; based on the Chinese press and other sources.

73. Fei Hs'ao-t'ung, "China's Multi-National Family," *China Reconstructs,* Peking, May–June 1952, pp. 23–29. An article by a famous anthropologist, now with the regime, on China's minorities and what the Communist regime is doing to aid them.

74. Fried, Morton H., "Military Status in Chinese Society," *American Journal of Sociology,* 57, January 1952, pp. 347–357. An article to some extent challenging the idea that military status was considered low in Chinese traditional society in that the peasants often used it and viewed it as a means of moving up in the social scale. It refers to the pre-Communist period.

75. Galegin, V., and I. Markov, "Trade-Union Construction in the People's China," *Soviet Press Translations* 6, February 1, 1951, pp. 54–57. Translated from *Professionalnive,* 10, 1950.

76. Green, O. M., "Communist and Peasant in China," *Eastern World,* April 1954, pp. 20–23. Comment on the increasing demands on the peasantry since the new "General Line."

77. Gould, Randall, "Shanghai during the Takeover, 1949," *Annals of the American Academy of Political and Social Science*, 277, September 1951, pp. 182–192. A vivid write-up of the takeover trials of the editor of the only American daily newspaper published in Shanghai.

78. Gourlay, Walter E., *The Chinese Communist Cadre: Key to Political Control*, Cambridge, Russian Research Center, Harvard University, 1952, iv, 122 pp.

79. Han Suyin (pseudonym), *A Many Splendored Thing*, Boston, Little, Brown & Co., 1952, 366 pp. An excellent statement of the plight of the westernized Chinese, and descriptions of both city and village life on the mainland in the early days of the regime, interspersed with what is primarily a Hong Kong love story.

80. Harding, T. Swann, "Politics and Economics in Chinese Agriculture," *American Journal of Economics and Sociology*, 10, January 1951, p. 220.

81. Hsiao Ch'ien, "My Determination to be a Warrior in Mao Tse-tung's Cultural Army," *Soviet Press Translations*, 7, April 1, 1952, p. 197, translated from *Hsin Kuan ch'a*, January 1, 1952.

82. Hsü, Francis L. K., *Religion, Science, and Human Crises: A Study of China in Transition and Its Implications for the West*, London, Routledge and K. Paul, 1952, x, 142 pp. (International Library of Sociology and Social Reconstruction.)

83. Hunter, Edward, *Brain Washing in Red China, The Calculated Destruction of Men's Minds*, New York, Vanguard Press, 1951, 302 pp. (Revised edition, October 1953, 341 pp.) An emotional path-breaking account of value as a careful description of how brainwashing is actually done.

84. Hutheesing, Raja, *The Great Peace*, New York, Harper & Bros., 1953, 240 pp. and appendix. A relatively objective job of reporting by an Indian businessman, brother-in-law of Nehru, who was in China on two conducted tours in October 1951 and May–June 1952. He covers various aspects, economic, political, social. This is an informative first-hand account, one of the most useful available.

85. Johnson, Hewlett, *China's New Creative Age*, New York, International Publishers, 1953, 192 pp. A commentary on conditions in Communist China based on the "Red Dean of Canterbury's" trip to China in 1952. It is very pro-Communist and not accurate.

86. Kharkhov, V., "The Chinese Countryside Is on a New Track," *Soviet Press Translations*, 6, July 15, 1951, pp. 405–407, translated from *Sotsialistitcheskoye Zemledeliye*, May 15, 1951.

87. Keim, Jean A., "Les Musulmans Chinois," *France-Asie*, 956, Avril–Mai 1954, pp. 604–606.

88. Kierman, Frank W., Jr., *The Chinese Communists in the Light of Chinese History*, Cambridge, Center for International Studies, Massachusetts Institute of Technology, June 1954, 44 pp.

89. Kierman, Frank W., Jr., *The Chinese Intelligentsia and the Communists*, Cambridge, Center for International Studies, M.I.T., June 1954, 24 pp.

90. Kierman, Frank W., Jr., *The Fluke That Saved Formosa*, Cambridge, Center for International Studies, M.I.T., June 1954, 13 pp. A description of the chaos wrought in the Communist army by a liver disease which may have helped save Formosa from invasion in 1950.

91. Kizer, Benjamin H., "Asia's Women Speak for Themselves," *Far Eastern Survey*, March 1954, pp. 45–47.

92. Landman, Lynn and Amos, *Profile of Red China*, New York, Simon and Schuster, 1951, 126 pp. A report which is mainly about Shanghai during the early takeover period.

93. Lee Shu-ching, "Agrarianism and Social Upheaval in China," *American Journal of Sociology*, 56, May 1951, pp. 511–518.

94. Li Ta, "Concerning the Thought Rehabilitation of University Professors," *Soviet Press Translation*, 7, February 1, 1952, pp. 86–89, translated from *Hsüeh hsi* for November 16, 1951. An official statement for consumption by study groups, presumably as psychological preparation for the 5-Anti campaign versus, among others, intellectuals.

95. Lindbeck, J. M. H., "Communist Policy and the Chinese Family," *Far Eastern Survey*, 20, July 25, 1951, pp. 137–141.

96. Lindsay, Michael, *Notes on Educational Problems in Communist China*, with supplements by Marion Menzies, Wm. Paget, and S. B. Thomas, New York, International Secretariat, Institute of Pacific Relations, 1950, 202 pp. A first-hand report of the Chinese Communists' educational theory and practice in "liberated areas" during the war. The supplements deal with 1945–1950 developments.

97. Lippa, Ernest, *Captive Surgeon, Adventures of a Doctor in Red China*, New York, Morrow, 1953, 280 pp. (From 3 articles in the *Saturday Evening Post*, April 28, May 5 and 12, 1951.) A strongly anti-Communist description with some illuminating insights into both traditional and Communist attitudes towards modern medicine.

98. Liu Shaw-tong, *Out of Red China*, translated from the Chinese by Jack Chia and Henry Walter, New York, Duell, Sloan & Pearce; Boston, Little, Brown & Co., 1953, 269 pp. A report of a liberal intellectual who worked at moderately high rank for the Communists during the civil war and then became disillusioned. It covers through 1949–1950. The translation is not altogether accurate and occasionally embellishes the original text. It is not analytical, but contains good reporting on various political and social aspects of the regime.

99. Magnien, Marius, *Au Pays de Mao Tse-toung*, Pref. de Marcel Cachin, Paris, Editions sociales, 1952, 351 pp. Pro-regime report by a Frenchman who has also contributed articles on China to *Cahiers du Communisme*.

100. Markov, I., "Cultural and Educational Work of the Chinese Trade Unions," *Soviet Press Translations*, 6, May 1, 1951, pp. 247–251, translated from *Professionalniye soyuzy*, No. 2, 1951.

101. *The Marriage Law of the People's Republic of China and Other Relevant Articles*, Peking, Foreign Languages Press, 1950, 41 pp. Text of the 1950 law by which the Communists have made a major assault on the traditional Chinese family. A basic social document.

102. McCammon, Dorothy, *We Tried to Stay*, Scottsville, Pa., Herald Press, 1953, 207 pp. An account by a young wife of a Mennonite missionary in Szechuan, 1947–1951. Mainly a personal story, generous and humorous, reporting a few interesting incidents.

103. Miao Chu-Hwang, "The Vacillation of the National Capitalist Class as Shown in China's Modern Revolutionary History," *Soviet Press Translations*, 7, June 15, 1952, pp. 275–281. Translated from *Hsüeh hsi* for March 16, 1952. Another official CCP text for study groups.

104. Min, Kyaw U., *Through the Iron Curtain via the Back Door*, Rangoon, Printed by the Burmese Advertising Press, 1952, 291 pp. A report of a trip in the spring of 1952 to Moscow via China by a Burmese businessman delegate to the International Economic Conference in Moscow. It was first published in newspapers and is written mostly from memory. Chatty in tone, it has no analyses of any import, though it is fairly impartial.

105. Montell, Sherwin, "The San-fan Wu-fan Movement in Communist China," *Papers on China* (Vol. 8), from the Regional Studies Seminars, duplicated for private distribution by the Committee on International and Regional Studies, Harvard University, February 1954, pp. 136–196. A report on the 3-Anti 5-Anti movement of 1951–1952, going into the historical, political, economic, and social aspects of this very important urban movement. A fairly thorough treatment, well documented.

106. Moraes, Frank, *Report on Mao's China*, New York, The Macmillan Co., 1953, 212 pp. The author is an Indian newspaperman who went on a tour of China in the spring of 1952 (at the same time as Raja Hutheesing, *op. cit.*). This is about the most useful semi-analytical account yet published about Communist China. The author goes into political aspects, including descriptions of the top leaders, and into economic and social affairs based on visits to such points as the Huai River project or a rural village. Although fundamentally skeptical about the loss of freedom, he attempts to report fairly.

107. Morrison, Esther, "A Comparison of Kuomintang and Communist Modern History Textbooks," *Papers on China* (Vol. 6), from the Regional Studies Seminars, duplicated for private distribution by the Committee on International and Regional Studies, Harvard University, March 1952, pp. 3–44. An analysis, based on Chinese sources, which reveals the differences in intellectual aims and climate. See also an unduplicated paper by the same author, "Two Years of Worker Peasant Education in Communist China," Spring 1952, 62 pp.

108. Moy, Clarence, "Communist China's Use of the Yang-ko," *Papers on China* (Vol. 6), from the Regional Studies Seminars, duplicated for private distribution by the Committee on International and Regional Studies, Harvard University, March 1952, pp. 149–188. A description of the simple dance which was used, especially in the early days, as a psychological weapon of good cheer among the masses, both urban and rural.

109. *Mutual Aid and Cooperation In China's Agricultural Production*, Peking, Foreign Languages Press, November 1953, 38 pp.

110. Noah, Lynn, "Chinese Communist Propaganda Technique towards Labor," projected, with revisions, for *Papers on China* (Vol. 9), from the Regional Studies Seminars, Harvard University. Present version, May 1954, 24 pp. and notes. An analysis of the laboring class in China and of the propaganda techniques by which the Communists attempt to mold them into the regime.

111. *People's China*, monthly, Peking (see Section IV, Part C). Frequent accounts of industrial or agricultural workers, etc., which are illuminating as a study of propaganda.

112. Priestley, K. E., "Chinese Communism and Christianity," *Far Eastern Survey*, 21, January 30, 1952, pp. 203–204.

113. Rand, Christopher, *Hongkong, the Island in between*, New York, Knopf, 1952, 244 pp. Various comments and accounts of actual experiences, especially in South China, by a well-known correspondent.

114. Rao, V. K. R. V., "Some Impressions of New China," *India Quarterly*, 8, January–March 1952, pp. 3–14. Also report on same trip in *The Nation*, April 5 and 12, 1952. A fairly pro-regime account.

115. *The Seventh Congress of the All China Federation of Trade Unions*, Peking, Foreign Languages Press, 1953, 141 pp. Report of the Congress held in the summer of 1953.

116. Schurcliff, Alice W., "Control of Industrial Labor in Communist China," *Monthly Labor Review*, 76, August 1953, pp. 821–825. A good short treatment of the subject.

117. Shah, K. T., *The Promise That Is New China*, Bombay, Vora, 1953, 342 pp. The diary of a 1952 visit to China by an Indian economist and trade union delegate. It is very favorable to the regime and against the United States.

118. Sister Mary Victoria, *Nun in Red China*, New York, McGraw-Hill, 1953, 208 pp. A Maryknoll nun's account of takeover, trial, prisons, and repatriation. False accusations and cruel treatment endured in South China are recounted with courage, but reveal a limited sphere of experience.

119. Skinner, G. William, "Aftermath of Communist Liberation on the Chengtu Plain," *Pacific Affairs*, 24, March 1951, pp. 61–76.

120. Skinner, G. William, "Peasant Organization in Rural China," *Annals of the American Academy of Political and Social Science*, 277, September 1952, pp. 89–100. Comments about land reform by an anthropologist who deals with the social changes brought about in the early days of the Communist rural program.

121. Stockwell, E. Olin, *With God in Red China*, New York, Harper & Bros., 1953, 256 pp. An account which covers the experiences of a Presbyterian missionary from November 1950 to November 1952. He was first stationed in Chengtu, Szechuan, and then spent a year in a Chungking jail. The author is occasionally tactless and sometimes overfacile. However, at his best he is a sharp and witty observer who has good background for understanding China and remained remarkably unembittered by his own experiences.

122. Stockwell, E. Olin, "What Is Chinese Brain-Washing?" *The Christian Century*, Part I, January 21, 1953, pp. 73–74. Part II, January 28, 1953, pp. 104–106. See note above.

123. Swarup, Ram, "The Myth of Social Surplus in China," *Thought* (published weekly, New Delhi), October 25, 1952.

124. Swope, Gerald and Richard J. Walsh, "Mass Education Movement and the JCRR," *Far Eastern Survey*, 20, July 25, 1951, pp. 145–148.

125. Tennien, Mark, *No Secret Is Safe behind the Bamboo Curtain*, New York, Farrar, Straus and Young, 1952, 270 pp. A report by a Maryknoll priest of his experiences under the Communists from November 1949 to January 1952, when he returned to the United States. He was in Shumkai in the eastern part of Kwangsi Province and had been in China since 1928. Although passionately anti-Communist, he is a shrewd reporter, both of land reform and of his prison experiences.

126. T. T., "The Intellectual in New China," written from Hong Kong, *Problems of Communism: China*, No. 2, 1953, pp. 1–7.

127. Townsend, Peter, *In China Now* (with introduction by Basil Davidson—*op. cit.*), London, Union of Democratic Control, 1953, 31 pp. An Englishman with some industrial experience making a brief pro-regime report.

128. *The Trade Union Law, together with Other Relevant Documents* (revised ed.), Peking, Foreign Languages Press, 1951, 38 pp.

129. Trewartha, Glenn T., "Chinese Cities: Origins and Functions," *Annals of the Association of American Geographers*, 42, March 1952, pp. 69–93. Useful background for the industrial classes on which material is very scarce.

130. Tsao Ching-hua, "A Fighting Friend of the Chinese People (Corky)," *Soviet Press Translations*, 6, July 15, 1951, pp. 408–410, translated from *Pravda*, June 18, 1951.

131. Van der Valk, Prof. Mr. M. H., "Problemen der rechtshervorming in China" (in Dutch), *Indonesië,* published in The Hague (quarterly, multilingual), Part I, October 1953, pp. 132–155; Part II, January 1954, pp. 199–208. Deals with legal reform in China.

132. Van der Sprenkel, Otto B., Robert Guillian, and Michael Lindsay, *New China: Three Views,* New York, John Day, 1951. Published in London, 1950. Comments on the takeover by a Dutch, a French, and an English observer, all with experience in China. The first is the longest and gives an account of Peking and Tientsin that is of interest. The authors were considered sympathetic to the Chinese Communists (at the time of publication), but they attempted to be factual.

133. Walker, Richard L., "The Working Class in Communist China," *Problems of Communism: China,* September–October 1953, pp. 42–50. A very useful account, summarizing events to the time written.

134. Wang Shu-ming, "The Development and Achievements of Chinese Literary Criticism within the Past Year," *Soviet Press Translations,* 7, January 15, 1952, pp. 48–51, translated from *Hsin Chien Sheh,* Peking, Vol. 5, No. 1, October 1, 1951.

135. Weakland, John Hast, "The Organization of Action in Chinese Culture," *Psychiatry,* Vol. 13, No. 3, pp. 361–370.

136. *Women in New China* (3rd ed.), Peking, Foreign Languages Press, 1950, 55 pp. Propaganda.

137. Wright, Mary C., "The Chinese Peasant and Communism," *Pacific Affairs,* 24, September 1951, pp. 256–265. A discussion, by a Sinologist, of early Communist actions towards the peasants and how the peasant has reacted and may continue to respond.

138. Wu Cheng-hsi, "An Analysis and Criticism of the Ideology of the Shanghai Capitalist Class," *Soviet Press Translations,* 7, July 15, 1952, pp. 313–315, translated from *Ching chi chou pao,* No. 6, 1952.

139. Yu Hai, "The Role of the National Bourgeoisie in the Chinese Revolution," *People's China,* 1, January 1, 1950, pp. 7–10; French version: "Le rôle de la bourgeoisie nationale dans la révolution chinoise," *Cahiers du Communism,* 27, Aôut 1950, pp. 87–92. An important policy statement concerning the coexistence of the bourgeoisie and the proletariat.

IX. Chinese Economy

Mainly Communist period, but including a few major background sources, and certain studies of the economies of the Soviet Union and other countries which are referred to in the text and are useful for comparisons.

1. Allen, G. C., and Audrey G. Donnithorne, *Western Enterprise in Far Eastern Economic Development: China and Japan,* New York, The Macmillan Co., 1954, 292 pp. Covers from mid-nineteenth century to the present. Comparisons between the two countries are emphasized; an accurate, useful, short summary.

2. Arnold, Julean, "Modern Industry in China," *Chinese Economic Journal,* October 1930, pp. 1066–1080. The author was an American commercial attaché in China.

3. Barclay, George W., "China's Population Problem, A Closer View," *Pacific Affairs,* 23, June 1950, pp. 184–192. (Reply to C. Y. Chang, see below.)

4. Barnett, A. Doak, "China's Road to Collectivization," *Journal of Farm Economics,* May 1953, pp. 188–192. A good analysis of Chinese agrarian and collectivization policy and of the institutional arrangements for fostering collectivization.

5. Baykov, Alexander, *The Development of the Soviet Economic System,* Cambridge, at the University Press, New York, The Macmillan Co., 1948, 514 pp. Author is an economist at the University of Birmingham.

6. Bergson, Abram, editor, *Soviet Economic Growth, Conditions and Perspectives,* Evanston, Ill., and White Plains, N. Y., Row, Peterson and Company, 1953, 376 pp. Proceedings of a conference of outstanding specialists in the field of Soviet economics.

7. Bergson, Abram, *Soviet National Income and Product in 1937,* New York, Columbia University Press, 1953, 156 pp. The author is a leading authority on Soviet national income.

8. Bergson, Abram, and Hans Heymann, Jr., *Soviet National Income and Product, 1940–48,* New York, Columbia University Press, 1954, 249 pp. (A research study by the RAND Corporation.)

9. Boldyrev, B., "Finances, Money, and Credits in the Economic Construction of the Chinese People's Republic," *Soviet Press Translations,* 7, January 15, 1952, pp. 35–47. Translated from *Voprosy ekonomiki,* No. 9, 1951. An interesting and careful review of the Chinese Communist financial policy and currency stabilization experience written from a Soviet point of view.

10. Brenier, Henri (correspondant de l'Institut), "La Prolétarisation de paysannat chinois et ses conséquences," *Politique Étrangère,* Avril–Mai 1954, pp. 195–210. A factual analysis on the economic, political, and social aspects of agricultural collectivization steps.

11. Brenier, Henri, "La réforme agraire en Chine," *Politique Étrangère,* 16, Mars–Mai 1951, pp. 167–175.

12. Brenier, Henri, "La situation Économique en Chine et à Hong-Kong," *France-Indochine,* 93, Janvier 1953, pp. 23–28. Comments on the economic aspects of agriculture, industry, and commerce.

13. Buck, J. L., *Land Utilization in China,* 3 vols., Chicago, University of Chicago Press, 1937. The standard source for factual data on mainland China's rural economy, based on a sample census.

14. Chang, C. C., *An Estimate of China's Farms and Crops,* Nanking, University of Nanking, 1932.

15. Chang, C. M., "Mao's Stratagem of Land Reform," *Foreign Affairs,* 29, July 1951, pp. 550–563.

16. Chang Chih-yi, "China's Population Problem: A Chinese View," *Pacific Affairs,* December 1949, pp. 339–356. (See reply by Barclay above.)

17. Chang Pei-kang, *Agriculture and Industrialization, The Adjustments that Take Place as an Agricultural Country is Industrialized,* Cambridge, Harvard University Press, 1949, 270 pp. (Harvard Economic Series, Vol. 85.)

18. Chao Kuo-chün, "Current Agrarian Policies in Communist China," *Annals of the American Academy of Political and Social Science,* 277, September 1951, pp. 113–123.

19. Chao Kuo-chün, "Chinese Land Policies," *Current History,* 24, June 1953, pp. 339–350.

20. Chao Kuo-chün, "Land Reform Methods in Communist China," *Papers on China* (Vol. 5), from the Regional Studies Seminars, duplicated for private distribution by the Committee on International and Regional Studies, Harvard University, pp. 107–174. (See also unpub. Cornell University Ph.D. thesis, September 1953.)

21. Chao Kuo-chün, Comp., *Source Materials from Communist China,* duplicated, Cambridge, Mass., 1952, Vol. I, *Agrarian Policy,* Russian Research Center, Harvard University, 41 pp. The three volumes are very useful translated collec-

tions of primary source materials. Vol. II. *Aspects of Economic Planning,* Russian Research Center, Harvard University, April 1952, 64 pp. Vol. III, *Fiscal, Monetary, and International Economic Policies of the Chinese Communist Government,* Center for International Studies, M.I.T., and Russian Research Center, Harvard University, October 1952, 96 pp.

22. Chen Chien-ke, "China's Outstanding Financial and Economic Achievements," *People's China,* Peking, October 16, 1951, pp. 9–11.

23. Chen Ta, *Population in Modern China,* Chicago, University of Chicago Press, 1946, 126 pp. Based primarily on a modern census of Yunnan in wartime, it also contains surveys of previous data and of other local censuses since 1911.

24. Cheng Cho-yuan, *Monetary Affairs of Communist China,* Hong Kong, Communist China's Problem Research Series, April 1954, 160 pp. (see Section II, No. 8).

25. Chia To-fu, "The Advance of China's Industry," *People's China,* Peking, June 1, 1953. Official Communist statement.

26. *China Handbook, 1950,* New York, Rockport Press, Inc., 1950, 799 pp.

27. *China Yearbook, 1948* (in Chinese), Nanking, China Yearbook Committee of the Chinese Nationalist Government, September 1948. Two volumes, Vol. I, 830 pp.; Vol. II, pp. 831–2080. (As translated by Chao Kuo-chün.) The most comprehensive source of Nationalist China.

28. *China Wins Economic Battles,* Peking, Foreign Languages Press, 1950, iii, 58 pp. Statements by Mao, Chen Yun, etc.

29. "China's Agriculture-Tasks for Transition," *The Economist,* March 13, 1954, pp. 782–783. Comments on plans for increasing both production and socialist controls. The author is relatively hopeful for China's success.

30. *China's Railways: A Story of Heroic Reconstruction,* Peking, Foreign Languages Press, 1950 (?), 45 pp. Propagandistic account.

31. *The Chinese Yearbook, 1944–1945,* Councils of International Affairs, the Commercial Press, Shanghai, for the period 1936–1945.

32. Chiu, A. K., "Agriculture," Ch. XXXII in *China,* edited by Harley F. MacNair, Berkeley, University of California Press, 1946, xxix, 573 pp. Thirty-four chapters on the history of Chinese politics and culture by various Far East experts.

33. Chou En-lai, "Report at the Fourth Session of the National Committee of the Chinese People's Consultative Council," in *Ta Kung Pao* (Impartiality Daily), Hong Kong, February 5, 1953.

34. Chou Ya-lun, "Chinese Agrarian Reform and Bolshevik Land Policy," *Pacific Affairs,* 25, March 1952, pp. 24–39.

35. Chun Chee Kwon, "Agrarian Unrest and the Civil War in China," *Land Economics,* 26, Wisconsin, February 1950, pp. 17–26.

36. *Communiqué on Rehabilitation and Development of National Economy, Culture and Education during 1952,* published by the State Statistical Bureau, Peking, September 29, 1953.

37. Cressey, George B., *China's Geographic Foundations, A Survey of the Land and Its People,* New York, McGraw-Hill, 1934, 436 pp. The best introduction to human geography.

38. Cressey, George B., *Asia's Lands and Peoples, a geography of one-third the earth and two-thirds its people,* 2nd ed., New York, McGraw-Hill, 1951, 597 pp.; 130 pp. are on China.

39. *The Crisis and Failure of Collectivized Agriculture under Communism,* published by the International Peasant Union, Forum, New York, 1953, Chicago, 1954, 28 pp.

40. Davis, Kingsley, *The Population of India and Pakistan,* Princeton, Princeton University Press, 1951, 262 pp. The authoritative source on this subject.

41. "Decision on the Development of Agrarian Production Cooperatives," of December 16, 1953, reported in *China News Analysis,* Hong Kong, February 12, 1954.

42. Delgardo, L., "Monetary Reform in China," *Eastern World,* February 1954, pp. 41–43. Review and Summary of R. Hsia, *Price Control in Communist China.*

43. "Economic Development in Mainland China, 1949–53," *Economic Bulletin for Asia and the Far East,* Vol. IV, No. 3, Bangkok, Siam, November 1953, published by the UN Economic Commission for Asia and the Far East, Research and Statistics Divisions, 56 pp.

44. *Economic Survey of Asia and the Far East, 1949, 1950, 1951,* Bangkok, Siam, published by the UN Economic Commission for Asia and the Far East.

45. Eckstein, A., *Conditions and Prospects for Economic Growth in Communist China,* Cambridge, Center for International Studies, M.I.T., 1954.

46. Erlich, Alexander, "Preobrazhenski and the Economics of Soviet Industrialization," *Quarterly Journal of Economics,* Vol. LXIV, No. 1, February 1950, pp. 57–88.

47. Fong, H. D., "Rural Industries in China," *Problems of the Pacific,* 5th Conference of the Institute of Pacific Relations, New York, 1933. A useful descriptive study.

48. Fong, H. D., *The Post-War Industrialization of China,* Washington, National Planning Association, 1942, 92 pp.

49. Gerschenkron, A., "Economic Backwardness in Historical Perspective," in *The Progress of Underdeveloped Areas,* ed. Bart F. Hoselitz, Chicago, 1952, x, 296 pp.

50. Ginsburg, Norton S., "China's railroad network," *Geographical Review,* 41, July 1951, pp. 470–474.

51. Gourou, Pierre, "The Development of Upland Areas in China," *The Development of Upland Areas in the Far East,* International Secretariat, Institute of Pacific Relations, New York, 1949. Comments by a geographer on the long-range possibilities of developing agriculture in China's upland areas.

52. Ho, Franklin L., "The Land Problem of China," *Annals of the American Academy of Political and Social Science,* 276, July 1951, pp. 6–11.

53. Hoeffding, Oleg, *Soviet National Income and Product in 1928,* New York, Columbia University Press, 1954, 156 pp. (A Research Study of the RAND Corporation.)

54. Holzman, F. D., "The Burden of Soviet Taxation," *The American Economic Review,* September 1953, pp. 548–571.

55. Hsia, Ronald, *Economic Planning in Communist China,* Cambridge, Center for International Studies, Massachusetts Institute of Technology, November 1953, 83 pp.

56. Hsia, Ronald, *The Role of Labor-Intensive Investment Projects in China's Capital Formation* (tentative title), Cambridge, Center for International Studies, Massachusetts Institute of Technology, summer 1954.

57. Hsia, Ronald, *Price Control in Communist China,* New York, Institute of Pacific Relations, 1953, 96 pp.

58. Hsia, Ronald, "Private Enterprise in Communist China," *Pacific Affairs,* 26, 4, December 1953, pp. 329–334.

59. Hsia, Ronald, "The Chinese Economy under Communist Planning," *Pacific Affairs,* 27, 2, June 1954, pp. 112–123.

60. Hsin Ying, *The Foreign Trade of Communist China,* Hong Kong, Communist China's Problem Research Series. March 1954, 161 pp. See Section II.

61. Hsin Ying, *The Price Problems of Communist China,* Hong Kong, Communist China's Problem Research Series, January 1954, 125 pp.

62. Hsu Hsueh-han, "China's Trade with European People's Democracies," *People's China,* Peking, No. 17, September 1, 1953.

63. Huang Yen-pei, "Progress in China's Light Industry," *People's China,* Peking, December 16, 1952, pp. 4–7.

64. Johnston, Bruce F., "Agricultural Productivity and Economic Development in Japan," *Journal of Political Economy* (bimonthly, Chicago), Vol. LIX, December 1951, pp. 498–513.

65. Kao Kang, "Report at the First Conference of Representatives of the Chinese Communist Party in the Northeast," Mukden, March 13, 1950, NCNA.

66. Ke Chia-lung, "China Builds a New Democracy," *People's China,* Peking, December 16, 1951.

67. Koh Tso-fan, "Capital Stock in China," *Problems of Economic Reconstruction in China,* China Council Paper No. 2, Institute of Pacific Relations, Eighth Conference, Mt. Tremblant, December 1952.

68. Kovalyov, E., "The Agrarian Policy of the Chinese Communist Party," *Soviet Press Translations,* 6, April 1, 1951, pp. 163–172. Translated from *Voprosy ekonomiki,* No. 10, 1950.

69. Levy, Marion J., Jr., *Some Social Obstacles to "Capital" Formation in "Underdeveloped Areas,"* to be published in New York by the National Bureau of Economic Research, Inc., 1954. The most suggestive examination of specific elements in Chinese and Japanese culture and social structure which are conducive or inhibiting to economic development.

70. Li Chang, "Railway Construction in China," *Far Eastern Survey,* 22, March 25, 1953, pp. 37–42.

71. Li Choh-ming, "International Trade," chapter in *China,* edited by H. F. MacNair, Berkeley, University of California Press, 1946, xxix, 573 pp.

72. Lieu, D. K., *China's Economic Stabilization and Reconstruction,* New Brunswick, N. J., Rutgers University Press, 1948, 159 pp. (Published under the auspices of the Sino-International Economic Research Center, New York, and the China Institute of Pacific Relations, Shanghai.)

73. Liu Ta-chun, *China's National Income, 1931–36,* Washington, D. C., Brookings Institution, 1946, 91 pp.

74. Lorimer, Frank, *The Population of the Soviet Union, History and Prospects,* Geneva, League of Nations, printed in Princeton, Princeton University Press, 1946, 289 pp. (Appendices pp. 203–258; Bibliography pp. 259–286, and index.)

75. *Manchukuo Yearbook, 1942,* Mukden, official publication of the Manchukuo Government.

76. Mitchell, Kate, *Industrialization of the Western Pacific,* New York, Institute of Pacific Relations, 1942, xv, 317 pp., Part III of *An Economic Survey of the Pacific Area.* The best single survey in English of industrialization to 1940, although it suffers from some inaccuracies.

77. Miyazaki, S., "New China's Five Year Plan," *Taiheiyo Mondai,* monthly, published by the Kansai Branch, Japan Institute of Pacific Relations, Osaka, March 1954, pp. 7–13 (translated in *Far East Digest,* Nos. 85 and 86, June 1954). An account by a member of the research staff of the *Asahi* newspaper giving statistics on production and future estimates.

78. Morikawa, Kiyoshi, "Industrial Recovery in Red China," *Oriental Economist* (Tokyo), 22, No. 520, February 1954, pp. 85–90. A pro-regime account of industrial

conditions in Fushun, Manchuria, by a Japanese industrial chemist repatriated in the spring of 1953. It emphasizes administration and the use of technical personnel.

79. Mukharjee, M., and A. D. Ghosh, "The Pattern of Income and Expenditure in the Indian Union, A Tentative Study," *Bulletin of the International Statistical Institute,* Vol. xxxiii, part III, December 1951 (published in Calcutta, India). Issue on International Statistical Conferences, India, pp. 49–68. Authors are with the National Income Unit, Ministry of Finance, New Delhi.

80. Murphey, Rhoads, *Shanghai, Key to Modern China,* Cambridge, Harvard University Press, 1953, xii, 232 pp. A treatment of the setting, growth, and functions of China's largest urban center by an economic geographer. The last chapter has brief comments on the Communist period.

81. *New China's Economic Achievements, 1949–52,* Peking, Foreign Languages Press, 1952, 285 pp. Policy statements of Po I-po, Minister of Finance, Chen Yun, and other important leaders. A useful source.

82. "Order of Government Administrative Council for Enforcement of Planned Purchase and Planned Supply of Grain," issued Nov. 23, 1953, reported NCNA, Peking, February 28, 1954 (CMP). Official Chinese Communist Government order.

83. Ou Pao-san, *Capital Formation and Consumers' Outlay in China,* Cambridge, Ph.D. thesis, Harvard University, 1948, 211 pp.

84. Ou Pao-san, "A New Estimate of China's National Income," *Journal of Political Economy,* 54, 6, December 1946, pp. 547–554.

85. Paauw, Douglas S., "Economic Principles and State Organization," *Annals of the American Academy of Political and Social Science,* 277, September 1951, pp. 101–112.

86. Pauley, Edwin W., *Report on Japanese Assets in Manchuria to the President of the United States,* July 1946.

87. Pei, Hsiang-yin, "Sino-Soviet Trade," *People's China,* June 16, 1953.

88. Po I-po, "Report on 1953 State Budget of the People's Republic of China," supplement to *People's China,* Peking, March 16, 1953.

89. Remer, C. F., *The Foreign Trade of China,* Shanghai, the Commercial Press, Limited, 1926, 269 pp. The most reliable source for the period up to publication date.

90. Remer, C. F., *Foreign Investments in China,* New York, The Macmillan Co., 1933, 708 pp. The single most complete and reliable source for its period.

91. Riggs, Fred W., *The Economics of Red China,* New York, Foreign Policy Association, 1951. (62) 72 pp. (Foreign Policy reports, Vol. 27, No. 6.)

92. Robinson, Joan, "Industrialization Is China's Primary Objective," *Great Britain and the East,* section 1, October 1953, section 2, November 1953, p. 11. Comments by well-known British economist on British trade with China in the light of China's industrialization plans.

93. Rosse, Robert M., "The Working of Communist China's Five Year Plan," *Pacific Affairs,* 27, March 1954, pp. 16–26. A rather superficial survey.

94. Rowe, David N., *China among the Powers,* New York, Harcourt, Brace and Co., 1945, 205 pp.

95. Schumpeter, Elizabeth B., editor, *The Industrialization of Japan and Manchukuo, 1930–1940,* New York, The Macmillan Co., 1940, 944 pp. A standard compilation on the subject.

96. Schwartz, Harry, *Russia's Soviet Economy,* New York, Prentice-Hall, 1950, 592 pp.

97. Shen, T. H., *Agricultural Resources of China*, Ithaca, Cornell University Press, 1951, 407 pp. A valuable reference work on China's farm economy.

98. Shigeto, Tsuru, and Kazvshi Ohkawa, "Long-Term Changes in the National Product of Japan since 1878," *Income and Wealth*, Cambridge, England, Series III, pp. 19–44.

99. Shimkin, Demitri B., *Minerals, A Key to Soviet Power*, Cambridge, Harvard University Press, 1953, 452 pp.

100. *Statistical Yearbook of the League of Nations, 1942–44*, Geneva, 1945.

101. Steiner, H. Arthur, "Chinese Development Programme," *Eastern World*, July 1953, p. 17.

102. "Struggle for the Distant and Great Goal of Socialist Industrialization," Editorial in *People's Daily*, October 1, 1953, NCNA. The first statement of the new General Line.

103. Szczepanik, F. F., "On Economic Theory of Maoism," *Ekonomi Dan Keuangen Indonesia* (Economies and Finance in Indonesia), January 1954, pp. 4–16. Theoretical discussion by a Lecturer at the University of Hong Kong.

104. Teng Hsiao-ping (Minister of Finance), "Report on the 1954 State Budget at the Thirty-first Meeting of the Central People's Government Council," June 16, 17, 1954, NCNA, Supplement No. 204, London, June 24, 1954.

105. Thomas, S. B., "The Chinese Communists' Economic and Cultural Agreement with North Korea," *Pacific Affairs*, 27, March 1954, pp. 61–65.

106. Trewartha, Glenn T., "Chinese Cities: numbers and distribution," *Annals of the Association of American Geographers*, 41, December 1951, pp. 331–347.

107. United Nations, *Demographic Yearbook, 1952*.

108. United Nations, *World Iron Ore Resources and Their Utilization*, New York, 1950.

109. United Nations, *Economic Survey of Europe since the War*, Economic Commission for Europe, Geneva, 1953.

110. United Nations, *Study on Iron and Steel Industry*, Economic Commission for Latin America, Vol. II, E/cn, 12/293/Add 2 & 3.

111. United Nations, *World Economic Report, 1951–52*, New York, April 1953.

112. U. S. Department of Commerce, *Foreign Commerce Yearbook, 1937*, published in Washington, D. C., 1938.

113. U. S. Department of State, International Press Service, *Collectivization in Europe and the Far East, A Comparative Study*, referenced in State Department Circ. Airgram No. 2771, 20 March 1953.

114. U. S. Federal Power Commission, *Steam Electric Plant Construction Cost and Annual Production Expenses*, Washington, D. C., 1950.

115. U. S. Foreign Operations Administration, *World Wide Enforcement of Strategic Trade Controls*, Mutual Defense Assistance Control October 3rd Report to Congress, Washington, D. C., November 1953.

116. Volin, Lazar, *A Survey of Soviet Russian Agriculture*, Washington, D. C., U. S. Department of Agriculture, Agriculture Monograph 5, August 1951, 194 pp.

117. Winfield, Gerald, *China, the Land and People*, New York, issued in cooperation with the American Institute of Pacific Relations, W. Sloane Associates, 1948, vii, 437 pp.

118. Woytinsky, W. S. and E. S., *World Population and Production*, New York, Twentieth Century Fund, 1953, LXXII, 1268 pp. An encyclopedic reference work of great value.

119. Yamada, Yuzo, and Associates, *Notes on the Income Growth and the Rate of Saving in Japan,* mimeographed, Tokyo, 1953, 19 pp.

APPENDIX 1

Papers from the Center for International Studies (CENIS), Massachusetts Institute of Technology, Cambridge 39, Mass.

Borowitz, Albert, *Fiction in Communist China,* July 7, 1954, 124 pp.

Borowitz, Albert, *Fiction in Communist China, Summary,* June 1, 1954, 5 pp.

Chao, K. C. (Chao Kuo-chün), *Land Policy of the Chinese Communist Party, 1921–1953,* 300 pp.

Chao, K. C., *Northeast China (Manchuria) Today,* 1953, 131 pp.*

Chao, K. C., *Mass Organizations in Communist China,* November 1953, 157 pp.*

Chao, K. C., *Mass Organizations Summary,* 1954, 12 pp.*

Chao, K. C., *The Chinese Communist Elections,* Summer 1954.*

Dai, Shen-yu, *Peking, Moscow and the Communist Parties of Colonial Asia,* July 23, 1954, 167 pp.*

Eckstein, Alex, *Conditions and Prospects for Economic Growth in Communist China,* Summer 1954.*

Hsia, Ronald, *Economic Planning in Communist China,* November 1953, 83 pp.*

Hsia, Ronald, *Economic Planning Summary,* 1954, 12 pp.*

Hsia, Ronald, *Labor Intensive Investment in Communist China,** Roads, Railroads, Water Conservancy, Summer 1954.*

Kautsky, John, *Moscow and the Communist Party of India,* Summer 1954.*

Kierman, Frank A., Jr., *The Chinese Communists in the Light of Chinese History,* June 1, 1954, 44 pp.*

Kierman, Frank A., Jr., *The Chinese Intelligentsia and the Communists,* June 1, 1954, 24 pp.*

Kierman, Frank A., Jr., *The Fluke That Saved Formosa,* June 1, 1954, 13 pp.*

McVey, Ruth T., *The Development of the Indonesian Communist Party and Its Relations with the Soviet Union and the Chinese People's Republic,* May 1954, 97 pp.

Nivison, David, *Communist Ethics and Chinese Tradition,* Summer 1954.

Pye, Lucian W., *Some Observations on the Political Behavior of Overseas Chinese,* June 1, 1954, 24 pp.

Rostow, W. W., *A Comparison of Soviet and Chinese Communist Society,* Summer 1954.†

Schwartz, Benjamin, *China and the Soviet Theory of "Peoples Democracy,"* 1954, 20 pp.*

Tsukahira, Toshio, *The Postwar Evolution of Communist Strategy in Japan,* Summer 1954.*

APPENDIX 2

Papers on China from the Regional Studies Seminars, Committee on International and Regional Studies, Harvard University.

Ayers, William, "Shanghai Labor and the May 30th Movement," *Papers on China,* Vol. 5, May 1951.

Borowitz, Albert, "Anti-imperialism as a political weapon: the official Russian views on China, 1945–1950," 41 pp. and notes, Regional Studies *201,* 1952.

* Papers written at CENIS.   † To be completed: titles provisional.

Callahan, Paul F., "Christianity and Revolution as Seen in the National Christian Council of China," Vol. 5, from the Regional Studies Seminars. Mimeographed for private distribution by the Committee on International and Regional Studies, Harvard, May 1951, pp. 75–106.

Callahan, Paul F., "T'ai Hsü and the New Buddhist Movement," *Papers on China*, Vol. 6, March 1952, pp. 149–188.

Chao Kuo-chün, "Land Reform Methods in Communist China," *Papers on China*, Vol. 5, May 1951, pp. 107–174.

Kennedy, Melville T., Jr., "The Chinese Democratic League," *Papers on China*, Vol. 7, February 1953, pp. 136–175.

MacFarquar, Roderick L., "Collectivism and the Traditional Agriculture: A Comparison," Regional Studies *201*, May 1954, 37 pp. and notes.

Montell, Sherwin, "The San-Fan Wu-Fan Movement in Communist China," *Papers on China*, Vol. 8, February 1954, pp. 136–196.

Morrison, Esther, "A Comparison of Kuomintang and Communist Modern History Textbooks," *Papers on China*, Vol. 6, March 1952, pp. 3–44.

Morrison, Esther, "Two Years of Worker Peasant Education in Communist China," Regional Studies *202*, 1951–1952, 62 pp. and notes.

Moy, Clarence, "Communist China's Use of the Yang-ko," *Papers on China*, Vol. 6, March 1952, pp. 112–148.

Noah, Lynn, "Chinese Communist Propaganda Technique toward Labor, 1949–1954," Regional Studies *202*, May 1954, 24 pp. and notes; projected, with revisions, for Vol. 9, *Papers on China* for 1955.

Pon, Alexander C., "Agricultural Construction in the Northeast, 1949–1950," Regional Studies *202*, May 1951, 66 pp. and notes.

Rounds, Frank W., Jr., "Russian Accounts of the Life of Mao Tse-tung," May 1950, 36 pp., notes and appendix.

Stockdale, Margaret, "Anti-American Themes on Chinese Communist Radio, June to December 1950," Regional Studies *202*, 1951, 48 pp., notes and appendix.

Wagner, Edward S., "The Korean Colony in Manchuria and International Rivalries in Northeast Asia, 1869–1951," Regional Studies *202*, May 1951, 55 pp. and notes.

Williams, Lea E., "The Korean-Manchurian Industrial Base," Regional Studies *202*, May 26, 1951, 62 pp. and notes.

APPENDIX 3

Unpublished *Studies in Chinese Communism*, papers under the direction of Theodore H. E. Chen, Department of Asiatic Studies, University of Southern California. Inquiries should be addressed to Commandant, Human Resources Institute Air University, Maxwell Air Force Base, Montgomery, Alabama. (Reference: Contract AF 33 (038)-25075.)

Project Terminated August 31, 1953.

Series I
No. 1. Courts and Police in Communist China, Henry Wei, adv. ed., hectographed.
No. 2. Agrarian Reform in Communist China, Shao-er Ong, adv. ed., hectographed.
No. 3. The Propaganda Machine in Communist China, Frederick T. C. Yu, adv. ed., hectographed. Supplement, Pro-Soviet Propaganda in Communist China. Adv. ed.

No. 4. The Resist-America Aid-Korea Campaign in Communist China, Wen-hui C. Chen, adv. ed., hectographed.

Series II

No. 1. Mao Tse-tung's "Lean-to-one-side" Policy, 89 pp., by Henry Wei. Supplement, October 15, 1952, by Henry Wei, 10 pp.

No. 2. A Study of Agricultural Taxation in Communist China, Shao-er Ong, August 15, 1952, 105 pp.

No. 3. Strategy and Tactics of Chinese Communist Propaganda, Frederick T. C. Yu, October 15, 1952, 146 pp. Supplement to No. 3, A Report on the Home Service Broadcasts of the Central People's Broadcasting Station in Peking, by Frederick T. C. Yu, October 15, 1952, 8 pp.

No. 4. "Mass Movements" in Communist China: Nationwide Campaigns in Communist China in Support of the Korean War, 169 pp., by Wen-hui C. Chen. Supplement by Wen-hui C. Chen, October 15, 1952, 15 pp.

No. 5. The Christian Church in Communist China, Helen Ferris, August 15, 1952, 144 pp.

Series III

No. 1. Organization and Structure of the Chinese Communist Government, Henry Wei, MS, October 1953.

No. 2. The Communist Party of China: Its Organization and Structure, ? Tang, MS, October 1953.

No. 3. Key Leaders in Communist China, Frederick T. C. Yu, May 1953, 152 pp.

No. 4. The Treatment of the United States in Four Chinese Communist Newspapers, Sin-ming Chiu, February 1953, 60 pp.

No. 5. Labor Problems in Communist China, Shao-er Ong, February 1953, 152 pp.

No. 6. The Family Revolution in Communist China, Wen-hui C. Chen, MS, October 1953.

No. 7. Reactions in Communist China: An Analysis of Letters to Newspaper Editors, Charles K. A. Wang, MS, October 1953.

INDEX

COMMUNIST CHINA

International boundary
International boundary indefinite
Administrative area boundary *
Provincial boundary
⊛ Communist capital
⊙ Communist provincial capital

*To be abolished, following announcement of June 19, 1954

0   100   200   300   400
Statute Miles